W9-CLU-604

Gift of the

SAMUEL P. HUNT

FOUNDATION

ARGENTINA'S "DIRTY WAR"

Argentina's "Dirty War"

An Intellectual Biography

by Donald C. Hodges

 UNIVERSITY OF TEXAS PRESS, AUSTIN

Copyright © 1991 by the University of Texas Press
All rights reserved
Printed in the United States of America

First Edition, 1991

Requests for permission to reproduce material from this
work should be sent to Permissions, University of Texas
Press, Box 7819, Austin, Texas 78713-7819.

∞ The paper used in this publication meets the
minimum requirements of American National Standard
for Information Sciences—Permanence of Paper for
Printed Library Materials, ANSI Z39.48-1984.

Library of Congress Cataloging-in-Publication Data
Hodges, Donald Clark, 1923–
    Argentina's "dirty war" : an intellectual biography / by Donald C.
Hodges. — 1st ed.
        p.   cm.
    Includes bibliographical references (p.   ) and index.
    ISBN 0-292-70423-2 (cloth)
    1. Argentina—Politics and government—1955–1983. 2. Argentina—
Politics and government—1983– 3. Government, Resistance to—
Argentina—History—20th century. 4. Argentina—Military policy.
5. Violence—Argentina—History—20th century. I. Title.
F2849.2.H63   1991
982.06—dc20   90-44074
                                                                   CIP

To Abraham Guillén
anarchist, communist, teacher, friend

Contents

Preface

THE "DIRTY WAR" of 1975–1978 was of special significance in Argentine national life as it brought to a head social tensions that had been accumulating since the launching of the military era by Argentina's first successful coup of the century in September 1930. As early as December 1924, Argentina's poet laureate, Leopoldo Lugones, heralded the coming "Hour of the Sword," when the military would begin its sixty-year stint of intermittent interventions in public affairs.

Although popular resistance to military intervention did not acquire momentum until the September 1955 coup, since then it has continued to respond to military pressures under civilian as well as praetorian governments. More recently, this continuing resistance went beyond merely reacting to praetorianism and took initiatives of its own. The result was not only a revolutionary war to which the dirty war responded, but also the revival of subversion after the return to democracy in 1983.

A microcosm of international politics, Argentina has experienced domestically the hostilities that citizens of other states experience mainly in the area of foreign relations. More than any other nation, since World War II it has been a battleground of ideas competing for supremacy—liberalism, democracy, socialism, communism, fascism, and the social teachings of the Catholic church—ideologies contributing to a climate of social and political chaos. In Argentina their encounter reached a pitch of violence unsurpassed in the hemisphere. Argentina can boast of the two largest, best-organized, and best-financed urban guerrilla formations on record—the Ejército Revolucionario del Pueblo (ERP), and the Montoneros. The response to their revolutionary war was also record-breaking—the military's dirty war, a revival of the methods of the Spanish Inquisition, and the most systematic form of state terrorism in the New World.

The dirty war had a covert as well as a declared objective. Publicly, it was initiated by a constitutional government that authorized the armed forces to use any and every means to eradicate armed subversion. Secretly, it was a link in a chain leading to the replacement of the constitutional government by a military regime having for its immediate goals the reversal of established economic policies, the permanent crippling of the majoritarian populist party, and the dismantling of organized labor and the protective mantle of social legislation.

The dirty war became the springboard to the armed forces' Process of National Reorganization, popularly known as the Military Process (1976–1982). The assignment of executive powers to the military in a national emergency whetted the generals' appetite for a still-larger share of responsibility in the nation's affairs. With their forces mobilized against subversives, they also turned against those they held responsible for subversion. Thus while the constitutional government shifted its responsibility for military repression onto the guerrillas, the armed forces blamed the government for the coup that toppled it in March 1976.

Although ostensibly limited to the elimination of Argentina's guerrilla organizations, the dirty war also targeted unarmed subversives. Thus its ramifications extended to the military's "disappearance" of political undesirables and to the crackdown on labor militancy. The hidden agenda of the dirty war aimed at extending it to the factory floor, universities, political parties, and the rest of Argentine society. Its final objective was to annihilate the rear guard of subversion, although the armed forces were initially authorized to eliminate only the vanguard.

Toward this end the Military Process fostered a climate of generalized terror that covered a wide range of persons linked to the guerrillas, such as family members, friends, and associates. While its tentacles reached out to embrace virtually everyone, they were especially felt by those professions considered subversive because of the level of the enemy's infiltration, mainly trade union organizers, teachers, lawyers, journalists, and psychiatrists. With the military's defeat of the guerrillas, the dirty war supposedly came to an end. In fact, it was turned over to the intelligence services and shifted to the political plane.

The military rebellions under the civilian government of Pres. Raúl Alfonsín (1983–1989) had as one of their purposes the vindication of the "antisubversive struggle"—a euphemism for the dirty war. Those rebellions testified to the armed forces' continued perception of their struggle as both licit and moral. For professional soldiers it was not the shameful episode that other sectors of Argentine society would prefer to forget. From a military standpoint torture was both a response in kind to the guerrillas' dirty tactics and the only effective means of extracting information from internal enemies who refused to cooperate with the authorities.

The dirty war was not a momentary aberration or a pathological deviation within the armed forces, but the expression of long-term tendencies, mounting intransigence, and the instability of Argentine political life. Argentina has been a battleground of more than one war against subversion. There was a dirty war in the remote southern province of Santa Cruz in the wake of World War I and the Bolshevik Revolution. The ensuing massacre of some fifteen hundred armed workers, surrendering in return for a promised amnesty, was a warning of things to come.

The dirty war must be seen as a response to the "Argentine question," the combined problems of economic decline since the Great Depression, political instability because of the assault on democracy, and the specter of subversion coterminous with the military era. During this period Argentina became a laboratory for testing responses to acute economic, political, and social problems. The generals' imposition of restricted democracy alternated with the populist solution of repairing abuses and with direct military rule. Their finest moment came with the dirty war, when they intervened first against armed subversion on a scale hitherto unknown and then against its immediate causes in political misrule and economic mismanagement.

Just as the guerrillas' revolutionary war was a delayed response to the Russian Revolution, so was the dirty war. But there are still missing connections to be made, and the full story has yet to be told. This book follows a chronological order for the purpose of establishing those linkages. Thus it shows how the return to democracy was conditioned by the Military Process, how the latter grew out of the dirty war, how the dirty war responded to the revolutionary war, how the revolutionary war emerged from resistance to an earlier military regime, how the resistance was sparked by military intervention against a populist government, and how this government and its populist predecessor responded to questions highlighted during earlier phases of the military era. The historical order also raises the issue of the dirty war's outcome, organized labor's resistance to the Military Process, the guerrillas' shift from armed struggle to political resistance, the defenestration of the generals, and their final humiliation.

This, then, is a study of the political origins and outcomes, ideological roots, attempted solutions, and fundamental issues of Argentina's dirty war. To understand the dirty war one must examine the generals' and the guerrillas' intellectual frameworks and perceived interests, their political clout, coalitions, and conflicts, the parameters within which they operated, and the dimensions of the Argentine question to which they responded.

Taking contemporary Argentine political history as its field of study, this work claims to be philosophical in three fundamental senses: as an in-depth investigation of the reality behind the appearance of events; as an attempt to understand the complex web of economic, political, and social happenings as a whole; and as the expression of an ultimate concern for the life-and-death issues that matter most in this world. Its examination of the mind-sets and intellectual shaping of the main protagonists satisfies the first condition. Its investigation of the causal relations between the Peronist phenomenon, revolutionary war, dirty war, and related Military Process and resistance satisfies the second condition. Its focus on the "final solutions" to the Argentine question satisfies the third condition.

I have assembled diverse but complementary methods with these objectives in mind. If a method may be likened to an instrument, then this study has more than one axe to grind. The phenomenological method is used for understanding the motives, judgments, and rationales behind the behavior of the principal actors. Besides description, structural and genetic explanations, this study relies on the dialectical method for discovering the role of reciprocal causation among the various contestants, and on analysis and criticism of rival accounts of the main events. Finally, attention is given to what is historically important, to the principal dimensions of the Argentine question and to the role of human agency in determining political outcomes.

The research leading to this book began during a trip to Argentina in 1976, when the dirty war was already under way. For several months I lived under a concentrated state of siege. This was not the Argentina I remembered from my youth, the country where I had been schooled from 1929 to 1941. What had happened since my school days to transform this once-civilized nation into a boiling cauldron of hostile ideologies with no peaceful resolution in sight?

Documents of the dirty war are now generally accessible, but one cannot say the same for those of the revolutionary war. The internal documents of the guerrillas and their political counterparts are hard to find and it is still a crime to possess them. As late as May 1985, under the benign democracy of Raúl Alfonsín, even such materials published abroad qualified as "illicit." Some could be had through political exiles in Mexico and Stockholm, but even with assumed identities, revolutionaries risked their freedom by talking to outsiders. The following is an acknowledgment of my most unusual sources, inaccessible to the armchair investigator.

For documents of the Montoneros and Montonero-dominated Partido Peronista Auténtico (PPA) and Juventud Peronista–Regionales (JP–R), I am obliged to Adriana Puiggrós of the former Casa Montonera in Mexico City; Montonero defense lawyer Ana Comas; editor Ricardo Curten of the Montonero monthly *Latino América*; the director of the Montonero archives, Alicia Giraudo; the JP–R's general secretary, Carlos González; the JP–R's organizational director, Nilo Gambini; Santa Cruz's former governor Jorge Cepernic; and the number-one public enemy during and since the dirty war, Mario Eduardo Firmenich.

Other documents pertaining to Peronismo en la Resistencia, the Juventud Peronista en la Resistencia, and the Juventud Peronista Unificada (JPU) were provided by Rodolfo Galimberti's former lieutenant Jorge Reyna, the editor of *JOTAPÉ*, Daniel Llano, and the acting secretary of the Unified Peronist Youth (JPU), Patricia Bullrich. A related debt is owed to the Trotsky Museum in Mexico City, the Centro de Investigaciones en Ciencias Sociales (CICSO) in Buenos Aires, the editors of *Combate* in Stockholm, Nelson Marinelli of the daily *El Tiempo*, María Seoane of the fortnightly *El Periodista*, Francisco Provenzano of the monthly *Entre Todos*, editors Daniel Molina and Ernesto Tiffenberg of the monthly *El Porteño*, Norberto Rey of the Partido Revolucionario de los Trabajadores (PRT), and the PRT's National Directorate for documents and data covering its armed vanguard during the resistance.

These were not the only participants in the armed and unarmed struggle whose information seemed vital to a balanced account of what happened. Besides my debt to those already mentioned, special recognition is due to Raimundo Ongaro and Osvaldo Villaflor of the Federación Gráfica Bonaerense (FGB), Córdoba's former governor Ricardo Obregón Cano, Argentine Communist party (PCA) national secretary Irene Rodríguez, the veteran trade unionist and former Peronist congressman from Catamarca, Isauro Molina, and the secretary of state and secretary general of the Partido Justicialista, (PJ) of La Rioja, Nubelio Valentín Brizuela.

Further acknowledgment is due to Florida State University for financial assistance in initiating this research and to Robert M. Levine, editor of *South Eastern Latin Americanist*, for permission to reprint my prison interview with Mario Firmenich. "The Montoneros' Past, Present, and Future" was published in the March 1986 issue, vol. 29, no. 4, and is reproduced in the Appendix.

Readers may be interested to learn the subsequent fate of some of my informants. After being found guilty of double aggravated homicide, kidnapping, and extortion, Firmenich was sentenced to life imprisonment by the federal court in San Martín, Province of Buenos Aires. Then, in the second proceeding against him for homicide with two aggravating circumstances, he was sentenced by the federal judiciary in the capital to a second term of life imprisonment—both limited to thirty years by the government's extradition agreement with Brazil. Although there was speculation that he might be amnestied, among the 279 individuals pardoned by the presidential decrees of October 7, 1989, Firmenich's name was conspicuously missing.

The militants I talked to from the Movimiento Todos por la Patria (MTP) fared even worse. A founder and member of its national directorate, Francisco Provenzano sided with those in late 1988 who incorporated into the movement's leadership the ERP's former commander, Enrique Gorriarán Merlo. On January 23–24, 1989, Provenzano helped direct the MTP's assault on Infantry Regiment No. 3, based in La Tablada on the outskirts of the capital, resulting in its partial takeover by more than fifty armed guerrillas. Nine soldiers and two policemen died in this action along with twenty-eight of the attackers. Although eighteen were identified as having surrendered, in a revival of the tactics of the "dirty war," Provenzano and five others were summarily executed.

List of Acronyms

AAA Alianza Anticomunista Argentina (Triple A)/Argentine Anti-Communist Alliance (Triple A)

ALN Alianza Libertadora Nacionalista/Nationalist Liberating Alliance

APA Agrupación Peronismo Auténtico/Assemblage of Authentic Peronism

APDH Asamblea Permanente por los Derechos Humanos/Permanent Assembly for Human Rights

CADHU Comisión Argentina de Derechos Humanos/Argentine Commission on Human Rights

CELS Centro de Estudios Legales y Sociales/Center of Legal and Social Studies

CGT Confederación General del Trabajo/General Confederation of Labor

CGTA Confederación General del Trabajo de los Argentinos/General Confederation of Labor of the Argentines

CICSO Centro de Investigaciones en Ciencias Sociales/Center of Social Science Investigations

CNA Comando Nacionalista Argentino/Argentine Nationalist Commando

CNT Comisión Nacional de Trabajo/National Labor Commission

CONADEP Comisión Nacional Sobre la Desaparición de Personas/National Commission on the Disappearance of Persons

CSLA Confederación Sindical Latinoamericana/Latin American Trade Union Confederation

CUTA Conducción Unica de los Trabajadores Argentinos/United Leadership of Argentine Workers

EGP Ejército Guerrillero del Pueblo/People's Guerrilla Army

ELN Ejército de Liberación Nacional/National Liberation Army (Bolivia)

ERP   Ejército Revolucionario del Pueblo/People's Revolutionary Army

ESMA   Escuela de Mecánica de la Armada/Naval Engineering School

FAL   Fuerzas Armadas de Liberación/Armed Forces of Liberation

FAO   Frente Amplio de Oposición/Broad Opposition Front (Nicaragua)

FAP   Fuerzas Armadas Peronistas/Peronist Armed Forces

FAR   Fuerzas Armadas Revolucionarias/Revolutionary Armed Forces

FAS   Frente Antiimperialista por el Socialismo/Anti-imperialist Front for Socialism

FGB   Federación Gráfica Bonaerense/Printers' Union of Buenos Aires

FOIC   Federación Obrera de la Industria de la Carne/Meatworkers' Union

FPN   Frente Patriótico Nacional/National Patriotic Front (Nicaragua)

FREJULI   Frente Justicialista de Liberación/Justicialist Liberation Front

FREPU   Frente del Pueblo/People's Front

FRIP   Frente Revolucionario Indoamericano Popular/Popular Indo-American Revolutionary Front

FRP   Frente de Resistencia Popular/Popular Resistance Front

FSLN   Frente Sandinista de Liberación Nacional/Sandinista Front of National Liberation

GOU   Grupo Obra de Unificación/Work of Unification Group

IMP   Intransigencia y Movilización Peronista/Peronist Intransigence and Mobilization

IP   Intransigencia Peronista/Peronist Intransigence

JI   Juventud Intransigente/Intransigent Youth

JP–R   Juventud Peronista–Regionales/Peronist Youth–Regional Organizations

JPRA   Juventud Peronista de la República Argentina/Peronist Youth of the Argentine Republic

JPU   Juventud Peronista Unificada/Unified Peronist Youth

JSP   Juventud Sindical Peronista/Peronist Trade Union Youth

LADH   Liga Argentina por los Derechos Humanos/Argentine League for Human Rights

LAP   Ley de Asociaciones Profesionales/Law of Professional Associations

LCT   Ley de Contrato de Trabajo/Labor Contract Law

MAS   Movimiento al Socialismo/Movement toward Socialism

MEDH   Movimiento Ecuménico por los Derechos Humanos/Ecumenical Movement for Human Rights.

MID   Movimiento de Integración y Desarrollo/Movement of Integration and Development

MIR   Movimiento de Izquierda Revolucionaria/Movement of the Revolutionary Left (Chile)

MLN   Movimiento de Liberación Nacional (Tupamaros)/Tupamaros (Uruguay)

MNRT   Movimiento Nacionalista Revolucionario Tacuara/Tacuara Revolutionary Nationalist movement

MPM   Movimiento Peronista Montonero/Montonero Peronist movement

MPU   Movimiento Pueblo Unido/United People's movement (Nicaragua)

MSB   Movimiento Sindical de Base/Movement of the Trade Union Rank and File

MSP   Movimiento Sindical Peronista/Peronist Trade Union movement

MTP   Movimiento Todos por la Patria/All for the Homeland Movement

MUSO   Movimiento de Unidad, Solidaridad y Organización/Movement of Unity, Solidarity, and Organization

OAS   Organisation de l'Armée Secrète/Secret Army Organization (French Algeria)

OLAS   Organización Latinoamericana de Solidaridad/Organization of Latin American Solidarity

OPM   Organización Político-Militar/Political Military Organization

OSPAA   Organization of Solidarity of the Peoples of Asia and Africa

OSPAAL   Organización de Solidaridad de los Pueblos de Asia, Africa y América Latina/Organization of Solidarity of the Peoples of Asia, Africa, and Latin America

PB   Peronismo de Base/Rank-and-File Peronism

PC   Partido Conservador/Conservative party

PCA   Partido Comunista Argentino/Argentine Communist party

PDN   Partido Demócrata Nacional/National Democratic party

PDP   Partido Demócrata Progresista/Progressive Democratic party

PI   Partido Intransigente/Intransigent party

PJ   Partido Justicialista/Justicialist party

PM   Partido Montonero/Montonero party

PO   Palabra Obrera/Workers' Word

PO   Partido Obrero/Labor party

PPA   Partido Peronista Auténtico/Authentic Peronist party

PRT   Partido Revolucionario de los Trabajadores/Revolutionary Workers' party

SERPAJ   Servicio de Paz y Justicia/Service of Peace and Justice

SMATA   Sindicato de Mecánicos y Afines del Transporte Automotriz/ Automobile Workers' Union

UCR   Unión Cívica Radical/Radical Civic Union or Radical party

UCRI   Unión Cívica Radical Intransigente/Intransigent Radical party

UCRP   Unión Cívica Radical del Pueblo/People's Radical party

UD   Unión Democrática/Democratic Union

UF   Unión Ferroviaria/Railroad Workers' Union

UOCRA   Unión Obrera de la Construcción de la República Argentina/ Construction Workers' Union

UOM   Unión Obrera Metalúrgica/Metalworkers' Union

ARGENTINA'S "DIRTY WAR"

1. The Argentine Question

THE ARGENTINE question is a product of the three great problems that generated it: the reversal in Argentina's economic development; political instability; and social unrest compounded by the specter of subversion. As formulated by Raúl Alfonsín before he became president in 1983, the question is why Argentina, a rich and democratic nation in the 1920s, reverted to a process that moved it toward underdevelopment, authoritarianism, and violence.[1] Once the most economically developed country in Latin America, with a model democracy and a quality of life envied even in Western Europe, Argentina reverted to Third World status. Many Argentines ask themselves what went wrong? They also ask what is to be done? The dirty war constitutes an answer to both questions.

The Argentine question first came to national attention during the 1970s. The dirty war and the related Military Process heightened Argentine awareness that the climate of violence associated with chronic economic decline and political instability was part of a uniquely Argentine predicament. Closely linked, the crisis of democracy dating from the 1930s, economic stagnation since the 1950s, and armed subversion beginning in the 1960s would henceforth become the principal focus of conflict among the country's major interest groups.

Would-be solutions to the Argentine question were of political consequence on two critical occasions during the 1970s and 1980s. The March 1976 coup and the launching of the Military Process had for their objective the resolution of the Argentine question once and for all.[2] The Peronists' first defeat in a presidential election occurred in October 1983, in part because of Alfonsín's call for a "Third Historical movement" also aimed at a definitive answer to the country's problems.

The armed forces' solution to the Argentine question responded to burgeoning social tensions and subversion accentuated by economic slippage and political stalemate. Stamping out armed subversion meant striking at its roots in political instability and economic mismanagement—or so the military reasoned. By the middle 1970s it had articulated its "final solution" to each of these predicaments, but the remedy only aggravated the malady.

The protagonists of this drama addressed all three facets of the Argentine question, but assigned different weights to each. The economic question took precedence for leaders of the business community. The Radical party, a bastion of liberal democracy, gave priority to the political question, mainly the defense of civil liberties. Meanwhile, the Peronist movement highlighted what it called "social justice," centered on a redistribution of the national income as one salient aspect of the social question. The parties of the Left focused on another aspect, the exploitation of Argentina's workers by the multinationals and the native capitalists; this became the basis of their propaganda for a "socialist homeland." By the 1970s the armed forces, too, were calling attention to the social question, but to the aspect of armed subversion.

Economic Decline

Blessed with a temperate climate, the heartland of Argentina stretches in a great arc from the capital of Buenos Aires approximately five hundred miles inland. Within this area lies the country's principal natural resource, the grasslands of the pampas, the fertile topsoil of which is some three meters deep, among the richest in the world. The eighth-largest country in the world, Argentina before World War I was economically closer to Canada and Australia than to any other Latin American nation. It was also on a par with most of the leading countries of Western Europe. A settler nation of primarily European immigrants, it had a predominantly urban population in 1913 and boasted the highest literacy rate in Latin America. By 1929 it had also won the reputation of a model democracy in the Western Hemisphere. A country in which all the indices of modernization were present made Argentina the envy of its neighbors until Mexico and Brazil began catching up and an unparalleled wave of violence washed over it.

In *La cuestión argentina*, Alfonsín begins by focusing on the fifty years of decadence that began after Argentina reached the pinnacle of its success in 1930. In 1880 few could have imagined that this remote, poor, and underpopulated country would become by 1930 the first nation of Latin America and renowned for its culture, its democratic stability, and its "position among the top five nations of the world in per capita income."[3] Again, few could have imagined in 1930 that the country would degenerate in the next fifty years to a second-class nation in Latin America, that not four but some forty countries would outrank it in the international community.

Representing former president Arturo Frondizi's Movimiento de Integración y Desarrollo (MID), MID's first vice-president Rogelio Frigerio has also attempted to deal with the question of Argentina's economic decline. His *Diez años de la crisis argentina*, covering the decade from 1973 to 1983, focuses on the same enigma: a country that has seen not only its relative position decline, but also its absolute position. While other countries have had difficulty keeping up with the rest of the world, Argentina is unique in being "the only country that has followed a course the inverse of that followed by the history of humanity."[4] Unquestionably the number-one country in Latin America in the 1930s with respect to Gross Domestic Product (GDP), Argentina had slipped by 1982 to third place, representing approximately 11 percent of the Latin American total, behind Brazil (34 percent) and Mexico (26 percent).[5] In 1950 the Argentine GDP matched the combined GDPs of all its immediate neighbors: Brazil, Chile, Uruguay, Bolivia, and Paraguay. Thirty years later it represented barely one-third of Brazil's GDP and only one-fourth of the total.[6]

Today it strains belief that in 1913 Argentina's per capita product was comparable to that of Switzerland, larger than that of Sweden, France, and Austria, twice as large as that of Italy, and five times that of Japan.[7] From having grown at a rate of 4.6 percent per annum from the turn of the century to the Great Depression, the country's GDP increased barely one percent from 1950 to 1983.[8] Thus by 1978 its per capita product had fallen to less than one-sixth that of Switzerland, half that of Italy, almost one-fourth that of Japan, and one-fifth that of Canada.[9]

Why did a land of recent settlement supplying beef and grains to Europe evolve so differently from its peers, notably Canada and Australia? In answer, David Rock points to the breakdown of Argentina's complementary partnership with Britain after World War II, which in past decades had contributed to its economic progress.[10] But he attaches more importance to the Spanish colonial heritage, which contrasts so markedly with the Anglo-Saxon in its economic consequences. Unlike the British settlers in North America, the Spaniards imposed an imperial system based on the exploitation of indigenous colonial peoples by an alien white elite. Tributary institutions contributed to the emergence of a simple agropastoral economy incapable of diversifying and developing. It was no lack of raw materials that blocked the country's industrialization, but the persistence of those tributary institutions. "Had those institutions been different, the resources would have sufficed for the emergence of a small farmers' commonwealth"—as in Canada and Australia.[11]

The landed oligarchy in Argentina was not displaced by a social upheaval like the Mexican Revolution or its U.S. counterpart, the smashing of the Southern plantocracy during the Civil War. Rather, the traditional hacienda economy eroded while the oligarchy of landowners metamorphosed into a modern agribusiness elite under the influence of foreign capital and the modernizing process. A shift in the mode of extracting the economic surplus occurred between 1880 and 1912, known as the period of the oligarchy. The lack of reliable statistics makes the exact date uncertain. The most that can be said is that a capitalist agroexport economy developed on the foundations of the traditional landowning class.

Previously, the oligarchy had depended for its revenues on a tribute for the use of land, rent that passed into the costs of agricultural products whether paid in money by tenant farmers, in labor services by the landowner's peons, or as a fee charged by the landowner. Later, profits from capital improvements and the direct exploitation of a rural proletariat became the chief source of revenue. The term *"estanciero"* is loose enough to include both traditional and modern landowners—but they belong to different classes. The biggest landowners underwent a mutation to become a new capitalist oligarchy; traditional landowners survived, but they no longer occupied the driver's seat.

In Western Europe and the United States, industry developed independently of the landowners through a process of capital accumulation. Industrial growth took place through the reinvestment of profits obtained in industry, without the help of landowners and often without assistance from banking capital. Profits were obtained the hard way, through fierce competition and technological innovation. The original enterprises were small and became large mainly through displacing and absorbing less-efficient units.

The Argentine experience has been quite different. There, as throughout most of Latin America, the traditional oligarchy took the initiative in conjunction with foreign capital and the multinational corporations in developing capitalism from above. Argentina's industrial establishments did not emerge from a long competitive struggle, but were monopolistic from the start and inextricably tied to the oligarchy and to foreign interests. Although Argentine industry was only a little more than fifty years old by World War II, its degree of concentration and centralization was already greater than that in the United States and other developed countries.[12]

The symbiosis of the traditional landed families and the new class of industrial entrepreneurs was a crucial factor in holding back Argentina's modernization process. Even so, Argentina belongs with Uruguay, Brazil, and Colombia in a group of specially favored countries that were able to develop a sizable and comparatively independent industrial bourgeoisie without a Mexican-type revolution.[13] In Mexico a weak bourgeoisie had been compelled to seek peasant and labor support in a violent confrontation with the landed oligarchy. Argentina escaped that predicament thanks to a new stratum of industrial entrepreneurs from the ranks of recent European immigrants. Having achieved an advanced degree of modernization, its economy evolved into a capitalist one without a major social explosion. That itself is part of the predicament—the country's failure to break with its colonial past.

The combination of stagnation and hyperinflation is of course typical of other Latin American and Third World countries. The distinctive feature of the Argentine case is that until recently no other Third World nation remotely approximated the economic status of the major European powers. But one may wonder whether Argentina's unique status before World War II was perhaps even more freakish than its subsequent decline. Argentines may believe the country belongs with Canada and Australia among the rapidly developing nations, but in fact "it only enjoyed the transient benefits of a bilateral relationship [with Britain] which could not be favorable in the long run."[14] That umbilical cord was damaged during the Great Depression and severed after World War II, and Argentines learned that their sense of greatness bore little relation to their real place in the world.

Without attempting to survey, much less assess, the alternative explanations of Argentina's economic decline, one should at least note some of the issues currently under discussion. Recent studies in particular underscore the complexity of the question and its connection with noneconomic factors. Thus one can reasonably claim that ideological factors play a crucial role in accounting for the country's economic backsliding along with responses to the social and political questions—and that these became an integral part of the chain of events culminating in the Military Process.

In *Gran Bretaña, Estados Unidos, y la declinación argentina, 1942–1949,* Carlos Escudé argues that the country's vital trading links with Great Britain were deliberately scuttled by the United

States in line with its foreign policy toward Argentina during and following World War II.[15] Virtually the same policy of economic boycott and political destabilization was applied to Argentina during the 1940s that would be applied to Cuba in the 1960s and to Nicaragua in the 1980s, with the same telling effects. Argentina's economic decline is interpreted as a product of political as well as economic factors, U.S. imperialism in particular. In response to U.S. foreign policy, Perón opted for economic autarchy, a solution that appeared rational at the time but that ended by compounding the country's economic difficulties.

Perón's autarchic industrial policy—his efforts to break out of the stranglehold of dependency while only partially addressing the causes—would become an additional factor in Argentina's decline.[16] Instead of continuing with a model of industrialization based on integration into the world economy, postwar Argentina adopted a policy of import substitution and protection for noncompetitive native industries oriented to the internal market. The economic consequences of this hothouse capitalism were high growth rates in the short run until the captive market became saturated, but sluggishness afterward.[17]

Corresponding to this policy of protectionism for the national bourgeoisie was a strategy of protectionism for labor based on the organization of powerful trade unions under state control. The immediate economic consequences of this strategy were the expansion of employment and of labor's share of the national income. Although it was momentarily placated, organized labor would become an autonomous and delegitimating force in the long run, when it could no longer count on protection from Peronists in the government. Thus Carlos Waisman concludes that it is in the realm of political policies and ideologies linked to nationalist and fascist schemes, rather than in the economic structure of dependency, that one must seek the explanation of Argentina's reversal of development.[18] Those policies, too, would become part of the problem.

The novel feature of Waisman's discussion is the connection he makes between Perón's case for radical import substitution and the social question: "Perón contended that a manufacturing sector developed on the basis of blanket protection would help prevent a revolution."[19] To avert a social explosion, Perón argued, the economic elites must make substantial concessions to the workers. They must guarantee that there would be virtually no unemployment and that the workers' standard of living would improve.[20] But for that, the country had to industrialize and provide the necessary jobs. Only the state could do that, but at the cost of subsidized industries isolated from the pressures of the world market. That meant the inefficient allocation of scarce resources and the failure to keep pace with technological change. Thus one consequence of the Peronist solution to the social question was to aggravate an already incipient economic predicament.

A similar assessment of the Argentine question was set forth by José Martínez de Hoz, the economy minister during the first five years of the Military Process. The country's economic predicament was traced to Perón's populist measures of economic autarchy and radical protectionism after World War II.[21] This was also the military's view of the matter. Thus in his speech on 30 March 1976, Gen. Jorge R. Videla justified the March coup as "the end not only of a government, but also of a historic cycle"—the cycle associated with Peronist and post-Peronist interference in and mismanagement of the economy.[22]

On 2 April 1976 the armed forces announced a program aimed at an economic solution to the Argentine question. The formerly closed economy isolated from every innovating current would be opened and reintegrated into the international economy, while public overspending, with its train of monetary emissions and inflation, would stop.[23] But again the results diverged from the expected. The long-term consequence was the dismantling of native industries rather than their upgrading to meet international standards. In effect, Argentina reverted to a preindustrial policy that further accentuated the economic question, making it even more troublesome to resolve.[24]

Ironically, one of the indices of economic success would subsequently become an index of failure. To modernize the economy, said Martínez de Hoz, it would be necessary to reach record levels in foreign borrowing. The foreign debt had remained at modest levels because of lack of international confidence in the country's future. For Argentina to have maintained an evolution of its external debt comparable to the growth of the international market, he argued, it should have risen to fifty billion dollars by 1976 instead of the shameful eight billion left as a legacy by the displaced Peronist government.[25] In 1976 this record low was cited as an instance of Peronist mismanagement of the economy. But by 1983, when the debt had soared to a record high of forty billion dollars, the new debt level had become an integral part of the economic crisis.

By the end of 1979 the dirty war had achieved its declared objective of eradicating armed subversion in Argentina. But the economic question that underlay the country's political and social problems and that had generated the revolutionary war was now virtually insoluble.

Political Instability

Since 1930 the salient fact of Argentine political life has been instability. Argentina holds the record in the Western Hemisphere for unstable political institutions during the twentieth century. What other nation can claim nine elected governments between 1928 and 1983, only two of which were permitted to complete their terms in office? Significantly, the exceptions were headed by generals. Prior to Alfonsín, the last civilian president to survive the waves that have periodically rocked the ship of state was Marcelo T. de Alvear, elected for a six-year term in 1922. Thus on taking office on 8 July 1989, Carlos Saúl Menem became the first in this coup-ridden nation to succeed an elected head of state in sixty-one years.

A major index of Argentina's record of political instability is that military regimes have proved to be as impermanent as civilian governments. It is the pendular swing from one to the other that has made a shambles of Argentine political life. A continuing military regime with or without the façade of elections, as in Stroessner's Paraguay or Pinochet's Chile, is not a sign of instability even under conditions of political resistance—hence the uniqueness of the Argentine case.

If one takes the Peronist decade (1946–1955) as an exception to the prevailing tendency of ungovernability, then there were two distinct periods in the deviation from stable governments. During the first, from 1930 to 1946, seven presidents served an average of two years apiece. During the second period, from 1956 to 1983, there were eighteen presidents, for an average of only one and a half years each. By then political instability had reached the critical point.

During the second half of this century there have been twenty-two years of military rule, nineteen years of restricted democracy or pseudoconstitutional governments when the majoritarian party was proscribed, and only eleven years of democracy. Besides the recurring shifts, each period was also destabilized by internal bickering. To summarize the political uncertainties that define the Argentine political riddle, "Argentina wavered between authoritarian or exclusionary regimes and populist-corporatist ones, all highly unstable."[26]

In addition to these direct factors, there were other more subtle ones indirectly contributing to political imbalance: "the lacerating experience of a now unmuffled, now muffled, violence, but always present."[27] Since Argentina was second to none in firepower and the sheer size of its political-military vanguards, its urban guerrillas also matched the record of the generals. Not even Nicaragua can boast of twenty-four years of intermittent armed resistance to democratic as well as military and pseudoconstitutional governments. Nor is there any other Latin country whose established political parties when out of power have made a rule of egging the armed forces to intervene on their behalf. Thus the Radical party incited and supported the coups against Perón in 1945, 1955, and 1976; Peronists supported a coup against the Radical government in 1966.

Economic decline alone cannot account for these phenomena. Political and social factors also played a role. But as in the case of the economic dimension of the Argentine question, the conditions that explain the country's unique predicament would eventually become an integral part of that predicament. Among the conditions defining Argentine political culture in the twentieth century are stalemate, intransigence, and outright lawlessness.

The huge influx of immigrants, rapid modernization, and the electoral reforms of 1912 that ended two decades of political abstention created a situation in which popular demands outstripped the capacity of political institutions to meet them. A political stalemate resulted between social classes and elites in which no group was able to govern as it would like, but each was strong enough to block effective action by its rivals. The periodic destablizing effects of this stalemate partly account for the succession of military coups in 1930, 1943, 1955, 1962, 1966, and 1976, not to mention the palace coups within each. Although an economically developed country, Argentina has experienced one political crisis after another because of the ramifications of this political deadlock.

Political stalemate was compounded by the tendency for foreign politics to shape domestic politics. As late as the Great Depression, this settlers' paradise barred almost one-third of the population from political participation and more than two-thirds of urban entrepreneurs and businesspeople who retained their original citizenship.[28] Not being Argentines, they identified with their nation of origin: the predominantly Italian stock with Mussolini's fascism; Spaniards with both sides during the Civil War; Germans with Hitler's national socialism; and British and Americans with the Anglo-American tradition of liberal democracy. Thus the foreign enemy became internalized.

In regions whose people are comparatively unified by a political consensus, as in the United States and Western Europe, compromise is the rule. Political stalemate results from the absence of such a consensus. Since the middle 1930s Argentina's internal divisions have become exacerbated in response to political-military confrontations elsewhere. During the Spanish civil war, Argentine loyalties were divided between support for the Republic and the generals' rebellion. World War II witnessed a corresponding schism between those backing the Allies and the Axis powers. This division was perpetuated in the 1946 elections, which Perón won against the Democratic Union of Conservatives, Radicals, Socialists, and Communists. To this day the country is divided between the partisans of a corporatist or semicorporatist solution to Argentina's predicament and a liberal solution.

Argentina's colonial status contributed to aggravating these divisions. By the turn of the century the La Plata region, despite its formal independence, was being described in British circles as Britain's model colony and as "British Argentina."[29] Thus Argentines became divided into Anglophiles and Anglophobes, depending on how they saw themselves vis-à-vis Great Britain—as imperial middlemen or colonial subjects.

Consequently, when World War II erupted, many welcomed it as heralding the end of British domination in Argentina, as a substitute for a second war of independence, this time staged in Europe with Hitler and Mussolini cast in the roles of the country's early liberators. Argentine nationalists looked to them as saviors. The reasoning behind this perception was not farfetched nor was it basically different from that of the generals during their dirty war. If Europe could become the theater of an Argentine war of liberation during World War II, then Argentina might become a battleground of the two superpowers in World War III. And if Nazi Germany and Fascist Italy served objectively as the country's allies in the struggle against British domination, so the United States might serve in a similar capacity in the struggle against international communism. Thus the stalemate between the superpowers became introjected into Argentine political life.

Although isolated from the mainstream of international politics, Argentines have not been immune to disruptive foreign influences. Leopoldo Lugones put his finger on this feature of his country's political culture in noting that Argentines lived "de afuera para adentro" instead of "de adentro para afuera" (from the outside looking in instead of from the inside looking out).[30] Most discussions of the Argentine stalemate center on the role of indigenous factors in the country's makeup. But if Argentina fits the model of a fundamentally colonial or dependent country, then more than a passing account must be given to endogenous factors.

Argentina's cultural dependence must be considered in understanding Argentine political culture. Spanish political culture played a pivotal role until independence, after which the tradition of British liberalism would shape the thinking of Argentina's most prominent politicians. However, liberalism suffered a major setback during the 1930s as a result of an emerging Catholic nationalism and Franco's crusade against communism. To the impetus given to Catholic social doctrine by the Spanish Falange and to Argentine nationalism by Italian fascism and German national socialism must be added the impact of the Cuban Revolution and the Chinese Cultural Revolution on Argentina's youth. Nowhere in the Western Hemisphere did these new doctrinal winds stir up more controversy and dissension than in Argentina.

Political stalemate signifies contention, not stability. Politics can be the salvation of a people, but it can also lead to their ruin when strife becomes the destiny of a country and political factions persist in doing what others insist on undoing. This is borne out by the militarization of Argentine political life after 1930.[31] During the 1970s and 1980s the press periodically bewailed the "Lebanonization" of Argentina and the "Beirutization" of its capital, Buenos Aires. Without a protagonist to deliver a knockout blow, Argentina has had to suffer through a seemingly unending series of military coups.

Argentina ranks first among all nations in the number of political parties and tendencies that during the twentieth century have adopted the label "intransigent." The Unión Cívica Radical (UCR) first gave currency to the term in its struggle for electoral reform. Then in the 1930s Leopoldo Lugones's Guardia Argentina adopted a program of "intransigent nationalism."[32] Subsequently, the Radical party (UCR) split into two wings, one calling itself the Unión Cívica Radical Intransigente (UCRI), later simply the Partido Intransigente (PI). During the first resistance to military dictatorship, the deposed president, Juan Domingo Perón, also adopted a line of "absolute intransigence" for his political party.[33] Peronist militants followed suit. In response to a second resistance to military dictatorship in the early 1980s they organized Intransigencia y Movilización Peronista (IMP), also known as Intransigencia Peronista (IP).

Perón personified a peculiar Argentine syndrome: "I cannot strike a bargain with conservatives for a very simple reason: I aim to destroy them."[34] Although intransigence antedates the formal appearance of the Argentine question, it made its debut as state terrorism as early as June 1956.[35] The military government responded to the Peronist uprising led by Gen. Juan José Valle by breaking with tradition and sending civilians as well as soldiers involved in the conspiracy to the firing squad. The police in the province of Buenos Aires also detained a number of workers without any established links to the rebellion. They were taken to a garbage dump and shot without even the pretense of a trial.

No small part of the ten years of terrorism beginning with the return to constitutional government in 1973 may be attributed to political extremes that converged in their interpretation of Argentina's time of troubles. There is a startling resemblance between Lugones's apocalyptic vision of the "Hour of the Sword" and that of Che Guevara almost a half century later in the epigraph borrowed from José Martí, the "Hour of the Furnaces."[36] Each also provided a rationale for intransigence.

Because their respective practices played into each other's hands, they are identified by many Argentines as the two devils of Argentine politics. The generals supposedly had more in common with the guerrillas than with advocates of the rule of law. Concerning the notorious "Butcher of Buenos Aires," Gen. Ramón J. Camps, the editor of the English-language *Buenos Aires Herald* observed: "Like Firmenich [the equally notorious guerrilla chieftain], Camps feels contempt for *bourgeois materialism* and makes a cult of purifying death. Like him, he is convinced of the need to eradicate the vices of society through a painful but necessary surgical operation. Both find modern Western society corrupt and consider the United States to be degenerate. A puritanical streak runs through the heart of Argentina that under given circumstances produces fanatics who find their fields of action in terrorism and repression."[37] Each played the part of an enlightened savior of society, but the consensus holds that each failed to assess the Argentine situation realistically.

Whatever its social origins, intransigence is today deeply ingrained in the national character. What Marxists call the class struggle has been exacerbated by the presence of intransigence and the related posture of arrogance. Dubbed the peculiar Argentine malady, arrogance shows up politically in intransigent claims for one's social class and particular party.[38] Because they are exorbitant, such claims cannot be met. Thus political stalemate plus intransigence have become an argument for lawlessness in Argentina.

The role of law is different in countries where the eruption of the masses onto the political scene has been successfully contained than in a country like Argentina, where the guardians of law and order have yet to domesticate the masses. One is apt to forget that in

England, the fountain of modern liberalism, democracy was likened to a beast, the raging leveler depicted by Thomas Hobbes in his *BEHEMOTH.*[39] It took several centuries for England and several generations for North America and Western Europe to moderate popular demands within the framework of liberal institutions. In Argentina that has yet to occur and may well never happen. As in seventeenth-century England and eighteenth-century France, in Argentina democracy and liberalism are at loggerheads.

Missing in Argentina is the liberal's respect for the rule of law. What Tocqueville said of America in comparison with Europe in the nineteenth century applies to the comparison with Argentina in the twentieth. In the United States, he noted, "that numerous and turbulent multitude does not exist, which always looks upon the law as its natural enemy."[40] Just as Tocqueville perceived that the European scale of authority was inverted in North America, so in Argentina the attitude toward law continues to be the inverse of that in the United States.

In democracies where the wealthy are placed in a position analogous to that of the poor under oligarchical regimes, according to Tocqueville, "it is the opulent classes which frequently look upon law with suspicion."[41] But the wealthy do not rebel if, as in England and America, their interests are sufficiently protected and there are curbs against the tyranny of the majority. Only where those curbs are felt to be insufficient, as in Argentina, has the oligarchy repeatedly conspired with the military to unseat popularly elected governments.

There the continual shift in the locus of sovereignty from the oligarchy to the people and back has accentuated disrespect for law on all sides. Instead of one form of lawlessness, there are several. As Perón acknowledged: "The Argentine question that interests us . . . [is] the struggle without quarter between the people and reaction."[42]

For the armed forces, Peronist intransigence had compounded the country's problems. But Peronism was not the only offender. As Videla's successor, in October 1981 Gen. Roberto E. Viola set forth the military's political solution to the Argentine question: "Our task will not be over on eradicating subversion, but also aims at removing all those factors that since 1930 have prevented our political life from taking place within the channels of stability."[43] The date is important, for it pushed back the historical cycle associated with the crisis of democracy to the military coup of 1930—and Peronism could not be blamed for that.

The Argentine question, Alfonsín believes, has resulted in an "iron dilemma."[44] The reasonable alternative to a sterile oligarchy, a military obsessed with national salvation, a Radical party deaf to the claims of social justice, and a Peronist movement overcome with authoritarianism would be for each to have acknowledged its respective errors. Instead, they transformed their vices into virtues, leaving no way to escape the horns. To make matters worse, when these four protagonists planted this dilemma, "the tragic project of subversive terrorism appeared on the scene."[45] Thus the Argentine question is tied to the problem of subversion, whose effect was to make the solution of the dilemma even more difficult.[46]

The Specter of Subversion

A once-hospitable and democratic society, Argentina would become a political inferno of social unrest and armed subversion bordering on civil war. While partly a response to deteriorating economic conditions, violence was even more closely tied to the "failure to satisfy legitimate social aspirations, the frustration of human longings, and the deprivation of elemental necessities."[47] Together these nourished a situation favorable to the proliferation of tendencies toward social dissolution: "Chaos, political anarchy, the breakdown of productive activities were jumbled together in the vortex of disintegrating tendencies. . . . Indiscriminate repression without any legal foundation became functionally tied to subversion and thus contributed to the chaos."[48]

Like the political question, the social question in Argentina predates recognition of a uniquely Argentine question, but today they are inextricably intertwined. From the earliest appearance of the social question as a public issue it was a response to subversion and fears of social unrest. In Argentina it acquired notoriety with the publication of *La questione sociale,* edited by an Italian anarchist in exile, Errico Malatesta. Originally published in Florence, his journal also appeared briefly in Buenos Aires.[49] Malatesta's more than four years in Argentina (1885–1889) helped pioneer the anarchist movement in that country. Partly through his efforts the gospel of insurrection through a general strike caught on among Argentine workers, leading to the country's first general strike, in November 1902.[50]

For Malatesta, the social question stemmed from the misery in which most workers had to live.[51] He also underscored the collective effect of human misery on social unrest. "Conflict may be open or latent; but it always exists since the government does not pay attention to discontent and popular resistance except when it is faced with the danger of insurrection."[52] If the government does not give way by making concessions, the people will end by rebelling. But if the government does give way, then they will "make ever increasing demands, until such time as the incompatibility between freedom and authority becomes clear and the violent struggle is engaged."[53] Such is the iron dilemma of subversion that Argentine governments also had to address.

Understanding the social question in Argentina is basic to understanding both the guerrillas' response and the generals' dirty war. The least-understood and most-controversial component of the Argentine question, the social question has several dimensions. At the most elementary level it signifies no more than poverty and its train of human misery in the form of homelessness, inadequate food and clothing, overwork, unemployment, unsafe and unsanitary conditions, disease, mental depression, demoralization, and premature death. But these phenomena are not inert facts independent of human agency, as if the destitute were always with us.

One is apt to forget that the social question does not exist for primitive peoples, that it is confined to civilized society, and that civilization rests historically on slavery and its long-term consequences, which continue to take their toll. Today, as in the past, the submerged masses in Argentina are used to lay golden eggs for their masters. Those too weak, chronically disabled, or unable to work are discarded. José Peter, a common laborer who became secretary of the meatworkers' union, compared the lot of workers to that of other domesticated animals: "Such is the situation of the worker, who is treated by the enterprises with less consideration than the animals that work for them. The animals have to be bought, labor-power is only ill-paid when it serves for something. Afterwards it is thrown into the street . . . like a dirty rag."[54] In short, some people are poor and miserable because they exist to make others comfortable and contented.

The conditions just described operate as stimuli that are less important for our purposes than the response. Crime and prostitution appear as individual responses, and social unrest as a collective response to the same fundamental frustrations. The social question becomes acute when the victims become aware that somebody is to blame. At that point mass discontent escalates into industrial sabotage, guerrilla warfare, mass violence, and partial insurrections—as in Argentina following the coup within a coup that banned the majoritarian political party and shut down the General Confederation of Labor in November 1955.

When expressions of social discontent are repressed, they tend to reappear in more virulent form. As a result, the social question is compounded through a vicious cycle that becomes part of the problem. This is nowhere more manifest than in the contrasting solutions to the social question defended by the guerrillas and the armed forces in Argentina. Although the economic and political questions played a role, the specter of subversion was the immediate factor behind the generals' dirty war. The complex product of diverse circumstances, the guerrillas looked to a final solution to the social question that would exorcise not just the symptoms but the causes.

The social question is sometimes understood as the control and management of social ills underlying social unrest. At issue are not only humanitarian concerns, but also the avoidance of a social explosion that may topple the foundations of law and order. Argentine politicians in particular have been preoccupied with real or imagined threats of revolution. For them, as for members of the business community, the social question is not a problem for social workers but fundamentally the management of social discontent.

This question appears in a different light from the perspective of the victims. In his memoirs, José Peter identified the management of social discontent as also part of the problem: "Completely lacking in the knowledge of social problems—so that we had to carry on our backs all the consequences of a brutal regime of exploitation whose secrets were jealously hidden from us—it was easy for the companies to deceive us."[55]

The British and American managers raised the specter of the "Russians" as a way of fomenting divisions between native and foreign workers and of disparaging the Russian Revolution. As Peter recalled: "The problem of management was to divide the meat packers in order to prevent their united struggle; our problem was to join together."[56] Peter's response was to fan the flames of social unrest through agitation and class struggle. His veil of ignorance, he acknowledged with gratitude, was gradually removed thanks to the intervention of militants belonging to the Communist party.

As head of the meatworkers, Peter was instrumental in submitting a memorandum to the Argentine Congress in July 1939 directed against the Taylor system of scientific management installed in Swift slaughterhouses, cold chambers, and processing plants more than a decade earlier. The memorandum read in part: "The worker has had to accelerate the rhythm of work to such a degree that it has become a grave danger to his health . . . suffering from malnutrition, he is within a few years incapable of working any more, a condition aggravated by his having incurred incurable illnesses—asthma, tuberculosis, rheumatism. To this must be added the destruction of his nervous system by the inhuman rhythm of work and by a life of continued misery and hardship. In such conditions he loses the faculty of thought, all possibility of culture, the joy of living, including his mental balance."[57] Obviously, social workers cannot do anything about this aspect of the social question.

In an early essay on the social question, Karl Marx called the danger of pauperism England's national epidemic.[58] But in recognizing it as a social malady, he identified the social system divided into classes as the "root of the evil."[59] Among the first to venture a final solution to distress in the modern world, he denied that public charity and administrative measures could effectively cope with it. "Nothing less is required than the *abolition of the proletariat. . . . Revolution* in general—the *overthrow* of the existing power and *dissolution* of the old [social] relationships"—an eminently political act that Argentina's guerrillas have taken to heart.[60]

Since ownership defines social class, Marx concluded, there can be no social peace without a solution to the "property question."[61] He would later reaffirm this claim and the futility of stamping out subversion by repression. Nothing less is required than the abolition of bourgeois property: "The soil out of which it [proletarian class struggle] grows is modern society itself. To stamp it out, the governments would have to stamp out the despotism of capital over labor— the condition of their own parasitical existence"—a lesson Argentina's generals have yet to learn.[62]

It is instructive to compare the Argentine generals' approach to the social question with that of British imperial politicians at the turn of the century. The chief difference is that Britain had a safety valve for social unrest in the colonies, where it could funnel its poor and unemployed. As Lenin cites Cecil Rhodes's proposed solution to the social question: "My cherished idea is a solution for the social problem, i.e., in order to save the 40,000,000 inhabitants of the United Kingdom from a bloody civil war, we colonial statesmen must acquire new lands to settle the surplus population. . . . If you want to avoid civil war, you must become imperialists."[63] Lacking this distinctive privilege, Argentina's armed forces were driven to more drastic methods, which Britain might have adopted if its circumstances had been different. To save the twenty-five million inhabitants of Argentina from a bloody civil confrontation, they rooted out the dissidents and potential troublemakers at the relatively modest price of, by some estimates, thirty thousand "disappeared."

This kind of political reasoning was first made famous by Thomas Hobbes. For Hobbes the social question was a matter not only of poverty, but also of agitation threatening to turn society upside down. Concerned less with the fact of poverty than with its potential for social unrest, he was the first modern philosopher to write a treatise on subversion and to proffer a final solution to the subversion problem. Noting that Presbyterian ministers and agitators were to blame for the deaths of some one hundred thousand during the civil wars, he added: "Had it not been much better that those seditious ministers, which were not perhaps 1000, had been all killed before they had preached?"[64] That such a small "massacre" would have saved lives compared to the larger one was also used to justify Argentina's Military Process.

Most responses to the social question focus on one of its two principal dimensions. When symptoms are of major concern, the social question takes the form of the subversion problem. But underlying the subversion problem lies the redistribution problem, and behind it, the property question. In claiming that no revolution has ever liberated humankind from the distress of poverty and exploitation, Argentine liberals simply reiterate the age-old adage that both the redistribution problem and the property question are basically insoluble.

The first Argentine statesman to face up to the Argentine question and to work actively to solve the social question was Juan Domingo Perón. Summarized in his slogan "Political sovereignty, economic independence, and social justice," the Justicialist solution to the country's ills gave prominence to the social question. To the question: "What is the problem in the Argentine Republic that should take precedence over all others?" he answered: "A social cataclysm."[65] Because social peace is the foundation on which to build constructive solutions to every other national problem, the first priority of the Justicialist movement was the establishment of social justice.[66]

With its roots in economic inequality, the social question does not become fully articulate until the masses begin clamoring for their rights. In past ages misery in the midst of abundance was tolerated because the poor could do nothing to relieve their condition. Without the right to participate in political affairs, they submitted to the powers that be. All that changed with the French Revolution, the spread of democracy in the nineteenth century, and mass agitation against social injustices. As Perón observed: "Misery in the midst of plenty is now intolerable and a question that demands a final solution once and for all."[67]

The social question became a political problem in Argentina when elites began to deceive the people with fraudulent elections and the proscription of the majoritarian parties while simultaneously defending democracy.[68] But those remedies no longer work; Argentina has become ungovernable. "As long as the government is not surrendered to whoever wins, there will be uprisings and insubordination. No solution will be reached and the country will move ever closer to the abyss. That is the fundamental problem."[69]

However, many Argentines believe that the Peronist phenomenon is part of the problem. Peronist efforts to ameliorate the condition of the masses not only stirred up unwanted controversy, but also backfired. Behavior guided by fear of revolution responded to an interpretation of social unrest that did not always correspond to reality.[70] Thus in a discussion of the intellectual dimension of the Argentine question, Waisman ties the breakdown of liberal democracy to the state elites' allegedly distorted perception of the specter of subversion.[71]

For the military the threat was a real one. Convinced that human life had suffered under the curse of poverty and misery since time immemorial, it despaired of any final solution to the social question. Without having read Hannah Arendt on revolution, it concurred that "no revolution has ever solved the 'social question' and liberated men from the predicament of want"; furthermore, "the whole record of past revolutions demonstrates beyond doubt that every attempt to solve the social question with political means leads into terror."[72]

Instead of a final solution to the social question, the armed forces attempted a final solution to the subversion problem. Officially designated the "final resolution," it included Nazi techniques of "disappearing" people in mass graves along with new methods of disposing of political undesirables.[73] Ostensibly occupied with combating terrorism, it ended by intimidating the entire population. Here, too, the cure appeared to many to be worse than the malady.

Without a revolutionary redistribution of the economic surplus, there can be few prospects for social peace in Argentina. Subversion feeds on poverty and misery in the midst of plenty. To remove the cause is to cancel the effect, but it takes a revolution to do so. There will be social peace, says the head of the printers' union, Raimundo Ongaro, only with the advent of a republic of equals.[74] Few share his optimism about a coming reign of equality. But there is no denying his conclusion that a world without privilege, a fundamental leveling from the top down as well as the bottom up, is the only final solution to the social question.

2. The Military Era

THE GENERALS' dirty war cannot be understood apart from military repression in Argentina, nor can the latter be understood apart from the country's first experiment in democracy and the tide of subversion unloosed by the Russian Revolution.[1] In October 1916 Hipólito Yrigoyen became president for a six-year period at the head of the nation's first populist movement, the Radical Civic Union. Yet within a few years his populist policies were held responsible for opening the floodgates to the January 1919 *porteñazo*, the mass uprising in the port city of Buenos Aires. Since the police were unable to quell the riots, the president directed the armed forces to intervene. An example had been set for the military. Beginning with the coup that toppled Yrigoyen during his second term of office in 1930, the armed forces began intervening on their own.

The military era that began in September 1930 momentarily put an end to Argentina's brief essay in democracy. The September coup was the first of its kind since the armed forces had become professionalized following the military reform laws of 1900 and 1905. It was the first to have the backing of professionally trained officers instead of military *caudillos*. By World War I a professional army was already being formed. Since the turn of the century its lowest-ranking officers had been required to be graduates of the Military College. In 1900 the Superior War College had been founded for the purpose of preparing officers for the army's general staff. Military officials came to resemble professionals in other fields: engineers, architects, physicians, lawyers. Thus a military technobureaucracy emerged whose first successful coup in 1930 marked the beginning of an era distinct from military rule in the nineteenth century.

In Argentina military intervention became institutionalized. The Supreme Court set a precedent for the military era by ruling in 1930 that the armed forces may legitimately oust an elected government because they alone have the task of protecting life, liberty, and property in the event the established order breaks down. The military may exercise this right when it states the reasons for its intervention, when it outlines its course of action, and when it swears under oath to obey the constitution and uphold existing legislation.

In searching out precedents for legalizing the September coup, the Supreme Court turned to Roman law. According to Roman law a dictator could lawfully replace the decisions of an elected assembly in a time of national emergency. But the process of selecting the dictator did not envision his imposition by a military coup. Moreover, the dictator was bound by the body of existing laws and the constitution in ways that a military junta is not. In short, there was no Roman precedent for the Argentine court's extraordinary decision.

The effect of this court ruling was to legitimate prospective coups in advance, provided they were successful. The Supreme Court's ruling also encouraged disaffected elements and political parties to engage in intrigue and conspire with the armed forces. Virtually every political party had a reason to cultivate military support for its projects. The precedent set by the Supreme Court made Argentina an exception to the rule of law practiced among civilized nations. Beginning with the coup of September 1930 and continuing through the coup of March 1976, military governments presented their cases before the Supreme Court, which made them legal retroactively.

The coup that toppled Yrigoyen perpetuated in open or concealed form the rule of the armed forces until their most recent decision to abdicate in December 1983. This is not to say that the military era is over. Even when Perón finally returned to power in 1973, he did so with the blessing of the armed forces as their last hope of quelling the subversive virus provoked by successive military interventions. Caution requires that judgment be postponed until the present fluid situation in Argentina has had a chance to crystallize. An end to the military era was prematurely announced in 1973. Only the PRT-ERP questioned this presumption. Ironically, history confirmed the judgment of an extremist party against all the counsels of political moderates. A decade later the same general optimism surfaced when the military abdicated. Today that mood has all but vanished.

The Crisis of Democracy

The history of Argentine democracy begins with the 1892 founding of the Radical Civic Union (UCR) and the emergence of Yrigoyen as its leader. Nicknamed the *peludo* (armadillo) for his behind-the-scenes talent as an organizer, Yrigoyen became the chief architect of his party's strategy of political abstention as a means of securing electoral reform. This strategy called for boycotting the presidential elections of 1898, 1904, and 1910 on the grounds that electoral fraud and the buying of votes made them unrepresentative. Backed by threats of a "revolution for democracy" and by a succession of Radical-sponsored military rebellions in 1890, 1893, and 1905, Yrigoyen's strategy of intransigence eventually bore fruit in the Sáenz Peña electoral reform of 1912.

The secret ballot helped to nullify electoral bribery and the introduction of compulsory voting and guaranteed minority representation contributed to reducing abstention. Previously, a combination of electoral fraud, bribery, and abstention guaranteed that the oligarchy would win and the winner would take all. The reforms provided that the party that ran second would share in the distribution of seats in a ratio of one to every two seats for the victor. Although foreigners made up the bulk of the industrial bourgeoisie and the urban proletariat and could not vote, those who could vote were induced to develop electoral machines to mobilize the popular will.

Ironically, the advent of democracy precipitated a rash of political, military, and economic crises that, beginning in 1930, have plagued Argentina ever since. Each crisis has involved a loss of control and a failure in performance. Although the agroexport oligarchy was able to conserve its economic privileges, it lost the reins of political power. By 1916 it had split into two wings. The "traditionalists" backed the mainstream Partido Conservador (PC)—which in 1931 would rename itself the Partido Demócrata Nacional (PDN). Because this was only a change of face, it would still be referred to as "Conservative." The "modernizers" supported the 1912 electoral reform, but their Partido Demócrata Progresista (PDP) never caught on among the electorate. Thus in the 1916 elections, the Progressive Democrats won only 22 percent of the vote. Although Conservatives and Progressive Democrats together polled some 45 percent of the total, the Radical Civic Union alone accounted for some 48 percent.

The resounding victory of the Radicals, repeated in the presidential elections of 1922 and 1928, finally motivated a Conservative backlash. Favoring elections only as long as they could win them or participate in a compromise government, Conservatives began to conspire against the democratic regime. The result was a new type of crisis that questioned the underlying norms of the electoral process and the constitution. This crisis of legitimacy, compounded by the Great Depression and the fear of mounting social unrest, provoked the military to intervene in September 1930.

Originally a questioning of the rules of the political game by the oligarchy, the crisis was perpetuated by the military's lack of confidence in democracy. Under conditions in which a stable two-party system of the British type could not be assured, there was no way of guaranteeing the periodic and peaceful transition to power by a loyal opposition. The crisis of democracy became aggravated by fears of a breakdown of authority and the spread of subversion. Whenever these fears aroused visions of a repetition of the mass violence under Yrigoyen or the threat of a popular government in Argentina, the military intervened.

Military intervention was encouraged by the specter of subversion after World War I. In Argentina fears of communism were heightened by the presence of an urban working class consisting primarily of foreigners. Mostly immigrants from Italy and Spain, they were strongly influenced by anarchist doctrines that shared common ground with Russian bolshevism. Anarchists were among the first to support the October Revolution of 1917, and in many countries they joined with left-wing socialists to form the nucleus of new Communist vanguards. In Argentina the influx of Russian Jews addicted to Marxism compounded the fears of imminent social unrest. The Jewish community in Buenos Aires was becoming the second largest in the world after New York City's. With mounting fears of Communist subversion this also fanned the flames of anti-Semitism.

A highly politicized and militant labor movement emerged during and after World War I, supposedly encouraged by the demagogy of the populist party in power. Populism provided an excuse for subversion, according to Conservatives, with the implication that the democracy of the polls was illegitimate. It also provided an excuse for military coups aimed at repressing the conditions of subversion in populist demagogy.

Italian fascism had led the way in the struggle against populist and socialist ideologies in Europe. It also provided a model for countering subversion in Argentina, whose population of predominantly Italian origin naturally looked to Italy for inspiration. As early as 1925 Alfredo Rocco, with Mussolini's endorsement, traced the intellectual roots of subversion to the spread of democratic ideology. The logic of fascism was clear: to control subversion one must put an end to democracy, and to uproot democracy one must target the liberal philosophy that gave it birth.[2] This meant replacing the liberal doctrine of human rights with traditional Catholic values, giving precedence to the claims of society over those of individuals.

In this perspective the crisis of democracy came to be linked with the causes of subversion. Western European democracy had provided fertile ground for the spreading Communist virus, while fascism showed the way to its eradication. The constant factor, common denominator, and justifying rationale of the military coups from 1930 on was in each case the so-called scourge of subversion. For the most part, even the military's negotiated abdications were motivated by fears that to remain in power would encourage social unrest.

Like the influenza epidemic that took the lives of some ten million Europeans and another half-million Americans in 1918, the Communist virus spread by the Russian Revolution had gotten out of hand. In Argentina as elsewhere, efforts were made to immunize the local population. A succession of red scares prompted the Radical government to call on troops to crush the workers. The military did its duty but complained that the Radical party had encouraged workers to make excessive demands. If the country had been governed properly, it reasoned, the police could have quelled the riots and the army need not have intervened.

During the 1919 red scare the country experienced its first proletarian uprising. In a rash of violent demonstrations in the nation's capital during the week of January 9–16, 1919, known as the *semana trágica* (tragic week), more than a hundred died and hundreds more were wounded by the army and right-wing death squads hired by employers. The spark that ignited this first *porteñazo*—a second *porteñazo* occurred in January 1959—was the death of five workers in clashes with hired thugs during a strike at the Pedro Vasena Metallurgical Workshops. A general strike was declared in protest. The struggle culminated in pitched battles between workers and the armed forces. The workers who had occupied the workshops were machine-gunned by troops commanded by a young lieutenant, Juan Domingo Perón.[3]

The second red scare erupted late in 1921 and continued through January 1922 in southern Patagonia. There the rural workers rebelled against British and Argentine sheep ranchers because of oppressive work conditions and low pay. Many Chilean migrant workers joined the general strike that paralyzed the entire province of Santa Cruz. Massive layoffs sparked the unrest. Led by anarchists influenced by the Bolshevik Revolution, the workers armed themselves and established a de facto soviet in control of the major cities and the countryside. The army was sent to intervene in the nation's first dirty war involving the unprecedented massacre of some fifteen hundred strikers following their surrender. Their bodies were never recovered because they were interred in mass graves. The headquarters of the mass rebellion was Río Gallegos, the provincial capital. Having grown up on a nearby sheep ranch at the beginning of the century, Perón had firsthand knowledge of the oppressive social conditions that contributed to the uprising.[4]

The army was enraged when the commanding officer of the punitive expedition, Col. Héctor B. Varela, was assassinated in revenge. The Argentine military has been committed to a struggle against subversion ever since.

Distress concerning the future of democracy in Argentina suggests a replay of Alexis de Tocqueville's misgivings about the future of the Great French Revolution. As he noted in his *Recollections:* "The Constitutional Monarchy had succeeded the Ancien Regime; the Republic, the Monarchy; the Empire, the Republic; the Restoration, the Empire; and then came the Monarchy of July. After each of these successive changes it was said that the French Revolution, having accomplished what was presumptuously called its work, was finished; this had been said and it had been believed. Alas! . . . here is the French Revolution beginning over again!"[5] He also wondered whether the 1848 revolution was destined to achieve an even more far-reaching social transformation than that of 1789 or was "destined simply to end in a condition of intermittent anarchy."[6]

In Argentina the sequence of military governments, restricted democracies, and tyrannies of the majority in the wake of its first crisis of democracy presents an even more disconcerting spectacle than that described by Tocqueville. Three Radical governments from 1916 to 1930 succeeded the oligarchical regime; the 1930 dictatorship replaced the last Radical government; restricted democracy replaced the 1930 dictatorship; the 1943 military regime replaced the restricted democracy; a Peronist tyranny of the majority replaced the 1943 military regime; in 1955 a liberal backlash replaced the tyranny of the majority; the 1966 dictatorship replaced the liberal backlash; in 1973 a renewed tyranny of the majority replaced the dictatorship; the 1976 Military Process replaced the new tyranny of the majority; and then came the Radical government of 1983. Like France in 1848, which had to repeat the work of 1789, Argentina was back where it had started in 1916.

In several ways the political history of Argentina from 1930 to 1983 is a rehash of French political history from the Restoration to the Third Republic. As in France during the nineteenth century, there was a crisis of democracy and an unstable political situation characterized by a four-way collision between Conservatives (Liberals), Radicals (Democrats), Peronists (Bonapartists), and the country's political-military vanguards (Blanquists).[7] Although historical analogies are risky, the same social classes were at loggerheads, as were their corresponding political ideologies.

In the events leading up to the electoral reform and universal suffrage for men, Argentina's elites were aware of the unfolding similarities between French society and their own.[8] In 1848 the provisional government installed by the February revolution had passed the first universal suffrage law for men in European history. According to the head of the provisional government, democracy signified a "conservative liberty . . . [a] better order . . . than in a government by a few for a few.[9] In Argentina, too, democracy found favor among the elites as a dike against social unrest. "If political exclusion were maintained," they argued, "the nation risked a repetition of the upheavals of the early 1890s."[10] Thus universal suffrage for men was designed "to contain and control the effects of social change and to buttress their own position."[11]

The elites were also impressed by the British experience. It is noteworthy that the dominant ideological influence behind the electoral reform derived from the liberalism of John Stuart Mill.[12] Like Mill, the reformers expressed an ambivalent attitude toward democracy, fearing what Mill called a prospective "tyranny of the majority,"[13] hence their concern to limit the sphere in which it is legitimate for democracy to interfere in individual liberties. The unrestrained will of the people left open the frightening prospect of what the Argentine poet-statesman Leopoldo Lugones called "barbaric majoritarianism," "the democratic degeneration of universal suffrage abolished by the Greeks and Romans after exhausting its possibilities."[14]

Although Mill rejected the earlier liberal doctrine of natural rights, he believed that democracy ceases to be legitimate when it violates what can reasonably be assigned to people as their rights. These include freedom of thought, expression, and association, along with freedom to do anything we please as long as others are not injured by it.[15] This was interpreted by Argentine liberals as respect for people's property as well as their opinions.

By the middle of the last century European liberalism had become discredited because of its ambivalent assessment of democracy. Even Mill proposed plural votes for the educated.[16] Almost uniformly, "classical liberals not only restricted political rights to the propertied or educated but opposed extending equality into the social and economic spheres."[17] A similar situation occurred in Argentina after the electoral reforms proved disappointing to the Conservatives, who were not returned to power. In their judgment the vote had been a gift to citizens who had betrayed their trust and forfeited their right to use it. The franchise was not a birthright, they believed, but must be earned individually or by past family members who bequeathed it to their heirs. That was the attitude of British Liberals in the nineteenth century, an attitude underlying the curtailment of Argentine democracy and its suppression in the twentieth.

Restricted Democracy

The sequence of military coups that has dominated Argentine political life for half a century got its start during the Great Depression. The military feared that massive layoffs might generate a wave of labor unrest. This resulted in the third red scare, of 1929–1930. In a brief memoir published in *Panorama* (14 April 1970), Perón acknowledged that the overthrow of President Yrigoyen "had been prepared by the tragic week of 1919."

In his monumental study on the Argentine military, Alain Rouquié explains Argentina's third red scare by a combination of factors, including memories of the anti-Bolshevik panic of 1919.[18] In May 1929 the Confederación Sindical Latinoamericana (CSLA), the regional organization of the Red Trade Union International, was founded in Montevideo. The following month the first Conference of Latin American Communist Parties met in Buenos Aires. Legalized by the Radical party, the Argentine CP had polled more than 2 percent of the vote in the nation's capital and close to one percent in the country during the 1928 elections. Although the figures were not themselves alarming, the massive unemployment and deteriorating social situation in 1929 aroused fears that the Communists might take advantage of mounting labor discontent.[19] These fears were exacerbated by a recrudescence of social banditry and anarchist bands specializing in counterfeiting and armed holdups.[20]

Instead of remaining firm against social pressures, Yrigoyen chose concessions. By launching a comprehensive program of reforms, including an eight-hour day and a forty-eight-hour week, in August 1929, he was criticized for fueling mass unrest. Such was the background to the 1930 coup, which had for its principal objective the annulment of the electoral reform of 1912 and a return to restricted democracy.

The idea of a coup was first implanted by civilians, who approached retired general José Félix Uriburu late in 1927 in the hope of preventing Yrigoyen from being reelected. Uriburu's civilian supporters included the Patriotic League, founded in January 1919 to hunt down strikers and rioters during the *semana trágica*. The Republican league, founded by Catholic nationalists in 1929 to restore republican institutions eroded by the plague of Yrigoyenism, also provided support. So did admirers of Leopoldo Lugones, who favored an authoritarian and military solution to the country's problems.

Lugones traced the doctrines of communism to the democratic ideology of the French Revolution inspired by Jean-Jacques Rousseau. Since the belief in political equality prepared the way for the Communist doctrine of economic equality, he argued, the only effective response to the Communist threat was to place restrictions on democracy.[21] It was his article in *La Nación* (24 May 1931) that first coined the expression "struggle against the internal enemy."

Convinced that democracy was a breeding ground of subversion and that liberalism was the fountainhead of democracy, Uriburu tried to install a fascist-type corporative regime modeled on Mussolini's Italy. A state of siege was imposed during which he dissolved the trade unions controlled by anarchists and Communists and had their leaders arrested en masse. Those who were still unnaturalized he forcibly deported. Members of the legal Socialist party also were arrested and harassed by the government. The anarchist Di Giovanni, convicted of counterfeiting and armed robbery, was given the death sentence. Repression of subversion became an excuse for strikebreaking, for ignoring past labor legislation, and for destroying the Radical party. The president and vice-president were imprisoned, Radical functionaries were fired on the pretext of administrative reorganization, and prominent leaders of the party were forced into exile.

The military regime of 1930–1932 was supported by the army under the active direction of Gen. Agustín P. Justo. But neither he nor most of his officers shared Uriburu's corporatist panacea. Uriburu hoped to reform the 1853 Constitution, but Justo was a liberal committed to preserving it. Under pressure from the army and its Conservative allies, elections were called in four provinces in April 1931. The state of siege was lifted, but after the Radicals won in the province of Buenos Aires in April, it was reimposed and the remaining elections were canceled.

Even these actions failed to satisfy the army's liberals. Thus in a virtual palace coup on April 17, manipulated from behind the scenes by General Justo, Uriburu was given an ultimatum: resign or convoke presidential elections before the end of the year.[22] National elections were then scheduled under conditions of restricted participation.

To assure that the Radical Civic Union or Radical party would not win again, the military government invited the opposition parties to form a broad front including anti-Yrigoyenist Radicals. But the UCR reunited despite the government's efforts to divide it. In July, Radical military officers staged an abortive uprising in Corrientes in response to suspended elections in their province. The government then banned the Radical party. This set the stage for the unprincipled Concordancia, an electoral alliance dominated by anti-Yrigoyenist Radicals and Conservatives. In August the anti-Yrigoyenist Radicals launched the candidacy of General Justo, an action ratified at their convention in September. Justo also received support from the mis-named independent Socialists, whose candidate for vice-president, Julio A. Roca, became Justo's running mate.

With the majoritarian party momentarily banned, the only op-position to Argentina's first "Great National Accord" came from an alliance of Lisandro de la Torre's right-of-center Progressive Demo-cratic party (PDP) and Nicolás Repetto's Socialist party. Since both had condoned the September coup, they could hardly hope for exten-sive Radical support. Meanwhile, Justo's supporters believed that to ensure victory the November elections had to be rigged. And so they were, in one of the most disgraceful and fraudulent elections in the nation's history—the price of saving the 1853 Constitution.

The September 1937 presidential elections saw a repeat perfor-mance. In addition to behind-the-scenes fraud, the secret ballot was replaced by public voting in the key provinces of Buenos Aires and Santa Fe without election tellers for the opposition. Even so, new elections had to be called in no less than nine provinces to bring about the Radicals' defeat.

Justo had deliberately chosen a weak candidate to succeed him, the anti-Yrigoyenist Radical Roberto M. Ortiz. Isolated from his party, President Ortiz had no political base of his own. Faced with the option of being a shadow president or governing the country as he wished, Ortiz realigned himself with the UCR. On the eve of con-gressional elections in March 1940, he astonished the nation in a speech repudiating the electoral methods of the Concordancia. As a consequence, the Radicals won 80 of the 158 seats in the lower chamber—a clear majority. Thus radicalism was again perceived as a threat by military officers.

Many were relieved when in July 1940 the president, because of illness, was obliged to delegate powers to the Conservative vice-president, Ramón S. Castillo. When Ortiz was pressured to resign in June 1942, Castillo became president. By replacing anti-Yrigoyenist Radicals in his cabinet, he effectively set up a new government dominated by Conservatives. This new government had even less credibility than the one it replaced.

During World War II there was a new upsurge in labor discontent. The number of strikes more than doubled between 1939 and 1942.[23] The victory of the Popular Front in the Spanish elections of 1936, followed by the establishment of a "Red Republic" and the ensuing civil war, caused apprehension concerning a future popular front in Argentina.

These fears were fostered by the embryo of a popular front of Yrigoyenist Radicals, Socialists, and Communists aimed at contesting the ill-reputed Concordancia. In November 1941, the Tenth Congress of the Argentine Communist party had formally adopted the thesis of a popular front. The Socialist party and the Progressive Democratic party accepted the idea, followed by the UCR at the end of 1942. Since these parties called for supporting the liberal democracies and their Communist ally in World War II, when it appeared that the allied powers might win the war, there was even further cause for consternation.

The prospect of a democratic alternative to the unpopular Concordancia evoked extremely negative images among Argentine officers. The Spanish civil war and the French defeat were blamed on their respective popular front governments, which had tolerated Communist propaganda. Army officers fretted over the prospect of postwar revolutionary subversion encouraged by a similar front in Argentina. "The colonels of 1942–1943 vividly recalled the 1919 *semana trágica* in Buenos Aires and the rebellions in Patagonia, according to them the result of lack of government foresight."[24] Some of them had occupied positions of first rank as lieutenants or captains in the repression of those popular movements.

The military lodge dominated by Colonel Perón, the Grupo Obra de Unificación (GOU), aimed to prepare Argentine officers for the anticipated postwar struggle against a Communist upsurge. Its articles of foundation explicitly acknowledged the "menace of a Communist revolution of a popular front type."[25] As the second number of the GOU's bulletin pointed out, the army would be the antidote to the "poison of the pseudodemocratic alliance made up of communizing elements."[26] Thus military officers geared themselves to resist the supposed threat to their country.

Fear of a popular front victory at the polls was not the only catalyst of President Castillo's downfall. Another was the aura of moral corruption that surrounded the government and undermined its authority. Several cabinet ministers and prominent personalities close to the government became involved in shady financial speculations. Politicians had been amassing private fortunes from war profits, artificial scarcities, and the black market since the United States entered the war in December 1941, at a moment when the government could not provide the wherewithal for the nation's defense. Because of its policy of neutrality the government was excluded from receiving military aid from the United States, yet it had been wholly ineffectual in obtaining such aid from the Axis.

Although General Justo had urged the president to declare war in the hope of receiving aid, his unexpected death in January 1943 deprived the army's liberal wing of influence on the government. At the same time, Catholic nationalists had little reason to rejoice over the prospect of a popular front defeat achieved through fraudulent elections and morally corrupt politicians. The GOU in particular was committed to eliminating corruption in government on the grounds that it encouraged cynicism, undermined loyalty, and left the nation morally defenseless in the ideological struggle against communism.

Pro-Allies and pro-Axis officers alike were confronted by a dilemma posed by the 1943 presidential elections: if honest, the elections would result in victory for the popular front, whose unprincipled demagogy would open the door to subversion; if dishonest, they would perpetuate the climate of moral lassitude in a government whose lack of legitimacy might also provide fuel for subversion. Thus both army liberals and Catholic nationalists resolved on a military coup that would dissolve Congress and postpone elections.

Tyranny of the Majority

Nobody could have guessed on 4 June 1943, the day of the coup, that its liberal head, Gen. Arturo Rawson, would be replaced within two days by a second coup representing the minoritarian nationalist current in the armed forces. Not only would Catholic nationalists gain ascendancy, but they would also look in desperation to organized labor to counter the tidal wave of opposition from the established political parties. Of the fifteen top army officers who launched the uprising, only two belonged to the GOU.[27] Thus the country was taken by surprise when the moderate Catholic nationalist general Pedro Ramírez was appointed president on June 6, and when he in turn was deposed in a coup led by nationalist hard-liners in February 1944. But the biggest surprise was yet to come. An army colonel with Fascist proclivities, Juan Domingo Perón, triumphed in the February 1946 elections to become the advocate of the most extreme democracy in the country's history. How it happened is one of the great puzzles of Argentine politics.

Matters came to a head when President Castillo dismissed his war minister, General Ramírez, on 3 June 1943.The dismissal was taken as an insult by all sectors of the armed forces. Ramírez's refusal to resign and the army's support of his decision led directly to Castillo's overthrow. Ironically, the organizer of the coup was General Rawson, whose political ties were neither with the pro-Allies Radicals nor with the pro-Axis nationalists but with members of Castillo's party.

As nominal head of the military conspiracy, Rawson repeated Castillo's mistake of appointing a cabinet dominated by Conservatives. Not one of the coup's original organizers received a government post. The colonels in direct command of troops had been relegated to the sidelines. But it was not their intention that pampered oligarchs and members of the Jockey Club should be abruptly removed and then returned to power. The colonels hurriedly met at the initiative of the GOU and demanded that General Rawson appoint another cabinet before being sworn in as president. When he refused, they obliged him to resign.

The GOU selected General Ramírez, the colonels' friend, to succeed him. As a result of this coup within a coup, the GOU's program became the program of the military government. The GOU became the vehicle by which a small group of middle-ranking officers wormed their way into key government positions and took over the reins of the army through their control of the decisive Ministry of War. It was a conspiratorial organization dominated by Catholic nationalists.

The colonels rejected the Concordancia for being soft on corruption, and the majoritarian Radical party for being soft on subversion. Opposed to all political parties, they naturally favored direct rule by the armed forces. In this respect they reaffirmed the objectives of Uriburu's 1930 coup. However, they tacitly repudiated the informal alliance between the armed forces and the agroexport oligarchy that, cemented by General Justo as well as by Uriburu, had dominated Argentine political life for more than a decade.

The crackdown on subversion and excessive labor demands began on June 4 with a wave of arrests of Communist party leaders and militants. General Rawson set the tone by ordering the detention of the editor of the Communist newspaper *La Hora* and his execution by a firing squad. On June 6 the leaders of the meatworkers' union, Federación Obrera de la Industria de la Carne (FOIC), were arrested and their local closed. Its general secretary, the Communist José Peter, was imprisoned without trial for almost a year and a half. In July the government dissolved the labor federation encompassing the biggest unions responsive to political activists in the Socialist and Communist parties and in August it removed the general secretary and supervisory council of the railroad workers in the Unión Ferroviaria (UF). Perón, who was completely identified with the military regime, was not averse to repression. On the contrary, he considered it necessary to break the stranglehold of exotic ideologies on the proletariat preliminary to his project of "nationalizing" the working class.

Labor was not the only target of the military. Corrupt politicians insensitive to national interests also came under fire. On June 5 the government dissolved Congress. Later that month it removed all elected provincial authorities, replacing them with military delegates. Elections were indefinitely postponed, and on June 18 the military government stopped referring to itself as provisional. On December 31 it banned all political parties and established control over the mass media. Uriburu's dream was taking shape as Catholic nationalists pushed aside Justo's clan of liberals to gain control of the armed forces.

At the same time, under the leadership of Colonel Perón as secretary of labor and welfare, a sector of the army moved from a mainly authoritarian position to a form of military populism. These military reformers shared the basic premises of Catholic nationalists but hoped to attack the causes of subversion, not just its symptoms. Instead of relying on repression to achieve their goals, military populists made concessions to the working class that effectively lost them the support of the oligarchy. Although Catholic nationalists were skeptical of the outcome of the new strategy, their alliance with the army's reformist wing was to continue for the next decade.

Perón propelled himself into a decisive position in the government in February 1944, only eight months after the coup that ousted General Rawson. In January, under pressure from the United States, President Ramírez had broken diplomatic ties with the Axis. The GOU and other nationalist officers reacted to this move with indignation. Several weeks later, the president turned against his nationalist critics by demanding Gen. Edelmiro Farrell's resignation as vice-president and war minister. But Perón with other officers at the War Ministry retaliated by forcing Ramírez's resignation and by delegating his mandate to the vice-president. Perón then became the new war minister and was appointed vice-president in June. At the same time, he retained his earlier position as secretary of labor and welfare.

Because the U.S. State Department interpreted this new coup as the work of pro-Axis elements angered by the rupture with Germany, it refused to recognize the government and made preparations to oust it. During the inter-American conference at Chapultepec, Mexico, in February 1945, the conditions for diplomatic recognition were spelled out. Argentina would have to declare war on the Axis and repress Nazi-Fascist activity inside the country. The United States demanded that national elections be scheduled and that the government be transferred to the Supreme Court. Although the government declared war on the Axis and diplomatic relations were restored in April, the newly appointed ambassador, Spruille Braden, arrived in May committed to ending fascist military control of Argentina.

With Braden as their inspiration and the tacit backing of the United States, the political opposition began to gel. In May the state of siege in effect since December 1941 was lifted. Braden pressured Perón to release political prisoners and to lift censorship of the press. His conviction that Perón and his associates were Fascist and Nazi sympathizers was picked up by the political opposition and by July had begun influencing younger officers. Responding to pressure from the army's rank and file, President Farrell announced on July 6 that elections would be scheduled, that there would be no fraud, and that the military would respect the people's will.

But these concessions failed to placate the opposition. Demonstrations against the military regime became a daily affair. In August, university students took to the streets while Socialists led the campaign for transferring government powers to the Supreme Court. Shortly afterward the state of siege was restored. Such was the political background of the third coup within the coup, this one by army liberals who issued an order for Perón's arrest and forced his resignation from the government on 9 October 1945.

The exhilaration of the political opposition that resulted from having overcome the forces of "fascism" lasted only a few days. For most military officers the new government's decision to return them to the barracks amounted to unconditional surrender—a betrayal of the revolution of June 1943. Although they feared the consequences of Perón's demagogy, as a defender of the armed forces he appeared the lesser evil compared to a revived Concordancia or a Radical victory in a popular front with Socialists and Communists. This explains their response to the general political strike called by the Confederación General del Trabajo (CGT) for October 18. It began on the seventeenth when hundreds of thousands of workers converged on Plaza de Mayo to demand Perón's release. The leaders of the coup were pressured to abdicate not just by workers, but also by Catholic nationalists and reformers in the army. The sole concession to the opposition was President Farrell's promise to schedule elections in 1946, when Perón would become the armed forces' candidate to guarantee military hegemony.[28]

Perón's project for enlisting labor support to nullify the anticipated postbellum wave of subversion was the only realistic option for the military. The resolution of the October crisis did not impose Perón as the army's candidate, but it did make evident his usefulness and virtual indispensability to the military, because of the pressure for elections that could no longer be feasibly postponed. As Rouquié comments, the October crisis revealed the existence of an autonomous military power jealous of its responsibilities and intent on delegating them in a way most advantageous to its corporate interests.[29]

The February elections were the fairest in Argentine history to that date. Perón defeated the unprincipled alliance of Conservatives, Radicals, Socialists, and Communists in the Unión Democrática (UD) by a margin of some 300,000 votes. It was not an overwhelming triumph, but it was enough to capture 304 of the 376 votes of the Electoral College and to pack the lower chamber with two-thirds of his delegates. Thus began the country's initiation into the first democratic steamroller, which stopped short only of making the opposition illegal. Indeed, the only curb to Perón's ambitions of scrapping the old political order and its system of political parties came from the military.

At least one political historian characterizes Argentina's perfect democracy as a "Dictatorship" with Perón as "Dictator."[30] By the time he was inaugurated his Secret Service numbered thirty thousand, and within a few years its goons, identified by their brown suits and gabardine raincoats—the supposed equivalent of Hitler's Gestapo—had tripled in number.[31] An unrestricted but illiberal and repressive democracy, according to its critics, Argentina under Perón systematically silenced political opposition.

Perón started by purging the civil service and judicial system. "Soon, no civil servant remained in his post who was suspected of any reservations in his personal loyalty towards the President, and all non-Peronista judges disappeared from the Bench."[32] The process began in September 1946 with the impeachment of members of the Supreme Court, until by the end of 1949 more than seventy federal judges had been replaced by judges responsive to Perón.[33]

In May 1949 a new constitution went into effect, permitting the president to serve consecutive terms. In September a gag law was pushed through Congress aimed at muzzling the opposition. The Ley de Descato, or contempt law, increased the penalties for slander and defamation against constituted authorities while denying the accused the right to present evidence in defense.[34] Although members of the opposition were already being purged from Congress for bad behavior—the Radical leader Ricardo Balbín was expelled in August 1950—that was not enough. Thus when the new law was invoked against him in November he received a five-year prison sentence.

The gag on the press also led to raids on the principal metropolitan newspapers beginning in November and December 1949. These were followed by the nationalization of all newsprint in February and outright expropriation of *La Prensa* in January 1951.[35] About the same time the Bicameral Investigation Commission on Un-Argentine Activities began its deliberations while another judicial monstrosity, the 1950 Law against Espionage, Sabotage, and Treason, broadened the definition of crimes against the state and the powers of police to investigate them. Thus, as the erosion of civil liberties became more and more evident, other prominent leaders of the opposition had to seek refuge in exile.

With such tactics Perón increased his stranglehold on Congress. In the first Peronist-dominated assembly (1946) there were 109 Peronist delegates and 49 representing the opposition—almost all Radicals. In the presidential elections of November 1951 the Peronists won 141 seats, leaving only 14 for the opposition, or a 9 to 1 ratio. They also obtained 100 percent control of the Senate. With such institutional support from both chambers and, given the new pyramidal or verticalist chain of command within the Peronist party, there was virtually no limit on what the leader could do. But there was a price to be paid for this democratic absolutism or totalitarianism, as Perón's enemies depicted it. Throughout the campaign the media were harnessed and the opposition hounded, their meetings broken up and dissenters silenced with arrests for contempt.[36]

Argentina's tyranny of the majority neither escaped nor disowned the military legacy that made it possible. The decisive influence of the military on Perón's first administration is exemplified by the fact that half of his cabinet consisted of army officers.[37] Nor is it simple coincidence that the army doubled its strength between 1943 and 1951, and in some instances offered higher salaries than even the United States Army.[38] But the repressive features of Peronist democracy were also due to the mobilization of workers even more willing than the military to crack down on the opposition.

Perón was the candidate of organized labor and simultaneously the military's constitutional dike against subversion. Both factors were indispensable to his continuation in power. He never lacked support from organized labor, but he could not always count on backing from the armed forces. Ultimately, the latter would be his undoing when the Catholic nationalist sector of the military deserted him.

The Military Liberal Backlash

Against Perón and the Peronist party, military intervention responded to two principal complaints: populist demagogy, and moral backsliding. Demogogy has been a constant of all Peronist governments, but the charge of moral lassitude has varied with the circumstances. In October 1945 Perón was charged with nepotism and financial scandals compounded by his immoral assistance to Nazi war criminals. In September 1955 he was charged with having sexual relations with a fourteen-year old protégée who lived with him in the presidential mansion, and with challenging the moral authority of the church with legislation making divorce and prostitution legal. These became the pretexts for a military coup.

Peronism also came under suspicion for harboring and encouraging subversive tendencies. The military became progressively alienated by Perón's coddling of organized labor, which he regarded as the backbone of his movement. When the workers responded to an unsuccessful military coup in June 1955 by destroying churches, rampaging through the streets of the capital, and firebombing the prestigious Jockey Club, Peronism became identified with an ideology even more repugnant to devotees of traditional order than Yrigoyen's Radicalism. Three months later Perón was forced to abdicate. Backed by military liberals but led by Catholic nationalists, the September coup was directed at containing and subduing this new internal enemy.

The new military government presided over by Gen. Eduardo Lonardi lasted barely fifty days. He, too, was deposed by a military rebellion. Led by the army's and navy's liberal wings, the November 13 coup was catalyzed by Lonardi's efforts to pack the government with Catholic nationalists. Military liberals also berated him for failing to crack down on organized labor and on so-called *perocomunismo*, the Peronist modality of totalitarianism.[39]

His successor, Gen. Pedro E. Aramburu, made no bones about his antipathy to Peronism. On November 16, only three days after the coup, the General Confederation of Labor (CGT) was intervened, and on November 30 the Peronist or Justicialist party was banned. Although elections were held in February 1958, they took place without the participation of the majoritarian party. At most, the military consented to revive a pseudodemocracy reminiscent of the Infamous Decade. With the Peronists out of commission, the Radicals were their indisputable successors. But when each of two Radical presidents appeared to be "soft" on Peronism, neither was allowed to complete his term of office.

The Radical party had publicly supported the coup of September 1955. But a year later it began to split on how to respond to the military regime. While the faction headed by Arturo Frondizi tried to reach an uderstanding with Peronism, the faction led by Ricardo Balbín favored collaboration with the dictatorship. Consequently, when Frondizi became the party's presidential candidate at its national convention in November 1956, Balbín organized his faction into a separate party. Henceforth there would be two radicalisms: Frondizi's Intransigent Radical party (UCRI) and Balbín's People's Radical party (UCRP).

As the representative of transigent rather than intransigent radicalism, Balbín's party enjoyed a comfortable margin over its rival. In the elections of delegates to reform the 1853 Constitution in July 1957, his party polled 250,000 votes more than Frondizi's. But a secret pact with Perón in January 1958 threw the weight of Peronists behind Frondizi, who triumphed in the February elections by a margin of some 1,500,000 votes. Later, Frondizi was obliged to return the favor by allowing Peronists to run their own candidates. This won them the governorship of Buenos Aires in the 1962 congressional elections. The military then intervened to nip in the bud this new threat of subversion.

By then the influence of the Cuban Revolution had borne fruit in the flow of Peronist militants to Havana for training in guerrilla warfare. After the Bay of Pigs fiasco in April 1961, the Cuban danger became a continuing preoccupation of military liberals as well as nationalists. The Soviet Union had established a permanent beachhead in the Americas and the United States appeared to be the only power capable of containing it. Counterinsurgency and hemispheric security became the military's most important concerns.

The military ousted Frondizi in March 1962, and Catholic nationalists staged a coup in August that gave them control of the government. But in September the liberal wing prevailed, as it had in 1931 under General Justo and again in 1955 under General Aramburu. Thus new restricted elections were held in July 1963. But having lost the support of Peronists, Frondizi's party also lost the elections. The winner by a margin of more than eight hundred thousand votes was the UCRP's candidate, Dr. Arturo Illia.

The new president was to share the same fate as his predecessor.

His first serious mistake was to permit Peronists to run candidates under cover of political front organizations in the 1965 congressional elections. Then, for underestimating the menace of Castro-Communist subversion on a continental scale, he further lost the confidence of the armed forces. Under the influence of the Pentagon, Gen. Juan Carlos Onganía had made the defense of ideological rather than geographical frontiers the armed forces' number-one commitment. He had urged President Illia to send an Argentine force to assist the United States in occupying Santo Domingo in May, but the president refused.

By March 1966 preparations for a coup were already under way in anticipation that the Radicals, who had repeatedly lost to the Peronists, would be defeated in 1967.[40] Restricted democracy had not worked as the generals hoped. Consequently, Illia was forced out of office in June in a coup led by retired army chief-of-staff General Onganía.

Military State and Military Party

The military state of 1966–1970 was a landmark in Argentine political history and also a preview of the future Military Process. It was the first time the military had seized power with the capacity of retaining it for an indefinite period. It was the first occasion on which rival tendencies in the armed forces healed their ideological differences through an informal pact that would enable each to share in the spoils. And it was the first Argentine example of a military-industrial complex directly managed by the military.

Inspired by the example of Spanish dictator Miguel Primo de Rivera, General Uriburu had aspired to a corporative state in Argentina. But General Onganía effectively established one. Assisted by the Catholic doctrine of moral re-armament in the form diffused by Spain under Gen. Francisco Franco, military pseudofascism, or *franquismo*, during the 1960s gained new converts, among them General Onganía. The "Argentine Franco" adopted a bureaucratic-authoritarian ideology relying heavily on the doctrine of the Spanish Falange and its founder, José Antonio Primo de Rivera. "Though [Miguel] Primo de Rivera was Spain's first dictator of the twentieth century, and Franco her second, the line of descent from one to the other was indirect."[41] José Antonio, the first dictator's son, was the ideological link and likewise the inspiration of General Onganía.[42]

The rationale for the coup was contained in a "Message to the People" on 28 June 1966. The military supposedly intervened "to reestablish an authentic representative democracy in which order reigns within law, justice, and the interest of the commonwealth."[43] The message complained of the lack of authentic authority, the prevalence of a vitiated electoralism, and the threat of anarchy as well as inflation. A follow-up document in July, entitled "Objectives of the Revolution," further complained of the "subtle and aggressive Marxist penetration in all areas of national life."[44]

Despite these banalities, there was a genuine intent by the military to modernize the economy through a change of structures.[45] Immense authority was given to the technocrat Adalbert Krieger Vasena, who had served in earlier military governments and was appointed economy minister because of his international connections. An economic liberal, Krieger Vasena contended that "the Argentine economy was plagued by incredible inefficiencies in the private as well as public sector, most of them induced by excessive subsidization, overextended welfare programs, and an undisciplined working class."[46] Illia's government was called into question for its discredited state interventionism, its demagogic ideology of a more equitable redistribution of wealth, and its interference with industrial development. A decade later similar complaints would be used to justify economic restructuring under the Military Process. As Rouquié puts it, the "subsidiarization" of Argentina within the framework of neocapitalist redistribution of investments in the nations of the periphery had run up against an unforeseen obstacle . . . a nonclimate of confidence unpropitious for foreign investments."[47]

Pretentiously labeled the "Argentine Revolution," the experiment in modernized industrial development supported by the financial community and the multinationals was cut short by resistance from organized labor. Despite success in reducing inflation, the government's efforts to eliminate obstacles to a free market and to cut costs had an adverse effect on Argentine workers. Their standard of living deteriorated as price controls on essential commodities were lifted, wages frozen, social benefits canceled, and strikes discouraged because of compulsory arbitration in which the government habitually favored management. Retirement age was raised from sixty to sixty-five years. Concurrently, the universities were purged of Marxist professors, a new law abolished university autonomy and student participation in decision making, and students were barred from all political activities. Added to cuts in university budgets and student subsidies, such measures contributed to radicalizing instead of neutralizing student politics and were partly responsible for the wave of armed resistance by youth groups in support of their own and worker interests.

The repression became insufferable. Tension mounted until the industrial city of Córdoba exploded in a popular insurrection and was briefly taken over in May 1969. The police were overwhelmed and the army had to intervene to restore order. Known as the *cordobazo*, this event rivaled the general strikes during the *semana trágica* of 1919 and *Patagonia rebelde* in 1921–1922. The *cordobazo* disrupted the hegemonic project of the military-industrial complex, shattered the unity of the armed forces, and became a catalyst for political-military vanguards committed to armed resistance.

In June 1970 Onganía was pressured to resign in the face of a coup by the army's commander, Gen. Alejandro A. Lanusse, a military liberal who had preferred concessions to Onganía's call for a show of force in 1969. Onganía's successor, Gen. Roberto Marcelo Levingston, was similarly shocked out of office by a military coup in response to a second *cordobazo* in March 1971. Finally, the country's new president, General Lanusse, negotiated Perón's return to power in an effort to forestall an impending *argentinazo*. And so the story continues after the Peronist electoral triumphs of 1973, through a second experiment in "barbaric majoritarianism," to the fall of the Peronist government in March 1976 in a coup by the reunified armed forces.

The establishment of a military-industrial state hinged on a continuing rather than a momentary pact between rival military tendencies. Unlike the September 1955 coup, in which the alliance between military liberals and authoritarians dissolved within a few months, the 1966 coup preserved the ties between them. For four years the interests of military liberals and authoritarians coincided. "Politics were suppressed by decree in the name of an ideology that evidently could not be liberal; but liberalism prevailed in the economic order and, for the new order, there was no antinomy between one and the other."[48] Authoritarians established their hegemony in the political sphere, liberals in matters of economics through a division of labor that put an end to the incessant quarrels between rival tendencies in the armed forces. The emergence of a distinctively military party dates from this event.

With the eclipse of military reformers in 1955, the armed forces have become increasingly homogeneous. But like other political parties, the military party exhibits different internal tendencies. Although solidly anti-Peronist, the two military currents interpret the Peronist phenomenon differently. For military liberals Peronism is abhorred for its abuses of power and its demagogy and class sectarianism, which supposedly encourage subversion. For Catholic nationalists its excesses and demagogy are intolerable, but Peronism is considered a national and Christian force that exonerates it.

The concept of a "military party" has become part of the standard vocabulary for understanding Argentine politics, but it is not a contribution of the country's social scientists. It was the extreme Left that first identified and denounced the formation of a military party. The concept was used informally by the PRT's secretary, Mario Roberto Santucho, in a November 1972 interview involving the principal leaders of the ERP, the Montoneros, and the Fuerzas Armadas Revolucionarias (FAR)—all of whom apparently adopted it.

For Santucho the military party made its debut in 1966 with Onganía's coup and the establishment of a "dictatorship with a fascist retinue."[49] Montonero Fernando Vaca Narvaja in the same interview used "military party" to designate the army's "homogeneous characteristics that differentiate it from other Latin American armies, except that of Brazil."[50] And Roberto Jorge Quieto of the Revolutionary Armed Forces (FAR) traced the party's origins to 1956, the army's post-Peronist efforts at political indoctrination, exemplified by "the training of officers in military schools of the Panama Canal Zone and the United States . . . and by the selecting of American-oriented professors and programs for Argentine military schools and the Superior War College."[51]

The first formal use of the term as an analytical tool dates from an article by Santucho in 1974, further elaborated in a follow-up article entitled "The Military Party." in 1966 the officialdom of the armed forces under General Onganía boldly "united around a political project . . . whose central proposal was to organize the country economically and socially in order to stabilize and develop the bourgeois economy . . . [and] to strike at the roots of the revolutionary awakening that was insinuating itself in the midst of the working class and the people."[52] By then a financial oligarchy linked to the foreign monopolies had replaced the landed oligarchy as the hegemonic influence within the ruling class,[53] hence the search for an instrument that would replace the defunct Conservative party—a new party of cadres with direct access to the means of violence indispensable to keeping the working class in its place.

The military party would become a continuing feature of Argentine political life during the next two decades. But was it autonomous? To modernize the economy, it needed to attract foreign capital by offering the prospect of stable and high returns under conditions in which organized labor had become a major contender for political power.[54] Since high profits were likely to be blocked by labor unrest and the incessant struggle for higher wages, to guarantee investment opportunities for foreign capital short of the imposition of a military dictatorship was nearly impossible. Would, then, the military's dependence on foreign capital induce it to take a back-seat to civilian technocrats appointed to oversee the modernization program?[55]

The military party emerged as the natural successor to the Conservative party. Like the latter, it shared the same fear of unrestricted democracy and the same commitment to fighting subversion. But it would be a mistake to conclude that it served the same interests. During both World Wars I and II the military and oligarchy were at loggerheads over the issue of neutrality versus intervention on the side of the British.[56] The army constituted a rival oligarchy based on selection and merit rather than inherited wealth, which also set them apart.[57] It was the traditional defender of Argentine independence, which sooner or later brought it into collision with the oligarchy's dependence on foreign capital.[58] Thus their coincidence of interests on political issues testified at best to a common front against the two mass-based civilian parties.[59]

The military party had its own interests, which only partly coincided with the oligarchy's. During periods when it wielded power directly, as from 1966 to 1973, its partnership with the financial oligarchy gave it a predominant role. The financial sector and foreign corporations were under its thumb, not conversely. When it chose to, as when it replaced Onganía with Levingston in June 1970, it adopted a different economic policy adverse to their interests.[60] Since it considered the oligarchy to be politically incompetent and always retained the final decision, "evidently the leadership of the process was not the oligarchy's but rather the army's."[61]

The military party is unique among military establishments in the Third World in having its own economic base. "Few militaries anywhere in the world operate as many industries and utilities as Argentine officers do"—even when civilians are in power.[62] In 1943 the military government authorized the creation of Military Factories (Fabricaciones Militares) with a board of directors resembling that of an industrial conglomerate. Although the rationale was to make Argentina independent in the production of armaments, Fabricaciones Militares also encroached on the private sector.

Eventually, they were producing everything from armchairs, subway cars, electrical conductors, lumber, petrochemicals, iron, and steel to armored vehicles and military aircraft. By the 1980s they were employing over forty thousand workers and their products represented 70 percent of total sales to the private sector.[63] The military party's share of economic power amounted to some two billion dollars in sales, or 2.5 percent of the GDP—in some years as high as 5 percent.[64] Indeed, the military's economic power was so substantial that it effectively blocked all efforts to privatize it. Neither Krieger Vasena nor Martínez de Hoz, the top technocrats of Onganía's "Argentine Revolution" and the Military Process, respectively, were successful in applying their free market strategies to Military Factories.

Three Military Projects

Three projects for containing and eradicating subversion have dominated military thinking since the first and second red scares prepared the armed forces for the military coup of 1930. First, military liberals settled for the moderate solution of banning the majoritarian parties and returning to a nineteenth-century restricted democracy in line with eighteenth-century republicanism. Their principal claim to fame is the fraudulent democracy of the Infamous Decade and the restricted democracy under Radical governments after the banning of the Peronist party in 1955.

Second, Catholic nationalists committed to an authoritarian solution had no use for either modern liberalism or democracy. Representing the military corporative or pseudofascist option, they played a prominent role during the dictatorships of Generals Uriburu and Onganía and, to a lesser extent, during the late Process of National Reorganization.

Third, military reformers led by Perón opted for still another solution aimed at eliminating the economic causes of subversion by giving workers a major stake in society. Instead of combating populism, Perón proposed to harness it in order to nullify subversion. Such was his response to the crisis of democracy from 1946 to 1955 and again from 1973 to 1974.

These military projects departed from the established social and political order to varying degrees. The liberals came closest to reviving the status quo ante. After restoring order, they returned to the sidelines, where they kept a vigilant eye on the restricted democracy they had created.

Catholic nationalists went further by banning all political activity while excluding the economically dominant class from sharing power. Their project was tantamount to a political revolution in the sense of a transfer of political power from one class to another, from professional politicians responsive to the oligarchy to professional soldiers defending their own interests. Thus there is a basic difference between liberal or oligarchic-dependent governments and military-authoritarian regimes.

The most radical of the military projects was unquestionably that of the military populists. The persistence of the objective conditions of subversion during the Infamous Decade became a pretext for the military to introduce not only a new political order, but also one that dangerously eroded the privileges of the agroexport oligarchy. The new order guaranteed bureaucratic political hegemony, but had the advantage over military-authoritarian regimes in having a mass political base. It incorporated the labor bureaucracy into the government, boosted the number of government technocrats by expanding the public sector, and provided opportunities for other segments of society to share in political power. In this way the entire professional and managerial class acquired a stake in the new order.

Under bureaucratic-populist rule capitalists and workers were disciplined. Perón's new order differed from that of classical European fascism in preserving the national Congress and the role of political parties. In this respect, it resembled the formative period of Italian fascism from 1921 to 1925, but not its later development. Perón's first two administrations questioned the irresponsible character of the capitalist system and contributed to its erosion. But because Perón challenged the economic hegemony of the agroexport oligarchy and favored the interests of organized labor, the Peronist option ended by dividing instead of uniting the Argentine people.

All three military projects targeted subversion. But unlike their liberal colleagues, both military authoritarians and populists launched political revolutions. They did so under Fascist influence. The specifically Fascist component of the military era is evident in the heritage of Spain's two principal variants of *falangismo:* the original populist variant modeled on Mussolini's national syndicalism by the Falange's founder, José Antonio Primo de Rivera; and Gen. Francisco Franco's antipopulist version, which demoted the Falange to a mere auxiliary of military policy. The Peronist regimes of 1946–1955 and 1973–1976 were clearly inspired by Primo de Rivera, whereas the military regimes of 1943–1945, 1966–1970, and 1976–1982 were at least partly indebted to General Franco's military substitute for fascism.

In order of importance or influence, how should these projects be ranked? The armed forces' priorities during the military era indicate that restricted democracy was at the top of the agenda, a democratic opening, at the bottom. The project of military liberals won top honors, while reform of the social structure proved to be a military nightmare.

The covert coup of April 1931, which compelled General Uriburu to call national elections or resign, was the prelude to eleven years of restricted democracy, while the coup within the coup of November 1955 opened the way for another eight years of partial democracy until stopped in its tracks by the coup of June 1966. It is also worth noting that General Lanusse's coup of March 1971 aimed at a restricted democracy, as did the March 1976 coup led by General Jorge Rafael Videla. Thus the liberal wing of the armed forces was hegemonic during almost two-thirds of the period between September 1930 and December 1983.

Although as many successful military coups during this period were initiated by the military's illiberal wing, they had difficulty consolidating them. Catholic nationalists sought a solution to the crisis of democracy through a radical overhaul of the political superstructure directly managed by the military. The coups by Uriburu, the GOU, Lonardi, and Onganía all pointed in that direction, as did the coup within the coup by Gen. Leopoldo F. Galtieri in December 1981. Because the resulting military regimes remained in power only eight years compared to almost thirty-two years when military liberals held sway, they played an evidently subordinate role during the military era.

There was only one military coup that had for its objective the restoration of unrestricted democracy in Argentina. The coup by Gen. Eduardo J. Avalos in October 1945 not only compelled Perón to resign as vice-president, but also pressured the government to call immediate elections that would guarantee the rights of political parties opposed to Perón's presidential ambitions. The only other democratic openings occurred when military liberals faced a crisis of legitimacy in 1972–1973 and again in 1982–1983, which could be resolved only by permitting Peronists to compete in elections that were initially intended to be restricted.

Altogether, Peronists were in power some twelve years, which exceeded the tenure of the military's illiberal and antidemocratic wing. But tenure in office is not the sole index for ranking military priorities. The continuity of a particular project within the armed forces also carries weight. The Peronist sector prevailed from 1945 to 1955, but was virtually wiped out by the end of 1956. Nor did it make a successful comeback during its second experience in office, from 1973 to 1976. Thus it cannot compare in significance to the nationalist and authoritarian sector. If Peronism endured as a political movement after 1955, it is because by then it had ceased to be a military project.

3. The Peronist Phenomenon

INSERTED WITHIN an era of competing military projects, the Peronist phenomenon was alone among them in acquiring a popular basis. In this respect it resembled its European progenitors, Italian fascism and German national socialism, spawned by the military experience of World War I. Like them it represented a position opposed to both liberal democracy in the West and the red menace in the East. While it claimed to be making a preventive revolution against communism, it further boasted of a solution to the social question under capitalism. A dike to subversion, Peronism simultaneously built up pressure for social change until others began using it as a springboard for revolution.

Although the generals' dirty war came in response to the guerrillas' revolutionary war, the Military Process responded to the consequences of Peronism in power from 1973 to 1976. For the generals, the Peronist threat posed by organized labor heralded a new form of subversion. The Peronist formula of preventive revolution depended on unwilling concessions by the business community to the so-called mafia in power, while the escalating demands of the trade unions likewise came to be perceived as extortion. Thus the unintended consequences of the Peronist project included the delegitimation of democracy and the eventual intervention of the military. Since the unintended consequences responded to the intended ones, an understanding of both the generals' dirty war and the Military Process hinges on an accurate account of the Peronist phenomenon.

Like fascism, Peronism boasts of an intellectually flexible and diversified political philosophy. Its diagnosis of the world situation helped generate a justicialist or ideological Third Position, whose adjustment to the changing times after the defeat of the Axis powers was responsible for the formulation of successive Peronist doctrines and strategies for implementing them. Thus Peronism hoped to outlive the military era to which it responded. But did it or could it? In fact, it contributed to the periodic return of the military to power.

The Coming to Power of the Working Class

Perón's diagnosis of what was happening in the world during the interwar years is basic to understanding why his proposed solution to the social question came to be viewed as subversive. On the one hand, he interpreted history as the rise and fall of particular social systems representing stages in the evolution of humankind, on the other hand, as periodic movements back and forth between the political extremes of individual freedom and state authority.[1] Within this conceptual framework revolutions occur when there is a shift from an old to a new historical cycle and a shift in the political pendulum in the opposite direction.[2] For Perón those shifts happened to coincide.

Two great cycles of evolution have dominated the modern age, according to Perón. The French Revolution was the first. Its heroic phase began in 1789; it suffered a major defeat in 1814–1815, but the resulting social changes endured for another century.[3] A new stage began in 1917, the cycle of the Russian Revolution. It succeeded in Russia in 1918 and reached epic proportions after its victories during World War II; hence the rhetorical question: "Will not its influence extend for a century over the world's future development and evolution?"[4]

What does this cyclical theory portend for Argentina? "The French Revolution finished with the government of the aristocracy and gave birth to the government of the bourgeoisie. The Russian Revolution finished with the government of the bourgeoisie and opened the way for the proletarian masses. The future of the world belongs to them."[5] The world was in the midst of a social revolution, Perón believed, and Argentina was an integral part of that world.

But the revolt of the masses was not the only revolution of the twentieth century. The political revolt against liberal democracy and its focus on the isolated individual was another.[6] Perón interpreted this shift from individualism to statism as a movement from political left to right.[7] But because statism is at the opposite extreme from individualism, it, too, is unsuited to a condition of equilibrium. Thus history teaches that social evolution gravitates toward a position at the political center, "the vertical position of the pendulum."[8]

Both the cyclical and the pendular movements of history, Perón observed, had thus far occurred within the context of social struggles between privileged minorities and unprivileged majorities. Since all revolutions were the work of activating minorities, even the Russian Revolution did not empower more than a small fragment of the class of those who work. What, then, did the advent of the masses in world history mean for Perón?

Perón anticipated the overcoming of class conflict under conditions of inequality. That the future of the world belonged to the masses meant the end not of class domination but of class despotism, "in a word, that the working class, which until now has been a spectator, shall also participate in the government, administration, and legislation of the state. . . . Not because we believe that no class has rights over other classes, but because what a class is in fact capable of conquering [by force] the other classes cannot legally deny it."[9]

Although the masses have had to suffer through the tribulations of absolutism, capitalist exploitation, and totalitarian annihilation, each stage has been an improvement on its predecessor.[10] Historical evolution is cyclical and pendular, and also testimony to human progress.[11] Underlying the historical antagonism between individual and state is the clash between people and oligarchy.[12] During the Middle Ages the state was at the service of feudal landowners and opposed to the interests of peasants and serfs. In the Modern Age the liberal-democratic state favored capitalists at the expense of wage earners. In the Contemporary Age this antagonism has been compounded by a totalitarian state that favors a state bureaucracy. Thus the "antagonism between the people and the state reaches its point of maximum tension" and is resolved only by a social democracy in which the people are sovereign.

Perón claimed that both capitalism and communism were systems that had been superseded by events. "We conceive of capitalism as the exploitation of man by capital, and of communism as the exploitation of the individual by the state. Both 'insectify' the person by means of distinct systems. We believe further . . . that the abuses of capitalism are the cause and that communism is the effect. Without capitalism, communism would have no reason to exist. We also believe that without the cause, the effect would also begin to disappear."[13]

This cycle of social revolution would occupy Perón's attention throughout the rest of his life. Two world wars and the revolutions of communism, fascism, and national socialism had paved the way for the "Hour of the Peoples."[14] By this he meant the replacement of liberal democracy by people's democracy, the end of the rule of money, and the overcoming of imperialism through national liberation movements. The Peronist revolution of 1945–1955 and the resistance that followed were part of this revolutionary cycle, which was perceived as subversive.

Perón identified three main forces contending for power in the contemporary world. Besides the Western powers defending the antiquated structure of liberal democracy and Soviet imperialism trying to impose a Communist solution to the social question, a bloc of nonaligned nations had emerged representing the interests of countries belonging to the Third World. But the first two worlds had formed a unholy alliance to contain the third. Not only in foreign policy did the United States and the Soviet Union come to terms in carving up the world between them;[15] in the form of popular fronts during the 1930s and 1940s, demoliberal and Communist parties also made common cause for the purpose of halting fascism and kindred movements such as Peronism in Argentina.

In both domestic and foreign policy, Perón contended, Italian fascism and German national socialism represented a *via media* between traditional demoliberalism and the new floodtide of change unleashed by communism. Perón considered them progenitors of today's nonaligned nations confronted by the two superpowers.[16] The mutually hostile internationals led by the United States and the Soviet Union had called a momentary truce in their worldwide political match in 1938 in order to contain and then defeat the first bloc of nonaligned nations led by Mussolini's Italy and Hitler's Germany.[17] It was only the German attack on Poland that upset the equilibrium and led to the collapse of what Perón depicted as "in ideological matters a third position . . . a third in discord."[18] However, history would repeat itself: "The formation of the Third World, impelled by the express or tacit union of those who struggle for liberation on both sides of the Iron Curtain, leads now as in 1938 to a rapprochement of the imperalist powers."[19]

The revolution of the twentieth century that began with the Russian Revolution had thus taken other more viable forms. "In the case of internal evolution, each people has its own characteristics so that each tries to destroy demoliberalism by different means. Russian communism, Italian fascism, German national socialism, like British laborism and the American New Deal, are distinct forms of the revolution. But the end is the same: the destruction of liberal democracy and its replacement by new forms more compatible with modern needs."[20]

This political transformation was being accompanied by an economic transformation that would gradually bury the capitalist system. "The rule of the bourgeoisie over the world has come to an end;

the government of peoples begins. Demoliberalism and its foreseen consequence, capitalism, have closed the cycle. . . . The victors will be those who reconcile the collective planning required by the times with the guarantee of individual liberty that is man's inalienable right."[21] Although justicialism differed markedly from the form of socialism adopted in the Soviet Union, "our movement forms part of a great world process that marches with the rest of humanity toward a *universal socialism*."[22] To this Perón added: "I have not the least doubt that in the twenty-first century the world will be socialist . . . whether it is called populism, socialism, or justicialism."[23]

The unacknowledged source of Perón's philosophy of history may be traced to Mussolini's 1932 *Doctrine of Fascism:* "The 'Liberal' century, after having accumulated an infinity of Gordian knots, tried to untie them by the hecatomb of the World War. Never before has any religion imposed such a cruel sacrifice."[24] Because liberalism was leading states to certain ruin, the whole world had tended to become antiliberal. Consequently, Mussolini expected this century to be a Fascist century, "a century of the 'Right.'"[25] Furthermore, "If the nineteenth century was the century of the individual (Liberalism means individualism) it may be expected that this one may be the century of 'collectivism' and therefore the century of the State."[26] Thus the pendular shift sketched by Mussolini coincides with the cycles of the French and Russian revolutions sketched by Perón.

Mussolini was initially silent concerning the outcome of the Russian Revolution. But it was not long before he identified Stalinism with a surreptitious variant of fascism. He began by acknowledging the gradual convergence between Stalinist "collectivism" and his own and ended by suggesting that the "phased involution of the Leninist system had produced an involuntary and inconsistent fascism."[27] Thus Mussolini interpreted actually existing socialism in the Soviet Union as a phenomenon of the political Right.

Among the other sources of Perón's philosophy of history, he placed the works of Oswald Spengler and Arnold J. Toynbee at the top of the list.[28] What did Perón learn from them? "In the first place, one must grant that all countries are agitated [internally] by an evolutionary process . . . and that, on the international plane, the second important factor is the decadence of imperialism."[29] These two factors, he acknowledged, were fundamental to understanding the great changes transforming the present world.[30] In Spengler's words, the "Western Civilization of this century is threatened, not by one, but by two world revolutions of major dimensions . . . one comes from below, the other from without: *class war and race war*"—the revolution of the discontented masses inspired by Marxist ideology and the revolt of the colonial peoples against European domination. "In the next few centuries both will fight side by side, *possibly as allies.*"[31] This gloomy prediction of the decomposition and decline of the West was later seconded by Toynbee in his monumental *A Study of History.* Corresponding to Spengler's two forces of world revolution, Toynbee distinguishes an "external" from an "internal" proletariat. A civilization is endangered and must pass through a "time of troubles," he argued, when the formless masses within and beyond its frontiers no longer accept its established institutions and civilizing mission.[32]

Perón adopted this scenario but rebaptized it the "Hour of the Peoples."[33] During the 1960s, he claimed, the peoples of the Third World had joined the exploited masses of the West in rebelling against the oppressive structures blocking their demands for freedom.[34] In the absence of concessions from their oppressors, they had turned to violence. Thus Perón anticipated that Argentina too would be consumed by revolutionary wars and a war of national liberation if no solution to the social question were found.

Was this projection realistic? Waisman argues that it was not—at least not during the 1940s, when Perón first articulated it.[35] But Perón's time span for the cycle of the Russian Revolution to spend itself extended beyond the immediate postwar era well into the twenty-first century. A preventive revolution takes several decades to prepare. The fear of subversion may have been exaggerated at the time, but in the long run it turned out to be realistic for most of the Western Hemisphere, including Argentina. The emergence of national security states in response to revolutionary wars in Brazil, Chile, Uruguay, Argentina, and the revolutions in Cuba and Central America confirms it.

The Ideological Third Position

What is the bearing of Perón's philosophy of history on his perception of Argentina's national interest? "We have described the synthesis befitting our revolution as humanist. It considers man above every other consideration as long as doing so is not prejudicial to the state. And it is statist with respect to everything that does not tyrannize over man. In other words, our position is centrist."[36] The Third Position is a fully articulated ideology of equilibrium supposedly combining the strong points of the extremes without their defects. "The dominant principle of our ideological system is the harmony of opposites, the equilibrium between extremes, the Third Position."[37]

Political extremes were responsible for "a world divided into two opposed camps . . . into two ideological positions: liberal individualism and totalitarian collectivism."[38] Those extremes had proved unstable and therefore unviable.[39]

Basic to Perón's Third Position was the concept of the "nation in arms."[40] The theme of a 1927 Argentine edition of Gen. Colman von der Goltz's *Das Volk in Waffen,* Perón adopted it in order to ensure not only the nation's defense, but also domestic tranquility through the "integral mobilization and organization of every citizen."[41] Its fundamental premise was that modern warfare is less a function of armies than of a people's morale and social well-being.[42] A nation cannot defend itself against foreign pressures, he argued, if its citizens are victims of capitalist exploitation and a liberal democracy that refuses to take responsibility for the social question. Without national unity, which depends in turn on social justice, there can be no military defense of the country's political and economic interests on the international plane; thus Argentina would remain a semicolony.[43]

Until the end of his life Perón continued to describe his faith in social justice as an intrinsically Argentine ideology.[44] "Like the people, justicialism is national, social, and Christian."[45] Presented at the First National Congress of Philosophy in Mendoza in April 1949, *La comunidad organizada* continues to be the classic statement of justicialist ideology.[46] But a more comprehensive exposition is to be found in notes dictated in 1954 for Perón's classes on Peronist philosophy.

Within an organized community each individual fulfills a social function in the service of all, and each of our faculties performs a special task that contributes to individual happiness. On both scores Perón took his cues from Aristotle, for whom virtue was a mean between extremes and for whom ethics culminated in politics.[47] For Perón, as for Aristotle, individual well-being was a function of social well-being, and vice-versa.

Perón likened a human being to a centaur, "half human, half brute, the victim of opposed and hostile desires, looking upward to heaven and at the same time galloping among clouds of dust."[48] History is testimony to the struggle between these two tendencies. "The evolution of human thought recalls the image of the centaur under the tension of high ideals during long periods of history, and during others condemned to profound obscurities as the slave of sordid material appetites."[49] Pursuing the same metaphor, Perón concluded that it takes an organized community to reestablish the equilibrium between people's two natures. "If there were epochs of exclusive accentuation of the ideal [Middle Ages] and others of the material

[Modern Age], our own must realize its ambitious and noble aims through *harmony*. One cannot reestablish a Centaur Age on the basis only of bestial muscles or of the human brain, but rather through a *sum of values*, through the harmony of those purely physical forces and those responsible for the miracle that makes even the heavens familiar to us."[50]

Neither refugees among the altars, monasteries, and convents nor victims of brute passions and a desacralized state befit humankind's ambivalent nature.[51] That is Perón's message, which calls for overcoming the narrow religious worldview in which faith is confused with superstition, and the equally narrow materialistic view vainly seeking felicity through things. On the one hand, extreme poverty and desolation "allow man no other escape than that of gazing upon and placing his hopes in another and transcendent world."[52] On the other hand, an abundance of commodities and a focus on consumption results in people's "thingification" and resulting "nausea."[53] Thus Perón aspired to a synthesis of the Middle Ages and the Modern World by "restoring the harmony between material progress and spiritual values."[54]

I have stressed Perón's philosophical debt to Aristotle and emphasis on proportion, harmony, and equilibrium (which most commentators have singled out as fundamental), but there is another debt no less important associated with the philosophical contribution of Christianity. "The Greek idea could not be completed without a new vision of human society from a more elevated perspective. That contribution was reserved for Christianity . . . the maxims that there is no innate inequality among human beings, that slavery is an opprobrious institution, that women should be liberated."[55] It was Christianity, according to Perón, that attributed to each man and woman a soul created in the image of God, a soul with ends transcending material life. "Christianity, which constituted the first great revolution, the first act of human liberation, was fortunately able to rectify the Greek conception. . . . It enriched the personality of man and made human emancipation, until then theoretical and limited in application, a universal possibility."[56]

What, then, is justicialist philosophy? As defined in Perón's justicialist catechism: "Justicialism is a new philosophy of life, simple, practical, popular, profoundly Christian, and profoundly humanistic."[57] The basic elements of Peronist ideology are wrapped up in this definition.[58] Peronist philosophy is simple because it is accessible and intelligible to everyone, not only to the educated. It is practical because it is a philosophy of action rather than abstruse contemplation, and it responds to the problems of everyday life. It is popular because its principal concern is to guide workers, to serve the nation, and to provide for human wants. It is profoundly Christian because it hopes to liberate as well as to save human souls and accepts the social implications of the Gospel for this world. Finally, it is profoundly humanistic because justicialism "centers its ideology and preoccupation on . . . the primacy in our country of a single class, the class of those who work."[59]

In this account, Aristotle is the first of Perón's intellectual precursors but Christ is the second. With respect to humankind's social nature, "justicialism identifies itself with the Aristotelian concept."[60] Yet nothing could be more foreign to justicialism than the social inequalities justified by Aristotle, so that Christianity was required to correct Aristotle's elitist bias.[61] "We believe that there are only two philosophies in the world that can embrace and give direction to the major ideological orientations: one is Christian philosophy, which is already 2,000 years old and has continued to sustain itself through 20 centuries; and the other is Marxist philosophy, which is the philosophy of communism. . . . There is no other."[62]

Every age has a dominant ideology, Perón maintained, dogmas that persist for many generations, even centuries. "There have been ideologies for the Middle Ages, for the capitalist stage, and now for the socialist stage. . . . Our ideals of social justice, economic independence, and political sovereignty are fixed and, at least for a long period of our history, will remain unchanged."[63] Although the ideals of economic independence and political sovereignty are not unique but are shared with liberal democrats in the West, they are necessary in the justicialist synthesis to prevent socialism from degenerating into a form of totalitarianism. As the most extreme totalitarianism, communism deprives people of even the most elemental freedoms. Fascism and national socialism are closer to justicialism in respecting basic liberties.[64]

Justicialism is the Third Position in the sense not of a compromise but of a just mean between body and soul, individual and state, liberalism and totalitarianism, capitalism and communism.[65] It is also third because the equilibrium it establishes came after capitalism and communism.[66] In other words, the First Position is capitalism, which got us into this mess; the Second Position is communism, which failed as a solution; and the Third is justicialism, which moderates their excesses and "ceases to be individualistic without becoming collectivistic."[67] Thus justicialism conforms to what most Argentines want: *"the people's happiness and the nation's greatness."*[68]

But that is not how Argentina's armed forces interpreted it. A counterfeit of both traditional Christianity and modern humanistic values, justicialism appeared to them as a sop to subversion.

Christian National Socialism

Military liberals and the mainstream of the Radical party have repeatedly characterized Peronism as either Fascist or crypto-Fascist. Initially, Perón's field studies of Italian fascism and German national socialism during a two-year tour of duty on the European mainland from 1939 to 1941 weighed more heavily than what he assimilated from British laborism and the American New Deal. Subsequently, he gave precedence to the latter. But the two versions of Peronism had enough in common that Peronists continued to describe themselves as Christian national socialists.

Perón's peculiar brand of socialism played down the socialist label in favor of its national and Christian sources. Peronists were wary of becoming branded as "socialists," he explained, because Argentine Socialists were among the political allies of the oligarchy.[69] Socialism was also distrusted by workers because of its much-touted atheism, which earned it the enmity of the church. Consequently, Perón settled for the term "justicialism."[70]

The odds clearly favored his Christian and humanist version of socialism. "Our revolution in process coalesced behind symbols too sacred for it to fail. Our emblems are: God, Fatherland, and Social Justice. We follow God by acknowledging the words of the Divine master, by encouraging men to love their neighbor as themselves. . . . The moral content of our revolution adheres to that finality. For that reason we have repeatedly affirmed that our doctrine is the Christian social doctrine."[71]

By Christian doctrine Perón had in mind the two most important papal encyclicals on the social question prior to World War II: Pope Leo XIII's *Rerum Novarum* ("On the Condition of Labor"), and Pope Pius XI's *Quadragesimo Anno* ("On the Reconstruction of the Social Order"), a restatement of the leading principles of Leo's encyclical on the occasion of its fortieth anniversary in 1931. Perón responded to the problems of private ownership, employer and employee, the dignity of labor, the state, workers' rights, hours of labor and wages, and workers' associations in the same spirit as Leo XIII.[72] He was no less indebted to Leo's principle of placing capital at the service of social interests. "It is now more than 60 years since the theories of socialist syndicalism began to yield results in the struggle between labor and capital and that extraordinarily authorized opinions, such as those of . . . Leo XIII, became the basis of new doctrines which should make that useless struggle disappear."[73]

Even more important was the influence of Pius XI, whose indictment of nineteenth-century capitalism as well as communism went beyond that of his illustrious predecessor. According to Pius XI it was unjust that capital claimed all the products and profits. Here lay the source of Perón's principle that labor and capital should share in the ownership and management of the enterprise as well as its income. Thus Pius XI advised that the wage contract should be modified by a contract of partnership: "In this way wage-earners are made sharers of some sort in the ownership, or the management, or the profits."[74] At the same time he warned workers against falling into the excess of socialism or collectivism. "There is, therefore, a double danger to be avoided. On the one hand, if the social and public aspect of ownership be denied or minimized, the logical consequence is Individualism. . . ; on the other hand, the rejection or diminution of its private and individual character necessarily leads to some form of Collectivism."[75] Perón's effort to reach a just mean between these extremes was anything but original.

Unlike Leo XIII, Pius XI distinguished a moderate from an extreme version of socialism. Extreme socialism, or communism, was rejected without qualification, but moderate socialism was interpreted as converging on Christian social doctrine. Moderate socialism condemns recourse to violence and accepts within limits the right of private ownership. Consequently, "its programs often strikingly approach the just demands of Christian social reformers . . . [and] it may well come about that gradually the tenets of mitigated Socialism will no longer be different from the program of those who seek to reform human society according to Christian principles."[76] He then added that private ownership involving excessive power over others should be replaced by public property, a demand for justice that is not peculiar to socialism. This was the opening Perón needed to equate justicialism with "Christian national socialism."[77]

The Christian variant should not be confused with the German variant of national socialism. Unlike British laborism and the American New Deal, both Italian fascism and German national socialism held that governments should assume overall direction of social, economic, and political activity. The result, Perón argued, had led to "administrative centralization carried to the extreme; the absorption of all private or semiprivate entities (cultural association, universities, etc.); absolute militarism; a closed and directed economy."[78]

At the same time, he credited both Italian fascism and German national socialism with having developed an alternative to capitalism and communism. The papal encyclicals had talked about such a new order, but Mussolini and Hitler were the first to establish one. Despite the totalitarian excesses, each favored a middle ground between free market capitalism and the command economy of socialism, while assigning the state the role of arbiter in harmonizing the interests of workers and employers. Ironically, although the Christian elements in Perón's political synthesis derived from the church, responsibility for implementing them was the work of European fascism.

Perón was not the first to synthesize these elements. It is noteworthy that few biographies of Perón contain any reference to the political thought of José Antonio Primo de Rivera, founder of the Spanish Falange. The Falange doctrine of national syndicalism is scarcely mentioned in Perón's writings, although it was a major precursor of the Peronist synthesis.

In a speech on 10 August 1944, Perón recalled two postulates of the June 1943 military coup that were to serve as the polar star for the Argentine people: first, the union of all Argentines; second, the principle of social justice.[79] The name he subsequently chose for his political organization, the National Justicialist movement, was inspired by these two principles. Tantamount to a synthesis of tradition and revolution, the political Right and Left, they testified to the supposed uniqueness of Peronism as a political philosophy. But it was not unique. It was an Argentine adaptation of Article 26 of the 1934 Program of the Spanish Falange.[80]

Consider the two pillars of the Falange, the nation and social justice. "We will not have a *nation* as long as each of us considers himself the bearer of a distinct interest," wrote Primo de Rivera. "We will not have *social justice* as long as each of the classes . . . wants to impose its domination on the others."[81] Formulated in somewhat broader terms: "Spain has latent within it . . . *a revolution with two veins: the inspiration of a profound social justice that must be implanted without fail; and the inspiration of a profound sense of the traditional, which must be rejuvenated at any cost."*[82]

Primo de Rivera anticipated Perón's Third Position. *"The National Syndicalist movement is confident of having found a just way out: neither capitalist nor communist. . . . against the Right, against the Left."*[83] The Falange sought a similar balance between body and soul, economic materialism and religious idealism. "If the *socialist revolution* consisted of nothing else than the implantation of a new economic order, we would have no fear. What has happened is that the socialist revolution is . . . the triumph of a *materialist sense of life and history.*"[84] Christian national socialism promised to overcome that defect.

How, then, was Primo de Rivera's philosophy adapted to Argentina? Article 6 of the Falange's program proposed to abolish the system of political parties and the accompanying electoral system.[85] Article 9 proposed a corporative state in which the trade unions, instead of serving the workers' class interests, would be restructured vertically to include managers and owners in each branch of production.[86]

But unlike Spain, which had just emerged from the Middle Ages, Argentina had an established tradition of political parties and powerful and independent trade unions that defied adaptation to such a model. Primo de Rivera had rejected the fascist label, but his critique of liberal democracy was nothing less than fascist.[87] The corporatist and antidemocratic elements of the "national syndicalist state" were also more than Perón could stomach. Although he agreed with them in principle, political realism demanded that he seek an accommodation with Argentine national traditions.

Justicialism also shares important features with Mussolini's "national fascism." In contrast to justicialist ideology, which places itself within the Christian and Aristotelian traditions, justicialist doctrine has more in common with political pragmatism and relativism. Boasted Mussolini: "Fascism is a superrelativistic movement because it has never attempted to clothe its complicated and powerful mental attitude with a definite program." Political doctrines are neither true nor false, he contended, but projections of human sentiments and longings. They all have some appeal that may be put to political use. "We are aristocrats and democrats, revolutionaries and reactionaries, proletarians and antiproletarians, pacifists and antipacifists."[88] Here, too, we have an anticipation of Perón's Third Position.

Like Mussolini, Perón prided himself on his doctrinal flexibility and elasticity.[89] Although the principle of social justice is enduring, its content changes in response to changing times.[90] Despite Perón's professed "centrism," he rejected the label "centrist" as too confining.[91] His metaphor of the vertical position effectively dissociated justicialism from both the political Left and the Right. But on at least one occasion Perón claimed that a centrist position is sectarian while Peronists are totally antisectarian: "Our Third Position is not a centrist position. It is an ideological position that is in the center, on the left or on the right, according to the circumstances" (*La Nación*, 6 September 1950).

Perón owed an additional debt to German national socialism. Certainly, he did not share the Fascist doctrine of the state as having a consciousness and will of its own by which it organizes the nation.[92] He subscribed to the Nazi doctrine of the state as the juridical instrument of the nation, a machine that functions within and serves the nation, not conversely.[93] Thus he did not demobilize the masses as Mussolini did, but followed the Nazi example of politicizing them.

It is understandable that the German sources of justicialism have been passed over in favor of the Italian and Spanish. But as Perón reminisced from exile in Spain: "The moment one entered Germany one realized that nowhere in Europe was there anything that worked so perfectly and precisely. I studied the social and political phenomenon in depth . . . what had emerged was an unprecedented social phenomenon, National Socialism, in the same fashion as Italy had given birth to Fascism. . . . That is how I created the whole doctrine. . . . People will say that it was a simple reflection of what was happening in Europe and I will answer that that is so."[94]

Among Perón's German sources one deserves special mention: Gottfried Feder's manifesto against usury and interest slavery. It was not necessary for him to have read Feder's tract in order to assimilate its ideas. They were incorporated in *Mein Kampf*, which Perón had read not once but twice in Italian and Spanish translations.[95]

Capitalism is the hegemony of finance capital, Feder contended, a system of exacting tribute from the producers made possible by the mere ownership of money.[96] The principal forms of this tribute consist of interest, dividends, and rents from the leasing of land. Opposed to the plutocracy is the working population of wage earners, salaried functionaries and employees, independent professionals working for a fee, and small entrepreneurs whose profits serve as reward for wholesome work.[97] "The scourge of humanity is not capital but capitalism."[98] As the antithesis of capitalism but not of productive capital, Feder concluded, socialism depends on the expropriation of the financial oligarchy and the abolition of interest slavery.

Perón predicated his doctrine on virtually the same distinctions. "We divide the country into two categories: one, those who work, and the other, those who live off those who work. Faced with this situation, we have openly taken the side of those who work."[99] Where do the owners of capital fit in this scenario? "We do not support the worker against wholesome capital [*capital sano*]."[100] As he explained: "We are not against capital but exploitation."[101] Since the productive use of capital is neither unwholesome nor exploitative, the enemy is not capital but exploitative capitalism. "Many times I have said we need hands, brains, and capital. But humanized capital, which extracts wealth from the land through productive work . . . [not] cold and calculating supercapitalism."[102]

In principle, Perón agreed with Hitler that socialism should be limited to the struggle against unproductive capital. "As I listened to Gottfried Feder's first lecture about the 'breaking of interest slavery,' I knew at once that this . . . sharp separation of stock exchange capital from the national economy offered the possibility of opposing the internationalization of the German economy without . . . a struggle against all capital." [103] Although the corporative features of justicialism are traceable to Italian sources, Perón's distinction between wholesome and unwholesome capital had a national socialist origin.

For Feder, the socialism of the national community is opposed not only to plutocratic capitalism, but also to "insectifying" communism. The latter represents a violent and brutal reaction to capitalism tantamount to performing surgery on a patient "by amputating his head, arms, and legs." [104] But the Bolshevik ant heap is not the only alternative: "To this Bolshevik fury, to this insensate subversion, we must oppose a new and organic mode of thought that vigorously unites all the productive classes in order to expel this venomous substance that had infected the world." [105] This was also Perón's critique of communism, predicated on a national Christian version of socialism.

Is justicialism, then, a form of fascism? Perón conceived of his doctrine as a successor to that of the Axis powers during World War II. While sharing the fascist critique of liberalism and demoliberalism, however, he did so in the name of democracy rather than authoritarianism. Democracy for Perón meant "doing what the people want." [106] Perón aspired to the role of leader, not dictator of Argentina's national revolution. Because European fascism was essentially elitist and authoritarian, on these two issues he parted company with his Fascist precursors.

In view of both its gradualism and its concern for striking a balance between extremes, justicialism has more in common with the American New Deal than with either Italian fascism or German national socialism. Thus Perón acknowledged his debt to Roosevelt: "The 'New Deal,' of which that great fighter Roosevelt wisely spoke, is not a hypothetical aspiration; it is a palpable reality. Those who are neither persuaded nor convinced by this profound and general transformation in present day society are like those unfortunates who have eyes but do not see or do not wish to see." [107] That is not his only reference to Roosevelt's political legacy. "Personally, we prefer the idea defended by Roosevelt . . . that the economy has ceased to be an end in itself to become a means of resolving social problems." [108] In social and economic matters, "I am proud to have implemented the only policy that appears capable to me of realizing the principles that ought to govern the world in the future: support for the just claims of the workers, a better distribution of wealth in all its aspects, conciliatory procedures for reducing the conflicts between capital and labor, interventionism by the state in all social problems, and also in economic matters when the system of free enterprise threatens the interests of the collectivity."[109] This policy agreed in fundamentals with that of Roosevelt.

Despite its kinship with European fascism, Peronism evolved into an Argentine version of British laborism and European social democracy. The challenge of the Peronist Left alerted Perón to the danger of characterizing his national revolution as socialist even in the most tepid sense. In response to that danger, he devoted his last efforts to redefining Peronist doctrine as a prelude to institutionalizing the Peronist movement.

The new doctrinal orthodoxy followed the lines sketched in Perón's last and posthumously published work, El proyecto nacional. Despite its subtitle, "My Political Testament," it was printed in only limited editions during the government of Isabel Perón. Rather than a reaffirmation of the doctrine enunciated during his first two terms as president, it redefines justicialism in the light of European social and political developments during his years in exile. Those years witnessed the resurgence of social democracy throughout most of Western Europe. Perón's "Argentine Model" reflects that resurgence.

How did Perón's new national project differ from his original one? The fundamental objective of the Peronist movement was defined not as a native brand of socialism, but as a national consensus based on compromise. The fundamental enemy no longer included the native oligarchy in league with foreign interests."[110] Perón's new project favored a model characterized as "Christian, national, and social"—social, not socialist.[111] But the distinction escaped most Peronists.

The objective of national consensus excluded class struggle. Consequently, the Argentine Model sought to co-opt business sectors traditionally hostile to justicialism by offering the prospect of moderate state intervention and a mixed economy open to foreign capital.[112] The Argentine Model also frowned on earlier schemes for expropriating big landowners and nationalizing the banks. Thus agrarian reform was removed from the justicialist agenda.[113]

How is social democracy defined in the Argentine Model? Democracy is social when the organized people "make the decisions and are the artificers of their own destiny."[114] For all sectors to be represented, there must be intermediate organizations between the individual and the state: first, a plurality of political parties, provided each has a numerically significant and ideologically coherent constituency; second, a plurality of social organizations representing definite economic functions, mainly trade unions, business chambers, and professional associations. Thus Perón's original preference for a corporative state based on purely functional representation gave way to a compromise with the traditional system of political parties.[115]

Based on consensus, this new social arrangement presupposed the eventual democratization of the Peronist movement, the end of its cult of leadership and principle of verticality for controlling the Peronist rank and file. "The social democracy we want is not founded essentially in the image of charismatic leaders, but rather on a permanent state of representativity of the popular masses!"[116]

In his ambition to be president of all the Argentines and not just the winning candidate of a political movement, Perón dropped the label "national socialism." A thorn in the side of his political enemies, national socialism had become a symbol of the strong-arm methods of both the Peronist armed formations and the fascist elements in the movement. But the two basic postulates of justicialism remained in force: national unity, and social justice. Hence Perón's new social democratic doctrine did not challenge the nationalist and socialist premises of justicialism. Although the new boost he gave to political pluralism signified a repudiation of his fascist origins, Perón's basic program retained its subversive ring to both the military and the business communities in Argentina.

Preventive Revolution

Perón was the first to admit that the doctrinal principles of his movement had been improvised.[117] But in practice he discovered example to be the best teacher. Since there is no guarantee that the course of events will conform to human intentions, improvisation has the advantage of adapting to the real world while leaving the leader free to resolve each problem as it presents itself. "In other words, deeds are performed, their lessons are assimilated, and . . . on that basis a doctrine is crystallized. That is the system we have followed. I never spoke of a doctrine until after we had realized what we had in mind."[118]

Principles are the doctrinal or programmatic articulations of ideals. For an ideology and its ideals to preserve their vigor, they must be articulated in principles that continue to evolve. Hence it is necessary to prepare each generation to become accustomed to new and different doctrines. Based on the political, economic, and social reforms initiated by Colonel Perón as secretary of labor and social welfare from 1943 to 1945 and then as president, a justicialist doctrine was improvised that effectively embodied the fundamentals of justicialist ideology.

Like the ideological Third Position, Perón's doctrinal responses to the world situation were predicated on the fear of revolution. The persistence of an oppressive and defunct economic and political order in the face of the Bolshevik Revolution, two world wars, and the politicization of the masses supposedly threatened the Argentine republic with a proletarian conflagration unless something was done soon. "Faced with this new phenomenon we are not going to wait for a new seizure of the Bastille. By suppressing the economic absolutism that is leading us toward a second French Revolution, we shall make the necessary changes before the Bastille is assaulted."[119]

Specifically, Perón sought a remedy for social unrest, class struggle, and communism. "The agitation of the masses is an effect of social injustice. The remedy is to be found neither in deceiving them nor in submitting them to force, but in doing them justice. . . . We seek to suppress the class struggle by a just agreement between workers and owners under the just protection of the state."[120] Neither exhortation nor threats of violence suffice to combat communism, because what intimidates capitalists has little effect on the working class. Only two recourses are effective: military repression and elimination of the causes of social unrest.[121] Because Perón believed that repression works only in the short run, after which subversion reemerges with even greater force, he favored a program of preventive revolution based on long-overdue political, economic, and social reforms.

The basic postulates of preventive revolution had been traced by Perón's own hand on the eve of the June 1943 coup.[122] The first postulate, "national unity," was his antidote to social dissolution fostered by political factionalism and the struggle among political parties.[123] The second postulate, "social justice," was his response to class struggle and Communist subversion. Other postulates were added covering the specifically economic and political content of justicialism. A third postulate was "economic independence," without which "there is no possibility of social justice."[124] Lacking the wherewithal to fill empty stomachs, one cannot implement the principle of equilibrium.[125] This postulate depended on a fourth, the postulate of "political sovereignty." "It is vain to seek economic independence without the nation's being in charge, without people's sovereignty as opposed to oligarchical rule."[126] These four postulates constituted the doctrinal essence of justicialism.[127]

This is not the order in which they were implemented. The Peronist program of preventive revolution had to begin by giving the workers a stake in the government. Without the masses in a position of political power it would be impossible to support a program of economic independence, in turn a condition of social justice, "which gives to each what is due one as a social function."[128] This improvised ordering of the postulates of justicialist doctrine—political sovereignty, economic independence, and social justice—was the inverse of their ranking as principles.

Politically, Perón's reforms aimed at establishing a people's democracy in place of the spurious democracy of the oligarchy.[129] The political reforms came in response to three "Creole lies": that the government was republican, representative, and federal.[130] It was not republican because power did not reside in the electorate; it was not representative because elected officials did not represent the interests of the voting public; and it was not federal because the central authority rode roughshod over the interests of the provincial governments.

Blocking the way to political reform was a system of competing political parties and a government by politicians seeking "to divide in order to rule."[131] The political reforms set matters right by placing politics at the service of the nation instead of the nation at the service of politics. Thus the working class was able to use political power for its benefit and a civil war was avoided.[132] This was one way to prevent revolution.

Besides political reforms, Perón's first government set itself the tasks of economic independence and economic development. Why this order? Because "if we produced goods valued at 10 billion pesos per annum, 6 billion would have been taken from us [by foreign interests] and we would be left with only 4 billion . . . , if we produced 100 billion, 96 billion would have been taken, leaving as always 4 billion. So what would be gained by producing more?"[133] Although the example was farfetched, foreign capital was the suction pump divesting the country of its wealth; hence Perón's argument for proceeding directly to the nationalization of foreign capital and the liquidation of the foreign debt.[134]

Economically colonized countries like Argentina are characterized by being at the service of capital, another factor impeding their development.[135] According to established theory, economic development occurs for the sake of profit. But if industry yields less than the required return and production is curtailed, the people will go hungry; eventually, they will rebel and create a disaster. To prevent a revolution, production would have to be increased even should it be unprofitable.[136]

During World War II Perón estimated that Argentina produced approximately twice what it consumed.[137] What would happen after the war, when it no longer exported to the belligerents, who would have reconverted to peacetime production? "There will be a paralysis of 50 percent and we will see a million Argentines unemployed. . . . There will be no other remedy than . . . [to] raise wages and salaries, so that each person can consume more than he does at present and each industrialist can produce as much as today without being obliged to stop the machines and fire the workers."[138]

For Argentina to overcome its economic vassalage, it had to develop native industries.[139] Contrary to reliance on the market, this called for a program of radical protectionism and subsidies.[140] It also called for putting the entire population to work, because only a fraction of the people produced anything. Disgracefully, most adults were freeloaders: "10 million out of 16 million Argentines spend and consume without producing like drones in the hive, while only 6 million make honey."[141]

How did Perón propose to achieve social justice? First, by making the nation wealthier; second, by redistributing the wealth. Since neither the government nor the workers were in a position to undertake the first alternative, the second was chosen with the expectation that it would make possible the first.[142] The objective was to raise effective demand as an incentive to increasing the supply.

It would have been logical to begin with an agrarian reform, followed by industrial reorganization aimed at developing the country's wealth, and then by a general increase in the workers' standard of living. "But it was imperative to change the order . . . [because] social reform could not be postponed."[143] Delaying reform would have left some workers to perish from malnutrition, while others would have withdrawn their support from the government. Although social justice is an effect of economic independence, Perón argued, in extreme instances it also operates as a cause.[144]

Social justice would help prevent revolution. First, nobody would go without the basic necessities, so that a living wage for the submerged population would take precedence over raising the standard of living of those who had emerged.[145] Second, labor would no longer be treated as a commodity.[146] Finally, differences in income and wealth would be drastically reduced, so that "there will no longer be people who are either too poor or too rich."[147]

The rationale for Perón's various reforms may be traced to his speech to the Military College on 7 August 1945. He argued that the principal cause of social unrest is that some people have more than they need and others do not have enough. Consequently, the solution is to take from the rich to give to the poor. Although this option was bound to be rejected by the wealthy, the wealthy were their own worst enemies. Thus he warned that, should they refuse to give up 30 percent of their riches voluntarily, they would be forced to surrender everything—and their ears as well! [148]

Perón also tried to mollify subversion by stealing its thunder. Instead of stamping out Communists, he opted to buy them out by pensioning their leaders, providing paper for their publications, and helping them to survive politically. [149] "My real purpose was to ensure that Communists would serve the preventive function of antibodies. Mankind would have disappeared thousands of years ago but for the pathogenic agents that combat mortally infectious germs. I try to preserve my quota as a warning." [150]

Potential heresies during the Middle Ages—among the Franciscans in particular—had been neutralized by the church's device of incorporating them into monastic orders. Confronted by an enemy that could not be destroyed, Perón believed, the West could survive only by absorbing, assimilating, and digesting the Communist experience. As he used to say: "If you can't kill your enemy by force, then strangle him in an embrace!'" [151]

Perón urged army officers to develop a doctrine, theory, and strategy of embrace and absorb. Although the mechanisms for embracing and absorbing communism were first applied by European fascism, the suicidal war in which Germany and Italy were defeated meant that Europe was again vulnerable to Communist subversion. Perón's only remaining hope was that the victorious powers might "regenerate in themselves those same mechanisms of absorption they had destroyed in the vanquished." [152] To save the West from the Communist peril, he sought to remake Argentina into a geopolitical *bunker* for preserving the fascist legacy and holding out during the anticipated postwar Communist assault. [153]

This explains the remarkable intellectual cocktail, the bizarre concoction that makes Peronism different from almost all other political doctrines. It aimed to orchestrate the four poles of Christian humanism, liberal democracy, communism, and fascism. This combination exceeded the wildest dreams of either Hitler or Mussolini. In its effort to become all things to all people, it literally had no competitors. As Perón was fond of saying, his mission was not to divide but to unite. [154]

The practical foundation of this seemingly Machiavellian doctrine may be traced to Perón's chosen vocation. "Politically, I am an amateur. It is in matters of leadership that I am a professional."[155] Unlike the politician, who serves special interests, a conductor must be adept at orchestrating differences that stretch from the Right to the extreme Left. But because a preventive revolution also embraces and absorbs revolution, it cost Perón the support of his military peers.

The Syndicalist State

To counter the influence of subversive ideologies on Argentine workers, Perón accomplished through deeds what Socialists and Communists had promised in words. Trade union membership jumped spectacularly from 1943 to 1946, and more than doubled between 1946 and 1950.[156] By 1955, when Perón was removed by a military coup, the overall unionization rate was 42 percent—a record for Latin America.[157] This was the first step toward establishing a syndicalist state, the end result of which was that by the early 1970s "fully half of the total workforce belonged to trade unions."[158]

Thanks to Perón's stress on social justice, real wages increased more than 25 percent between 1943 and 1948, while the share of wages and salaries in the national income rose to 50 percent in 1950.[159] Paid annual holidays, paid sick leave, redundancy and dismissal compensation, compensation for workplace accidents, the famous *aguinaldo*, or thirteenth-month bonus, as a Christmas present, and the extension of the pension system to all employees were also part of the justicialist package of labor reforms. This was the second step toward a syndicalist state.

Perón's goal of a syndicalist state was predicated on collective agreements between labor and capital, with the state acting as intermediary. It depended not only on collective bargaining by industries, but also on an act of national compromise, or "Social Pact." An equilibrium between labor and capital was an essential part of Perón's economic program. For labor it signified an increasing share of the national income until the military intervened in 1955. "This ascending scale was being raised by us until it reached fifty-fifty. The percentage declined during the 18 years after 1955 to 33 percent."[160]

A major index of a postcapitalist economy is the distribution of the national income. The minimum objective of a justicialist economic order was set at 50 percent for labor, anything less being interpreted as the prevalence of capitalist relations of production. Although it is possible to creep into socialism of the non-Marxist variety, Perón believed the threshold must be high enough so that so-called workers' income matched and then exceeded that from the ownership of capital.

The Peronist project became crystallized in a trade-union doctrine befitting labor's special interest: "The trade union organizations have their *own* doctrine, because they also have a special function to perform."[161] I have mentioned the principal labor reforms Perón promised and implemented during his various terms in office. But was that the extent of his trade union doctrine?

Within a week of Perón's landslide vote in the November 1951 elections, he promised his followers that the syndicalist state, until then only a dream, would be gradually implemented.[162] This would enable Argentine workers to participate in both the legislature and the administration through representatives belonging to the trade unions. As a token of the coming syndicalist era, in December the province of the Chaco received a syndicalist constitution under which half of the legislature would be chosen by the provincial electorate of some two hundred thousand and the other half by the thirty thousand–strong provincial CGT.[163] That seems to have been the extent of the experiment, which retained little more than symbolic value. But the significance of this gesture should not be underestimated. Although it was still a long way from the goal of a workers' state, if carried out on a national scale it would have given labor a 50 percent stake in the federal government corresponding to its 50-50 share in the national income.

As Perón recalled from exile in November 1958, he had repeatedly told the leaders of organized labor that "the final objective of justicialism is the 'syndicalist state,' and that the forms adopted by the Peronist movement were destined to realize that metamorphosis by degrees without falling into useless excesses and without provoking violent transitions." In illustration he cited the evolution of the Peronist government and congress toward forms that were progressively syndicalist, because of the "effective preponderance of the labor Central [CGT] within national institutions."[164] Two provinces were singled out for special mention, the Chaco and La Pampa, for giving the edge to organized labor without having to resort to violence.

This was a far cry from Fascist versions of the syndicalist state as representing both owners' associations and the trade unions. With functional representation limited to trade unions, Perón's democratic recasting of national syndicalism favored organized labor. Meanwhile, he cautioned that the most prudent strategy for labor was not to provoke opposition, but to gain the support of other sectors. The evolution of Peronism into a "classist" party would be counterproductive if it divided instead of united the nation. In effect,

Peronist strategy would have a classist outcome without taking a classist form or relying on classist methods.[165]

In retrospect, several leaders of the Peronist party and of the CGT regarded the failure to eliminate the "partidocracy" as the fundamental mistake of Peronism in power. "The justicialist state had to operate within the institutional framework created by the oligarchy. . . . It limited itself to giving new meaning to obsolete forms . . . without suppressing the party regime . . . without destroying capitalism."[166] It did not bring about a change of structures by implementing the syndicalist state. It only partly removed the roots of subversion and therefore failed as a form of preventive revolution. This, too, played into the hands of Argentina's armed forces.

Counterrevolution and Resistance

Faced by rebellious army generals and a hostile navy in 1955, Perón's only hope of retaining power was to arm the workers. One reason for not doing so was that it would lead to civil war. After witnessing the effects of the Spanish civil war when he passed through that country in 1941, a Pyrrhic victory was not what he wanted.

In 1955 his government fell because he believed the costs of defending it were too high: "a civil war that would have set the country back some 50 or 100 years, and would have caused the death of one or two million Argentines."[167] He pointed out that "at best [those counties that had made a violent revolution] were worse off than before! On this score we have always been pacifists. I have declared it all my life." He claimed that war in any form was not an intelligent way to settle differences: "The French Revolution cost half the population of Paris; the Spanish civil war took a million lives; the Mexican Revolution cost a million and a half dead; in Russia the first year alone killed more than 12 million; in China Mao was accused of assassinating 10 million, a figure the Chinese have corrected and placed at 20 million."[168]

As Perón recalled in a speech to the CGT in November 1973, the defense of the people's interests "always develops according to two fundamental ingredients: time and blood."[169] The violent struggle consumes blood; the peaceful and organized struggle contributes to saving it, but needs time to succeed. In any case, it is "much better to spend time and to save blood, which tends to be spilt in vain."[170] The sole justification for spilling blood, he believed, was if it promised to be the lesser violence.

Hesitating to push for an Argentine equivalent of the Mexican Revolution, Perón chose to abdicate. Whatever his other reasons for abdicating, he later questioned this decision. As he admitted to his biographer: "I fear that the Argentine Republic, which rejected a rational evolution toward a change of structures . . . , must pass through a bloody revolution."[171] By postponing the ordeal, Argentines would have to suffer the additional violence, repression, and frustration of overt and covert dictatorships and the reversal of labor's hard-won gains.

While Perón continued to promote a peaceful strategy, he believed that under extraordinary circumstances violence might be the most humane alternative. The violence of events varies directly with the time required to incubate it. "Consequently, we must hurry up the violent outcome even though it seems a little bloody. If we wait, worse will come."[172] Without violence there can be no peace and the anarchy may prolong itself for many years. "If you must kill without fail, it is better to do so rapidly, as quickly as you can."[173] The preferred option, a drawn-out resistance, could help save blood, but if blood had to be spilled, then one should save time.

But Perón was not always consistent. "The more violent we are, the better. Terror cannot be vanquished except by another superior terror."[174] Under the pressure of circumstances he momentarily settled for a strategy incompatible with the lesser violence. "We will see who loses with the general ruin!" he exclaimed.[175] Certainly, it is difficult to square these and similar utterances with his philosophical commitment to balance and moderation. Notwithstanding his argument for the lesser violence, behind his strategy for provoking chaos was a proclivity to lawlessness. He hoped his strategy would compel the generals to resign before matters got out of hand, but he was willing to take the risk that they would not.

Reinforcing the generals' assessment of Perón as a political extremist, his correspondence contains still other samples of this syndrome. "Revolutions like ours must always begin with chaos; therefore, instead of fearing chaos, we should try to provoke it."[176] "Everything or nothing!"[177] "Fall who may fall, cost what it costs!"[178] "Sabotage, consumer boycotts, exhausting the water supply, destruction of telephone and telegraph wires, disruptions of every kind, strikes, work stoppages, tumultuous protests, pamphlets, rumors of all types, slowdowns, civil disobedience, violations of laws and decrees, refusal to pay taxes, insidious sabotage of the public administration, etc., are tactics that, when well executed, can in a few days bring down any government."[179] "We have to create . . . a permanent state of insurrection."[180] For the generals of the Military Process such intemperate language smacked of political subversion.

Raúl Alfonsín was not the first president of Argentina to contemplate punishing the generals for crimes against citizens. Perón favored the trial and punishment of all officers who had participated in the September coup. He also recommended a new military code that would effectively prevent future coups. "When the commanders-in-chief of the army and air force are to be removed, I don't mean to suggest that you get rid just of a few, but rather that you should eliminate hundreds. You must also apply a new rod for breach of discipline, which is the scourge that will totally and definitively destroy the army, air force, and finally the navy. They are the real powers that betrayed the people and they must pay for their transgression."[181]

Although this was among the most outrageous of Perón's directives, it was not the only outrageous one. Recalling Napoleon's efforts to instill morale in ragged and hungry troops by offering them the prospect of sacking Piedmontese villages and violating their women, Perón suggested doing something similar in Argentina. Thus all the possessions of the oligarchs and "gorillas" would be expropriated. This total confiscation without reparation would be applied as follows: first, "those who seize a house belonging to the oligarchs, and detain or execute its owners, shall keep it for themselves"; second, "those who seize an estate under the same conditions shall keep everything belonging to it, as also those who take over the businesses of the 'gorillas' and enemies of the people"; third, "uncommissioned officers who kill their superiors and take charge of their troops shall command them in the future, a rule that also applies to ordinary soldiers who perform a similar action."[182]

With such secret directives the 1956–1973 resistance got under way. But the directions were not just subversive; they were downright criminal. As Perón threatened in a major document of the resistance: "Rather than allow the [dictatorial] canaille to have things their own way, we prefer to destroy everything so that in the end we may all be equal, even if it be in misery."[183]

There is a strong dose of anarchism in these exhortations to unloose the popular Behemoth. As Perón acknowledged in his taped memoirs: "I was always a revolutionary and even a little bit of an anarchist. I always respected anarchism, despite its idealism, which doesn't permit it to do anything more [than to overturn]. Because it deserves respect."[184] These remarks were hardly in keeping with justicialist doctrine. But for the moment he believed that the urge to chaos might be an asset in making a revolution. The time for controlling it would come later, in consolidating power and institutionalizing a new order.

According to one political observer, Perón played for a year and a half at making a Russian revolution.[185] From the middle of 1956 to the end of 1957 "he placed the country in the serious risk of a civil war, which at bottom he did not want."[186] This assessment is confirmed by Perón: "I, too, was a pacifist until June 9, but after the crimes committed by the tyrants supported by the political parties, I no longer have hopes of a bloodless solution. The hatred and desire for vengeance that these predators have awakened in the people will one day come out into the open . . . only afterward will it be possible to think of pacification."[187]

The crimes of the dictatorship and the onslaught against the trade unions had turned Perón's thoughts to revolution. Argentine workers also did an about-face. Their first response was to accept the coup, but no sooner had Perón abandoned the country than a group of Peronist militants calling themselves "Peronist Resistance" went into action. Between September 1955 and the elections of February 1958, some seven thousand explosive artifacts were detonated in acts of sabotage against the military regime. According to the review *Confirmado* (24 December 1975), that was more than the number of bombs exploded during the entire Algerian war of independence over a period twice as long.

In response to the Peronist resistance organized by John William Cooke, Perón was persuaded to give the workers what they wanted. Once they asserted themselves, he took the initiative of issuing directives on how to topple the dictatorship. Even so, he stopped short of Cooke's strategy of general insurrection. Publicly, he endorsed guerrilla warfare only as a last resort under conditions in which it might do a minimum of harm. Thus his justification for violence was ambivalent.

Perón's faith and trust in the masses were restored. "Although some Peronist leaders defected in response to defeat, many millions of loyal Peronists remained firm and defended the cause. The fall from power has served to purify the movement."[188] The masses had replaced their leaders. "Parallel to the bloody and usurping reaction of September 16 and after the people's initial moment of astonishment and listlessness had passed, a state of popular insurrection began surging up 'from below.'"[189] The strength of the Peronist movement, he concluded, lay in this spirit of intransigence and readiness to revolt.

When Cooke became Perón's political heir in 1956, Perón gave him a carte blanche to act in his name. "I have a blind faith in you," he said of the party's outstanding militant.[190] Cooke was ideally cast for the role of leader. Arrested in October 1955, he secretly directed the resistance from behind bars. After a spectacular escape from the Río Gallegos prison in southern Patagonia in March 1957, he fled to Chile, where he continued to conspire and prepare for armed struggle. In May 1958 he returned to Argentina to launch a new wave of hostilities against the pseudoconstitutional government of President Frondizi. Mounting street riots and incendiarism prompted Frondizi to declare a state of siege in November. Cooke was again detained, but soon released. Then came the labor riots of January 1959, in a replay of the first major red scare in the nation's capital in January 1919. Obliged to flee the country, Cooke took refuge in Castro's Cuba, where he arranged for the training of Argentine guerrillas.

In November 1956 Perón formally appointed Cooke to head the resistance.[191] As Perón explained the reasons for Cooke's appointment: "Dr. Cooke was the only leader who sought me out, the only one who openly took a position of absolute intransigence, which is what I believe suits our movement at this moment. He was also the only leader who, without wasting time, organized a group for struggle in the capital . . . and who, despite his displacement from one prison to another, was always able to reach me with his information and the only one I was able to reach with my directives."[192]

Perón chose Cooke to head the resistance knowing that Cooke favored even more extreme measures than his own. After the unsuccessful navy and air force coup of 16 June 1955, Cooke had supported a proposal by the trade unions to organize popular militias in defense of the government. Then on the advice of Abraham Guillén, the Spanish anarchist and civil war veteran collaborating on Cooke's review *De Frente*, he had presented to Perón an alternative plan for irregular forces that would operate clandestinely and independently of the regular army.[193] Although Cooke's plan was vetoed by Peronist military officers jealous of their professional monopoly, it would later be implemented in Perón's name.

Perón's "General Instructions to Leaders" (January 1956) is the single most important document of the resistance. As Perón underscored their importance, "nobody can consider himself a Peronist if he does not know, if he does not apply and get others to carry out those directives, which only repeat what the people want and Peronists aspire to achieve in this dark hour of our country's destiny."[194] The instructions provided the strategy for civil and armed struggle from 1956 to 1973 and again from 1976 to 1983. Perón's document reads like a manual of subversion. With few exceptions its strategy, if not the final objective, corresponded to that of the Cooke-Guillén guerrilla plan of 1955. Perón's strategy may be summarized under the following points corresponding to the document's main divisions.[195]

Plan of Action

Resistance to a military coup must be implemented through successive stages. The first step is to organize a surreptitious and insidious struggle aimed at hitting the enemy where it hurts, but without exposing oneself to retaliation. Organized by civic groups and the trade unions, sabotage should aim at undermining both the public order and the productive process. During work it can take the form of slowdowns, work stoppages, and strikes; after work, of boycotts, demonstrations, generalized protest, and civil disobedience. The second step is to intensify the struggle by grass-roots organizations and to extend it throughout the country. The third step must prepare for the coming showdown. Finally, in the event the country is paralyzed but the camarilla in power refuses to abdicate, guerrilla warfare must be launched.

Resistance

The key to successful resistance is united action and the people's resolve to destroy everything, if necessary, to bring down the dictatorship. Thus the country will belong to everybody, or it will belong to nobody. This struggle may be individual or organized. Small individual acts of sabotage may be carried out in all places at all times: at home, in the street, at work, at play. Although each act of moral and material depredation may be miniscule, the sum of millions of such acts is tantamount to "integral warfare," enough to reduce any tyranny to indecisiveness and helplessness. Organized resistance may be of four general kinds: military, in demoralizing or winning over officials and subofficials of the armed forces; economic, in undermining production and distribution and in accentuating waste and pollution; social, in disturbances of the public order provoked by work stoppages and strikes; political, through continued agitation, provocation, and infiltration. Although in part legal, it also relies on clandestine organizations specializing in active sabotage, intimidation, armed attacks on persons and institutions, and the enforcement of so-called people's justice.

Organization

The clandestine regrouping of old cadres, the formation of new ones, and the establishment of a communications network between the underground organizations of the Peronist movement and the trade unions dissolved by the military authorities are fundamental to the resistance. Since secrecy is paramount, the resistance should be organized according to the cell system. Violent measures must be taken against traitors and infiltrators to assure that secret organizations and their leaders are not endangered. The strict completion of orders is essential. When the people are at war, it is necessary to proceed on a warlike basis. This calls for the organization of clandestine task forces for threatening the properties and intimidating the persons and families of the camarilla in power.

Revolutionary General Strike

The resistance has three principal objectives: first, to undermine and wear down the dictatorial regime; second, to strengthen popular opposition to the regime by organizing the unorganized and by improving existing forms and methods of organization; third, to prepare and coordinate the country's complete paralysis. When these three conditions have been fulfilled, it is time to declare a revolutionary general strike that will remain in force until the government abdicates. No government can continue for long in the face of total breakdown, but if the strike is only partial or gives way to government intimidation, the paralysis may be overcome. Unless the strike is both resolute and total, it is better not to strike at all. To launch a revolutionary general strike and fail is to imperil the entire resistance by losing the decisive battle.

Guerrilla Warfare

To add force to such a strike and to accelerate the final showdown, preparations for guerrilla warfare must already have begun. When the time comes to launch the armed struggle, the guerrillas must have the independence, initiative, proficiency, and resources for sustaining it. These may be achieved through armed operations, small enough and disconnected so as not to attract public attention. It is not necessary to organize rural guerrillas. Urban guerrillas backed by the local population, through surprise actions and the rapid displacement of their forces, present an invisible target to the enemy and are virtually invincible. Guerrillas should be recruited from the most decisive and audacious cadres, from those already organized for acts of sabotage and attacks on the persons and goods of the leading agents of repression. When the moment arrives to launch guerrilla warfare, those cadres will already have been trained as guerrillas.

Special Operations

Since the rule of terrorism is appropriate to those who fear terror, the resistance must reply in kind: first, by intimidation and violence; second, by informal trials and punishment. Like vipers, those responsible for executing loyal Peronists and slaughtering innocent people must be stamped out. The "gorillas" must reach the conclusion that they have been condemned to death by the people, that their families' lives are endangered, that their properties will be destroyed through incendiarism, bombs, and vandalism, that nothing is secure. Their names and addresses must be made public by means of pamphlets, so that they come under constant surveillance by those intent on killing them. The greater the violence, the better— but it is preferable for a "gorilla" to die from poisoning or from a hit-and-run driver than from a direct attack on his house, from which he may escape unharmed. Each such action must be minutely planned without improvisation by persons of absolute confidence, acting together in secret and without leaving any trace. A secret society calling itself "The People's Justice" must be organized on a permanent basis. It should include the parents and friends of the persecuted, dispossessed, imprisoned, and dead—all of whom have a moral obligation to punish the guilty. This society shall be organized in territorial, trade-union, and political brotherhoods, each with a list of personal data targeted on the enemies of the people. The list shall be headed by Gen. Pedro Aramburu and Adm. Isaac Rojas, who were responsible for the military coup of September 1955. The obligation of the "brothers" is to apply the penalty. They will be protected by their anonymity, known by a number and a key word in place of their name and surname. All their meetings will be secret and their faces covered with a hood to prevent recognition. They will be carefully screened before joining, they will not be allowed to desert, and all traitors and infiltrators will be mercilessly killed.

Here we have the model for the Montoneros' sect of twelve persons, who announced themselves to the world with a dramatic kidnapping in May 1970. The victim had already been fingered by Perón: General Aramburu, who had unleashed during his two and a half years in office a major offensive against the trade unions and had been directly responsible for the execution of loyal Peronist officers in the unsuccessful revolution of June 1956. That he was finally tried and executed by his captors in June 1970 was in strict conformity to Perón's "General Instructions." The irony is that a major statesman, the most popular president Argentina ever had, and an outspoken critic of subversive terrorism should have relied on such methods.

How did Perón's strategy differ from Cooke's? Perón did not count on urban guerrillas to set in motion a mass resistance; he relied on mass resistance to organize and activate the guerrillas. More important, the Cooke-Guillén plan aimed at preparing a popular insurrection.[196] But Perón's strategy envisioned the abdication of the generals in response to economic paralysis and social chaos. Perón expected to use the resistance as a trump card in negotiating the military's orderly withdrawal from power. Although his "Instructions" warn of a general insurrection, he did not advocate one. Prior to the 1955 coup Cooke had asked for arms to defend the government. Perón had other ideas. It would have been easy to give the workers arms—the problem was to get them back.

Cooke was put in charge of implementing Perón's "Instructions," but he interpreted them in the light of his and Guillén's guerrilla plan of 1955. His continuing commitment to this plan is evident in a sixty-five-page document inserted in a letter to Perón dated 28 August 1957. Entitled "General Report and Plan of Action," its principal objective was a general insurrection.[197] Only an armed vanguard could catalyze the people to take up arms through a "permanent campaign of alarm."[198] But it was not a protracted struggle that Cooke had in mind: "A lightning civil war offers the best strategy . . . but for that, popular support is necessary on a national scale."[199]

Perón's response to Cooke was to agree nominally with the strategy of an insurrectional movement—something he had not done in his "Instructions." We have to create the germs, he wrote, of a "permanent insurrectional situation."[200] He cited the Bolshevik Revolution as an example. "Consider what transpired during the second Russian Revolution of October 1917. From 1906 to 1917 a condition of social insurrection was prepared so that, when the first World War undermined the power of the state, it was enough for one thousand men enacting audaciously and without force to bring about a coup and the triumph of the most important social revolution of all time."[201] He then advised: "We must follow that same technique. We already have an insurrectional situation. We only need to extend and to intensify it . . . [until] the dictatorship becomes weakened to the point that it can be annihilated."[202]

Was this the mass or general insurrection defended by Cooke? No, because Perón abhorred the Spanish civil war as a virtual holocaust and rejected it as a model. Under no circumstances could he agree to apply the final section of the Cooke-Guillén guerrilla plan: "A military uprising against a popular government is an occasion for transforming usurpation into civil war. The Spanish civil war began in this way and offered multiple possibilities of victory by the popular forces."[203] Although Perón encouraged Cooke to go ahead with the "Plan of Action," it was because he expected it to generate an insurrectional climate that would pressure the military to abdicate—not an insurrectional war.

These differences were far from trivial. An insurrectional war would have shifted the locus of power from the Peronist political and labor bureaucracies to the revolutionary organizations, whereas an insurrectional climate promised to be, and in fact was, the prelude to a negotiated transfer of power involving elections and the restoration of the status quo ante. Cooke did not relish such an outcome. Consequently, when he persisted in giving an insurrectional interpretation to Perón's "Instructions," he was discreetly replaced.

The primary document of the resistance addressed to Peronist leaders was followed in mid-1956 by Perón's "General Directives for All Peronists."[204] Although both documents are undated, in a letter to Cooke on 12 June 1956 Perón indicated that five months had passed since launching his "Instructions."[205] That would place their date around the beginning of January 1956. The "General Directives for All Peronists" appeared some six or seven months later in the wake of the "most villainous executions in the country's history."[206] This passage and others concerning the killing of defenseless prisoners and sadistic assassinations in prisons and concentration camps refer to the unprecedented bloodbath in June 1956 in retaliation for the unsuccessful military revolt of two Peronist generals, Juan José Valle and Raúl D. Tanco. Instead of jailing the rebels, the government chose to shoot them. Military officers were not the only victims. Imprisoned workers were dragged from their cells and mowed down by firing squads because of their Peronist sympathies.

The "Directives" acknowledged the consequences of believing in a bloodless revolution: "We were mistaken and have had to pay a high price for our humanitarianism."[207] Nonetheless, Perón perceived a bright side to this dismal picture. Without this initial error the justicialist revolution would have continued to backslide. "It was the pruning that would recover our revolutionary dynamism."[208]

After that initial error there was only one option left: "We must face up to the consequences of fighting for a *definitive social revolution* destined to achieve its objectives through active combat until the reaction is totally disarmed and absolutely extinguished."[209] But despite Perón's inflammatory language and endorsement of violence, his objectives were comparatively modest: the end of repression, the recovery of the workers' rights, and the restoration of the

1949 justicialist constitution abrogated by the military in April 1956.[210] Two related strategies were proposed for achieving those ends: first, "civil resistance that wears down the enemy, while we organize our clandestine forces and then proceed to paralyze the country and seize power by any means including the provocation of chaos"; second, in the event that this first strategy should prove unfeasible, "political action by our mass organizations by which they can obtain a foothold in the government and from there implement our real objectives."[211]

Some fifteen years later the hour of decision arrived.[212] At that point Peronists were in need of a new set of directives. Perón's 1972 *Actualización política y doctrinaria para la toma del poder* consisted of an updated version of the "General Directives for All Peronists," with the difference that it aimed not at launching the struggle but at carrying it to completion.[213] Like his earlier directives, it addressed three principal topics: the objectives, strategies, and concrete tasks of the resistance.

Perón aligned himself with movements of national and social liberation throughout the Third World, and with the principal socialist experiments in Latin America epitomized by Castro's Cuba and Allende's Chile.[214] Taking his cue from Mao Tse-tung's "On the Correct Handling of Contradictions among the People," he distinguished the friends of the people from their enemies both inside and outside the Peronist movement.[215] To succeed against Yankee imperialism and its native allies, he urged supporters to avoid sectarianism and to coordinate their separate struggles toward a common goal.

The immediate operational problem was how to cope with a dictatorship in retreat, how to negotiate the enemy's withdrawal from power without succumbing to its demands for some form of restricted democracy. With the enemy on the defensive, Perón ordered the popular movement to harass the government by whatever means, at all moments, and in all places.[216] Special attention was given to the Peronist armed organizations as indispensable to waging a revolutionary war. Their slogan: "Where force is present, nothing; where absent, everything, striking where and when it hurts."[217]

Perón's 1972 document contains the most revolutionary guidelines ever issued in his name. Its rejection of Russian communism did not preclude the acceptance of Fidel Castro and Mao Tse-tung as allies in the struggle against U.S. imperialism. A new doctrine was proposed consistent with Christian national socialism but adapted to the new era of liberation movements in the Third World, a doctrine whose hostility to capitalism and U.S. hegemony in Latin America exceeded that of any of Perón's earlier or subsequent utterances on the subject. Although the new doctrine lost currency with the return of Peronism to power in May 1973, it helped to mobilize and arm the Peronist Youth during the last year of the resistance.

Each of these major documents of the resistance rested on doctrinal revisions of the Third Position. Few people were going to risk life and limb in a revolutionary war whose only objective was to restore social stability. John William Cooke, the principal protagonist of armed struggle, was also the first to warn Perón that the movement would disappear if it did not alter its doctrine.

The first hint of a revolutionary interpretation of the Third Position appeared in a letter from Cooke to Perón dated 24 July 1961. In it, he criticized the original doctrine for being "Christian, Occidental, and Anticommunist."[218] It was pointless to try to revive the original alliance with the church and the armed forces, he argued, because they were no longer with but against the popular forces. Peronism could no longer be an alternative to communism without defining itself as a movement of the Left. Otherwise, Cooke warned, "like a strange bug that is on the Left but tries to ingratiate itself with the Right, we will last as long as you do, after which will come the Diaspora with our movement fractured into particles and with nothing to offer."[219]

In a follow-up letter on the same topic, Cooke claimed that there was no longer any place in the movement for the doctrine of a just mean. "What will be is not the 'conciliation of classes,' social equilibrium, or anything of that style. Because that was possible in a conjuncture that no longer exists. Multiclass national fronts are still feasible but only with the revolutionary classes in command—workers, peasants, intellectuals, petty bourgeois. . . . The forces are polarizing and there is no intermediate position."[220] To overcome capitalism, Cooke insisted, one could no longer rely on the "astute Machiavellians of equilibrium."[221] A movement for national liberation like Peronism could become the vanguard only by identifying itself with the "extreme Left."[222] To stop the Communists, the Peronist movement would have to support them in the struggle against capitalism. As he summarized his new conception of the Third Position in a letter to Perón on 18 October 1962, "thirdism [*tercerismo*] implies independence with respect to the two blocs—capitalist and Communist—but not *equidistance*."[223]

Although Perón sensed the danger of Cooke's challenge from the Left, his first response was to embrace and absorb it. Only when this strategy failed did he revise his original doctrine by concessions to the Right. As he recalled in a speech to the CGT: "When we were impatient and wanted to go too fast, we ran into a wall created by the opposition!"[224] Thus Perón was not taken off guard by the September 1973 coup that toppled Pres. Salvador Allende in Chile. "What happened in Chile demonstrates that Allende fell victim to sectarianism, to policies that encouraged excesses," whereas "we apply the law of counterbalance."[225]

But the damage had already been done. Perón's strategy of armed resistance had confirmed suspicions that he was an unscrupulous opportunist who could not be trusted and that he had created a monster he could not tame.

Social Dissolution instead of National Unity

Perón predicted that what happened in Chile would not happen in Argentina. But there was a coup only two and a half years after he made his pronouncement. Perón's vaunted doctrinal flexibility turned into a nightmare not only for the Justicialist movement, but also for the Argentine nation. Instead of national unity, it led to national disintegration. Prior to the Peronist phenomenon, the burden of capital accumulation had been borne by the working masses. Perón's reforms changed all that by giving organized labor an effective veto over economic policies hitherto benefiting the interests of big capital and the landed oligarchy. Argentina has yet to recover from the unintended effects of this stalemate.

Despite Perón's authoritarian efforts to bring organized labor under state control, the boost to the trade unions at the factory level contributed to democratizing the workplace. Factory committees emerged consisting of shop stewards, who served as workers' delegates elected in open assemblies in each shop or department. These factory committees functioned as organs of a workers' democracy that "gradually took away more and more of management's prerogatives . . . [and] directly threatened management's 'right to manage.'"[226]

Perón hoped to neutralize exotic ideological and revolutionary currents in the labor movement. By granting workers much-needed improvements, he expected them to moderate their intransigence. Instead, class struggle intensified as the working class gained in numbers, organization, and confidence based on a "dense network of social and political ties which could not be broken by repression."[227] Although workers in March 1976 were in no mood to defend a Peronist government they no longer trusted, the failure of the government to contain the combativeness of the working class within a framework of national unity was a major cause of the coup.[228]

From the end of March to the beginning of July 1975, sustained political activism by organized labor reached a level that had not been seen since the *semana trágica* and *Patagonia rebelde*. The trouble began when the government denounced a subversive plot involving the local leadership of the metalworkers' Unión Obrera Metalúrgica (UOM) in Villa Constitución and San Nicolás, the heart of the nation's heavy industry, some fifty kilometers south of Rosario on the Paraná River. On March 20 this government-styled "Red Serpent of the Paraná" was occupied by federal and provincial police forces estimated at about four thousand, the unions were intervened, and their leaders arrested.

The response of the workers was to declare a strike aimed at releasing their leaders and restoring the unions to their elected officials. It lasted almost sixty days. "The resistance was everywhere," recalled Leonardo Lezcano. "The resistance was organized with the participation of the workers . . . , with industry paralyzed, with the support of shopkeepers and of all the sectors of the city. . . . Recalling what the resistance was like during those two months, I am really amazed at how we could have held out such a long time in a situation in which our lives were in danger."[229]

This most important industrial strike in the country's history was to become the prelude to the first massive labor demonstrations against a Peronist government. Pressured by the rank and file, which demanded an end to the repressive policies of the cabal headed by the minister of social welfare, José López Rega, the CGT convoked a huge demonstration in Plaza de Mayo on June 27—the largest of its kind since the mobilization that inaugurated the Peronist era on 17 October 1945. This action was followed by the CGT's general strike of forty-eight hours on July 7 and 8, which pressured López Rega to resign along with the minister of economy, Celestino Rodrigo. Known as the *rodrigazo*, it also alerted the armed forces to the specter of labor ascendancy within the Peronist government.

It was the CGT's general strike that prompted what Ricardo Obregón Cano, the former governor of Córdoba, called the armed forces' invisible coup against the Peronist project. Awaiting trial for subversion in the same prison as the generals and admirals of the Military Process, Obregón Cano dwelt briefly on the succession of covert coups that had paved the way for the open coup of March 1976: the palace coup against President Cámpora in July 1973; the palace coup by López Rega in July 1974; and the internal coup by the armed forces in August 1975, when Peronist general Alberto Numa Laplane was deposed as commander-in-chief in a move led by General Videla. By August 1975 the top military brass had concluded that only the armed forces could stop the CGT and its political arm, the "62 Organizations," from blackmailing the government with threats of labor mobilizations. Thus in his Christmas Eve message, Videla threatened that, if the Peronist government did not take a firm stand against the forces of social dissolution, at the end of three months the military would intervene to restore order.

That Isabel Perón could not govern in accordance with a settled plan, that one cabinet after another fell, that inflation had gotten out of hand, all were laid at the door of organized labor. It was not only the government's vacillation and the near chaos to which it had led the country that troubled the military. Although these became the pretexts for the coup, the persistent threat of a labor veto and of a government hegemonized by the trade unions also weighed in the balance.

The military's worries over the subversion problem were matched only by its concern with the Peronist phenomenon. Prior to the Military Process the armed forces considered Peronism as their fundamental enemy. Four successful coups tried to dismantle the sources of Peronist power: the coup that toppled Perón in September 1955, the coup within the coup of November 1955, and the coups against Presidents Frondizi in March 1962 and Illia in June 1966.

Perón's claim to fame was having devised a final solution to the subversion problem. But it was a strange and roundabout remedy that prompted him to encourage subversion in the course of combating it. Reliance on a revolutionary war to end revolutionary war cut two ways. On the one hand, the promotion of revolutionary violence accelerated the abdication of the military and the return of Perón, who was "expected to deal with subversion in a more effective way."[230] On the other hand, Perón's anticipated "solution to the subversion problem . . . was brutally disproved soon after the elections."[231]

The Peronist electoral victories in 1973 contributed to restoring the government's legitimacy while undermining support for the guerrillas. But "the continuation of subversion produced just the opposite result, accelerating the downfall of the popular coalition and the return of the military."[232] Try as he might, Perón failed to discipline his own creation—the armed formations of the Peronist Youth.

The boost Perón gave to the Peronist armed formations spilled over to the Guevarist political-military vanguards. When the Montoneros returned underground in September 1974, their armed actions indirectly supported the latter. Subversion reached a peak in 1975, and in response the Justicialist government stooped to even more repressive actions than the dictatorship it had replaced. By then it was apparent that Perón's final solution to the subversion problem had boomeranged.

Ironically, Perón's policies of equilibrium aggravated instead of alleviated social tensions in the long run. Thanks to Perón, the trade unions became an independent contender for power: "It is the ability of the labor movement to protect its interests that has prevented so far the resolution of the stalemate through the hegemony of the big bourgeoisie and the agrarian elite."[233] In Argentina there were too many cooks, leading to endless and fruitless contention.

The fact remains that Peronism did not dare to scrap the capitalist system. Perón's goal was a labor-based government and the redistribution of wealth, not structural changes.[234] Labor had first to be organized and then mobilized. Yet even with limited objectives, Peronism was challenged at every step.[235] Abstractly speaking, it was a fiasco, but in the context of World War II and the immediate aftermath, it was the best that Argentina could offer: "Popular movements do not have ideal characteristics; they have those that social forces, struggles, and at times chance factors give to them."[236] Deadlock was the price of Perón's political, economic, and social reforms; it could hardly have been otherwise.

A broad view of Argentina's recent history suggests that the country was feeling the birth pangs of a new social order. Peronism introduced many new elements into Argentine life, of which the most important were the central roles given to state managers and the trade unions in shaping economic policy. The resulting redistribution of more than 10 percent of the GNP from landowners and capitalists to wage earners led to a bitter fight between Peronist and anti-Peronist forces that continues to this day.[237] The social cost of Perón's political, economic, and social reforms may seem exorbitant, but the reforms politicized the workers and gave them their first taste of power. Although his solution to the subversion problem was bankrupt from the start, it produced deadlock and the conditions for getting the country off dead center.

That hardly recommended it to the military. The officers in the armed forces viewed Peronism as the cause of Argentina's problems, not the solution. Military liberals perceived Perón's appeals to organized labor as an excuse for extortion. They accused his mafia of political gangsters of creating an artificial danger, and then of exacting protection payments to keep the threat under control. Failure to pay for this protection could bring harassment by the Peronist *patota* (armed thugs). Perón's strong-arm methods smacked of fascism, while his use of state power to obtain concessions for his mass followers qualified as totalitarianism.

Catholic nationalists in the armed forces had other reasons for resisting the Peronist project. For them the disquieting fact was Perón's aiding and abetting of democratic futility. His lies were bad enough, but even worse was his deference to the will of the masses. It was not Perón's fascism that bothered them, but his complicity with subversive and mass violence. The escalating revolutionary war and flourishing of armed gangs, they noted, coincided not with the absence of democracy but with its return after 1973.

Perón anticipated that giving the people what they wanted would bring social peace and an end to the military era. But his reforms created a vacuum of power and a climate of insecurity in which human lives as well as properties were threatened. As a result, Peronism brought on massive intervention by the armed forces. Instead of ending the military era, it reinforced the military's resolve to stop the Peronist steamroller in its tracks.

4. The Revolutionary War

BEHIND THE revolutionary war in Argentina was the revolutionary situation that nurtured it. In the wake of the November coup, which followed the coup that ousted Perón in September 1955, the workers found themselves dispossessed of their legitimate organizations. For almost sixteen years their political party was outlawed. With their unions intervened until February 1961, and again in 1967 and 1969, they were also deprived of legal channels to defend their economic interests. Since Perón had urged them to prepare for a protracted struggle culminating in a mass insurrection, a precedent was set that would eventually bear fruit in the armed formations of the Peronist Left.

In July 1966 the universities were intervened, which fanned the flames of student unrest kindled by the example of another eminent Argentine, Ernesto "Che" Guevara. It is noteworthy that on the heels of General Onganía's coup in June, Guevara appeared in neighboring Bolivia in command of a guerrilla organization, the Ejército de Liberación Nacional (ELN). Meanwhile, the military's ban on political activity, which lasted until 1971, further aggravated matters by pitting the civilian elites against the military. Thus to the objective conditions of a political crisis were added the subjective conditions, which account for the revolutionary war and its persistence even after the return of Peronism to power in 1973.

Central to understanding the revolutionary war is an accurate assessment of the protagonists. The guerrillas' perception of their role must be weighed alongside the opinions of their civilian detractors and military repressors. The only divisive issue among those who favored tough measures against armed subversion was whether the guerrillas could have been contained within the rule of law. As for the guerrillas, they disputed the stereotype of terrorists and fascists of the Left—a stereotype that made them responsible for their own repression—but they agreed with the generals that they could not have been defeated militarily without the dirty war.

Legacy of the Political-Military Vanguards

Argentina's guerrillas were ideologically, doctrinally, and strategically obligated to two principal figures. The Peronist armed formations were indebted to John William Cooke (1920–1968), and the Marxist-Leninist military vanguards to Ernesto "Che" Guevara (1928–1967). Because of Cooke's more than three years of exile in Castro's Cuba, he, too, came under Guevara's influence. Nonetheless, it would be a mistake to define Cookism as a Peronist adaptation of Guevarism, first, because of Cooke's pronounced nationalism as opposed to Guevara's internationalist orientation; second, because of Cooke's broad-front socialism as distinct from Guevara's left-wing communism; third, because of Cooke's reliance on the "myth" of a general insurrection.

In a letter to Perón on 14 November 1957, Cooke summarized the conditions for revolution: "A revolution requires a *revolutionary party, revolutionary leaders,* and a *revolutionary myth* on the one hand, and the occasion on the other."[1] The role he assigned to revolutionary leaders and a revolutionary party corresponded to Lenin's subjective conditions of revolution; that of a revolutionary occasion, to Lenin's objective conditions.[2] What was new is the significance he attached to a revolutionary myth.

A myth is distinct from a mystique in galvanizing human will and actions instead of feelings. As Georges Sorel defined it in *Reflections on Violence,* a revolutionary myth is a complex of symbols that predisposes us to act, that evokes the impulse to struggle and inspires us to fight.[3] This work disseminated by French, Italian, and Spanish anarchists eventually found its way to Argentina as part of the legacy of anarcho-syndicalism. For Sorel the revolutionary myth par excellence was that of the General Strike. For Cooke it was the myth of a General Insurrection.[4]

Since myths are not affirmations of a past, present, or future state of affairs, they are neither true nor false. In this respect they resemble mystiques. But they have to be convincing to be effective. As Cooke reminded Perón: "One of its [a general insurrection's] elements is viability, the people must be convinced that the insurrection is possible."[5] Because of theoretical emphasis on the objective conditions of revolution and the workers' self-interest, Marxist-Leninists have little use for either myths or mystiques. But for Cooke there was no Chinese Wall between the objective occasion and the subjective conditions of revolution: "What people do not understand . . . is that the revolutionary conditions will appear to the extent that we strengthen ourselves and persevere in revolutionary actions."[6] The multiplication of revolutionary energy contributes to producing revolutionary conditions, "to creating the mentality of victory in the revolutionary movement and to spreading defeatism in the ranks of the oppressor."[7]

In another passage suggestive of Guillén's influence, Cooke recalled that in Barcelona in July 1936 the anarchists defeated an army of thirty-five thousand thanks to the myth of a general insurrection.[8] This and other examples led him to conclude that, as a result of popular intervention, "a moment arrives in which material force, apparently concentrated in the hands of reaction, joins the side of the revolutionaries or offers only token resistance."[9]

These passages are remarkable in anticipating Guevara's revolutionary strategy. Wrote Guevara in *Guerrilla Warfare:* "It is not necessary to wait for all the conditions of revolution to be given; the revolutionary *foco* [vanguard] can create them."[10] This principle, a restatement of Cooke's thesis that the insurrectional effort helps to create the revolutionary occasion, also has an anarchist origin.

Although Cooke was indebted to Marxism, he rejected the Marxist label. Speaking of Marxists, he said: "We have little confidence in those pundits of history who give a preview of the end but never understand what happened yesterday or is happening now."[11] How do they know that the objective conditions of revolution are lacking in Argentina, or know in advance what is mere "adventurism," destined to fail, and what is "scientific," and destined to succeed?[12] There is no magic formula for assuring the right moment for launching an armed struggle, nor does armed struggle become possible except through launching it.[13]

Cooke also took an ambivalent stand on Peronism. Despite Perón's record in behalf of the Argentine worker, Cooke characterized him as "the main asset of bourgeois-democratic politics in Argentina."[14] A "pre-Marxist," Perón was not at that moment "destined to formulate a revolutionary policy, understood as a unity of theory, organization, and methods of struggle." He was more of a memory, a symbol of the revolutionary spring of the Argentine proletariat. Nonetheless, Cooke saw no reason for conflict between the old myths and the new. "The people will not find their Peronist loyalty incompatible with their adherence to men and groups of the movement who open for them new perspectives for continuing the trajectory that became blocked."[15]

Eventually, there would be a convergence of Cookism and Guevarism, but it was not Cooke's doing and it did not obliterate their fundamental differences. The Peronist adaptation of Guevarism by the Montoneros coincided with the adaptation of Peronism by the Revolutionary Armed Forces (FAR)—a Guevarist political-military vanguard. The fusion of these two organizations in October 1973 contributed to bridging the gap between the Peronist and Guevarist armed formations. Several crossovers also occurred. In 1974 a splinter group calling itself the ERP–22nd of August merged with the Montoneros, and that same year the Peronist Armed Forces (National Command) merged with the Guevarist ERP. But left-wing or revolutionary Peronism is not Guevarism.

Yet what they have in common overshadows their differences. Paradoxically, although Cookism is a revolutionary variant of Peronism, it has more in common with Guevarism. Before setting foot in Cuba and before Guevara developed a distinctive doctrine, Cooke made clear that the focus of his Peronism was the social question: "The struggle for liberation starts from the definition of the real enemy, imperialism that acts through the native oligarchy and the political, economic, and cultural mechanisms at its service . . . *the national question and the social question are indissolubly joined.*"[16] Perón, too, had tied these questions together, but in a different context and from a different perspective. Unlike Perón, Cooke shifted the emphasis from the amelioration to the obliteration of "social inequalities."[17] The solution to both questions became nothing less than revolution through the "liquidation of the oligarchy as a class."[18]

Although Cooke acknowledged class struggle to be a social problem, he did not treat it as a threat to national unity but as a condition for overcoming national disunity.[19] He rejected the dictatorship of the proletariat as utopian and an obstacle to the workers' becoming the axis of a new social order, but there is not the least suggestion that he considered it subversive of Argentina's national being. Indeed, he would later identify his solution to the national and social questions with subversion: "What is not deference is now subversion. The Left has always been subversive or at least has attempted to make its subversion effective."[20] That includes the Peronist Left, the revolutionary vanguard of Peronism.[21]

The Communists, he complained, were not subversive enough. "We know that they do not threaten the existing order, that in our country they are satisfied with constitutional guarantees, so that they may continue working like ants until the advance of world communism reaches Argentina. . . . Meanwhile, they struggle to establish electoral fronts, gathering money to publish foolishness, and making campaigns for peace."[22] In contrast, Peronists were a palpable danger with a combative working class behind them, without any theory of the bourgeois-democratic revolution or respect for demoliberal institutions blocking their path. They had a simple program aimed at seizing power and expropriating the possessing classes.[23] That is what made them subversive.

"To offer to save the country from communism is a stupid and malicious hypocrisy."[24] It was stupid because Peronists were the main threat to capitalism, and malicious and hypocritical because the struggle against communism was basically a trick by dishonest and reactionary governments to obtain dollars and military aid from imperialism. Except for the fact that Communists made common cause with liberals and democrats, Peronists should not make an issue of communism.[25] What was wrong with communism was not that it was subversive, but that Communists insisted on too many conditions before they embarked on a revolutionary course, while decrying those who did so as provocateurs and adventurists. Consequently, the revolution must be made without and despite them.[26]

There was a time, Cooke recalled, when Peronists represented the revolutionary vanguard in Latin America. In its day the Mexican Revolution was the vanguard in the anti-imperialist struggle; then it was Argentina's turn to lead the way. But now every movement of liberation was taking its cues from the Cuban Revolution.[27] Although in the Argentina of 1945 "*a revolution was possible . . .* , now it is possible to do what then was impossible."[28]

Until recently, according to Cooke, revolutionary movements in Latin America could not count on economic aid from the socialist countries. Since such aid now made the difference between a revolution that survived and one that drowned in the sea of imperialism, one must reassess the role of the Soviet Union and its allies.[29] The division between the capitalist and the socialist blocs made "the fate of the dominated peoples coincide with that of the socialist world."[30] Hence Peronists could no longer be neutral concerning the global struggle between the two superpowers, even though like Cuba they stood outside it.[31]

The essence of justicialism was not anticommunism, Cooke concluded, but anti-imperialism and social revolution.[32] "To reconstruct the '1945 front' we would have to renounce what characterizes us and gives us our reason for being . . . because those allies of yesterday [military and clergy] are now partners of imperialism in the holy war against communism and we would become their allies should we enlist in their ranks."[33] Nor would Peronists gain anything by it, because they were held in suspicion by the army and clergy who in conjunction with imperialism would be the beneficiaries of such a coalition.

Cooke redefined Peronism as a force for subversion instead of a dike against it. Only reactionaries within the Peronist movement insisted on identifying its essence with a crusade in defense of Western Christian civilization.[34] That made them accomplices of an army that had become part of the "continental police against revolutionary war and communism (which means us, too)," and of a church whose "saints have no other purpose than the destruction of communism" (which meant the dissolution of Peronism).[35] As for the defense of Western civilization, "the Occident now represents France against Algeria, the United States against Cuba and Latin America, Portugal against Goa and Angola, Great Britain against Kenya, and Belgium against the Congolese patriots."[36] In the same way, hemispheric solidarity meant "supporting imperialism in the exploitation of other peoples . . . [when] as anti-imperialists we have to take sides with the Algerians who are Muslims, with the Kenyans who are idolaters, and with the Cubans who are bearded!"[37]

The Peronists' third ally in the "front of '45"—the national bourgeoisie—had also done an about-face. As in all semicolonial countries, in Argentina the bourgeoisie was not the pioneering, risk-taking, and progressive class of the centers of world capitalism, but a class economically and culturally subjected to imperialism.[38] Although in 1945 it was revolutionary to form an alliance with the bourgeoisie as a condition of a new deal for labor, the effort to resurrect the same program during the 1960s would deprive the Peronist movement of both its strength and meaning.[39] Old solutions no longer worked. "What was then the height of audacity, the most violent assault against capitalist legitimacy, would now be a lukewarm reformism that would put us in bed with everybody."[40] There could be no liberation without a struggle against capitalism. If Peronists were to remain Peronists, they would go on socializing the wealth and being stigmatized for it. "Consequently, as a bulwark against communism, we are useless."[41]

The social question also had priority for Che Guevara. Even before he became a Marxist, he "dreamed of working tirelessly to aid humanity."[42] As a medical doctor who had traveled extensively throughout Latin America, he "perceived closely misery, hunger, disease—a father's inability to have his child treated because he lacks the money, the brutalization that hunger and permanent punishment provoke in man until a father sees the death of his child as something without importance."[43] In coming to the aid of the dispossessed classes, he became aware of a fundamental fact: "To be a revolutionary doctor or to be a revolutionary at all, there must first be a revolution."[44]

It was the duty of the revolutionary to make the revolution, Guevara declared, but one could not do so without certain favorable conditions. Those conditions he traced to what economists euphemistically label "underdevelopment."[45] Low wages and unemployment define it. Guevara called it "HUNGER OF THE PEOPLE: weariness from being oppressed, abused, and exploited to the maximum; weariness from selling one's labor day after day for fear of becoming a part of the great mass of unemployed—all so that the maximum of profit is squeezed from each human body only to be squandered in the orgies of the owners of capital."[46] Such was the social question to which communism and not just socialism, he believed, provided the answer.

Guevara rejected the solution to the social question in the Soviet Union and Eastern Europe as too tepid, as not going to the root of the problem. "Pursuing the wild idea of trying to realize socialism with the aid of the worn-out weapons left by capitalism (the market place as the basic economic cell, profit making, individual material incentives, and so forth), one can arrive at a dead end."[47] In other words, what was called socialism was a far cry from what revolutionaries originally intended by it, because it was not even the lower stage of communism and had failed to create the communist "new man" simultaneously with the economic base of the new society.[48]

Such was Guevara's "little heresy," which is hardly what Cooke had in mind. For Guevara, all existing forms of socialism provided a solution only to the social question as it presented itself under capitalism. That was not because socialism was national rather than international, but because it envisioned no more than expropriating the capitalists. Social inequalities persisted under socialism, because of the perpetuation of material incentives and personal gain in the form of exorbitant salaries rather than profits. Such was the watershed dividing Guevara's followers from Cooke's.

A Clear and Present Danger

It is noteworthy that the generals of the Military Process shared the guerrillas' estimate of the struggle as a revolutionary war. Gen. Ramón Díaz Bessone's *Guerra revolucionaria en la Argentina (1959–1978)* represents military opinion. It likens the "revolutionary war" to the revolutionary wars in Cuba and Nicaragua—although there subversion won and in Argentina it was defeated. "The truth is completely falsified when one pretends to compare the situation of our country with that of some European countries, in particular Italy, Spain, France, and Germany. In those countries terrorist gangs continue to 'enjoy good health,' but in no instance did an illegal organization have for many years the minimum capacity for creating a 'liberated zone,' such as the one attempted in our Tucumán. Nor did they have the capacity to take over and control towns, nor to seize garrisons and take arms."[49]

The Montoneros interpreted their struggle as the passage from armed resistance to a revolutionary war. As a Montonero document published in September 1971 acknowledged: "In 1969 the movement begins to pass to the offensive. It is the beginning of the war for power. . . . Everyone has a place and function in this contest, and all forms of struggle from insurrectional acts such as the *cordobazo* to bank assaults are part of a combined strategy aimed at developing the *revolutionary war.*"[50] Thus Díaz Bessone concludes that "the Montoneros' documents leave no room for doubt that they were at war with the national state, against its institutions, and in particular its armed forces."[51]

The ERP shared a similar account of the transition from resistance to revolution. At the Fifth Congress of the Revolutionary Workers' party (PRT) in July 1970, the founding document of the ERP was adopted: "Considering that in the course of the *revolutionary war* launched in our country, our party has begun to fight with the objective of disorganizing the armed forces and making possible the insurrection of the proletariat and the people, that the armed forces of the regime can only be defeated by opposing to them a revolutionary army, . . . that during a long period our *revolutionary war* will take the form of urban and rural guerrillas. . . , the Fifth Congress of the Revolutionary Workers' Party resolves to found the People's Revolutionary Army."[52] Evidently, the ERP's objective was not only resistance, but also revolution. As an article in the PRT's journal *El Combatiente* (12 June 1974) subsequently acknowledged: "It is now more than three years since the Argentine people initiated the process of *revolutionary war*, whose final objective is . . . the establishment of a socialist homeland."[53]

But were the guerrillas really a threat to the institutional fabric of Argentine society? Altogether, writes Díaz Bessone, the different guerrilla organizations succeeded in enlisting some 150,000 supporters, or less than one percent of the population. "But they were and are tremendously active, and they counted on important external support from Cuba, the U.S.S.R., the Communist countries behind the Iron Curtain, and Western Europe."[54] If they did not succeed in their sinister design, it was because the armed forces replied in kind.

The transition from armed resistance to an alleged revolutionary war dated, according to guerrilla accounts, from the *cordobazo* in May 1969. However, Díaz Bessone believes the first salvos were fired as early as December 1959.[55] That was the beginning of the first guerrilla *foco*, the Uturuncos ("tigermen" in Quechua) in the provinces of Tucumán and Santiago del Estero. Cooke, "the ideologue of this group," helped prepare the revolutionary war during its embryonic stage.[56] Later, Guevara's influence predominated, although behind Cuba could be detected a Soviet presence.[57]

Díaz Bessone attaches special importance to exogenous factors that, he believes, were indirectly responsible for the spread of revolution to Argentina. Significantly, Soviet strategy after World War II took a new turn in backing wars of national liberation and in spreading revolution to the Third World. This new strategy first made headway at the Bandung Conference in Indonesia in April 1955, convened by the Soviet Union and China for the purpose of promoting international committees of solidarity in support of the struggle against colonialism.[58]

From this conference emerged the Organization of Solidarity of the Peoples of Asia and Africa (OSPAA), which met in Cairo (1957) and afterward in Guinea (1960), Tanzania (1963), Ghana (1965), and Cuba (1966). At its meeting in Havana the organization was expanded to include delegations from Latin America. The Argentine delegation to the new Organization of Solidarity of the Peoples of Asia, Africa, and Latin America (OSPAAL), also known as the "Tricontinental," included John William Cooke along with representatives of the Argentine Communist party (PCA) and other Marxist-Leninist vanguards.[59] Thus Argentina gradually was sucked into the orbit of Soviet ideological influence.

The OSPAAL gave rise to the Organization of Latin America Solidarity (OLAS), which convened in Havana in July–August 1967. Prominent among the Argentine delegates led by Cooke were those who would later organize Argentina's urban guerrillas, Juan García Elorrio, Roberto Jorge Quieto, Fernando Abal Medina, and José Baxter, founders, respectively, of the Camilo Torres Commando, FAR, Montoneros, and ERP.[60] In the spirit of the OLAS's honorary president, Ernesto "Che" Guevara, it was agreed to organize in each country an Army of National Liberation (ELN) modeled on Guevara's army in Bolivia.[61] As the permanent headquarters of the OLAS, Havana would continue to provide military training, arms, intelligence, and a sanctuary for volunteers in the revolutionary war on a continental scale.

Díaz Bessone claims that the core of what promised to become Argentina's Army of National Liberation was organized in 1968 in the country's Northwest. On the basis of captured documents, he surmises that the Argentine guerrillas initially comprised three sectors or columns organized by Argentine delegates to the 1967 OLAS Conference.[62] Integrated into the Revolutionary Workers' party (PRT), the first sector would subsequently become identified with the ERP. The second sector consisted of dissidents from the established Communist party, the FAR and the earlier Fuerzas Armadas de Liberación (FAL). The third sector comprised the cadres of revolutionary Peronism, the Fuerzas Armadas Peronistas (FAP), and the Montoneros.

Although the documentation leaves something to be desired, the ideological impact of Che Guevara and the Cuban revolution on Argentina's political-military vanguards is well established. Few dispute that Cuba constituted a subversive beachhead in the Americas that helped sow the seeds of class violence in Argentina. Nor is there any reason to doubt that those seeds took root, sprouted, and flowered in a revolutionary war—in turn, the justification for the dirty war and related theory and practice of state terrorism during the Military Process.

After a decade or so of incubation during the first Peronist resistance, argues Díaz Bessone, the revolutionary war became a reality with the Montoneros' kidnapping, trial, and execution of General Aramburu in May–June 1970. Díaz Bessone divides the revolutionary war into three periods: the initial aggression with the complicity of General Perón that came as the culmination of the resistance (1970–1973); the continuing and intensified war by the guerrillas on their own account in opposition to the Peronist party in power (1973–1975); and the extension of the revolutionary war to the entire country that compelled the last Peronist government to authorize the intervention of the armed forces in February 1975.

In his judgment the threat posed by the guerrillas, especially the Montoneros and the ERP, could be countered effectively only with the backing of the civilian population. Otherwise, the armed forces were basically helpless, and "the revolutionary war would have triumphed."[63] The guerrillas had to be isolated and detached from their urban and rural bases of support. This required the active intervention of the military, for until it effectively took control in February 1975 the odds favored the guerrillas.

"In our country a supreme threat endangered the nation . . . vis-à-vis a languishing political power after the death of Perón."[64] As long as the guerrillas could count on various legal fronts and protection afforded by the Constitution, as long as the climate of terror persisted and the government found itself discredited, they could be expected to thrive. In Argentina the guerrillas were numerous, well organized, technically knowledgeable in electronics and mass communications, and logistically and militarily prepared to set their sights on the seizure of power.[65] In Western Europe that objective was always beyond reach. Police repression sufficed, whereas in Argentina harsher methods demanded the guerrillas' physical "annihilation."[66]

The armed forces were not alone in their depiction of a clear and present danger. The Peronist government and Radical opposition in Congress shared a similar assessment of the threat presented by subversion.[67] Even after the military launched its campaign of extermination, it took four years before the guerrillas' defeat could be assured. This fact alone supports the military's judgment that the revolutionary war could not have been defeated short of the suspension of constitutional guarantees.

Development of the Revolutionary War

A brief survey of the emergence of the revolutionary war in 1970 through its peak years in 1974–1975 substantiates this judgment. I begin with a sketch of the Montonero armed struggle followed by that of the PRT-ERP.

When the Montoneros' founders, Fernando Abal Medina and Carlos Gustavo Ramus, died in an ambush in September 1970, the Montoneros consisted of only a dozen or so cadres. José Sabino Navarro had infused new blood into the organization when his Córdoba Commando merged with it early in 1970. He had also provided indispensable military training. But the occupation of La Calera, Córdoba, in July led to more than half a dozen arrests. By year's end the guerrillas were still barely able to survive. Thus when Sabino Navarro was killed in a shoot-out in July 1971 and was succeeded by Mario Eduardo Firmenich, there was as yet no indication that within a few years the Montoneros would become the largest and most influential guerrilla organization in Latin America.

The massive growth of the Montoneros was made possible by a variety of factors. In vain had they and other recently armed groups tried to join the prestigious Peronist Armed Forces (FAP), the first of the specifically Peronist armed formations to surface. Led by Peronist Youth leaders Envar El Kadri and Carlos Caride, the FAP rejected such overtures from motives that are still unclear, so the Montoneros had to shift for themselves.

The choice of the name "Montoneros" turned out to be a godsend in attracting not only revolutionary Peronists, but also Catholic nationalists and disaffected Marxist-Leninists. The name evoked images of Argentina's nineteenth-century Montoneros, the landless gauchos and impoverished miners who fought for the independence of the country's interior provinces against the landed oligarchy and against British merchants in the port city of Buenos Aires. This powerful symbol of Argentine nationalism provided a national identity for a revolutionary current that might otherwise have been branded as alien.

However, it was not just the name but the spectacular kidnapping, trial, and execution of former president Pedro Aramburu (the *aramburazo*) that attracted national attention and support from the Peronist rank and file. Three features of this operation especially recommended it to opponents of the military regime: it had Perón's specific endorsement; it was carried out successfully; and it catalyzed the military coup that toppled General Onganía and paved the way for new elections.

Along with Cooke's revision of the Third Position, the Montoneros leaned heavily on Perón's documents of the resistance and subsequent declarations on revolutionary war. To reassure themselves that the *aramburazo* met with Perón's approval, they sent him a letter on 9 February 1971 justifying their action as a strategic application of justicialist doctrine. They especially wanted to know if Perón agreed with their conclusion that "the only possible road for the people to seize power and install national socialism is total, national, and prolonged revolutionary war . . . [following] the methods of rural and urban guerrillas."[68]

Perón responded on 20 February 1971, endorsing the Montonero action and also giving carte blanche to continue operating in any way they saw fit. Besides the surface organizations of the Justicialist movement engaged in acts of provocation, he recognized the need for clandestine groups "engaged in 'revolutionary war' . . . in which everything is justified provided the end is useful."[69] He also conceded that the Montoneros' strategy had successfully adapted Peronist doctrine to the special conditions created by the military dictatorship. It was not their reliance on violence that he found objectionable, but their claim that revolutionary war was the "fundamental axis and motor of Peronism."[70] With that, he discreetly disagreed.

Commenting on Perón's correspondence with the Montoneros, Díaz Bessone cites a 1980 statement by a former defense minister in Perón's government claiming that Perón knew the "*armed formations had a Marxist-Leninist ideological source*" and accepted their support "*simply because they were 'enemies of our enemies.'*"[71] But they cost the Justicialist movement dearly, for while Perón made use of the Montoneros, they made use of Perón to further their revolutionary war.

Perón's endorsement of the Montoneros accounts for their subsequent spectacular growth. The various armed groups that had unsuccessfully sought to merge with the FAP approached the Montoneros with a similar intent. In mid-1972 the Descamisado Political-Military Organization under the leadership of Horacio Mendizábal and Norberto Habegger joined them. In October 1973 it was the turn of the FAR, and in June 1974 a wing of the FAP led by Carlos Caride merged with the Montoneros.

But the big leap came from another quarter: support from the Peronist Youth–Regional organizations (JP–R), which became the Montoneros' legal front under the leadership of Rodolfo Galimberti. At a 9 June 1972 rally in the stadium of the Argentine Boxing Federation, a crowd of some ten thousand Peronist Youth chanted: "The FAR and the Montoneros are our Comrades!" As Firmenich recalled, he was in hiding in a shantytown and could not believe his ears when he heard of the event: "Ten thousand Montoneros! It was incredible."[72]

The other major armed formation surviving from the 1956–1973 resistance was the Guevarist-oriented ERP. It developed at a faster pace to lead the pack in the number of military operations from 1970 to 1975 and to become the chief target of the armed forces. The ERP's founding came in response not only to the OLAS declaration and the May 1969 *cordobazo*, but also to the adoption of a resolution on the armed struggle in Latin America at the Ninth World Congress of the Fourth International (Unified Secretariat). The resolution urged Latin American Trotskyists to increase the number of rural guerrilla nuclei and to launch military actions in the big cities.

This resolution played into the hands of the PRT's Guevarist current, led by Mario Roberto Santucho. His followers regarded Guevara rather than Trotsky as their spiritual mentor and were more susceptible to Cuban propaganda than to that of the European-based Trotskyist International. The successor to the first Guevarist-oriented guerrilla formation in Argentina, the Ejército Guerrillero del Pueblo (EGP), the ERP adopted virtually the same name and appears to have been christened in its honor.

Unlike the PRT, a vanguard party of Marxist-Leninist cadres, the ERP was an armed front broad enough to include militants of virtually any radical persuasion. Although subordinated to and directed by the party, it was not the PRT's armed branch, since its militants did not have to become party members. Nor was it a branch detached from the trunk, since every member of the PRT belonged to the ERP. It was a novel organization consisting of the rudiments of an irregular army led by a political party. The pride of the Fourth International, the ERP would soon break with international Trotskyism to follow an independent course. The formal rupture occurred in June 1973.

Except for armed actions, these different military vanguards had more in common with their respective political counterparts and ideological kin than they had with one another. The ERP had acknowledged links to the Uruguayan Tupamaros, or Movimiento de Liberación Nacional (MLN), the Chilean Movimiento de Izquierda Revolucionaria (MIR), and the survivors of Bolivia's National Liberation Army (ELN). It also had strong ties to Cuba and was the leading exemplar, along with these other movements and Nicaragua's Frente Sandinista de Liberación Nacional (FSLN), of the Guevarist project of a continentwide revolution. Its links to the Cuban Revolution and indirectly to the Soviet Union opened it to the charge of being part of an international terrorist conspiracy. This was in sharp contrast to the Montoneros, who had begun as Catholic nationalists, who prided themselves on being patriots, who rejected exotic imported models of revolution, who were less vulnerable ideologically, and who, partly for that reason, were not the principal target of the military's dirty war.

Another crucial difference between the ERP and the Montoneros was strategical. The ERP was not seeking to restore political democracy or to return Peronism to power. Unlike the Montoneros, it could not obtain political leverage by fighting for a Peronist government. It did not have close ties to Juan Abal Medina, the youthful secretary-general of the Justicialist movement appointed by Perón in October 1972, nor did it have access through him to the president-elect's inner circle. Thanks to an electoral pact that December, the Peronist Youth secured a beachhead within the new government. With a claim to one-third of electoral offices at all levels, it became in principle the equal of the Peronist political and trade union branches. Thus in May 1973 the Montoneros obtained six governorships of their choice, including those in the key provinces of Buenos Aires and Córdoba, and two cabinet posts, the Foreign Ministry and the crucial Ministry of the Interior.[73]

The ERP could not hope for any significant concessions from a Peronist government, and in the March 1973 elections did not support the justicialist candidates. Its strategy was to prevent the "mask of 'democracy'" from shelving the question of revolutionary power.[74] Since both the landed oligarchy and the big bourgeoisie preferred to govern without force, Guevara argued, the revolutionary's task was to oblige the government "to resort to violence, thereby unmasking its true nature as the dictatorship of the reactionary social classes."[75] This meant forcing the ruling classes "to retreat or to unleash the struggle—thus beginning the stage of long-range armed action."[76] Once the armed struggle began one should persist in it, because a revolution that did not expand invariably regressed. Such was the strategy of the ERP as distinguished from the strategy of the Montoneros, both before and after the military abdicated in May 1973.

While the Montoneros momentarily abandoned the armed struggle in May 1973 and did not return underground until September 1974, the ERP continued to develop its military capacity. Thus it reached its peak performance in 1974–1975, whereas most of the Montoneros' military operations occurred during the last six months of Isabel Perón's government and the first year of the Military Process.

Notwithstanding the abdication of the military and the return of the Peronist party to power, the ERP intensified instead of phasing out its military operations. As Díaz Bessone relates, the immediate effect of the military's abdication on 25 May 1973 was an upgrading of the revolutionary war. In June alone the ERP was responsible for five successful acts of extortion and related kidnappings of business executives, three major seizures of arms and munitions, a dozen occupations and expropriations of industrial and commercial enterprises, and three assassinations of prominent figures.[77]

The political amnesty decreed by the new government immensely strengthened the hand of the guerrillas. Approximately 370 of some 2,200 subversives already sentenced or awaiting trial were released on May 25 alone.[78] More than a third of them belonged to the ERP. Of those released from the Villa Devoto Penitentiary that same day, the last column to leave consisted of 72 of the ERP's experienced fighters marching behind their flag with clenched fists raised.[79] And as many arrived in the capital on May 26 among the 173 prisoners released from the Rawson Penitentiary in Chubut.

Such was the background of the ERP's major frontal attack on the military post of Sanidad in the nation's capital in September. This was followed by a full-scale invasion of the military base of Azul in the province of Buenos Aires in January 1974. Then came the news of a world record in ransoms from the kidnapping of ESSO executive

Victor Samuelson in March. The fourteen million dollars paid for his release was used to finance the simultaneous assault in August on the seventeenth infantry regiment in Catamarca and the army's munitions factory in Villa María, Córdoba.

These actions were followed by the most significant and prolonged operation of all, the launching of rural guerrillas, the establishment of a "liberated territory," and the battles with army units in the mountains of Tucumán. Beginning in December 1974, the rural guerrillas occupied the army for more than a year. In a related action on 13 April 1975, the ERP successfully assaulted the 121st military arsenal in the vicinity of San Lorenzo, Santa Fe. Finally, when the ERP's rural guerrillas became hard-pressed to survive, they regrouped for the abortive assault on the army garrison in Monte Chingolo on 23 December 1975. Located on the outskirts of the nation's capital, Monte Chingolo was the scene of the largest single action by urban guerrillas in the nation's history.

That the ERP rather than the Montoneros became the armed forces' chief preoccupation is evident from President Videla's address to the nation on 24 September 1976—in celebration of the military junta's first six months in office. Delivered in the capital of Tucumán Province, the message began by recalling Gen. Manuel Belgrano's emancipatory struggle for independence from Spain launched from the same soil on the same day in 1812. Under the code name "Operation Independence," a similar struggle was being repeated against foreign-inspired rural subversion. "In Tucumán, precisely, subversion concentrated its maximum efforts toward disintegrating the national territory and implanting its law of hatred and terror. . . . Its leaders have been destroyed [Mario Roberto Santucho, the ERP's top commander, along with José B. Urteaga and Domingo Menna on 19 July 1976] and to a considerable extent its logistic and propagandistic apparatus. . . . Its annihilation has top priority as an indispensable condition of security."[80]

The ERP's operations in Tucumán were responsible for Isabel Perón's directive to the military in February 1975 to use any and all means for combating the rural guerrillas. With Operation Independence began the so-called dirty war. In retaliation for the ERP's frustrated attack on the army's command post in the town of Famaillá, the army turned the town's school into the first clandestine concentration camp for the disappeared. From February 1975 to April 1976, after which the methodology of disappearance, interrogation, and torture was extended to the rest of the country, this chamber of horrors processed hundreds of the ERP's militants from all over Argentina.

In February 1985 I visited the *"escuelita de Famaillá"* and talked to some of the residents in the neighborhood. Located at the town's west end, it was still surrounded by barbed wire. Nor had the climate of fear dating back to 1975 completely dissipated. A center of torture and disappearances? No, it was used as a military base in the "war against subversion." Thus the military's perception of the revolutionary war was shared not only by the guerrillas, but also by sectors of the civilian population forced into serving as witnesses.

Terrorists of the Left

Did the Montoneros resemble the "terrorist gang" depicted by James Neilson in *La Semana* (29 December 1983)? Was the ERP, as Jacobo Timerman characterized it, a "terrorist Trotskyite group" of the "lunatic Left"?[81] The conviction that the guerrillas were "terrorists" and worse was shared by the country's new president. Said Raúl Alfonsín: "To our moral condemnation of terrorist subversion we must add its political condemnation. . . . If an experience of democratization was born in 1973, terrorism came to strangle it and made even more difficult the solution to the country's dilemma."[82]

The grounds for these claims were the standard meaning of terrorism as the use of violence and intimidation for political purposes. Precisely, this was the sense given to the word by Argentine liberals, social democrats, and the new Radical government. By indicting as terrorists the principal leaders of the Montoneros and the ERP along with the generals and admirals responsible for the Military Process, the president made a point of adhering to conventional usage.

What is terrorism? As currently defined, it is the "use of terror and violence to intimidate, subjugate, etc., especially as a political weapon or policy." The term is "usually applied to organized acts or threats of violence for intimidating opposition or publicizing grievances."[83] Although the term dates from the Reign of Terror during the French Revolution, it also encompasses the violence of reactionary regimes with the deliberate aim of creating a climate of fear in order to paralyze resistance.[84] Today its meaning has been further extended to include the revolutionary effort to overthrow tyranny, as well as random bombings, kidnappings, airplane hijackings, the taking of hostages, and assassinations with a political purpose.

The Argentine guerrillas have been faulted for relying on the tactics of gangsters and stooping to revenge and senseless killings. The Montonero tactic of *apriete* (squeeze) was used to justify acts of vandalism as well as assassination.[85] The 1975 firebombing of two bars and almost a thousand pleasure launches in the resort town of Tigre was a warning to the government of what might happen if the Montoneros' legal avenues should be closed. The squeeze also lay behind the Montoneros' assassinations of CGT boss José Rucci and former interior minister Arturo Mor Roig. These assassinations aimed at extracting concessions in future negotiations with General Perón and Radical party leader Ricardo Balbín.[86] But the reliance on intimidation had the opposite effect and hardened those who were expected to soften.

Carlos A. Brocato claims that both the Montoneros and the ERP departed from the norms of revolutionary war established by Fidel Castro in the Sierra Maestra. Castro imposed the inflexible rule that, if prisoners could not be guaranteed the minimum conditions of physical sustenance and medical care, they should be released—even when it meant they would return to fight the guerrillas.[87] Brocato commends Castro for repudiating the unrestrained use of violence in favor of clemency and respect for human rights, first, because his policy distinguished the Cuban revolutionaries from the brutal practices of the Batista regime; second, because it prevented them from degenerating to the same level as the enemy; third, because it gained the respect, sympathy, and support of the population.[88] But in Argentina the guerrillas' hostages were not always cared for and were sometimes shot in retaliation.

Along with revolutionary trials and executions, Brocato questions the practice of kidnapping civilians and holding them for ransom.[89] The Cuban guerrillas did not stoop to such terrorist tactics. Nor were assassination and revenge, as in the notorious case of General Aramburu, ever condoned by the rebel army.[90] Brocato further questions the presumed justification of bank assaults as revolutionary "taxes" or "expropriations." Robbery, he contends, is not part of the methodology of mass mobilization and class struggle.[91]

In Argentina even attacks on military garrisons smacked of terrorism. The army's troops were not professional soldiers or mercenaries, as in Batista's Cuba, but youthful conscripts performing their year of military service.[92] Since the children of the wealthy were not usually assigned to garrisons, the killing of ordinary conscripts was widely repudiated. That was not the way to endear the guerrillas to the masses. Only attacks on police stations—the Montoneros' favorite tactic—would appear exempted from this criticism.

Brocato imputes to the guerrillas the Machiavellian dictum that the end justifies the means.[93] Giussani charges them with something even more terrible: turning Machiavelli on his head and making "the means justify the end."[94]

These charges ignore the subtleties of Machiavelli's thesis. Machiavelli argued that in war one must act like a beast.[95] In Greek mythology Achilles was turned over to Chiron the centaur, half man and half beast, to be educated on how to be a prince. To act as a beast, he was instructed to imitate the fox for astuteness and the lion for boldness. The well-instructed ruler not only uses force on his enemies, but also fraudulently appears "to be all mercy, faith, integrity, humanity, and religion."[96] That is the context in which Machiavelli defended the thesis that the end justifies the means. His means give a privileged place to conventional morality, which is necessary to legitimize power. Thus Machiavelli also believed that the means justify the end. But that is hardly an argument for terrorism.

Richard Gillespie deplores the Montoneros' terrorism against their own members. In a country where capital punishment is frowned on, the guerrillas applied it to Fernando Haymal, whose "crime was simply human weakness."[97] Roberto Quieto, the FAR's top commander and number three in the Montonero hierarchy, was similarly sentenced to death by a revolutionary tribunal for betraying vital information. This death sentence for a revolutionary hero with an international reputation stunned many Montoneros and appalled innumerable sympathizers.[98]

The revolution had begun to devour its children. Paradoxically, the Montoneros' idealism, modeled on Che Guevara's romantic notion of a "new man," was accompanied by a Stalinist contempt for the intricacies of the human condition.[99] Their cult of self-sacrifice associated with moral heroism had its flip side in an apparent disregard for human life. Nowhere was this more evident than in a statement by Firmenich in the Cuban journal *Bohemia* on 9 January 1981: "We have lost five thousand cadres, but how much more mass support have we won?" From this admission, Gillespie concludes that the Montonero leadership had succumbed to total cynicism, the sacrifice of the revolutionary vanguard in a desperate gamble to achieve some distant political payoff when the Peronists might return to power in Argentina.[100]

The guerrillas' alleged cult of violence was supposedly based on a cult of death that sacralized their resort to terrorism.[101] The Montoneros, Giussani speculates, would repudiate the result of their actions if it could be achieved by peaceful means, for their "idolatry of the means" makes of their vaunted end little more than an alibi.[102]

The attribution of a cult of death to the guerrillas lacks veracity. It is one thing to glorify death in action; it is another to become resigned to the possibility. Even Guevara's panegyric to revolutionary love concludes with the invocation: *"Patria o muerte"* (Fatherland or death).[103] Death is justified by the end it serves: *"Venceremos!"* (we will overcome) As Lenin pointed out, for a revolution to take place a majority of workers, or at least the revolutionary vanguard, not only must realize that a revolution is necessary, but also must "be prepared to die for it."[104] That is not a cult of death.

What were the limits, if any, that Argentina's guerrillas placed on the use of terror? Broadly speaking, they were the limits imposed by the revolutionary tradition from Lenin through Trotsky to Guevara. Because as Lenin criticized the inconsequential terrorism of anarchists, the guerrillas thought it futile to dissipate energies on the terrorist acts of individuals.[105] Nor did Lenin condone massive terrorism against an exploiting and oppressive class: "the 'Jacobins' of the twentieth century would not guillotine the capitalists. . . . It would be enough to arrest fifty to a hundred financial magnates and bigwigs . . . *to expose their frauds."*[106]

Trotsky shared a similar view. Because permissible violence *"really* leads to the liberation of mankind," it follows that *"not* all means are permissible."[107] Violence must have a sympathetic response among the masses and must be widely perceived as necessary. "To the terrorist we say: it is impossible to replace the masses; only in the mass movement can you find expedient expression for your heroism."[108]

Guevara too had reservations concerning terrorism. "It is imperative to distinguish clearly between sabotage, a highly efficacious revolutionary war measure, and terrorism, inefficacious and generally indiscriminate in its consequences, since in many cases it victimizes innocent people and costs a large number of valuable lives for the revolution."[109] Although he justified individual terror against repressive figures notorious for their cruelty, he did not advise it when it "brings as a consequence an overflowing of repression and its sequel of deaths."[110] Terror, yes; terrorism, no.

These citations dear to the ERP may suffice to absolve it from belonging to a "lunatic Left." But how do the Montoneros respond to the charge of terrorism? Firmenich has admitted to being subversive, because of his involvement in the armed resistance. However, he defines terrorism as "a policy for controlling sectors of the population by means of terror," adding that the Montoneros never practiced such a policy.[111]

Since there are numerous kinds of terrorism, the factual question is to pinpoint their differences. Although the Montoneros believed their violence served a popular cause, that cause was not generally perceived as such. Nonetheless, the subversive terrorism of the Montoneros belongs to a different genre from both the illegal and legal use of terror by the armed forces. State terrorism is evidently more massive, systematic, and consequential than guerrilla terrorism.[112]

One way of distinguishing between terrorisms is by their magnitude. The estimated ten thousand to thirty thousand disappeared by the Military Process and the five thousand to ten thousand "executed" are examples of political genocide, the intent to eliminate physically a racial, national, social, religious, or political group. In Argentina torture was the prelude to genocide. For every person who disappeared or was executed, Amnesty International estimates that four times as many were tortured and released. The guerrillas did not come close to matching this record. That their use of terror was indiscriminate, that they were no less guilty of flagrant violations of human rights than the military and the Argentine Anti-Communist Alliance (AAA), is a gross caricature of reality.

Another falsehood disseminated during the government of Isabel Perón was that the great majority of actions by subversives resulted in death or injury, to which the legal forces responded mainly with imprisonment. In a painstaking study of armed actions in Argentina between May 1973 and March 1976, Juan Carlos Marín shows that the guerrillas were responsible for 827 actions resulting in death, injury, or detention. In contrast, the antisubversive forces were responsible for 2,118 actions resulting in human casualties.[113] Contrary to the reading of the same statistics by the government and most of the press, only 28 percent of the operations attributed to the guerrillas had human casualties compared with 72 percent by the forces of repression.

To buttress its case, the government chose to emphasize the contrast between its own and the guerrillas' responsibility for death and injuries compared to detentions. In this accounting the guerrillas were responsible for 624 deaths and injuries compared with 203 detentions (a euphemism for kidnappings), while the repressive forces were responsible for 693 deaths and injuries compared with 1,479 detentions.[114] Thus 75 percent of the guerrillas' operations caused death or injury compared with 30 percent by the government.

Marín breaks down these data into their components, which provides an altogether different reading. The guerrillas were responsible for 4,538 armed actions without casualties compared with 305 with injuries, 318 with deaths, and 203 with detentions—one case lacking information.[115] In contrast, the antisubversive forces were credited with 1,009 actions without casualties compared with 97 with injuries, 542 with deaths, and 1,479 with detentions. Thus 63 percent of the deaths resulted from antisubversive operations compared with only 37 percent attributed to the guerrillas.

Marín's sifting of the data also indicates that, unlike comparable actions by the repressive forces, guerrilla operations aimed at disarming and weakening the enemy were accomplished for the most part without death, injury, or detention.[116] He concludes that "the enemy sought the destruction of the popular forces through the annihilation of their persons . . . [whereas] the armed action of the people gave priority to weakening the enemy materially and to avoiding human losses."[117]

It is fair to say that the Montoneros and the ERP did not select their victims randomly, did not torture them, did not disappear them or engage in anything remotely resembling genocide. They made a special effort not to kill innocent people. Apart from those caught in cross fire, their victims were clearly associated with either the forces of repression or specific acts of repression. Although the identification of all police officers and members of the military as enemies of the people might seem an exception, as the power behind the Military Process they shared responsibility for the repression and were accessories to its crimes. Cruel and massive intimidation were not part of the guerrillas' repertoire.

In view of these differences between state-inflicted terror and the armed actions of guerrillas, it is misleading to lump them together. "Terrorism" is a politically loaded term, an epithet for what people perceive as an unjustified use of violence. Since the violence of the guerrillas was not vindicated by a military victory, their fate was to be doubly victimized in words and deeds. The victors got away with terror, while the word *terrorist* applied mainly to the vanquished. Ironically, when the armed forces abdicated in December 1983, the generals and admirals of the Military Process became cast in the same role as the guerrillas.

Most assessments of the guerrillas mistakenly assume that what subversive and state terrorism have in common overshadows their differences. It is noteworthy that neither the repressive forces nor the guerrillas made this mistake.

Were the Guerrillas "Red Fascists"?

Were the Montoneros and the ERP fascist or fascist-inspired? The Montoneros are vulnerable to this charge in view of their fascist pedigree, but it is not merely their origins that are incriminating. The alleged cult of violence shared with the ERP would seem to brand both as fascist. They supposedly exhibit the same Marxist heresy attributed to Mussolini, a commitment to heroism, sacrifice, and action for its own sake, which defines the original ideology if not the institutional trappings of Italian fascism.

The Montoneros' family tree dates from their origins in a left-wing split in the Catholic Nationalist Tacuara, a fascist youth organization whose lineage goes back to the pro-fascist Civic Legion of the 1930s and the reactionary Patriotic League of the early 1920s. The Tacuara was frenetically anti-Communist and originally anti-Peronist, until a left-wing split surfaced in 1963 calling itself the Movimiento Nacionalista Revolucionario Tacuara (MNRT). The new Tacuara still upheld the ideology of the Spanish Falange represented by José Antonio Primo de Rivera; however, it looked to Peronism to implement the Falangist objective of a national syndicalist state.

The future leaders of the Montoneros were thus converted to Peronism. But in 1966 they came under the influence of former priest Juan García Elorrio. A fervent admirer of the Colombian guerrilla priest Camilo Torres, Che Guevara, and John William Cooke's brand of revolutionary Peronism, he represented a fusion of Camilist, Guevarist, and Cookist themes combined with the cult of Evita Perón. It was he who won the future Montoneros over to an adaptation of Cooke's and Guevara's social and political philosophies, reconciling Christian faith with the strategy of violent revolution. He also encouraged them to go underground to form the Camilo Torres Commando, the armed precursor of the Montoneros.

Curiously enough, the Montoneros' leaders began their political careers in the shock forces for combating Marxism but ended by espousing something akin to Marxism. How does one explain this anomaly? According to their critics, their ideological about-face had a common foundation in the cult of violence and authoritarianism found at both extremes of the political spectrum. The facility with which fanatics of the extreme Right swing to the extreme Left and conversely is exemplified by the merger of the Montoneros and the FAR, the latter with a Communist lineage led by Roberto Quieto. "It was only necessary that the fascist Firmenich should move a little more to the left and that the communist Quieto should move a little more to the right, for them to be able to unite with the same level of violence and blind activism in the common project of installing a totalitarian society!"[118]

Ricardo Masetti, head of the People's Guerrilla Army (EGP), supposedly is another example of this syndrome. Having acquired his first taste of politics as a militant in Juan Queraltó and Guillermo Patricio Kelly's quasi-fascist Alianza Libertadora Nacionalista (ALN) and as a journalist on the fascist newspaper *Tribuna*, he subsequently became a convert to Guevarism.[119] José Baxter, who headed the left-wing split in the Tacuara, similarly gravitated leftward to crown his political career as a commander of the ERP. Although not peculiar to Argentina, this syndrome appears to have flowered in a specifically fascist context: "It was no accident that the terrorism of the seventies surged forth in countries that had experienced fascism,"[120] for example, the Red Army faction in Germany, the Red Brigades in Italy, and the Montoneros and the FAR in Argentina.

The Montoneros combine Marxism and nationalism in a unique synthesis, which Timerman interprets as "fascism of the Left."[121] Giussani offers a similar account in comparing the Montoneros to Mussolini's originally socialist *fasci di combattimento*, and by discovering a parallel in Ernst Roehm's "Brown Shirts"—the socialist wing of the Nazi party.[122] Still others attribute to the Montoneros a species of "red fascism."[123]

The first time I heard this expression in reference to Argentina's guerrillas was in May 1971 in a conversation with Argentine journalist Horacio Daniel Rodríguez. He applied it to his fellow Argentine Che Guevara, also described by him as a *condottiero*, adventurer, a Don Quixote of revolution.[124] Guevara, a red fascist? The concept seemed to be misapplied. But it is implicit in the writings of other journalists, who consider Guevarism to be a distortion of orthodox Marxism. Thus Timerman includes the ERP as an example of "left-wing fascism," and Giussani includes the FAR under the same heading.[125]

The term "red fascist" first acquired currency in the wake of the Soviet-Nazi Nonaggression Pact of 1939.[126] Later, its implicit conflation of Stalinism and Hitlerism would acquire academic respectability under the seemingly neutral cover of "totalitarianism." However, Rodríguez's characterization of Guevarism as "red fascism" and Timerman's depiction of the ERP as "fascism of the left" grossly abuse political labels. At most Stalin appropriated nationalist symbols and encouraged the use of fascist methodology in the revolutionary struggle for power. Care should be taken not to confuse Stalinism with red fascism or left-wing fascism as these terms are used in Argentina.

I have already argued that it is a mistake to classify Peronism as a fascist movement. If my analysis stands up, then it is also erroneous to classify the different versions of revolutionary Peronism as fascist-inspired. Surely, there is a less-misleading way of characterizing Argentina's political-military vanguards. At the very least, a distinction should be made between Guevarist-Peronists (Montoneros) and Peronist-Guevarists (FAR).

Both Timerman and Giussani attribute to the Montoneros a cult of death. But the inspiration for Montonero violence was not the fascist idealization of war, the martial virtues, and action for its own sake. In part it stemmed from the heroic example of Che Guevara, whose ideology—a composite Marxism-Leninism and existentialism originating in the French resistance—was opposed in principle to fascism. But it also stemmed from the cult of Evita Perón.

From their inception the Montoneros were intrigued and captivated by the mythology surrounding the figure of the former actress. The vaunted heroine of Argentine labor, Evita was supposedly involved in mobilizing workers on that fateful day in October 1945, when their massive appearance in the Plaza de Mayo helped defeat the first military coup against Perón. Hunted down and imprisoned, Perón was freed on October 17, after mass demonstrations by his supporters and a general strike declared by the CGT threatened to explode in a popular insurrection. The revolutionary mobilizations of October 17 would become a model for Peronist resistance to future coups.

In response to the second coup against Perón in September 1951, Evita prompted the organization of the first workers' militias. Money from her charitable foundation was diverted to buying five thousand automatic pistols and fifteen hundred machine guns through the agency of the Dutch royal family, which had visited Buenos Aires earlier that year.[127] At least one hundred pistols were distributed before the plan was shelved by Perón, who preferred less provocative and more traditional ways of defending his government.

Evita's responses to the attempted coups differed from her husband's in that she called on workers to intervene directly in defense of their interests, instead of concentrating on balancing social forces and playing off the workers against their enemies. Her vitriolic tirades against the oligarchy had already earned her the reputation of harboring revolutionary impulses that would later sustain a left-wing variant of Peronism. Preaching death to oligarchs in her autobiography, she provided a rationale for the guerrillas' violence: "With or without bloodshed, the race of oligarchs, exploiters of mankind, will inevitably perish in this century!"[128]

Evita's claim that "Peronism will be Revolutionary, or it will be Nothing!" would provide fuel for the Montonero slogans "Evita—Perón—Revolution," "Evita, present in every combatant," and "if Evita were alive, she'd be a Montonera!" The heroine of labor until she died of cancer in July 1952, she later metamorphosed into Evita the guerrilla. Thus, beginning with the escalation of armed struggle in January 1975, the Montoneros' official organ took the name *Evita Montonera*.

With Evita Montonera as their namesake, they seemed to have a winning formula. The CGT had petitioned the Vatican to canonize Evita for her charitable works, and Perón had declared October 18 Saint Evita's Day. Millions of Argentines literally worshiped her as a saint.

What the cult of Evita Perón became for the Montoneros, the cult of Guevara became for the PRT-ERP. The Montoneros at least shared with fascism a strong commitment to nationalism. The PRT-ERP was not nationalist, but internationalist in outlook. Anti-Stalinist to the core, there is even less historical evidence for its supposed fascist cult of violence.

Consider its Guevarist origins. In 1959, in response to the Cuban Revolution, a proguerrilla faction led by Angel Bengochea emerged within the principal Trotskyist party in Argentina, Palabra Obrera (PO)—named after the party journal. Strongly influenced by Guevara's strategy of guerrilla warfare, Bengochea organized in 1964 the Buenos Aires Commando, an urban support group for Masetti's People's Guerrilla Army in the province of Salta. Although Bengochea perished when his commando's arsenal accidentally blew up in a Buenos Aires apartment house, his revolutionary line was carried forward by his followers and by Mario Santucho's Frente Revolucionario Indoamericano Popular (FRIP) centered in the sugar-growing province of Tucumán.

In 1962 Santucho made a trip to Cuba, which convinced him that only Marxism could serve as a reliable guide to revolution. This experience led to a working agreement between the FRIP and the PO in 1963, followed by their fusion at the founding congress of the PRT in May 1965. Since Workers' Word (PO) had belonged to the Fourth International (Unified Secretariat), after the merger the PRT continued to be recognized as its Argentine section.

Under Guevara's influence, Santucho favored a political-military organization of professional revolutionaries. But the party's reformist wing, led by Hugo Bressano (alias Nahuel Moreno), wanted a party of workers centered on the industrial trade unions in the nation's capital. At the PRT's 1968 congress Santucho's line prevailed, followed by the founding of the ERP at the PRT's Fifth Congress in 1970.

In a May 1973 interview with two of the ERP's official spokesmen (*Intercontinental Press*, 28 May 1973), the details of its personality cult were spelled out. "We recognize Ernesto Che Guevara as the top commander in the revolutionary war on which we have embarked. And this is not a mere . . . expression of personal affinity. It also stems from a general agreement with his strategic conceptions for developing the revolution: create two, three, many Vietnams, with one—or several—of them in Latin America." To this encomium the authors added that the ERP's starting point was Che's concept and exemplary practice of proletarian internationalism.

These passages indicate an implicit acceptance not only of the cult of Guevara, but also of Guevara's novel cult. First, there is an appeal to the Guevara mystique, a form of hero worship corresponding to the cult of Eva Perón. A prime example is Fidel Castro's speech on 18 October 1967 at the wake in memory of Guevara.[129] Second, there is an allusion to the doctrine of revolutionary sacrifice summed up in Guevara's essay "Socialism and Man in Cuba."[130] Third, there is an invocation of Guevara's Bolivarian or continental revolution, a Herculean and quite impossible task beginning with one or more Vietnams in Latin America.[131]

There is no doubt that Guevara's version of Marxism-Leninism was a far cry from that of the established Communist parties in Latin America. But to portray it as a form of red fascism and to consider the PRT-ERP as an example of left-wing fascism is at best a caricature. The PRT has considerably more in common with the Peronist-Guevarists of the FAR than with the original Montoneros. But unlike the FAR, its militants do not share the legacy of revolutionary Peronism. Thus the designation "red fascism" completely misses the mark.

In an effort to encapsulate Guevara's thought within the framework of Italian fascism, James Gregor focuses on its resemblance to Mussolini's "Marxist heresy."[132] As he characterizes Guevara's heresy and that of Cuban Marxists: "The original Marxist emphasis on economic determinants in historical development has succumbed to voluntarism and activism—and an emphasis on violence, sacrifice, and dedication."[133] From this rather modest beginning Gregor arrives at the starting pronunciamento: "Cuban radicals [in which group he includes Guevara] have resolved the dilemma of the nonrevolutionary proletariat and the historic role of nationalism by transforming classical Marxism into a Caribbean variant of fascism."[134]

The resulting distortion of Guevara's thought stems from a failure to make the following crucial distinctions. First, the fascism of Mussolini is uncritically identified with that of the National Fascist movement, which escaped his control, so that Mussolini's "Marxist heresy" is not a faithful representative of institutional fascism in

Italy. Second, Italian fascism culminated in a complete break with Marxism, and was a Marxist apostasy, not a heresy. Third, Guevarism is not Castroism, and its international and proletarian outlook cannot be traced to the nationalism of Cuba's José Martí.[135] Fourth, Guevara's emphasis on violence, sacrifice, and dedication went hand in hand with an acceptance of the Marxist determinants of historical development and of economic self-interest as a motivating force of revolution. In short, neither Guevara nor his followers were "red fascists."

It is a cheap academic trick to lump together fascism, national socialism, bolshevism, Maoism, Castroism, Guevarism, and Peronism as all members of the same family in the so-called new radicalism.[136] Even less convincing is the reduction of the various members of this constellation to expressions of so-called paradigmatic fascism.[137] In bracketing the differences that divide them one discounts their respective roads to power. Indeed, the Fascist alliance with the bourgeoisie as opposed to the Communist alliance with the working class transformed these two movements into mortal enemies.

Did Guerrillas Provoke the Military Coup?

The campaign by Argentina's liberals to discredit the guerrillas has laid at their doorstep the burden of responsibility for not only the dirty war, but also the March 1976 coup. But one should beware of attributing too much as well as too little importance to the guerrillas. The intriguing question is not whether they goaded the military to commit excesses, but under what circumstances the military intervened and in response to precisely what factors. The guerrillas' guideline, "the worse, the better," is open to misunderstanding. If wishes were deeds, they would have provoked the coup but not the atrocities of the dirty war. Then, after instigating a movement of popular resistance, the would have established a government of their own.

Guevara's strategy was designed to instigate a coup in order to unmask the hypocrisy of bourgeois legality.[138] Under the influence of this strategy, both the PRT-ERP and the Montoneros hoped to unmask the real nature of Peronist rule from 1974 to 1976 by pressuring the armed forces to intervene. As Julio Santucho recalled, the ERP attributed a "positive significance to the thesis 'the worse, the better.'"[139] It sufficed, the ERP believed, "to unmask the false leftism of a populist leader to reorient the laboring masses toward the correct socialist path."[140] As for the Montoneros, the Vaca Narvaja brothers welcomed the coup with the words: "we will win, we have pushed them onto our own terrain!"[141]

No government can tolerate for long illegal and violent challenges to its authority. "The protests of the guerrilla groups about the mounting of a campaign of repression seem therefore rather hollow; it is precisely the reactions that could be expected."[142] However, it is one thing to argue that the guerrillas incited the Peronist government and military into organizing secret and illegal death squads, and another to argue that they provoked the 1976 military coup.

As early as September 1973, the ERP "wanted to topple the democratically elected government and to induce the military to come to the forefront."[143] But does that mean that the coup came in response to the ERP's strategy? To assert that the guerrillas provoked intervention means that they took the initiative, and the armed forces merely responded. But other factors besides armed subversion were at issue in shaping the Military Process, notably the historical cycle of political instability since 1930 and the related cycle of economic decline since the 1950s—the other facets of the Argentine question.

The allegedly senseless provocations occurred after the military abdicated in 1973 and the Peronist party had returned to power. Thus Brocato claims that the ERP in September 1973 and the Montoneros a year later provoked the Peronist trade union bureaucracy and the Peronist right wing to organize death squads in retaliation.[144] But the death squads mounted by the trade union bureaucracy and by López Rega's Ministry of Social Welfare antedated the ERP's September attack on the armed forces. The armed thugs of the Juventud Sindical Peronista (JSP) in conjunction with the Lopezreguist gangs went into action at the Ezeiza International Airport on June 20. This was the baptism by fire of the right-wing action squads. The Ezeiza massacre responded to a mass mobilization of subversives who were demonstrating peacefully, not to an armed provocation.

Organized with a view to countering the wave of subversion dating from the 1969 *cordobazo*, these gangs also responded to the new Peronist arrangement for sharing power. Because of Perón's recognition of the Peronist Youth as the official fourth branch of the movement—in addition to the political, trade union, and women's branches—the Montoneros and their allies had the right to share in the spoils of victory. In the list of candidates of the Frente Justicialista de Liberación (FREJULI) in the March 1973 elections, 25 percent was allocated to the allies of the Peronist movement and the remaining 75 percent divided mainly among its political, trade union, and youth branches—the last dominated by the Montoneros—with women receiving only token representation.

In this corporative arrangement the principal losers were the political and the trade union branches, which felt injured in having their quotas reduced because of beardless upstarts. From the beginning, Perón's decision to create a fourth branch was stubbornly resisted by both the political and the trade union bureaucracy, which complained of ideological infiltration by newcomers infected with Marxist-Leninist ideas. Resentful at this encroachment, they began preparing an all-out assault on the Peronist Youth and the Montoneros in particular.

The offensive mounted against the youth branch by José Ignacio Rucci of the CGT and by the political sector responsive to José López Rega's Ministry of Social Welfare turned into a massacre. But the victims had to share the blame. Pressured by López Rega and the trade union bureaucracy, Perón repudiated the Montonero-dominated Peronist Youth by appointing in July the leader of the unrepresentative Juventud Peronista de la República Argentina (JPRA) as the youth's representative on the Justicialist Supreme Council. When he withdrew his official recognition of the youth branch in May 1974, its candidates were already being forced out of office. But the parting of ways came not because it provoked the government through armed resistance, but because its share of political influence was resented by the traditional sectors of Peronism.[145]

Did armed resistance induce the government of Isabel Perón into covering up for the death squads and then authorizing the military's dirty war? On this score both the ERP and the Montoneros now plead guilty.[146] But provoking a dirty war is one thing, and provoking an unconstitutional coup is something else.

How important, then, is armed subversion in accounting for the overthrow of the Peronist government? On the one hand, "*foquismo* [reliance on armed force by a political-military vanguard] became converted into an agent of military intervention, while also justifying it."[147] On the other hand, there were other factors behind the coup that "transcended and were of greater import than the guerrillas."[148] The influence of the United States and its doctrine of National Security as a counterweight to populist pressures was one factor. The concern of Argentina's financial establishment to defend its privileges was another. Important also were the military's concrete interests and response to the lure of power and economic privilege. Nor should one forget "the political corruption of Peronism, infested with canaille who had soiled the slogans of liberation during the long period of proscription."[149] In this perspective, the guerrillas did little more than add fuel to the fire.

Argentine trade unionists believed that the chief purpose of the repression was to undo the gains of organized labor.[150] The specter of subversion did not provoke, but provided a pretext for the coup against a government notorious for its prolabor policies.[151] As one eminent political historian interprets the Military Process, it was basically "a revolution in government whose aim was the total dismantlement of the Peronist state."[152]

This assessment coincides with that of President Videla's economy minster from 1976 to 1981. José A. Martínez de Hoz acknowledged that from the moment Perón assumed power after World War II until the collapse of Isabel Perón's government in 1976, the Peronist legacy of state intervention was mainly to blame for the economy's poor performance and failure to modernize.[153] In his judgment: "The armed forces were guided by the urgency not only to overcome a circumstantial crisis of tremendous gravity, but also to lay the basis for the country's healthy, stable, and progressive development that would remove it from its condition of stagnation and frustration."[154]

Brocato, too, believes that the guerrillas were not the fundamental factor behind the 1976 coup. Military coups in Argentina have invariably responded less to the radical policies of populist governments than to the failure of those governments to live up to their promises. It was their loss of popular support that in each case prompted the military to intervene.[155]

The military abrogated traditional rights as the only effective means against an enemy that relied on constitutional guarantees to continue operating.[156] But this was hardly the sole reason for its action. The Proclamation by the Military Junta on 24 March 1976 justified the coup in order to put an end to subversion and to government incompetence and favoritism. The document pointed to the growing power vacuum threatening the country. It also complained of the government's irresponsibility in dealing with the economy, a rate of inflation greater than that of Germany in 1921–1922, exacerbated by a failure to resist the pressures of organized labor. These themes were reiterated in another overview of the coup dated 7 April 1976. "Confronted with the tremendous vacuum of power capable of submerging us in dissolution and anarchy, with the government's incapacity to bring people together, with the repeated and successive contradictions evident in the adoption of arbitrary measures, with the absence of a global strategy for confronting subversion . . . , [we have decided] to put an end to misgovernment, conspiracy, and the subversive scourge."

Antonio Cafiero, the Peronist economy minister from August 1975 to February 1976, believed that Isabel Perón faced a crisis from the day she became president. "The day Perón died I already had intimations that a coup was in gestation."[157] In a meeting in which he participated, one of the top military brass asked: "Who is now in control of the country?" Indignant at the general's lack of respect, Cafiero responded: "What do you mean 'Who is in control'? . . . The nation's president!"[158]

From the beginning of Isabel Perón's government, the military indicated that she lacked the necessary authority to govern and would eventually have to be replaced. In the meantime the generals began to elaborate their strategy. The president mistakenly thought she could retain power by making concessions: "She believed in the 'Bordaberryzation' of the cabinet."[159] Originally, this term signified the incorporation of the military into a government nominally under civilian control. Juan María Bordaberry, Uruguay's president from 1972 to 1976, had agreed to military control of his administration in February 1973 and in June abolished Congress and replaced it with a Council of State. However, despite Bordaberry's civilian front, he was removed from office by what has come to be called a process of "Bordaberryzation"—a military coup by quotas.

Ernesto Corvalán Nanclares, former minister of justice and appointed at the same time as Cafiero, tells a similar story but believes that preparations for the coup began even earlier. Although some maintain that the machinations began the day Perón died, evidence suggests that "the conspiracy began the same day that justicialism won the elections in [March] 1973."[160] In confirmation he cites the declarations of the former Argentine ambassador to Uruguay, Guillermo de la Plaza. When interviewed by a United Press International reporter in Montevideo on 3 April 1979, the ambassador mentioned the creation during the first months of 1973 of an "Operation Fatherland," whose military leaders would later play a prominent role in the Military Process. Claiming to have been the only civilian in the conspiracy, he declared that the *"operation began when it became evident that Argentina might fall into a situation of political and social chaos . . . at that time plans were made that culminated on 24 March 1976, the date the Armed Forces seized power."*[161]

If we are to believe these reports, the guerrillas were an inconsequential factor leading to the coup. But if they did not provoke it, perhaps they accelerated it. On this score, too, Cafiero thought otherwise.[162] The immediate catalyst of military intervention was the cabinet crisis of July 1975, provoked by the CGT's first general strike against a Peronist government.[163] With the Peronist movement split at the seams and wages and prices out of control, the government became paralyzed. As Cafiero commented: "What better climate for a military coup?"[164]

By September the rebellion was already in progress. "Numa Laplane, the army's commander-in-chief, was displaced by a military conspiracy. . . . I realized it the day Videla was designated to replace him, because this was a concession by the constitutional government to the army." [165] That same day Cafiero met with the heads of the three armed services to ask for a statement of support for the government. But their declaration contained the following phrase: "The armed forces support the constitutional government at this moment, at this stage of the process of development." [166] When Cafiero asked what that implied, he was told it was support phrased in military jargon. Cafiero challenged them on the spot.

With or without the scourge of subversion, Cafiero concluded, the armed forces would have intervened. [167] But this claim is no more credible than the counterclaim that guerrillas provoked the coup. The fact of the matter is that the armed forces intervened in response to armed subversion as well as the other factors I have mentioned.

Feasibility of the Armed Struggle

Virtually all sectors of the military believed in the feasibility of the revolutionary war. As a leading protagonist of the dirty war summarized the prevailing military opinion in retrospect: "The revolutionary war in Argentina began to take shape shortly after Perón's fall in 1955. . . . Beginning with the assassination of General Aramburu [1970], subversion maintained the initiative in crescendo and without respite for five years. During that period its power increased constantly . . . while the armed forces, one of the principal targets of aggression, were kept in their barracks out of combat by de facto governments as well as de jure. The effort to contain the guerrillas with the police and courts failed. . . . The comparison of the situation in this country with the revolutionary wars in Cuba and Nicaragua is a valid one." [168] The military's predicament was how to contain subversion without resorting to illegal methods. [169]

For most students of the Argentine situation, the sustained actions of irregular armed formations during the 1970s were inconsequential in achieving the guerrillas' goals and therefore senseless. The Montonero and ERP projects were unfeasible, we are told, because they were incapable of combining military and mass struggles. [170] Even if the guerrillas had patiently accumulated forces from 1973 to 1976, their armed struggle would have gone unrewarded. [171] With few exceptions, political commentators and academic experts on guerrilla warfare agree with this judgment. Ten years of violence with nothing to show but a mountain of corpses! That, we are told, is the legacy and the lesson of urban guerrilla warfare in Argentina.

That was not the military's opinion of the revolutionary war. Although guerrillas were annihilated on the battlefield, "they were not defeated politically," but continued the war by other means.[172]

Among the handful of critics who concur with this assessment is Argentine sociologist Juan Carlos Marín. He sees no reason to despair about the linkage between armed and mass struggles in Argentina.[173] Not only does he defend the feasibility of guerrilla warfare during the 1970s, but also believes that armed struggle has awakened revolutionaries to its possibilities and to an awareness that in Argentina it has only just begun.

Marín's argument rests on the premise that a revolutionary situation emerged beginning with the *cordobazo* of May 1969.[174] Such a situation hinged on the existing crisis of legitimacy produced by fundamental divisions within the ruling class and on the deterioration in working conditions and the standard of living culminating in organized resistance to the regime. Although these factors had been present in varying degrees from the formal launching of the Peronist resistance in January 1956, it took the *cordobazo* to convince sectors of the Argentine Left that conditions were ripe for sustained armed operations. The revolutionary situation became intensified with the emergence of political-military vanguards and the sequence of urban uprisings that followed. The mass insurrections in Rosario and Cipolletti in September 1969, Córdoba again in March 1971 (known as the *viborazo* because the governor called revolutionary agitators *víboras,* or vipers), Mendoza in April 1972, and General Roca in July, were among the most notorious.[175]

General Alejandro Lanusse concurs that these events made up an insurrectional climate, contributing to the overthrow of General Onganía in 1970 and his successor a year later.[176] Thus when Lanusse opted for a way out by holding elections in March 1973, the guerrillas responded with alarm. Aware that elections were designed to pacify the masses and to disarm the political-military vanguards, they considered the democratic opening to be the counterinsurgency measure it really was.[177] Not to allow themselves to be disarmed became the revolutionary imperative of the moment.

The urban guerrillas were locked into a revolutionary situation. They also had strong reasons to believe they could continue to press their advantage. "The *devotazo* [the storming of the Argentine bastille of Villa Devoto on 25 May 1973] takes up the tradition of the *cordobazo* and signifies the peak in the upward movement of the masses during this period."[178] Who could know at the time that the ebb tide of the revolutionary process was about to set in? To their credit, both the Montoneros and the ERP refused to be disarmed. Nonetheless, when they appeared in force at the Ezeiza Airport on 20 June 1973—the largest mass mobilization in Argentine history— they were unprepared for the ensuing battle. It was not enough to retain their arms; they should have been disposed to use them.[179]

Marín recalls that it was the effort by the Versailles government to disarm the workers of Paris that led to the civil war of 1871.[180] Marx had warned the Parisian workers against launching an insurrection prematurely but when they did so he vigorously defended them. Citing Lenin, Marín defends both the French uprising in 1871 and the Russian experience in 1905. "If Marx . . . declared that the insurrection would be senseless, he nonetheless was able to appreciate that 'senselessness' as the greatest mass movement of the proletariat in the 19th century. So the Russian Social Democrats had a thousand times more reason to convince the masses that the struggle of December 1905 was the most necessary, legitimate, and important movement of the proletariat after the Commune."[181] Those uprisings, even though they failed, demonstrated that the people in arms "should attempt to seize and may succeed in acquiring power."[182]

In any case, the exercise of revolutionary war must precede the theory.[183] Since mistakes in revolutionary strategy can be demonstrated only post facto, there is no escaping the lessons of trial and error.[184] Although such lessons involved tremendous social and political costs, they were indispensable in carrying forward the revolutionary situation of 1969–1973.[185] The only alternative would have been capitulation, precisely at a moment when the scale of popular mobilizations favored the guerrillas and victory seemed around the corner.[186]

Prior to the Bolshevik Revolution, acts of insurrection responded to initiatives and opportunities created by the bourgeoisie. Lenin's contribution was to seize the initiative, to organize a political-military vanguard, and to plan for revolutionary war. The violence of the bourgeoisie, he believed, could be contained only by the counterviolence of the proletariat. For Marín, there is no escaping this predicament.[187] When vested interests are perceived as threatened, civil war results at the initiative of the possessing classes, who "'feel' attacked by each effort of the dispossessed sectors to conquer or recover social and political space."[188] Thus even peaceful efforts to transform society sound the alarm for a "pro-slavery rebellion."[189]

Admittedly, events followed a somewhat different sequence in Argentina. The revolutionary and combative cadres of the popular movement interpreted the *cordobazo* as a sign that the working class was prepared to defend its mobilizations by force. This realization, rather than the counterrevolutionary war that followed, braced them for "the task of preparing and practicing armed struggle."[190] The ruling class and armed services also interpreted the *cordobazo* as a prelude to armed hostilities.[191] The chain of urban uprisings that lasted until 1972 became the catalyst of kidnappings and assassinations not only by the guerrillas, but also by right-wing commandos and the armed forces.

The thorny question is whether the armed struggle after the March 1973 elections and the installation of a people's democratic government in May accomplished the objective of maintaining the momentum and continuity of the earlier armed resistance. In view of María Matilde Ollier's data for the period from 1970 through 1972, Marín's data for the period from 1973 to 1975 indicate that the momentum was definitely preserved.[192]

Ollier credits the revolutionary vanguards during the three years preceding the March 1973 elections with 1,243 armed operations. The peak occurred in 1971, with the last of the urban takeovers. The figures show 282 operations in 1970, 603 in 1971, and 368 in 1972.[193] Ollier's data indicate that during this three-year period the ERP led the pack with 262 armed actions compared with 67 for the Montoneros, 61 for the Marxist-Leninist FAL, 39 for the FAR, and 26 for the FAP.[194] Altogether these five guerrilla organizations were responsible for a little more than one-third of the total.

That the armed struggle continued to gain momentum is evident from Marín's figure of 5,364 guerrilla operations over the next three years—an increase of more than 400 percent.[195] These armed actions were overwhelmingly by the ERP and the Montoneros. Since most of the other guerrilla vanguards had closed up shop or otherwise merged with the two principal ones, it is safe to attribute some 5,000 operations to the ERP and the Montoneros alone—an increase of more than 1,000 percent. The ERP represented the lion's share of this growth.

Paradoxically, the fruits of the earlier armed resistance were reaped under the constitutional governments of 1974–1975. The guerrillas could not have developed and expanded their operations, Marín points out, without considerable mass support. Thus it is a mistake to dismiss the guerrillas as an insignificant minority. The armed struggle involved a "war between opposed social forces, not [just] between 'armed apparatuses.'"[196]

The generals of the Military Process had their own reasons for believing that armed actions were a feasible exercise. In an interview in *La Semana* (29 December 1983), General Camps acknowledged that the guerrillas had become so adept in the art of clandestine warfare that the armed forces had to resort to generalized terrorism, torture, and disappearances in order to save the country from subversion. This judgment, shared by other generals and admirals, substantiates in part Marín's vindication of the armed struggle. The guerrillas might still be carrying on their armed actions and propaganda were it not for the dirty war.

But were they in a condition to do so after the resounding defeat of the two biggest operations against the army's garrisons, by the Montoneros in Formosa in October 1975 and by the ERP in Monte Chingolo in December? According to more than one authority, the guerrillas were already decimated before the Military Process got under way.[197] But the guerrillas were not finished. Although the ERP never recovered from its defeat at Monte Chingolo, where it lost some one hundred of its best cadres, the Montoneros continued fighting through 1976.[198]

Marín's and Ollier's studies indicate there were two periods in the revolutionary war that began with the *cordobazo:* its emergence and consolidation (1970–1972), followed by its development and expansion (1973–1975). Although the linkage between mass resistance and armed struggle cemented during the first period gradually eroded during the second, it was not until the third period, the guerrillas' decline, defeat, and disappearance (1976–1979), that the linkage appears to have been broken. The dirty war and the Military Process were instrumental in breaking it.

5. Battleground of World War III

THE GENERALS thought of their dirty war as an integral part of a Third World War in defense of Western civilization. The immediate origins of this notion that World War III had already begun—a thesis popularized by former president Richard M. Nixon in *The Real War*—dates from the Doctrine of National Security elaborated by the Joint Chiefs of Staff during President Kennedy's administration.[1] Until then the East-West confrontation had focused on divided Europe, Korea, and China. But with the increasing realization that America's nuclear capacity had failed to stop the spread of revolutionary movements in Latin America, the new administration evolved an alternative strategy of counterinsurgency.

The Argentine generals who adopted this strategy would come to justify it on the grounds that Argentina was a battleground of World War III. This interpretation of the reality behind the appearance of U.S.-Soviet relations is basic to understanding the dirty war and the related Military Process. What, then, was the original theory of World War III, what were its supporting arguments, how did it become transmitted to Argentina, and to what extent is it credible?

The Global Scope of Internalized Warfare

As the military buttress of Kennedy's program of security and development adopted by the Alliance for Progress, counterinsurgency was conceived as both a military strategy and a strategy of civic action. It included a bundle of political, economic, and psychological measures in conjunction with military and paramilitary operations. In Argentina, as elsewhere, their purpose was to contain and defeat so-called subversion. Said General Videla: "Subversion is not a problem that requires only military intervention; it is a global phenomenon demanding a global strategy covering all areas: politics, economics, culture, and the military."[2]

Such was the strategy applied in Bolivia as well as Vietnam. But with the popular backlash in the United States and the suppression of peacetime military service, the doctrine was reformulated by giving priority to local forces of repression. Known as the Nixon Doctrine, the defense of Western civilization henceforth rested on the policing capabilities of the armed forces among U.S. allies in Asia, Africa, and Latin America against a supposed internal enemy. Formulated within the framework of the cold war, this doctrine understands the world as in a "permanent war in which the armed forces of the Latin American nations are committed to the defense of the West . . . in the struggle against subversion on a world scale."[3]

As the only organized force capable of containing subversion, the armed forces in each country became the pivot for applying the Nixon Doctrine. Concerned over the failure of democratic institutions to control popular pressures for higher wages, improved living conditions, and other unsatisfied demands that harbored the seeds of social resentment, the Argentine military once again turned to an authoritarian solution with the backing of the army's liberal wing. Thus the decisions of a military junta came to replace the bickering among political parties, while emergency measures were applied that effectively undermined the rule of law.

Violations of human rights were justified on the pretext of defending them. Since subversives had no compunction in using violence, the armed forces reasoned, why should their own hands be tied in the effort to restore order? As Gen. Adcel Vilas, commander of the Fifth Army Corps, acknowledged in a statement prior to the military coup: "The offensive against subversion presupposes in the first place freedom of action in all areas . . . *a series of special procedures*, an instantaneous response, a *persecution to the death*."[4]

These new modalities of struggle were justified on the grounds that classical methods of warfare learned in military schools were useless in the struggle against subversion. Confronted by an enemy that was neither visible nor identifiable and that had no respect for the rules of war, the generals chose to use the same drastic methods the subversives had used against them. As Lt. Col. Hugo Pascarelli justified those measures in March 1977: "The struggle we engage in does not recognize moral limits; it is beyond good and evil."[5]

What these statements failed to add was that the military's emergency measures included the regular use of torture. This was not a response in kind, since the guerrillas neither practiced nor condoned it. Nor did the guerrillas disappear their victims, detain them indefinitely without charges, and execute them without trial. Even in the case of property transgressions there was a noticeable difference.

Whereas the guerrillas robbed banks and supermarkets and collected ransoms from corporations whose executives they kidnapped, the armed forces victimized defenseless individuals without batteries of lawyers to defend their interests. The spoils of war encouraged the armed forces to violate the property rights of those presumed guilty merely because of their associations. This was not a tactic used by subversives.

Considerations of national security took precedence over personal security and individual rights. The militarization of society signified the suspension of such important civil liberties as freedom of movement and the press. To dragnets and roadblocks was added censorship, concealed as well as open, voluntary and imposed. Censorship applied to public radio, television, and cinema and to private correspondence, telephone conversations, and street talk. The classroom and meetings of professional associations came under surveillance. The "state of war" justified the indefinite suspension of habeas corpus, trial by jury, and respect for the property of the detained.

The political institutions basic to liberal democracy were annulled, suspended, or deformed to suit the interests of those in power. The Constitution ceased to apply, Congress was dissolved, political parties were suspended, and trade unions intervened. Even judgments by the Supreme Court were overruled when they failed to conform to the military's perception of the national interest. In effect, the armed forces became identified with the state, so that a challenge to one became a challenge to the other.

A clear statement of the international significance of the war against subversion was provided by General Camps in a series of two articles in *La Prensa*. In the first, published on 28 December 1980, he noted that the wave of subversion in Argentina was a product of the Soviet Union's strategy adopted after World War II, a strategy for extending its influence without a direct confrontation with the United States. This strategy was applied initially in the remaining European colonies in Africa and Asia, mainly against England and France, in the form of struggles for national liberation. It was later applied to Latin America, where there were no colonies in the traditional sense. Hence when Moscow opened its new front, it relied not on armed encounters of the conventional type but on a much more insidious strategy of subversion. Successful in Cuba, it was then applied to Venezuela in 1960, Nicaragua in 1961, Guatemala in 1962, the Dominican Republic and Peru in 1963, Colombia in 1964, Uruguay in 1965, Brazil and Bolivia in 1967, Chile in 1968, Mexico in 1973, and Paraguay in 1974.[6]

In a follow-up article published on 4 January 1981, Camps recalled that it was not until 1957 that the Argentine military began the organized study of Communist revolutionary war. It was the French experience in Indochina and Algeria that was the focus of those studies, the objective being to investigate the Marxist phenomenon throughout the world and the most effective means of containing its advance. Thus the French strategy of counterinsurgency and its later adaptation by the United States in Vietnam dominated Argentine military thinking until roughly 1975.

Camps acknowledged that first France and then the United States were the two great disseminators of antisubversive doctrines. "The United States in particular organized centers for teaching the principles of the struggle against subversion. It sent advisers, instructors, and disseminated an extraordinary number of bibliographies."[7] But the examples studied consisted mainly of defeats, so it was possible to analyze only what to avoid. Moreover, in Argentina subversion was not being fought on foreign soil. "That was the basic difference: the French and Americans fought outside their own territory, in countries with a different race, different language, different customs."[8]

American counterinsurgency strategy, Camps concluded, was defective in two principal respects: the United States failed to develop a global view of Communist strategy in its different and seemingly unconnected manifestations, and it relied almost exclusively on military means to combat it. Under U.S. influence the Argentine military adopted this mistaken strategy. Not until September 1975 was it finally able to develop a strategy of its own. At that point, "we came of age and applied our *own doctrine*, which definitely assured Argentina's victory against armed subversion."[9]

That repression had to be harsher in Argentina than in Western Europe would eventually be concluded by all sectors of the armed forces. For Europeans the principal locus of subversion was not at home but in their colonies in Southeast Asia and Africa. Armed subversion never mushroomed in the countries of Western Europe as it did in Brazil, Chile, Uruguay, Bolivia, and Central America. In Argentina, as among its neighbors, an extreme situation of subversion would require extreme measures to combat it. Not for nothing did the generals of the Military Process believe that Argentina had been chosen by left-wing terrorists as a battleground of World War III.

Jacobo Timerman recalls that in the clandestine prisons where he was held from 1977 to 1979, there were weekly sessions on the different features presented by World War III.[10] The substance of those sessions was that the Western liberal democracies were too internally divided to confront communism decisively, that "Europe would go red," and that only a response like that of Nazi Germany could be expected to stem the tide of subversion.[11] Timerman's impressions were not exaggerated. Said General Camps: "I maintain that Argentina has not just experienced a war, but rather that it was the battleground of a war that included the world. Today that war continues in other fields, as in Central America."[12]

According to the doctrine formulated in 1979 by the army's top commander, Gen. Roberto E. Viola, it was both necessary and legitimate for Argentina's armed forces to intervene militarily in other countries in defense of governments beleaguered by "internal aggression" and against duly elected governments believed to harbor subversive tendencies.[13] Thus the military junta lent ten million dollars to Pres. Anastasio Somoza for the purpose of fighting the Sandinistas, and after his fall in July 1979 another half million dollars for recruiting mercenaries to overthrow the Sandinista government.[14]

Argentina's armed forces subsequently intervened in support of the July 1980 coup in Bolivia to prevent the transfer of its government to the popular coalition led by Hernán Siles Suazo. Some seventy Argentine officers are estimated to have participated in the coup, three of whom were implicated in the assassination of socialist leader Marcelo Quiroga Santa Cruz.[15] Beginning in September the Argentine military also contributed to training paramilitary death squads in kidnapping, torture, and disappearance techniques intended to prevent the spread of subversion in Guatemala.[16] In 1982 the army's chief of staff announced its decision to succor militarily the government of El Salvador against the menace of the revolutionary war in that country, while in Honduras the Argentine military participated in training counterinsurgency teams and granted military aid amounting to more than four million dollars.[17]

Camps's belief that Argentina had become a battleground in an unconventional and undeclared Third World War was shared by other generals. The so-called Order of Battle issued by the Joint Chiefs of Staff on 24 March 1976 expressly declared that "Argentina is one of the battlefields of World War III—the war against subversion."[18] And on taking over as chief of the federal police in June 1976, Gen. Arturo Corbetta added that the Argentine police could not ignore its responsibilities in "this Third World War as it has been called, in which the theater of operations in the Argentine Republic . . . plays a leading role."[19]

Under the menace of international communism and its revolutionary wars, the generals ceased to be restrained by national boundaries.

Among the distinctive features of contemporary warfare was the defense of a new type of frontier, ideological rather than geographical. As General Viola characterized World War III: "Unlike classic wars, this war has neither a definite beginning in time nor a final battle crowning its victory. Neither does it have large concentrations of men, arms, and other materials of war, nor clearly defined battle lines."[20] It was an altogether new kind of war.

War or Witch Hunt?

The thesis of a Third World War and its corollary, the so-called dirty war in Argentina, was challenged in 1984 by Frontalini and Caiati's widely acclaimed *El mito de la guerra sucia*. According to the authors, armed conflict alone does not constitute war.[21] Neither the actions of Argentina's guerrillas nor the measures taken against them amounted to war in any academically respectable, dispassionate, or impartial sense of the word.[22] Unlike the revolutionary wars in Algeria and Vietnam, the operations of Argentina's urban guerrillas were too puny to qualify even as unconventional wars.[23]

For Frontalini and Caiati the keystone for distinguishing war from other forms of violent confrontation is the presence or absence of belligerent forces roughly commensurate in firepower.[24] The conflict between incommensurable forces, as in the case of the final solution to the Jewish question, is not war but genocide.[25] In the event of such a conflict, the loser is a victim of repression. "Graphically, one may speak of a struggle between a man and a bear, not between a man and a mosquito."[26]

The largest armed encounter with guerrillas between 1973 and 1983 took place in Tucumán during Operation Independence. An army force of five thousand surrounded and liquidated the ERP's rural guerrillas, estimated at about five hundred.[27] Since overall the ratio was much higher in favor of the military, the crushing of armed resistance by the regular army qualified as repression, not as the opening battle of World War III. Hence the authors' conclusion that there was a "hunting party" (*cacería*) but no "dirty war."[28]

As the word is currently used, *war* is synonymous with armed struggle between states, nations, or political factions. Its first or preferred meaning equates war with "open armed conflict between nations or states, or between parties in the same states, carried on by force of arms for various purposes; a conflict of arms between hostile parties or nations."[29] Armed robbery carried on by agencies other than a party or organized political group is not war but delinquency. The so-called gang wars between rival Chicago mobs during the

1930s fall outside the prescribed parameters, constituting at best a metaphorical application of the term. Similarly, the assassination of heads of state or other political notables by isolated individuals does not constitute an act of war.

Current usage agrees with Carl von Clausewitz's statement: "War is politics continued by other [i.e., forcible] means."[30] More precisely, it is a political instrument, whatever its particular purpose may be. Thus it includes the religious wars of the sixteenth and seventeenth centuries along with Islam's holy wars. As an armed conflict aimed at disarming an enemy, war's essence is a duel, except on a larger scale.[31] Clausewitz believed it must be large enough to involve hostilities between regular armies.[32] This restriction rules out the possibility of guerrilla wars, counterinsurgency wars, and so on. But current usage also encompasses armed conflicts between smaller political groups.

Although war is carried on by politically organized groups, the difference between war and no war is not measured by the number of shots exchanged. Guerrillas may have to confront a regular army, but in Argentina the armed struggle between the right-wing death squads of the AAA (Triple A) and the political-military vanguards of the Left occurred without the intervention of the military. Characterized by political commentators as a war of apparatuses, it was a war between political parties rather than armies.

Frontalini and Caiati give a Clausewitzian definition of war suited to their political purposes. The capstone of their argument is Oriana Fallacci's interview with Galtieri in *La Nación* on 12 June 1982.[33] Asked if he had ever personally experienced war, he replied: "Well, another kind of war." To which the reporter insisted: "No, I mean war, real war!" Galtieri lamely acknowledged that his experience was limited to unconventional war. Fallacci retorted that she had served as a war correspondent in three major wars, including Vietnam: "Therefore, I know what war is, I know what you don't know!" As if to say that the only real wars are big ones.

Struggle for the World

Far more controversial is the generals' claim concerning World War III. A careful assessment of it requires an examination of its principal source in the works of the leading theorist of World War III, the North American social and political philosopher James Burnham (1905–1987). "More than any other single person," writes George H. Nash, "Burnham supplied the conservative intellectual movement with the theoretical formulation for victory in the cold war."[34]

Much the same can be said of his influence on the Argentine military in shaping its notions concerning World War III.

Born into a family of devout Roman Catholics—his brother Philip would later become the editor of the Catholic magazine *Commonweal*—Burnham acquired international fame with his widely heralded bestseller *The Managerial Revolution* (1941). Then, after his definitive break with Marxism, he published his path-breaking *The Struggle for the World* (1947). The first of his trilogy on World War III, it also served as the theoretical basis of his column "The Third World War," published in *National Review.* Beginning in November 1955, Burnham's column ran until April 1970, and thereafter as "The Protracted Conflict" until he retired as senior editor in December 1978. In an article entitled "The Founding Editors," William F. Buckley acknowledged Burnham's contribution: "Beyond any question, he [Burnham] has been the dominant intellectual influence in the development of this journal."[35]

Burnham is unique among North American political philosophers in having had a major influence on U.S. foreign policy. His theory of a Third World War was based partly on studies during World War II for the Office of Strategic Services (OSS), the United States's first central intelligence agency.[36] E. Howard Hunt of Watergate fame remembers Burnham as a consultant from 1948 to 1952 to the CIA's Office of Policy Coordination, while historian Townsend Hoopes recalls that Burnham's work struck profoundly sympathetic chords among influential officials in the State Department, Defense Department, and CIA.[37]

Besides gaining a respectable hearing from influential government officials such as Richard Nixon and Sen. Joseph McCarthy, Burnham influenced military thought through his lectures at the National War College, the Air War College, and the Naval War College. In February 1950 the *New York Times Book Review* reported that he was officially on leave from New York University to do research in the nation's capital, research supposedly done for the CIA and for Senator McCarthy's witch-hunt of native Communists.[38] And in the CIA-sponsored plan that overthrew President Mossadegh of Iran and installed the Shah Mohammed Reza Pahlavi in his place, Burnham is further credited with having played a key role.[39]

For these and other services, Pres. Ronald Reagan awarded Burnham the Presidential Medal of Freedom in February 1983. The citation reads: "As a scholar, writer, historian and philosopher, James Burnham has profoundly affected the way America views itself and the world. Since the 1930's, Mr. Burnham has shaped the thinking of world leaders."[40] The first conservative intellectual to be so honored, Burnham as much as anyone provided the theoretical basis for the critique of liberal foreign policies and the adoption of a strategy of global anticommunism during the early cold war period.[41]

The Struggle for the World opens with the provocative statement that World War III began in April 1944.[42] That would be a year before the end of World War II. Ships of the Greek navy operating under the British Mediterranean Command were in the harbor at Alexandria when the Greek sailors mutinied. The mutiny, led by the military arm of a political front directed by the Greek Communist party, was the prelude to the Greek civil war. Burnham interprets the mutiny as the first armed skirmish between international communism and the British Empire. Although Britain and the Soviet Union were still allies against the Axis powers, he believes this skirmish signaled the beginning of another war.[43]

Was this war subsidiary to World War II, an accompaniment or aftermath, such as the colonial disturbances and movements of independence in the Far East? Subsidiary wars had followed in the wake of World War I from approximately 1917 to 1924, and the same was true of the postlude to World War II. But the Greek mutiny and civil war, the Chinese civil war, and the Iranian conflict were not part of that postlude, Burnham argues, because the alignment of enemy forces was substantially different from that during the Second World War.[44]

It is now generally recognized that the battles and campaigns of World War II did not begin in August 1939, but in Spain in 1936. Even the battles of 1939 were preliminary to the military climax from 1940 to 1945. World War III, Burnham contends, began in a similar way. Thus the absence of destruction on a massive scale between 1944 and the launching of the cold war in 1947 did not mean that "World War III" was only a metaphor.

Burnham claims that with Hitler's defeat imminent, the Soviet Union and the Communist parties responsive to it began preparing for the next war in their struggle for world domination: confrontation with their World War II allies.[45] Communist strategy throughout the Balkans noticeably changed during 1944 in Yugoslavia and Albania as well as Greece. Even Burnham's critics acknowledged the beginning of a cold war in the aftermath of World War II. But the term "cold war" is a euphemism for World War III and is misleading in suggesting that shots are not fired and blood does not flow, as flow it did in Greece, China, Indochina, the East Indies, and the Philippines during 1947.[46]

If the war was not cold, it seemed to many to be limited in scope—

local wars maybe, but not a Third World War. This argument, according to Burnham, confuses the limited application of firepower characteristic of war in its early stages with a war's scope and objectives.[47] The objective of world domination is surely not limited. Although it takes both sides in a dispute to make peace, one is enough to prepare for war and to wage it in ways that weaken the enemy's defenses and undermine morale. When the enemy finally becomes alerted to the danger, it is too late to respond effectively. Thus the West was caught napping when the Communist strategy of subversive political and ideological warfare surfaced without direct involvement by the Soviet Union.

Contemporary Communist warfare is deceptive, Burnham concludes, because the line of demarcation has disappeared not only between hot and cold wars, but also between war and peace. Subversive warfare in particular has no definite beginning or end. In the past there was a clear-cut distinction between military and civilian targets, but this distinction was obliterated by the nature of total warfare. World War III combines political, ideological, and psychological warfare as well as armed struggle.[48] As Clausewitz recognized, armies do not have to be continually in action for war to occur.[49] Although mass armies were not committed to Western Europe during 1941 and 1942, it is generally agreed that a war was in progress.

Bridges to Argentina

Burnham influenced the Argentine generals through three channels. The first route consisted of French military missions to Argentina and the training of Argentine officers in France using manuals of unconventional warfare written by the generals and colonels defeated in Algeria and Vietnam. The second channel consisted of books in translation on World War III, published in Buenos Aires. The Pentagon and the government's various programs of military aid, including the training received by Argentine officers at Fort Gulick, Fort Bragg, and elsewhere, amounted to a third avenue.

In France the chief disseminator of Burnham's views was the celebrated author and resistance leader André Malraux (1901–1976). As minister of culture in the Fifth Republic from 1958 to 1968, he owed his position to the military coup in Algeria on 13 May 1958 that brought down the Fourth Republic and paved the way for Gen. Charles de Gaulle's return to power. Publicly sharing Burnham's thesis of a long-term crisis involving the transition from capitalism to a new managerial society, compounded by a shorter but more acute crisis over the political structure of the new order, Malraux was in a strategic position to influence French policy during the Algerian War.[50]

In a published dialogue with Burnham in Paris in 1948 Malraux recognized the importance of Burnham's books, which showed that "behind the struggle between capitalists and proletarians, there has begun to develop a reality of an entirely different kind."[51] There was no point in defending capitalism, he believed, because the old economic order had become defunct. Nor was there any point in defending liberal political institutions or in reaching a political understanding with Communists, much less the Soviet Union, because "there has never been a fair competition . . . between liberals and Communists."[52] At issue for conservatives was the defense not of political liberalism, but of cultural liberalism in the effort to preserve the heritage of Western civilization against Communist Byzantinism and the heritage of the Eastern Roman Empire.[53] At least, that was a feasible exercise, Malraux concluded, whereas the defense of the older liberalism was sheer folly.

It is worth noting that both Burnham and Malraux equate the liberal "Third Force" in France, whose political manifestos began appearing in December 1947, with Perón's Third Position, enunciated a year or so earlier. "Perón tried to summarize through it Argentina's wish to remain independent, and to refuse to 'take sides' in the world struggle between the United States and the Soviet Union."[54] But realistically speaking, there can be no Third Force between Communist civilization and the West—that is the gist of their criticism.

The Burnham-Malraux connection subsequently established a bridge with the Argentine military. In 1957, with the collaboration of the French armed forces, the vice-director of Argentina's Superior War College organized the first systematic study of the strategies of revolutionary and counterrevolutionary warfare as practiced in Vietnam and later applied to Algeria.[55] "The objective was to make obligatory the study of Marxist developments throughout the world and the most convenient way of halting their destructive advance."[56] The lieutenant colonels of the French army who helped to organize this study specifically linked it to "indoctrination concerning the 'third world war against communism.'"[57] The original French source of that indoctrination is Malraux.

Several years after the appearance in April 1961 of the Organisation de l'Armée Secrète (OAS), notorious for its brutal campaign of terrorism against Algerians, its methods, too, became the subject of intensive study by the Argentine armed forces. Two of the OAS's chiefs traveled to Buenos Aires to give instruction. Their guide consisted of "texts of the generals and colonels Salan, Massu, Beaufre, Bonnet, Bonnost, Chateau-Jobert, and Trinquier—all of them defeated in North Africa and Vietnam—manuals that advocated torture to obtain information and the physical elimination of the 'agents of subversion.'"[58] Their efforts were assisted by an Argentine civilian, Ramón Luis de Oliveira César, who under the pseudonym of Alexis Martín had written a book on the French tactics of occult war, published in Buenos Aires in 1963.[59] This work complemented Carlos Fría's 1950 Spanish translation of Burnham's *The Coming Defeat of Communism*, the second volume of his trilogy on World War III, also published in Argentina.

Argentine officers traveled to Paris for specialized training in unconventional warfare and used the same manuals that had been translated into Spanish in Buenos Aires and Madrid. Gen. Adcel Vilas remembered with pride what he assimilated from those manuals and applied as the original chief of Operation Independence in Tucumán.[60] As former Montonero Juan Gasparini comments concerning this influence: "In essence we have here the source of 'our own doctrine' (Camps), the 'last resort' (Díaz Bessone) . . . it is nothing less than the systematic disappearance of the victim's corpse."[61]

When Burnham retired as senior editor of *National Review* his column was assigned to Australia-born Brian Crozier (1918–   ), director of the prestigious Institute for the Study of Conflict in London. A recognized authority on international subversion and an expert on national defense, Crozier had lectured extensively at war colleges in several countries. Because he considered Burnham as his political mentor and shared the same views concerning World War III, he too became a bridge between Burnham's political thought and the Argentine generals.

It is worth considering the Crozier bridge in some detail. At least four of his books became available to the generals in their own language. His *The Struggle for the Third World* (1966)—an evident play on the title of Burnham's 1947 work—was promptly translated and published in Buenos Aires in 1967. The original Argentine source of Burnham's theory of a "hot cold war," other than its diffusion by the Pentagon, Crozier's book provided the generals with a justification for the Military Process because of its thesis that Castroism-Guevarism is the agent of a Soviet-financed "conspiracy that extends, in one form or another, throughout the Latin American and Caribbean areas."[62]

This book was followed by a sympathetic portrait of the Spanish dictator, *Franco: A Biographical History*, translated and published in Madrid in several editions beginning in 1969. It defended the model of an authoritarian government that not only saved Spain from communism, but also made possible a return to liberal democracy.[63] Several years later Crozier's *A Theory of Conflict* was translated and published in Buenos Aires, followed by his *Strategy of Survival* in 1978 under the altered title *Occidente se suicida*, suggestive of Burnham's *Suicide of the West*. Although used to justify the dirty war in retrospect, Crozier's basic concern for the survival of the West was already familiar to Argentines from his earlier books.

In justification of the military dictatorships in Brazil, Chile, and Uruguay during the early 1970s, Crozier argues that repression is the only intelligent response to subversion. But it is not an easy matter to distinguish legitimate dissent from subversive and therefore illegitimate dissent, defined as a "systematic attempt to undermine society."[64] In the fight against subversion, he recommends that subversive intent as well as subversive organizations be repressed whether laws are violated or violence is merely advocated. It is enough that the rights to free speech and association are abused by systematically denigrating established values, eroding confidence in prevailing institutions, or discrediting the government.[65] Each statement, article, talk, or program may be within the law, but if the combined effect tends to create a climate of opinion conducive to public acceptance of Soviet foreign policy objectives, or to present events one-sidedly in ways that favor revolutionary change or undermine the will to resist subversion, then it imperils freedom and cannot be tolerated by free societies.[66]

The ultimate peril to a free society, Crozier contends, is the availability of freedoms used to destroy freedom. Consequently, a "relatively more tolerable (if only because less permanent) alternative to a democracy under threat is the authoritarian solution."[67] If subversion is recognized to be a problem in its early stages, most countries can cope with it by a determined use of existing laws. But if such measures fail, the only remaining resort is to introduce martial law.

It is generally accepted that when a country is at war with a foreign power it has the right to adopt emergency measures, to detain suspects without trial, and to introduce censorship. Internal war, according to Crozier, deserves the same consideration. "Is there not a parallel, peculiarly apt for the 1970s, between the situation of a country at war with an external enemy, and the country faced with a situation like Ulster, or Vietnam, or Turkey or Uruguay?"[68] Are countries in such situations no less at war than Britain and its allies during World Wars I and II? Although a sensible government will not resort to internal warfare unless there is a clear and present danger, "the danger often is that it fails to act when there is one, out of timidity or excessive deference to [liberal] tradition."[69]

Several years before Jeane Kirkpatrick's influential article (which would shape foreign policy during the Reagan administration), "Dictatorships and Double Standards" (*Commentary*, November 1979), Argentina's generals had already used the distinction between radical totalitarian governments and semitraditional authoritarian regimes to justify their dirty war. Implicit in Burnham's writings, this distinction is basic to Crozier's classification of political regimes.[70] Thus he distinguishes three political options in today's world: Western-style democracy, "totalist" or totalitarian states, and authoritarian rule.[71]

Despite popular beliefs to the contrary, Crozier holds that authoritarian and totalitarian regimes are political opposites.[72] First, authoritarian regimes depoliticize society, whereas totalitarian governments mobilize there entire populations in political activities. Second, most people are much freer and also economically much better off under authoritarian rule than under totalitarian. Finally, authoritarian governments are relatively unstable and, when pushed from within, are capable of evolving into Western-style democracies. "In contrast, no totalitarian regime has ever collapsed except as a result of a world war, and no Communist party, once in full national power, has yielded to democratic rule since Lenin seized power in 1917."[73]

To prevent defeat in World War III, Crozier recommends emergency measures that are basically illiberal. He urges a gradual weeding out of hidden and avowed Marxist-Leninists from opinion-shaping positions in schools, universities, newspapers, radio, and television.[74] He insists that only political parties unreservedly committed to a large and flourishing private sector in the economy should be allowed to present candidates in national elections.[75] Tantamount to banning not only Communist but also Socialist parties committed to a policy of gradual nationalizations, such a measure is justified by Crozier as a supposed sine qua non of a pluralist and representative system.[76] He also calls for laws against industrial subversion, such as politically motivated strikes. Finally, the Western democracies can no longer afford what he calls the "luxury of misplaced tolerance."[77] Telephone tapping and other similar measures are justifiable, he believes, despite the right to privacy. "We are after all at war . . . [and] an internal war can be no less damaging in its ultimate result than a war of physical destruction."[78]

One can imagine how the Argentine generals responded to such advice. If such measures were deemed essential to preserve freedom at the heart of Western civilization in liberal Great Britain and the United States, much more drastic measures would be required on the periphery. Crozier's arguments were especially relevant to military liberals who shared his basic premises. But they also played into the hands of Catholic nationalists like General Camps.[79] Camps's comments on World War III and the West's will to survive are strikingly similar to Crozier's, which suggests some familiarity with the latter's works.[80]

To his and Burnham's specifically political premises that all societies are ruled by elites and that popular sovereignty is a technical impossibility, Crozier adds Burnham's economic postulates with a bearing on contemporary politics. First, "control of the world is passing into the hands of managers . . . in business and government." Second, capitalism or the economic arrangement favoring the owners "will soon disappear . . . [because] it no longer works."[81] Thus Crozier accepts the thesis of economic convergence between East and West, but rejects the parallel thesis of political convergence. As he puts it, the "fundamental difference between the totalist bloc and the pluralist societies is political, not economic."[82]

Several of these precepts were shared by Argentina's generals. It was not their purpose to save a worn-out capitalist system from a professional-managerial elite that included themselves and threatened to replace the capitalists. Rather, it was to save what could be saved of free institutions in Argentina. The generals believed they were fighting a war in defense of Western values in a remote battleground of World War III. Defending the privileges of a financial oligarchy was not the issue.

The fundamental issue was political, not economic. For Crozier, "World War III really began with the Bolshevik seizure of power in 1917,"[83] hence his distinction between World War III and World War IV—the threatened nuclear holocaust directly involving the superpowers.[84] As for the intellectual origins of World War III, Crozier traces them to the *Communist Manifesto.* Thus he regards the period from 1848 to 1917 as the "prehistory of World War III," and the period from 1917 to the outbreak of World War III a quarter century later as the "preparatory phase of 'the struggle for the world.'"[85]

General Díaz Bessone concurs with Crozier that the "struggle for socialism is the most gigantic civil war that world history has ever known."[86] Under Crozier's influence, he interprets the revolutionary civil war in Argentina as a continuation not only of that unleashed by the Bolsheviks in 1917, but also of that proclaimed by Marx and Engels in 1848. Thus he agrees with their description of "the more or less veiled civil war, raging within existing society, up to the point where that war breaks out into open revolution, and where the violent overthrow of the bourgeoisie lays the foundation for the sway of the proletariat."[87] Commenting on this passage, Díaz Bessone says: "Here is expressed basically what is meant by *revolutionary war.*"[88]

What disturbs him is that Marxism is an ideology born and bred in the heart of the West that "proposes to destroy Western civilization (religion, political and social institutions, economy, education, etc.)."[89] After taking power in czarist Russia in 1917, it seized control of China in 1949. Were it not for the Soviet Union, Marxism might be contained without the need for drastic measures. But the Soviet Union does not hesitate to pursue its objectives through revolutionary wars in the areas it seeks to subvert. For that purpose it trains local Communists in the methods of guerrilla warfare.[90]

The Soviet Union's principal educational institutions for Third World revolutionaries were the Lenin Institute for Communist cadres and the Patrice Lumumba University for non-Communist trainees. According to Crozier's informants, both provided cover for intensive courses in guerrilla warfare, street fighting, assassination, sabotage, sharpshooting, explosives, and other arts of terrorism.[91] It had been known for some time that non-Communist revolutionaries were being processed through the Patrice Lumumba University and sent to camps at Tashkent, Baku, Odessa, and as far afield as North Korea. But what had only recently become known in 1973 was that Communist party members from Third World countries were also being trained in those methods.

Crozier's information came from defectors who may not have been trustworthy. However, in the summer of 1983 revolutionary exiles in Mexico confirmed his data for me. A militant in the Uruguayan CP, "Tachi," and some three hundred other Uruguayan Communists were trained over a period of several years in Moscow and other camps inside the Soviet Union. On returning home, he helped unload several tons of captured American-made arms and ammunition from a North Vietnamese vessel anchored off Uruguay's northern coast. These were subsequently distributed and concealed in caches throughout the country.

But the important point is that the Uruguayan Communist party was comparatively rare in Latin America in subscribing to armed struggle. Thus one cannot generalize from the Uruguayan example to Argentina or other countries of the Third World, as Crozier and Díaz Bessone do. Although the Lenin Institute provided guerrilla training on request, fewer than a handful of Latin American CPs encouraged such training, and the Argentine CP was not one of them. This is an important qualification of the Burnham-Crozier thesis concerning World War III and discredits the omnivorous role they assign to the Soviet Union.

Some of the Pentagon's top officials also made a point of disseminating Burnham's views concerning World War III. A case in point is that of an American military mission to Argentina in 1981. In a statement to the Argentine press, Gen. Edward Meyer, chief of staff of the U.S. Army, declared that "guerrillas and subversion are symptoms that World War III has begun."[92]

How relevant were Burnham's close connections with the CIA, the State Department, Sen. Joseph McCarthy, Pres. Richard Nixon, Pres. Ronald Reagan, the Defense Department, and U.S. military colleges and institutions for the Argentine military? An appendix to Frontalini and Caiati's work documents the role of U.S. military aid, military assistance, and missions to Argentina up to and including the Military Process.[93] For two decades beginning in 1950, close to three thousand Argentine military officers attended special courses at Fort Gulick and other U.S. bases. Although beginning in 1961 the U.S. stopped providing heavy arms to Argentina for defense against a hypothetical Soviet invasion, it continued to provide light weapons for counterinsurgency warfare against so-called internal enemies. And as late as 1983 U.S. military personnel occupied offices in the headquarters of the Argentine army's commander in chief, with separate telephones in the Operations Section, Overseer of Operations, and Central Division. Thus the web of U.S. infiltration into Argentine military institutions linked the generals to U.S. global policy in the struggle against international communism.

Among U.S. statesmen, Richard M. Nixon (1913–   ) was the most influential disseminator of Burnham's doctrine. In *The Real War*, he begins his discussion of World War III with a citation from Crozier, followed by a variation on the opening sentence and theme of Burnham's *Struggle for the World*.[94] As if that were not a sufficient index of his indebtedness, he ends the book with an allusion to Burnham's and Crozier's column in *National Review:* "The outcome of the 'protracted conflict' between East and West will depend on our military arsenals, our strategies, our vision, and our control of those material resources that are needed to build the weapons of war and the sinews of peace."[95] If the West loses World War III, it will be because of lack of willpower compounded by the "failure of the leadership class" and an "unwillingness to face reality"—themes also basic to Burnham and Crozier.[96] Although Nixon momentarily suspended work on his book because of the demands of his 1968 presidential campaign, much of the preliminary research "found its way into speeches, and the ideas I was developing in it found their way into the policies of my administration."[97]

This war called peace, Nixon argues, began in August 1944, when the Polish freedom fighters rose up against the Nazi occupiers in Warsaw, only to be abandoned by their Soviet ally.[98] Instead of aiding the liberation of the city, the Soviet army stood idly by for seven weeks until, cut off and helpless, the Western-supported forces of resistance surrendered to the Germans, thus opening the path to Soviet domination of Poland. Although there are strong reasons for believing that the cold war did not begin until March 1945, when the Soviet Union forcibly installed a Communist-dominated government in Rumania, the tensions between the United States and the Soviet Union "first surfaced in Poland."[99]

World War III is the longest war the United States has ever engaged in and, Nixon adds, the first truly global war, the first total war at every level of society, and the first war of international terrorism by remote control.[100] It is more than a cold war; "World War III has proceeded from the Soviet seizure of Eastern Europe, through the communist conquest of China, the wars in Korea and Indochina, and the establishment of a western hemisphere outpost of Soviet power in Cuba, to the present thrusts by the Soviet Union and its allies into Africa, the Islamic crescent, and Central America."[101] The coups that brought Soviet satellite regimes to power in Afghanistan and South Yemen, no less than U.S. interventions in Latin America aimed at containing Castro's export of revolution, were also "battles in that war."[102] For Argentina's generals this message was not new; they had already learned it from other sources.

Credibility of the Theory

To understand the sequence of events known as the dirty war it is imperative to examine the generals' perception of the revolutionary war. If their theory of World War III is credible, then it has an important bearing on our assessment of what transpired.

Most critics of Argentina's dirty war are unfamiliar with Burnham's thesis and its supporting arguments. Consequently, it is not surprising that they find the Argentine generals' conflation of the cold war and World War III preposterous. If the United States and the Soviet Union are the protagonists of World War III, how is one to explain that in the almost half century since World War II the United States has yet to become involved in an armed confrontation with the Soviets? Although the United States has been directly at war with the Soviet Union's allies, as in China, Korea, and Vietnam, not once has the Soviet Union waged war on an ally of the United States.

The alternative explanation is that the superpowers were involved in a cold war. The established view is that the cold war appeared with the onset of the bipolar Soviet-American antagonism, and that it was "precipitated and took form in eastern Europe, initially in disputes concerning the postwar status of Poland and Rumania."[103] Although the term first became popular in 1947, the antagonism can be dated from the last year of World War II—whether in Poland in August 1944 or Rumania in March 1945.[104] Later, the scope of the conflict expanded when the United States began suppressing national liberation movements and revolutionary wars throughout the Third World.[105]

At present, Communists distinguish three kinds of war: world wars involving large-scale conquest of foreign territory, which today threaten to turn into a nuclear holocaust; local wars confined to a limited area, such as the Korean and Vietnamese wars; and wars of national liberation or revolutionary wars with their corollary, counterinsurgency warfare.[106] In this perspective, there has been neither a local nor a world war between the United States and the Soviet Union since World War I. Hence talk of World War III is both politically irresponsible and a caricature of the real world—especially since the advent of *glasnost* and *perestroika* during the 1980s.

At most there was a worldwide conflict of arms between the United States and so-called international subversion, more accurately described as different expressions of national subversion. The enemy was not the original edition of subversion that issued in the Bolshevik Revolution, but the manifold new editions in the form of offspring throughout the Third World. The outcome was a war global in scope, but not the kind of war described by Burnham, Crozier, and former president Nixon.

Unlike World Wars I and II, which were conventional and of relatively short duration, this has been an unconventional war of some forty years duration whose end is only now in sight. In this respect it resembles the Hundred Years' War between England and France (1337–1453) and the Thirty Years' War involving the continental powers (1618–1648). Both of these wars were interrupted by peace treaties and by periods of relative inactivity. As Clausewitz acknowledges: "*Suspension* [of hostilities] and *inactivity* are the *normal condition* of an army in the midst of war, *action* constituting the *exception.*"[107]

For the State Department, the Greek civil war was a turning point. But it was not the mutiny of Greek sailors in April 1944 that precipitated the cold war. The precipitating factor was the British decision three years later to end its military involvement in Greece.[108] That signified abandoning the country to the Communist guerrillas entrenched in the mountains, who also controlled the rural areas outside the big cities. With a sanctuary in neighboring Yugoslavia and arms, munitions, and medical provisions from Bulgaria and Albania, a Communist takeover appeared inevitable. Such was the background of the Truman Doctrine of global containment of Soviet communism in a speech on 12 March 1947, described by the *Chicago Tribune* as the kind of speech that American presidents had made only "on the occasion of going before Congress to ask for a declaration of war!"[109]

In his cold war speech on March 12, Truman said that by exploiting human want and misery a militant minority had created a condition of political chaos in Greece. The "terroristic activities of several thousand armed men, led by communists," had created a situation with which the Greek government could not cope.[110] He spoke of free peoples struggling to maintain their free institutions against political movements seeking to impose a form of totalitarianism. That had already happened in violation of the Yalta agreements in Poland, Bulgaria, and Rumania. And he concluded that "it must be the policy of the United States to support free peoples who are resisting attempted subjugation by armed minorities."[111] Thus wherever a war of national liberation or a Communist revolutionary war developed, the United States would intervene against it before the people had a chance to support it. Containment of the Soviet Union and no more revolutions—that was the substance of the Truman Doctrine.

But America's military, economic, and ideological influence did not reach far enough to determine the fate of Eastern Europe. That was the great disappointment that prompted President Truman's cold war speech. "It was Russian control of Eastern Europe which alarmed the West and precipitated the Cold War. . . . Russian-Communist control of East Europe was the basis of the belief in the West that Russia was out to conquer the world."[112] World revolution was supposedly the means of achieving the Soviet goal of world conquest.

It is ironic that Burnham should have made so much of Soviet efforts at world revolution, for it was precisely Stalin's doctrine of socialism in one country, downplaying international revolution, that led Trotsky to found the Fourth International in 1938. Despite Burnham's Trotskyist past, he conflated the Soviet Union's goals with those of international communism. Hardly less surprising was his claim that "international communism is led, in all of its activities, from its supreme headquarters within the Soviet Union."[113] No Trotskyist could possibly agree to that claim when Burnham made it in 1947, nor could any dispassionate observer of world politics then or since.

In asserting that the Greek Communist party in 1944 was a section of the international Communist movement directed from Moscow, Burnham chose to ignore that the Comintern had been dissolved in May 1943.[114] With the shelving of the Third International as an obstacle to Soviet objectives, the Communist parties beyond the Soviet Union's immediate sphere of influence gradually emancipated themselves from their former tutelage. Thus Burnham discounted the development of Marxism-Leninism from a single world center with its headquarters in Moscow to the polycentric phenomenon of the postwar period.

It is in light of this development, both unforseen and dismissed by Burnham, that one is compelled to reject his characterization of World War III as a war between the United States and the Soviet Union. The war was between the United States and national subversion, which had no supreme or central headquarters and was only aided and abetted by Moscow. The Argentine military misperceived the character of their dirty war, because of a faulty understanding of the American-Soviet antagonism and of the war against "international terrorism."

In modern as well as contemporary usage, a world war must satisfy three fundamental conditions: first, it must be global in scope; second, it must be an international war between nation-states rather than a police or military action against a lesser contestant, as in the case of international terrorism; third, it must take the form of direct and open warfare between the belligerents rather than covert engagements through proxy wars or other indirect and auxiliary forces. Any other definition of "world war" qualifies as idiosyncratic and arbitrary.

The cold war meets the first condition, but fails to satisfy the second and third. Although occasionally hot on the periphery, it remained cold at the center. Contrary to its interpretation by the Argentine military, it consisted of a series of internationally significant and interconnected local wars, but not a world war.

On the premise that a third world war was not inevitable, the Soviet Union retreated on every major issue that might have led to armed confrontation with the United States. In the conviction that no amount of aggressive violence could stop its spread short of a suicidal nuclear war, the United States responded with a policy of dé-

tente that testified to a willingness to accept the fact of Soviet hegemony in Eastern Europe and parts of the Third World. Although in
principle committed to ridding the world of the "ideological bu-
bonic plague" that has decimated millions, even former president
Nixon no longer talks of World War III, but rather of peaceful competition between the two superpowers.[115]

One is driven to the ineluctable conclusion that Argentina was
not a battleground of World War III. Contrary to the prophets of
doom, a third world war never materialized, whether between the
United States and the Soviet Union, as Catholic nationalists maintained, or between Western Christian civilization and international
terrorism.

6. The Defense of Western Civilization

IDEOLOGICALLY, BOTH Argentine military liberals and Catholic nationalists believed in the defense of Western civilization against the forces of international terrorism aided and abetted by the Soviet Union and its allies. They further agreed that extraordinary measures might be justified in defense of Western values. The resulting convergence of outlooks and the emergence of a unified military policy encouraged them to take the initiative in launching the Military Process. But the differences dividing them were never really overcome.

Besides the Anglo-Saxon influence on Argentine liberalism, the intellectual foundations of the dirty war must be sought in the Spanish, Italian, and Catholic heritage of Argentine nationalism. What bearing did these origins have on the generals' rationale for repression? And was the defense of Western civilization really at stake?

Cold War Liberals

The liberal generals and admirals justified their emergency measures by the urgency of containing and eradicating the wave of subversion that began under the influence of Peronism and mushroomed in the wake of the Cuban Revolution. Because the liberties guaranteed by liberal and democratic institutions had been used by subversives to destroy freedom, liberals felt compelled to suspend those liberties in order to defend them. They demanded responsible democratic institutions and safeguards to freedom. As General Videla observed: "An aggressive and destructive nihilism tried to erase every form of legitimate pluralism . . . [hence] the elaboration of basic guidelines for achieving future political stability is a prior and indispensable condition of installing a democratic regime."[1]

Military liberals traced the crisis in Argentine society to the crisis of democracy following World War I. General Viola noted that the military's task was not only the eradication of subversion, but also the elimination of those factors that had destabilized national life since 1930.[2] This year is crucial for understanding the liberal viewpoint, according to which Yrigoyen's brand of radicalism was compatible with Argentine national traditions. Argentine political history after his overthrow was another matter. For military liberals the semi-fascist coup of September 1930 was a disgrace, as were the fraudulent elections during the so-called Infamous Decade and the populist plague that followed.

Since the time of General Justo, liberals in the armed forces have looked on the traditional liberalism of the Radical party with favor. This was true of Gen. Pedro E. Aramburu, who preferred Balbín's UCRP to the Yrigoyenist developmental and social policies of Frondizi's UCRI, and it was also true during Gen. Alejandro A. Lanusse's tenure as president from 1971 to 1973. Both Aramburu and Lanusse shared the UCRP's interpretation of Argentine history and assessment of Peronism as a break with the country's liberal past. The UCRP likened Perón to the former dictator Juan Manuel de Rosas; so did military liberals.

On assuming the presidency on 13 November 1955, Aramburu affirmed that the purpose of the liberating revolution was to "reestablish the rule of law and restore authentic democracy."[3] On December 31 he blamed Perón for the chaos, discord, and social disequilibrium that were prominent features of the former totalitarian regime.[4] He also justified the dissolution of the Peronist party by claiming it was an instrument of dictatorship. In February 1956, on the anniversary of Rosas's fall, he reaffirmed the principles of the 1853 Constitution while comparing the overthrow of Perón's tyranny with Gen. Justo José de Urquiza's demolition of the twenty-year Rosas dictatorship at the battle of Caseros in 1852.[5] And in a speech on May Day 1956 he likened Peronism to communism for transforming otherwise independent individuals into blind automatons, "drowning their individual wills and responsibilities so that they think with the same mentality."[6]

All liberals shared the view likening the Peronist tyranny to Rosas's earlier tyranny. All liberals were committed to what Aramburu called the "continuing struggle for liberty against despotism."[7] They also agreed on the need for exceptional measures to defend the Constitution against those intent on subverting it. But as General Lanusse acknowledged, defense of the Constitution did not mean unswerving obedience to constituted authority. In response to the 1969 *cordobazo*, which shook the foundations of the existing military regime, he confessed: "I had never believed—and I had never made others believe—that the army's obedience to those in power should be interpreted as unconditional."[8]

Lanusse agreed with the substance of President Onganía's 1964 speech at West Point, when Onganía still represented the liberal cause. This so-called West Point Doctrine defined the limits of obedience to civilian governments by authorizing the military to intervene in the following instances: first, during disorder in the affairs of government; second, during violent shifts in the domestic balance of power; third, after infringements of the liberties and rights of citizens; and fourth, during other exceptional situations.[9] As Lanusse quotes from Onganía's speech: "Not to react to such situations is to become a blind instrument to established power and to an authority that is illegitimate."[10]

Lanusse added another liberal tenet. While claiming that military intervention is occasionally justified, he defended the independent role of political parties and rejected the corporatist and authoritarian schemes of Catholic nationalists.[11] "A simple look at the world map shows that when dictatorships of one kind fall, they generate dictatorships of another type. During the 1970s the terrorist formations of the Left were largely nourished (almost exclusively in one case) by militants of hit squads previously in the service of the extreme Right. This is evident from the names of militants in the organization whose first action was the assassination of Gen. Pedro Eugenio Aramburu, and also from the antecedents of many members of the Trotskyist guerrilla organization."[12] To this extent military liberals shared with Radicals the theory of two terrorisms and its corollary, the theory of two totalitarianisms.

The credo of military liberals was aptly summarized by Lanusse: "I do not believe that you can fight the enemies of liberty by suppressing liberty, for in that case defeat is assured. I am convinced that totalitarianism of the Left flourishes on the soil of reactionary dictatorships. . . . Sane, open, free societies where dissent is possible have always defended themselves better against infiltration than submissive communities that have made free thought unlawful."[13] This passage is revealing in that it identifies the liberals' fundamental enemy while upholding civil liberties as an indispensable dike against subversion.

Similar but less generous sentiments were voiced by President Videla in a speech in Tucumán in celebration of the first six months of the military government. After noting that cultural freedom was the first victim of subversion, he added: "We have repeatedly indicated that one of the fundamental purposes of the Process of National Reorganization is to install at the proper moment a republican, representative, and federal democracy. . . . We must revitalize the institutional system for the purpose of ending, once and for all, the traditional pendular cycle of constitutional governments and military regimes—a process that will be long and difficult because of the profundity of the crisis. . . . [Therefore] we will not fall into the temptation of hurried electoral solutions nor permit the return of political fronts whose failure the country remembers." [14]

The last sentence constituted a slap at General Lanusse, first, for moving too fast in dismantling the former military regime and, second, for allowing Peronists to dominate the elections through the Justicialist Liberation Front—a political monopoly. Lanusse agreed with Arturo Mor Roig, his Radical minister of the interior, that elections should be held at the earliest opportunity. For Videla that was a mistake in view of the Peronist landslide victories in March and September 1973, which incubated a new crisis and a renewed wave of subversion more terrible than its predecessor. Premature elections favored the FREJULI and made a mockery of Lanusse's plans when the resulting Peronist monopoly of power was used to favor organized labor. This prompted the military to intervene again to restore equilibrium.

Videla's judgment of Lanusse had the advantage of hindsight but failed to consider the encouragement given to subversion by the military's outlived policy of banning the majoritarian party. In 1972–1973, subversion enjoyed the protective umbrella of Perón's personal endorsement and the support of the Peronist movement; in 1975–1976 subversion lost both. In 1972 the country was faced with a prospective *argentinazo* under orders from Perón and with the backing of the CGT, whereas such a prospect was only a remote possibility by the end of 1975. [15] Thus it is unlikely that Videla's policy of state terrorism, which worked after 1975, would have worked against a Peronist resistance in full bloom.

That the issue of subversion was no less central to Lanusse's thought is clear from his memoirs covering the period from the May 1969 *cordobazo* to the military's abdication four years later. The events in Córdoba indicated that Argentina had been chosen by international terrorists for launching a revolutionary war of continental dimensions, a plague of violence that would become, as General Videla later described it, "'the backdrop of all Argentine life.'" [16] But subversion "could not have found conditions propitious for going on the offensive if we [the armed forces] had not committed serious errors." [17] Above all, it was necessary to heal the breach between the armed forces and the general public, hence the imperative of a democratic opening that paved the way for Perón's return—all in the interest of combating subversion.

As Lanusse responded to the threat of what he called "substantial numbers of political immigrants from Nazi-fascism or Trotskyite Marxism," the strategical problem was to detach them from their mass support in the Peronist movement.[18] As long as Perón remained in exile, they would continue to operate in his name. If Perón returned, he would be obliged by his pragmatic calculations and habitual prudence to cast his lot with the reformist trade unions because of their greater political weight. Otherwise, he would die in exile glorifying his armed formations.[19] Lanusse did not underestimate the effect that would have on Argentine society. The worst possible alternative was that Perón should continue in his present role and that responsibility for the brewing civil war should rest not on his head but on the Argentine military.

In a masterpiece of Machiavellian strategy, Lanusse enticed Perón to return if he wanted to be a candidate in the elections, and then challenged him to return if he did not wish to appear a coward. "My intention was that Perón should return, once and for all, to put an end to the myth, to demonstrate . . . that nothing [ill] would happen to the country."[20] As anticipated, Perón's return created conditions for his confrontation with the guerrillas and ended the ambiguity of the resistance by compelling him to define himself.[21] That was how Lanusse undermined the myth of Perón as a revolutionary leader. It took the liberal establishment within the armed forces to set the trap and to call the leader's bluff. Thus the real Perón died in a general's uniform cursing instead of encouraging subversion.

A constant thorn in the side of military liberals, the survival of Peronism has contributed to dividing them into moderates and ultras. Although an ultraliberal from 1955 to roughly 1962, Aramburu metamorphosed into a moderate.[22] This signified a softening in his assessment of Peronism. His successor as leader of the moderates, General Lanusse, was even more firmly convinced of the need to legalize the Peronist party. He disagreed that Peronism was a cousin to totalitarianism and he rejected the ultras' claim that Peronism was incorrigibly subversive. While conceding that the abuses of Peronists in power were intolerable and should be suppressed, he agreed with Catholic nationalists that the national and Christian elements in Peronism had effectively saved Argentine workers from communism.

Because Lanusse believed in overcoming ideological barriers, he made his peace with Chile's president Salvador Allende.[23] Domestically, he stopped short of suppressing subversive ideologies. Rather than dissimulate an artificial unity among Argentines, he accepted ideological differences as the only way of reaching a national accord.[24] Thus he criticized the superstitious, fearful, and conservative anti-Communist law of Onganía's vaunted "Argentine Revolution" for having had an effect opposite the one intended.[25]

As for the defense of Western civilization, Lanusse interpreted it as the defense of liberal governments in the West independent of the religious question and the role of Christian values.[26] A classical liberal converted to the exigencies of the war against subversion, he rejected the corporatist and authoritarian clericalism of the Franco type. Thus he blamed the *franquista* current within the armed forces for "permanently encouraging military coups and proposing, as one of the objectives, the liquidation of political parties and their replacement by corporatist mechanisms."[27]

Lanusse hoped to reorganize the party system in order to overcome the chaotic civic life of previous decades. Toward this end he proposed to limit representation to four or five political currents. "Peronism, radicalism, conservative and centrist liberalism, federalism, and perhaps a moderate form of the legalistic Left."[28] Democratic Socialists and Communists would have the right to form political associations and to participate in political debates, but unless they marshaled the percentage of affiliates required to register under the reorganized rules they would not be recognized as political parties. Presumably, the limitation of political representation to the great currents of public opinion would not make a mockery of elections, as had the proscription of majoritarian parties and recourse to electoral fraud. Since the military would assure clean elections and the "rules of the game" after the elections, those who won could expect to complete their terms of office without the losers resorting to military coups.[29]

Suicide of the West

Although military liberals complain of the exotic character and alien influence of Marxist ideology, their own ideology represents a no-less-alien transposition to Argentine soil of Anglo-Saxon liberalism. On the one hand, it is a carry-over of the traditional British liberalism that gained converts among Argentine intellectuals in the nineteenth century and became institutionalized in the 1853 Constitution. On the other hand, it represents an infusion of cold war liberalism from the United States.

Unlike Catholic nationalists, military liberals looked to the United States for guidance. As General Videla acknowledged: "Argentina belongs to the West and we recognize the leadership role of the United States."[30] In fact, the type of liberalism prominent among Argentine officers was modeled on that of the State Department and the Pentagon: the cold war liberalism championed by Burnham and disseminated in Argentina through the writings of Brian Crozier. A thorough understanding of it is basic to understanding the Military Process.

The confrontation with Soviet communism represents a struggle between opposing civilizations, Burnham argued, not just nations. To the obvious difference between the Soviet Union's economic and political system and that of the nations of Western Europe, he added profound cultural and religious differences. Relying on the work of historian Arnold J. Toynbee, he counterposed Western civilization and its values to those of four other living civilizations: the Far Eastern, Hindu, Islamic, and Orthodox Christian, which includes the Soviet Union.[31] Despite the fact that the economic and political maps of the world have been partly Westernized, the cultural map today is substantially what it was some one thousand years ago.[32] Peter the Great, the Napoleonic Wars, the Holy Alliance, and the influence of Western technology brought Russia into the orbit of Western civilization.[33] However, "the combination of Byzantine, Asiatic and barbarian strains in her culture had prevented her from becoming organically a part of the West."[34]

What is Western civilization? Burnham defined it as the continuous development through space and time, in the center of Western Europe since approximately A.D. 700, of a social formation distinguished by a unique and coherent set of institutions, beliefs, and values.[35] Whatever Russia's relation to the West may have been before the Bolshevik Revolution, at the end of 1917 it became not just separate from but hostile to it. This separateness and hostility Burnham associated with the grotesque closing of the borders: "The new rulers understood their initial territory to be the base for the development of a wholly new civilization . . . destined ultimately to incorporate the entire earth and all mankind."[36]

Rather than the decline of the West, which suggests a psychological or moral judgment, Burnham underscored the West's contraction vis-à-vis the expanding new civilization of Soviet communism.[37] He distinguished two features of this contraction: the end of Western domination over non-Western societies, as in China, India, and Africa; and the eclipse of Western dominion within societies and regions formerly part of the West, as in Eastern and East-Central Europe and, more recently, Cuba.[38] In this perspective, Western civilization has shifted into reverse, having been thrust backward toward the original base from which it began its process of world expansion.

What explains this reversal in the fortunes of the greatest civilization known to humankind? Burnham's answer was that "what Americans call liberalism'"—meaning unrestricted democracy— "is the ideology of Western suicide."[39] As the prevailing ideology in the United States and Western Europe, it supposedly motivates and justifies the contraction while reconciling people to it. No lack of economic resources or of military and political power can explain the contraction, because the United States surpasses the power of the Soviet Union in all major areas, and with the combined resources of its European allies is virtually invincible.[40] The primary cause must be sought in intellectual, moral, and so-called spiritual factors. Burnham reduced them to a failure of nerve, the absence of a will to survive because of a pale and bloodless ideology.[41] Needless to say, that was not the liberalism of the Argentine military.

The liberals' unconditional commitment to abstract right offers no compelling motive to risk life for a powerful ideal.[42] The panacea of continuing progress and perfectibility allows no rationale for sacrifice without the prospect of earthly reward. The liberals' focus on peace and compromise discourages the necessary and efficient use of force against potential and actual enemies. Thus what Burnham identified as the liberal syndrome is incompatible with the moral stamina required for carrying out the responsibilities of empire, the moral courage to kill people "without collapsing into a paroxysm of guilt."[43]

Is there any political faith people are willing to die for? Having begun his political career as a Marxist-Leninist and gone through the ropes of the Trotskyist movement in the United States, Burnham conceded that communism was such a faith. His concern was how to combat it. The defense of the values of Western Christendom appeared to be the only political commitment on a par with what he called the "gigantic ideology of Bolshevism."[44] After his experience with Marxism-Leninism he was not going "to settle for the pigmy ideologies of Liberalism, social democracy, [and] refurbished laissez-faire."[45]

In Western civilization the primary social values, according to Burnham, are liberty, freedom, justice, and peace. By "liberty" he understood national independence or self-government; by "freedom," the rights of the individual to free speech, movement, and association; by "justice," social welfare and the curbing of gross exploitation and discrimination; by "peace," the absence of large-scale warfare among the major powers.[46] The problem was how to rank them.

For nineteenth-century liberalism the standard ordering was a compound of freedom and liberty followed by justice and peace.[47] For early-twentieth-century liberalism until roughly the Great Depression the ranking was justice, freedom, liberty, and peace.[48] For contemporary liberalism, or "democratism," the fear of a nuclear holocaust has resulted in ranking peace first, followed by justice, freedom, and liberty.[49] Thus the overriding tendency has been for freedom and liberty to take a back seat in the scale of Western values, which means there is "nothing left worth fighting big wars for."[50]

For overcoming this failure of nerve, Burnham believed the most effective Western ideology was an updated version of the "older liberalism."[51] In its ranking of the primary social values, liberty holds first place, followed by freedom, peace, and justice. To downgrade liberty, a process traceable to early-twentieth-century liberalism, is to dilute loyalty to the nation and to disavow the uniqueness and superiority of Western values.[52] It means concretely that "patriotism plus Christian faith are to one or another extent replaced by internationalism," that "the 'survival of mankind' becomes more crucial than the survival of my country and my civilization."[53] Thus Burnham sought to revive the ultraliberal values of liberty and individual freedom he associated with the stability and expansion of Western culture in the nineteenth century.[54]

In siding with liberty, Burnham linked the values of patriotism with the defense of Western Christian civilization.[55] Since the fate of one's nation hinges on that of the larger society to which one belongs, the corollary of patriotism is to defend that society come what may.[56] For Burnham that meant a struggle against the threat of atheistic materialism and the desacralizing effects of modern liberalism, which are responsible for morally disarming the West. Thus he defended pre-Renaissance Catholic philosophy against the main line of post-Renaissance thought, of which twentieth-century liberalism is the principal heir.[57]

Because this latter-day liberalism cannot cope with feelings of guilt that afflict civilized beings, Burnham argued, the liberal is morally vulnerable before the spectacle of the sorrows and demands of other, less-fortunate peoples. Consequently, "he often develops a generalized hatred of Western civilization and of his own country as part of the West."[58] It follows that the defense of Western values re-

quires an ideology that can redeem citizens from guilt and its unpatriotic consequences.

Independent of Christianity's claims to truth, "the traditional religion of Western civilization faces the reality of guilt, provides an
adequate explanation for it, and offers a resolution of the anxiety to
which it inevitably gives rise."[59] The only requirement is belief in
the Christian solution of the problem of guilt, whether or not it is
true.[60] This means a commitment to the "interlocked Christian doctrines of Original Sin, the Incarnation and Redemption, which constitute the Christian solution."[61] Since Burnham considered this solution vital to the defense of Western civilization, he relied on it as
an activating myth. Such is the gigantic ideology he believed to be
the only effective counter to contemporary liberalism, creeping socialism, and the prospect of Communist subversion.

Burnham's reaffirmation of a national tradition complemented his
rejection of twentieth-century liberalism. Whereas socialism prepared the way for totalitarianism, liberalism tends toward "Caesarism," or the unchecked rule of the executive.[62] Unlike Catholic
nationalists in Argentina, who found political salvation in military
intervention rather than in the rule of law, Burnham favored a strong
congress reinforced by a system of checks and balances.[63] Thus his
philosophy of government endeared itself to the liberal or moderate
wing of Argentina's armed forces, for whom the word *liberal* stood
for caution and moderation as opposed to the extreme measures advocated by military authoritarians.

It is clear from Burnham's repudiation of Caesarism that he had
little faith in military regimes. Within the emerging technocratic
and managerial society the typical political form is an increasingly
autonomous and pervasive governmental bureaucracy sanctioned
by mass plebiscites. This tendency toward Caesarism, he foresaw,
was "supported by a bureaucratized military and police apparatus,
[which] operates primarily through administrative decree while
using an assembly as recording device and sounding board."[64] Without parliamentary or congressional rule, there can be no defense of
liberty and civil rights. To ask whether Congress can survive is
equivalent to the question: "Can constitutional government, can
liberty, survive in the United States?"[65] Thus Burnham's rejection of
authoritarian solutions reinforced the liberal current within the Argentine military.

In the course of elucidating the different meanings of the word *liberal*, Burnham also contrasted the different uses of the word *democracy*. The strict or etymological meaning, popularized by the French

philosopher Jean-Jacques Rousseau, equates democracy with the un-limited and direct expression of the popular will.[66] But there is an-other more conservative meaning, in which democracy signifies constitutional government based on the rule of law, civil rights, and the indirect expression of popular sovereignty.[67] This is the sense in which Burnham defended it. Although this second meaning has no etymological justification, in England and North America it has come to rival and supplant the first.

This is the sense in which Burnham described Perón's government in Argentina from 1946 to 1955 as essentially non- and antidemo-cratic. He discounted the popular vote for Perón on the grounds that what was essential to democracy was not rule by the majority but due process and respect for civil rights. "We (we in the English-speaking countries, that is) call the totalitarian regimes of our times—the regimes of Hitler, Mussolini, Stalin and Perón—'dic-tatorships.'"[68] Even though Perón did not abolish the Argentine Congress, Burnham believed the epithet was justified because "bu-reaucratic democratism, whether or not fully Caesarian in form, finds a plebiscitary assembly to be an indispensable instrument of its managerial rule."[69]

In this perspective, what was true of Hitler's and Stalin's regimes was also true of the Peronist governments from 1973 to 1976. This negative assessment of mass democracy, or "democratism," as Burnham called it, supported the military liberals' preference for re-stricted democracy and justified their military coup. Paradoxically, even the dirty war could be justified up to a point, as indeed it was in defense of "democracy."

The Credo of Catholic Nationalists

Catholic nationalists shared a different rationale in defense of West-ern civilization. They traced the crisis in Argentine society to a loss of values dating from the Protestant Reformation and the "older lib-eralism" (Locke), in turn responsible for the corrosive effects of de-mocracy (Rousseau). Since these philosophies were the breeding ground of Argentine radicalism, traditional as well as contemporary liberals have come under suspicion as potential enemies of a well-ordered society.

Unlike military liberals, Catholic nationalists are not constitu-tionalists. Their assessment of the 1853 Constitution agrees with that of Leopoldo Lugones: "The Argentine Constitution is the ideo-logical poem of *alienation* [*extranjerismo*]. . . . The present Consti-tution affirms *the free navigation of the country's interior rivers under all flags . . . even during war.''*[70] The British are responsible for this humiliating clause. Far from representing the Argentine people, the Constitution is a continuing insult because of its servility to a liberal ideology imported from Great Britain and the United States.[71] Since Catholic nationalists concur with the need to reform rather than uphold the present constitutional order, they have few compunctions in violating it.

In interpreting Argentine history, they accept the work of historical revisionists in rehabilitating the dictator Juan Manuel de Rosas as one of the country's outstanding patriots.[72] Rosas defended Argentina's sovereignty by closing the principal rivers to British and French vessels. He also represented the interests of the interior provinces against British commercial interests in the port city of Buenos Aires. Defeated by Gen. Justo José de Urquiza with the help of Argentina's arch-enemy, Brazil, Rosas fled into exile in 1852. The Constitution was not his work but that of his Anglophile successors.

The 1930 coup was not an isolated event but wedded to an ideology that would justify the coups of June 1943, September 1955, June 1966, and March 1976. Influenced by his nationalist associates, Uriburu tried to become a new Rosas and to restore the role of the Catholic church in Argentina. His nationalist advisers deplored the alien effects of Anglo-Saxon liberalism on Argentine life, rejected the intervention of the masses in Argentine politics starting in 1916, and longed for a restoration of authority, hierarchy, and discipline. Since they were republicans rather then monarchists, a dictator seemed to be the only remedy for surviving the crisis and saving the country from an irresponsible democracy.

A model was at hand, the solution provided by the Spanish dictator Miguel Primo de Rivera (1923–1930), subsequently imitated by General Franco (1939–1975). A member of the oligarchy and a professional soldier influenced by the church, Primo de Rivera subscribed to the clerical doctrine of *hispanidad*. Based on the informal union of Hispano-American nations under the spiritual leadership of Spain, *hispanidad* aimed at restoring the church's influence, which was being undermined by liberal, democratic, and socialist ideologies. Like Primo de Rivera, Uriburu tried to impose something akin to fascism from above as distinct from Mussolini's fascism from below.[73] But the elitist influence on Uriburu was so strong that, unlike the Spanish dictator, he refused to enlist labor backing for his regime.[74]

Argentine nationalism in its contemporary sense dates from the intellectual movement that fueled Uriburu's military intervention against the Radicals' first experiment in democracy. The precise date of its appearance, says Federico Ibarguren, was the December 1927 founding of the journal *La Nueva República,* directed by Rodolfo and Julio Irazusta and edited by a team that included Ernesto Palacio.[75] Shortly thereafter, the directors and editors supported the efforts of a fellow journalist, Roberto de Laferrère, in organizing the movement's first volunteer militia, the Republican League.[76] The principal representatives of nationalist ideas, the new journal and nationalist militia conspired with General Uriburu to overthrow the Radical government of Hipólito Yrigoyen.

A synopsis of Catholic nationalist doctrine appeared in the journal's first-anniversary edition in December 1928. It urged putting an end to the social and political chaos engendered by democracy. Basically, nationalists believed in subordinating individual interests to the interests of the nation, and individual rights to the rights of the state. As the document explained: "This is enough to distinguish nationalism from the doctrines of political *pantheism,* characterized by the neglect of the essential end of all government—the COMMON GOOD—whose place has been taken by abstract principles: sovereignty of the people, liberty, equality, the emancipation of the proletariat."[77] In place of these abstract principles, nationalists called for a restoration of governmental authority. "Today in all countries *nationalist* movements are committed to the RESTORATION of traditional political principles, of the classic idea of government in opposition to the errors and disastrous consequences of doctrinaire democracy. Confronted with the unsettling myths of demagogues, these movements hold high the fundamental truths that are the life and grandeur of nations: ORDER, AUTHORITY, HIERARCHY."[78]

In keeping with the social teachings of the church, Catholic nationalists hoped to restructure society along corporatist lines. The fascist corporatist philosophy, which inspired Uriburu's coup, received the Vatican's blessing a year later with the appearance of Pope Pius XI's encyclical *Quadragesimo Anno.* The encyclical announced the church's support for the Italian corporative state and the political philosophy of national syndicalism undergirding it. As the pope described the new social arrangement: "The State here grants legal recognition to the syndicate or union . . . [which] alone can represent respectively workingmen and employers. . . . The corporations are composed of representatives of the unions of workingmen and employers of the same trade or profession, and as true and genuine organs and institutions of the State they direct and coordinate the activities of the unions in all matters of common interest. Strikes and lock-outs are forbidden. If the contending parties cannot come to an agreement, public authority intervenes."[79] Despite misgivings about the bureaucratic character of the Fascist state, he acknowledged its advantages: "peaceful collaboration of the classes, [and] repression of Socialist organizations and efforts."[80]

The Vatican had long rejected the liberal philosophy proceeding from the Protestant Reformation in the form of natural law and social contract theories in the seventeenth and eighteenth centuries. The Reformation doctrines of the importance of each person's conscience and the congregational structure of ecclesiastical authority were held responsible for the liberal focus on individual freedom and consent as the basis of political obligation. Common to Hobbes, Locke, Marx, and Lenin is an interpretation of society as a sum of individual wills. Although liberalism and its offshoots differ in their methods, they agree that the happiness of individuals is the supreme good and the state only an instrument.

During the 1930s Catholic nationalists were also drawn to the writings of José Antonio Primo de Rivera. Rejecting the liberal view of society as atomistic, inorganic, and antihistorical, he denied that Spain was the product of a social contract.[81] It was a sacred union of past, present, and future generations, a historical being with its own life and destiny. And by the same token, its purpose was not the happiness of individuals, but the fulfillment of a mission in the world defined by custom and tradition.

It is within the framework of such an organic theory of society that Catholic nationalists criticized the dissolution of the church's influence in the modern world and its replacement by the political philosophies of liberalism, democracy, socialism, and communism. Here too they took their cues from Primo de Rivera's interpretation of Catholic social doctrine. Although the liberal form of government began with enlightened despotism, in which parliament played a subordinate role and represented only the privileged orders, the suffrage later became broadened to include the propertyless masses.[82] But liberals began to cajole and flatter them, to give the people what they wanted instead of what might be best for them. Thus "*Democracy, the daughter of Liberalism, killed its own father!*"[83]

Subsequently, democracy would be killed and buried by its progeny. While capitalists accumulated immense fortunes, they drove millions of others to desperation. "Because matters could no longer go on that way, *socialism* emerged to . . . improve the condition of the proletariat."[84] But it did not stop at that. Demoliberalism with its political parties bequeathed to posterity the legacy of class struggle.[85] This legacy transformed socialism from a movement of redemption into a movement of revenge. Thus the end result was violent revolution and Communist dictatorship.

For Primo de Rivera and his Argentine acolytes the progression from liberalism through democracy to socialism and communism is the history of successive failures to achieve the same basic goal—individual welfare. Liberalism proved disappointing, because left to themselves most people foundered in a condition of misery from which they could escape only through state intervention.[86] Then democracy proved a disappointment, because individuals realized that political equality was not enough and that left to themselves they were ill-equipped to exercise power.[87] Afterward, socialism challenged the capitalist system, which divided people into a minority of exploiters and a majority of exploited and impoverished wage earners.[88] However, it failed to solve the economic problem and swallowed up the individual in the state.[89] So communism came to supplant socialism. But as a logical extension of the same underlying philosophy of individualism, it contributed to the replacement of capitalists by a class of bureaucrats who continued to sacrifice national goals in the pursuit of selfish interests.[90]

Peronism played a part in this sequence but was not what it pretended to be.[91] Perón claimed to have a Christian philosophy of history, but its highlight was not the thirteenth century, when Catholic spiritual and temporal power reached its zenith. Instead, Marxist ideology was an advance over the democratic ideology diffused by the French Revolution, itself a step forward compared to the doctrines of liberalism and individualism engendered by the Protestant Reformation.[92] Although rejecting demoliberalism, Perón did not turn his back on modernity. Besides being tarnished by its lack of concern for social progress, St. Thomas's philosophy was left behind by these developments of the modern world.[93] Catholic nationalists sharply criticized this modernist perspective.

Radical Counterrevolution

Unlike military liberals, Catholic nationalists did not consider their mission to be the defense of liberal institutions threatened by Peronist demagogy, the excessive demands of organized labor, and the guerrillas' revolutionary war. For them the defense of Western civilization signified first and foremost the defense of the Catholic faith against modern liberalism and its democratic, socialist, and communist progeny. Toward that end military intervention had to do more than merely annihilate the guerrillas and pull the teeth of Peronism. It also had to eliminate the liberal virus and prevent the return of the politicians to power. That called for a counterrevolution that would place the military permanently in authority through an alliance of the cross and the sword.

In common with Italian Fascists, Catholic nationalists defined the enemy as liberalism, democracy, socialism, communism, and anarchism. But as Federico Ibarguren noted, with few exceptions they stopped short of becoming Fascists.[94] In contrast to Fascist theory, "artificially generated in a laboratory of intellectuals by the totalitarian and desacralized sperm of the twentieth century, Argentine nationalism was nurtured by the old Hispanic cult of personality fertilized by Catholic tradition."[95]

Federico's father, Carlos Ibarguren, paid tribute to the ideas disseminated by Benito Mussolini, especially the need for strong government to defend the order, hierarchy, and discipline required to counteract the Communist menace.[96] But these ideas were not original to Italian fascism. They had already been spelled out by Charles Maurras (1868–1952), the founder of Action Française and Mussolini's political forerunner. As Carlos Ibarguren recalled: "French culture exercised a powerful influence among us through the mode of action and teachings of the great politician and nationalist Maurras and of Action Française—discounting the monarchist tendency. It provoked a turnabout here that attracted the profound interest of many youths and gave rise to definite political and social tendencies opposed to liberalism and parliamentarism."[97]

That was part of Maurras's appeal. His condemnation of modern political doctrines coincided with the church's animadversions concerning the same ideologies bred by modern liberalism.[98] Cited as heretical by Pius IX in his celebrated *Syllabus of Errors* (1864), those doctrines were denounced by Maurras for the preference they assigned to the interests of individuals over the claims of nation and state. Thus liberals, democrats, socialists, communists, and anarchists occupied the front rank in Maurras's classification of domestic enemies, followed by a second rank of Jews, Protestants, Freemasons, and atheists.[99]

Maurras argued that salvation from these two sets of internal enemies, religious as well as political, was basic to the defense of European civilization. Salvation lay in government by a natural aristocracy, an elite opposed both to a conventional aristocracy and to a democracy of the masses.[100] Convinced that in the absence of monarchy the military would have to intervene against the forces attempting to dissolve society, Maurras called for an alliance of the nationalist intelligentsia and the officer corps—an idea with ominous consequences for Argentina.[101]

Even more ominous than Maurras's influence was that of his Spanish predecessor, Juan Donoso Cortés (1809–1853). The principal inspiration behind Pius IX's *Syllabus of Errors*, Donoso exerted a direct influence on Argentine nationalism through his political writings. Scrutiny of the editorials of *La Nueva República* indicates few references to French influence.[102] Despite its having a column named "Politics" and a section called "Press Review," as Maurras's journal *Action Française* had, "more importance must be conceded to Donoso Cortés."[103]

Maurras's influence was mainly indirect. Virtually all the editors and collaborators of *La Nueva República* had read Donoso and were intellectually indebted to him, which could not be said of Maurras.[104] The Vatican's interdiction of Maurras's thought in 1925 lost him the support of many Catholics.[105] Thus Ernesto Palacio replied to accusations of Maurrasianism: "We cannot subscribe nor do we subscribe to a personality whose doctrine has been condemned by the infallible head of the church."[106]

Donoso had the further advantage over Maurras of writing in Spanish and upholding the cult of *hispanidad*. Although his political thought came under severe criticism by the liberal wing of the church, it prevailed over its rivals thanks to the intervention of Pius IX. Two pieces in particular made an impression on Argentine nationalists: Donoso's speech on dictatorship (4 January 1849), and his speech on Europe (30 January 1850). Coming in response to the rash of European revolutions in 1848 and to the first appearance of communism as an organized political force, these two pieces contain the heart of Donoso's reflections on what Carl Schmitt characterized as the revolutionary "terror" of 1848.[107]

Donoso had the unique distinction, Schmitt said of his Spanish predecessor, of being the "most radical of the counterrevolutionaries."[108] Unlike De Maistre, Bonald, and earlier restorationists as well as later ones like Maurras, Donoso was a political realist convinced that the epoch of monarchy, legitimist succession, and hereditary aristocracies was over. As Donoso interpreted European events, the revolutions of 1848 had seen the emergence of a new phenomenon under the names of socialism, communism, anarchism, atheism, and nihilism, evidence that the final battle in defense of European civilization was at hand.[109]

Confronted with this radical evil, Donoso believed only a dictator could save the world from anarchy,[110] hence Schmitt's assessment of

Donoso as a forerunner of contemporary theories of Nazi-Fascist dictatorship in opposition to the political philosophies of the Restoration.[111] Donoso represented a curious combination of political theologian, who saw in the struggle between atheistic communism and Western Christianity the approach of Armageddon, and cold politician, driven to support Napoleon III's December 1851 coup against a parliament too weak to govern.[112] Donoso's outlook was shared by Argentine nationalists, who also interpreted the struggle between Western Christianity and atheistic communism in apocalyptic terms.

In his speech on dictatorship to the Spanish Cortes, or parliament, Donoso argued that when legal measures could not save society from revolution, then by all means go to a dictatorship.[113] Democratic liberties, he prophesied, were dead. Like monarchy and hereditary aristocracy, the age of parliaments had passed.[114] The class struggles of 1848 presaged the advent of a demagogical and socialist world state, the most gigantic and desolating tyranny in the history of humankind, a prelude to total chaos that only military despotism might check.[115] The choice was simple: either a dictatorship of the "saber," which comes from above, or a dictatorship of the "dagger," which comes from below.[116] This was also the predicament faced by Argentine nationalists.

Donoso's speech made him an international celebrity overnight. It also contained the rudiments of a philosophy of European history. As long as the spiritual power represented by the Catholic church ruled over the temporal power, repression was interiorized.[117] There were few causes for social discontent, and liberty prevailed over strong government. But with the Protestant Reformation and the decline of the church in the sixteenth century, absolute monarchy made its appearance along with standing armies of slaves in uniform. As the church's decline continued, political repression became even more acute, with the creation of republics and an internal instrument of repression, the police.[118] What liberals and democrats esteemed to be liberty in the form of enlightenment and self-government, Donoso believed, was not freedom but a prelude to universal tyranny. In summary, religious and political repression vary inversely; that is Donoso's "law of history," with a European interpretation.[119]

Among the correspondence provoked by Donoso's speech, his letters to Count Charles de Montalembert elucidate the political theology that complements his political realism. In the first of the letters to Montalembert, Donoso claimed that people are so naturally vile, so consumed by original sin, that they can neither know what is good nor have the will to act accordingly even if they had the knowledge.[120] Consequently, "freedom of discussion leads necessarily to error, just as freedom of action leads necessarily to evil." By itself reason is blind and a servant of the passions, which are corrupt. People cannot know their best interests without an infallible authority to guide them, and they cannot will them unless their passions are disciplined by the fear of God. For Argentina's Catholic nationalists, this was the essence of political wisdom.

In a variation on Saint Augustine's *City of God,* Donoso interpreted Western history as a continuing struggle between Good and Evil, between Catholic civilization and its challengers. Since left to themselves people can only sin, the outcome of this struggle is predetermined: "Evil always triumphs over good in this world, while the victory of good is possible only through God."[121] It follows that good can triumph only through a miracle. In Donoso's periodization of world history, three such miracles averted total catastrophe. The first period, from the Creation to the Deluge, would have ended in the complete triumph of evil had it not been for God's direct and miraculous intervention. The second period, from the Deluge to the beginning of the Christian Era, would have ended the same way were it not for the miracle of Christ's Coming. And during the third period, beginning with Christ's Coming, the Final Judgment was "the crown of all miracles."[122]

Donoso's follow-up speech on Europe is important in clarifying the doctrinal statement on Argentine nationalism published in *La Nueva República* on the occasion of its first anniversary. Following Donoso, the editors classified doctrines that neglected the national interest as instances of political pantheism.[123] They were no less indebted to his philosophy of government. Thus it was from Donoso that they derived their secular trinity of "ORDER, AUTHORITY, HIERARCHY."[124]

Fundamental to Donoso's periodization of European civilization is the identification of evil with subversion of the religious and political orders.[125] Sin consists in disobedience, whose political counterpart is revolution. Since sin has become natural to people, revolution will ultimately triumph. Such was Donoso's thesis concerning the decline of the West, to which he added that "all the social forces of Europe together have not sufficed to do more than barely contain the Monster."[126]

It follows that evil is not in governments but in the governed, that "evil appears in the governed when they become ungovernable."[127] On the basis of these premises, Donoso distinguished two successive phases of Western civilization. After an initially positive or vital phase under the leadership of the Catholic church came a negative or decadent phase dominated by revolutions.[128] During the ascending phase people believed that God directly governed the world and that monarchs were his representatives on earth. In contrast, the descending phase negated God's authority and then government's.

The first expression of this negation was deism in religious matters—the doctrine that God reigns but does not govern.[129] Its political corollary was liberalism and a constitutional monarchy in which the king's powers were limited by parliament. The second negation was *pantheism*, the doctrine that God neither reigns nor governs.[130] Its political counterpart was republicanism based on a pantheistlike deification of the general will that makes the people instead of governments sovereign. Finally, pantheism degenerates into *atheism*.[131] Its political equivalent is anarchism.

Europe at mid–nineteenth century, in this interpretation, was entering the second negation of its descending phase. But the atheistic-communist-proletarian elements that surfaced in 1848 indicated that Europe was also en route to the third negation.[132] Although "a republic is a necessary form of government of peoples who are ungovernable," its fate is sealed in Donoso's apocalyptic vision of history.[133] Socialism, which he did not distinguish from communism, represents an advanced form of democracy, which makes it the threshold of anarchy. The triumph of "socialist revolutions" would be followed by the "looting of Europe," the end of patriotism and standing armies, and the dissolution of society into two armed camps: the party of the despoiled, and the party of the despoilers.[134] Europe would become so weakened by this internal strife that it would finally fall prey to Russia, which would then become infected with the revolutionary virus.

In the long run Donoso expected nihilism to triumph over Western civilization and to destroy its temporal and spiritual powers: the state and the papacy. At the same time, he did not believe that Catholics should sit idly by while this catastrophe unfolded. It was their duty to resist subversion as the incarnation of evil and to postpone the demise of Christendom as long as possible.

This called for a restoration of belief in the secular trinity of "Authority, Obedience, and Sacrifice," which presupposes the inviolability of order and hierarchy. Only among priests and soldiers, only in the church and the army did Donoso believe those ideas still carried weight.[135] Consequently, he looked to them as the guardians of European civilization against revolutions and the impending chaos he feared would destroy it.

These were the Donosian ideas adopted wholly or in part by the directors and editors of *La Nueva República* and by General Uriburu, one of its original subscribers.[136] They were also the basis of the nationalists' proposed alliance of the cross and the sword. Thus "Catholic" and "authoritarian" became the defining features of Argentine nationalism, which bears the principal intellectual responsibility for launching the military era. Donoso's ideology also provided an excuse for the mounting crimes of the Argentine military, which culminated in the Military Process. Precisely because the generals looked on revolution as a satanic conspiracy, they considered their mission a holy one.

The Fundamental Enemy

Catholic nationalists interpreted the liberals' defense of modern secular freedoms as playing into the hands of the enemy. It was not enough to defend Western civilization, they argued, without protecting the Western religious and cultural heritage.[137] Indeed, for those in the tradition of *La Nueva República*, which took its cues from Donoso Cortés and Pius IX's *Syllabus of Errors*, the fundamental enemy was the liberal culture of modernity stemming from the Protestant Reformation.

However, some Catholic nationalists believed that behind the ills of the modern world lurked a still more sinister threat to Western civilization. Such was the opinion voiced by among others General Nicolaides, who succeeded General Menéndez as commander of the brutal Third Army Corps in Córdoba after the latter's unsuccessful coup in 1979. In a widely disseminated statement Nicolaides declared that the Marxist monster was meeting with little or no resistance, but that this was not something new. *"The Marxist-Communist International has been operating,"* he claimed in what must have struck most of his readers as a patent absurdity, *"since 500 years before Christ!"*[138]

This was the basic outlook of the *Protocols of the Learned Elders of Zion*, which still finds a wide and receptive audience in Argentina. The *Protocols'* subversive ideas are not limited to Zionism, but also reveal the influence of the Bavarian Illuminati, revolutionary French Masonry, and Marxist notions of a classless society.[139] The Jews were believed to be at the bottom.

In this perspective, Jews rather than Communists were the fundamental enemy. The *Protocols* allude to the prophetic writings in which God chose the Jews to subdue and rule the nations of the earth.[140] It was Third Isaiah (60:11–12) that gave classic expression to this Jewish eschatology: "Therefore thy [Zion's] gates shall be open . . . that men may bring unto thee the forces of the Gentiles, and that their kings may be brought. For the nation and kingdom that will not serve thee shall perish." Written in Palestine about 500 B.C., this prophecy reassured the Jewish people—who had just returned from exile and rebuilt the second Temple in 516 B.C.–that their time had come. That 500 B.C. was chosen by General Nicolaides as the date of launching the "Marxist-Communist International" suggests a Jewish origin and responsibility for the subversion that has plagued humankind ever since.

Catholic nationalists had more solid ground than the *Protocols* for linking Judaism and subversion. The two most influential philosophers behind the Military Process were Father Julio Meinvielle and Jordán Bruno Genta. Meinvielle's works cover such controversial topics as the biblical peoples in their struggle for world domination, the rapprochement between the church and the Third Reich, the Jew in the mystery of history, and Marxist communism in the anti-Christian revolution.[141] Genta, although less prolific, also dedicated himself to diffusing his philosophy among the military. The most influential works for which he is still remembered focus on the revolutionary war and the armed forces' struggle against subversion.[142] Unlike Meinvielle, who died from natural causes in August 1973, in October 1974 Genta received his final reward from an ERP splinter group in retaliation for the Trelew Massacre.

Common to both philosophers is the identification of the high point of Western Christian civilization as the Middle Ages. The spiritual climax is associated with the *Summa Theologica* of Saint Thomas Aquinas (1225–1274), the temporal climax, with the reign of King Louis IX, otherwise known as Saint Louis (1214–1270). Since then, for both of them, civilization has gone progressively downhill.

Meinvielle examined the principal events responsible for this decline: the Protestant Reformation, the French Revolution, and Marxist communism.[143] A critique of this unholy trinity had already become part of official church doctrine. The novel element was Meinvielle's tracing of the origin of these three revolutionary events and ultimate responsibility for each to the collective Anti-Christ he associated with Judaism.[144]

It was bad enough that the Jews had "crucified our Lord." But what also disturbed Meinvielle is that they had been conspiring ever since at destroying Christianity and replacing it with their faith. Their supreme mission, he believed, was to provoke and disseminate social chaos during the entire two thousand years of the Christian epoch.[145] Although Protestantism had an independent origin, the Jews exploited it for their special purposes, as they would later exploit liberalism and democracy.[146] But their principal ideological weapon was Masonry, in turn responsible for the French Revolution. More recently, they had created Marxism. Anti-Semitism is thus the cornerstone of Meinvielle's philosophy of history.

To counteract Jewish influence, Meinvielle recommended fascism as the only viable option for Christians during the 1930s. But some forms of fascism were more akin to Christianity than others.[147] Although Mussolini was a political genius, he could not be trusted because of his pragmatism. German national socialism was even more objectionable for being saturated with paganism. The corporativism of Antonio de Oliveira Salazar, the Portuguese dictator, was profoundly Christian. However, it could not be adapted to Argentina because it was not rooted in uniquely Spanish traditions. Thus the only fascism that qualified was its Spanish variant, the *falangismo* of José Antonio Primo de Rivera, which aimed at installing a Christian national state. The Military Process was infected not so much by Nazi as by Christian anti-Semitism, as developed by Meinvielle in his controversial philosophy of history.

It is worth recalling that anti-Semitism has a built-in rationale from New Testament scripture. The founders of Christianity realized that the survival of Judaism threatened to undermine the church's legitimacy. If the church was really to replace Israel, the Jews had to be discredited, hence the New Testament canonization of anti-Semitism in Matthew 27:25, which lays the blame for Christ's murder both on the present generation of Jews and on all Jews for all time. Matthew puts words into the mouths of Jews present at the crucifixion: "Let his blood be on our heads and the heads of our children."

To this original Christian belief that every Jew is a Christ killer was added a second, hardly less compelling, motive for hatred of Jews. Thus the Gospel of John (8:43–44) explains the Jews' rejection and murder of Christ: "You are of your father, the Devil, and your will is to do your father's desire." Charged with deicide and collusion with Satan, the Jews have ever since been the prime moral and religious targets of Christian animosity. Consequently, when they were linked in the nineteenth century with the spread of revolutionary ideas, the specter of a worldwide Jewish-Marxist conspiracy led to emergency measures directed against them.

The same basic themes recur in Genta's works. Like Meinvielle, his principal obsessions were Judaism and Marxism, to which he added a special preoccupation with Masonry and a passionate hatred of the United States.[148] He believed that America's liberal democratic regime was dominated by Jews and Masons, and that U.S. intervention in World War II had opened the floodgates to Soviet communism. The anticommunism of the State Department was dismissed as superficial, for America's capitalist economic system and demoliberal ideology had, despite the professed aims, indirectly contributed to the spread of subversion.

Does it make sense, Genta asked, to wait for revolutionaries to make the first move? [149] Should they be protected by the Constitution so that they could continue to violate it? On the contrary, the only intelligent response would be to accept their challenge and to reply in kind. To this Genta added that the armed forces had a moral obligation to extirpate subversion.

Here was the philosophical justification the generals had been looking for. They, too, resented the artificial restraints imposed by Congress and by an irresponsible electorate, which had voted the Peronists into power. Genta taught them to reject popular sovereignty as a "satanic aberration" and to disregard its demagogical claims as the "empire of the lie."[150]

In the biographical preface to his political testament, his daughter María Lilia Genta recalls her father's chosen mission of indoctrinating the military for the coming war against subversion.[151] Based on the medieval doctrine of two swords, spiritual power in Argentina would be assigned to the Catholic church and temporal power to the armed forces. This automatically excluded political parties from a role in government. It also paved the way for a "National Crusade" against Argentina's infidels and for a military takeover along the lines of General Franco's assault on the Spanish Republic.[152] Her father's martyrdom did not bring his mission to a close, for the younger generation of officers might still benefit from his teachings.[153]

It may be objected that Meinvielle and Genta's philosophy of history lacks credibility. However, that the written legacy of subversion dates from the Prophetic books of the Old Testament is a matter of fact, not of ideology. Other Christians have traced their origins to Jewish sources and are proud of them. It is a pro-or-con attitude toward subversion that, superimposed on the historical data, is the basis of pro-Jewish or anti-Semitic political ideologies. It was the generals' obsession with eradicating subversion that accounts for their anti-Semitism, not their anti-Semitism that explains their hatred of subversion.

The appeal of Meinvielle and Genta's philosophy may be explained by their focus on Catholic ideology and the alien roots of revolutionary ideas. Such an orientation speaks directly to the military mind. It also speaks to Argentina's predominantly Roman Catholic population. If there is a gigantic ideology in Burnham's sense, one capable of containing the Marxist Behemoth and of making Western civilization worth dying for, this is it.

But are Protestants and Jews really the scourge of Western civilization? Within a Roman Catholic philosophy of history, the fate of Western civilization is tied to that of the church. So it was not unreasonable for Catholic nationalists to identify their enemy with the historical forces that contributed to the contraction of the church's influence. What was unreasonable was their perception of Western civilization as not simply civilization in the West, but Catholic Christian civilization.

Catholic nationalists blamed the spread of anarchist and communist ideas on liberal and democratic permissiveness. But why have those doctrines proliferated mainly where liberal and democratic traditions failed to take root? In the West those doctrines have flourished mainly in Catholic countries where the influence of the Protestant Reformation and its offspring made headway only belatedly, if at all. The alternative explanation is that they are substitutes for the liberal and democratic ideas spawned by the Reformation. Certainly, their diffusion in Catholic countries cannot be explained by the presence of liberal and democratic institutions, much less by the eclipse of Catholic power.

Behind both the Bolshevik Revolution and democratic institutions, Catholic nationalists perceived the insidious influence of the Jew. But Jews are no more responsible for subversion than any other people. Although they provided it with an ideological beachhead in religious scripture, sociological conditions of oppression and exploitation count more heavily than words in explaining the persistence and spread of a revolutionary culture in the West. The Jews cannot be blamed for that. Just as no reasonable person holds the Russian people responsible for the victory and spread of communism in their country, so no reasonable person holds the Jewish people responsible for the presence of subversive ideas among the Jewish community.

It seems that subversion is a global phenomenon characteristic of all civilized life.[154] The higher the level of civilization, the greater are the burdens and the more unbearable the conditions for those living a marginal existence, hence the tendency for subversion to spread with scientific, technical, and industrial progress.[155] It also appears that liberal democracy is a dike against rather than a catalyst of subversion. Communist ideas appear to catch on best where there are no competing liberal and democratic doctrines. For Perón the most effective way to extirpate subversion was to uproot its causes. To some degree both liberalism and democracy have already done so by sapping with reforms the vitality of more radical recipes for change.

7. The Military's "Final Solution"

AMONG THE principal justifications of the military coup of March 1976 was the failure of the Peronist government to quell subversion. Although a state of siege had been imposed since November 1974, the generals in charge of repression felt hemmed in by constitutional restrictions that allegedly played into the hands of the guerrillas. To attack subversion at its roots, they believed, required a total war against not only the two principal guerrilla formations, the ERP and the Montoneros, but also their actual and potential sympathizers. Since the guerrillas refused to wage a conventional war, the military reasoned, the armed forces should use every conceivable means to eradicate them. In such a merciless confrontation, the entire nation had to be geared for battle. This signified the adoption of emergency measures and the suspension of politics as usual.

Anticipations of State Terrorism

In tracing the origins of state terrorism in Argentina, Duhalde has discovered an embryonic form in the first systematic use by the police of explosives against the homes of known opponents of the 1970 military regime.[1] Between 1970 and 1972 a dozen or so disappearances anticipated the methodology that would be applied on a massive scale during the Military Process.[2] State-induced violence did not stop there. It was followed by the navy's massacre of sixteen defenseless political prisoners in the city of Trelew on 22 August 1972 and by the blossoming of parastate terrorism when the Peronists returned to power the following year.[3]

The Trelew massacre fades into insignificance beside the massacre at the Ezeiza Airport on 20 June 1973. In conjunction with security forces, the Ministry of Social Welfare planned to repulse by gunfire any attempt by the Montoneros and the Peronist Youth to occupy places adjacent to the platform where Perón was to address the welcoming crowd on his return from exile. The resulting confrontations cost the lives of more than 200. Although hardly a friend to the Montoneros, Giussani says "there were no indications that they responded to the gunfire."[4] The vast majority of the victims bore Montonero banners. At a clandestine press conference in 1975 their leader, Mario Eduardo Firmenich, placed the number of Montonero casualities at 182.[5]

State terrorism in Argentina took definite shape with the founding of the Argentine Anti-Communist Alliance (AAA). Masterminded by López Rega, it was organized in collusion with police commissioner Alberto Villar, who was responsible for parapolice repression from 1970 to 1972. Financed and armed by the Ministry of Social Welfare, its ranks included not only army officers and police officers on active duty, but also discharged police officers, enlisted criminals, and cadres of the right-wing Peronist Youth of the Argentine Republic (JPRA) and the quasi-fascist Peronist Trade Union Youth (JSP).[6] But ideological motives were not the only ones for joining the Triple A. More convincing than ideological appeals, "each assassination or crime was handsomely paid with funds reserved by the state."[7]

The Triple A is generally believed to have been organized behind Perón's back. It operated anonymously, intermittently, and did not take responsibility for its actions until after his death. However, Perón set a precedent in a classified document submitted by the Peronist Supreme Council to a meeting of the provincial governors on 1 October 1973.[8] This document would be used to authorize the removal of seven Peronist governors, the witch-hunt against the Peronist Left, and the murder of hundreds of Peronist militants.

The text contains sections worthy of a Torquemada.[9] Part one, "Situations," sketches the systematic but undeclared state of war launched by terrorist and subversive Marxist groups against the Peronist movement and its leaders. The war reputedly had taken several forms: first, a campaign of slander with the aim of ridiculing Peronist leaders and making them appear as traitors to General Perón; second, the infiltration of Marxist groups with the double objective of radicalizing Peronist doctrine and placing themselves at the head of the mass movement with the support of the Peronist Youth; third, threats and aggressive actions aimed at creating a climate of fear among Peronist cadres; and fourth, the assassination of outstanding Peronists.

Part two, "Directives," lists the measures for confronting the internal enemy, so that anyone who refused to collaborate might be separated from the movement. An intense campaign would be launched to reaffirm the general principles of Peronism and to clarify its fundamental differences with Marxism. The various organizations and sectors identified with Peronism would be asked to define themselves publicly in the war against subversion. During this state of emergency any criticism or questioning of the directives of the movement and government emanating from General Perón would be censured, and anyone linked to Marxism and its political positions or public demonstrations would be excluded from the party's organizations. Propaganda by Marxist groups presented in the name of Peronism would be prohibited, while participation in any actions favorable to such groups or even their toleration would be considered grounds for expulsion.

All of the foregoing measures were within the framework of the law. However, the "state of war" ceases to be a metaphor when one considers that "all means of struggle should be utilized that are considered effective according to each place and opportunity."[10] Who judges their effectiveness? That is left to the leaders in each district. Here we have a license for the expulsion of political infiltrators and their physical elimination.

At a cabinet meeting in January 1974 López Rega proposed to organize death squads—the future Triple A—but Perón vetoed the proposal.[11] Even so, the foregoing document clearly justifies them provided they are effective. Aware that they could boomerang and drive the Montoneros underground, which is precisely what happened after his death, Perón was reluctant to sanction such emergency measures. But that did not prevent López Rega from organizing the Triple A while Perón was still alive.

Because Perón could not rely on the armed forces, he had a reason for supporting the clandestine organization of the Triple A with government patronage and police protection. "The operations of repression required a special force . . . , because to facilitate the intervention of an alien force (the army) would place the government sooner or later in the hands of the military."[12]

Behind the sudden ascension of López Rega from first sergeant to general commissioner of the federal police was the hand of Perón. That, and the subsequent appointments in February 1974 of Alberto Villar as assistant chief of the federal police and of Luis Margaride as chief of federal security, contributed to making the police a willing accomplice of the Triple A.[13] Militarily weak and isolated, Perón had no other choice in combating subversion than to build a secret army with police recruits under police direction.

The Montoneros were quick to hold López Rega responsible for creating the Triple A. But could preparations for parapolice terrorism have taken place without Perón's knowledge and approval? His interests were being served by antisubversive commandos, and he did nothing to disarm them. He was ultimately responsible for their existence, for their operations, and for the disappearances that were not the invention of the Military Process.[14] The efficiency and impunity with which the Triple A subsequently acted is evident from the figures cited for the first seven months of 1975: 450 assassinations and 2,000 disappearances.[15]

The witch-hunt launched by Perón in October 1973 is reminiscent of Hitler's purge of the Nazi left wing in June 1934 and Mussolini's purge of left-wing Fascists in 1935, when those clamoring for socialism were forcibly registered as "volunteers" in the Ethiopian war. They also recall Stalin's purges of 1936–1938. In my interview with Firmenich, he alluded to Perón's assimilation of the strong-arm methods of Stalinism as well as Italian fascism. As the Lenin of Argentina's misnamed national revolution, Perón continues to be revered by the Montoneros. But he also played the part of Stalin in ordering the purge of the Peronist left wing.

The Triple A was not the only form of state terrorism mounted from within a Peronist government. On 5 February 1975 the government authorized the direct intervention of the armed forces against the spread of rural subversion. In a decree signed by Pres. Isabel Perón and her entire cabinet, the armed forces were directed in Article 1 "to carry out the military operations considered necessary to neutralize and/or annihilate subversive elements active in the Province of Tucumán."[16] This amounted to a carte blanche to proceed with emergency measures.

The resulting military intervention was the first to be undertaken in accordance with U.S. counterinsurgency measures, including torture and assassination.[17] "For the purpose of 'isolating' the guerrillas and discouraging their support by the local population, civilians were 'taught a lesson' by means of torture, kidnappings, and firing squads in the towns bordering the zone of operations."[18] Such measures were sanctioned by the presidential decree and took the form of civic actions and psychological warfare taught in the counterinsurgency program in the Canal Zone: "The Ministry of Social Welfare shall apply, in coordination with the Ministry of Defense (General Command of the Army), the necessary measures of civic action to the population affected by military operations" (Art. 5); and "The presidential press secretary shall apply, at the indication of the Ministry of Defense (General Command of the Army), the corresponding psychological measures that are needed" (Art. 6).[19]

In conformity with this decree, the armed forces launched their dirty war in Tucumán. Precisely there, between February 1975 and April 1976, occurred the first massive experiment in state terrorism, including secret concentration camps, illegal detentions, kidnappings, and torture of civilians.[20] The "Little School of Famaillá," on the outskirts of the town by that name, was selected to be the first concentration camp of this kind. It would become the model for several hundred other camps scattered throughout Argentina.

The stage was accordingly set for the governmental edict of October 1975, in response to the Montonero assault on the army garrison in the capital of Formosa. With Pres. Isabel Perón on sick leave, the initiative was taken by Acting Pres. Italo Argentino Luder. This second decree provided legal justification for spreading the system of state terrorism to the entire national territory.[21] Thus state terrorism associated with the Military Process had an alleged constitutional sanction going back to the last Peronist government.

Tactics of the Dirty War

To appreciate the difference between the military governments of 1966–1973 and 1976–1983, I shall briefly review the military's unique response to the wave of subversion that crested during the government of Isabel Perón but was subsequently eradicated by the Military Process.

The totalitarian controls imposed by the first military junta (1976–1978) aimed at intimidating the entire Argentine people.[22] In the name of combating subversion any number of Argentines might reasonably be eliminated, affirmed General Videla.[23] The obsession with rooting out subversion accounts for the thousands of disappeared persons, most of whom would be considered innocent by any standards other than those of the military assassins in power. Although some three thousand guerrillas met their death in the torture chambers of the armed services, to this figure may be added another seven thousand executions and from ten thousand to thirty thousand civilians who disappeared—a margin of error unimaginable unless it was deliberate.

How many did the military disappear from 1975 until after the dirty war officially ended? On assuming office, President Alfonsín ordered a full investigation of the atrocities. The National Commission on the Disappearance of Persons, chaired by Ernesto Sábato, documented 8,960 disappearances, but the list did not include the unreported and did not take into account the survivors' wish for anonymity.[24] The principal human rights groups and organizations of the Left estimated a number more than three times higher, rounding it off at 30,000.

Although this figure might appear exaggerated, at the Chacarita Cemetery in the nation's capital the number of cremations rose from 13,120 in 1974 to 15,405 in 1975, then jumped abruptly to 20,500 in 1976 and to over 30,000 per year in 1977, 1978, and 1979, falling back to 21,381 in 1980.[25] Considering the abrupt jump in 1976 and the nearly matching figure for 1980, it is a fair guess that the number of cremations of those dead from natural causes averaged around 20,000 per annum during the intervening years. In that case the number of illegal cremations may well have reached the 30,000 mark—in a single cemetery.

Notorious among the methods for disappearing political prisoners (today a transitive verb in Argentina) was the so-called transfer.[26] Prisoners were subjected to a form of triage, sorted out according to the danger they represented as political activists. If a prisoner had engaged in armed operations in factory or other takeovers, he or she was counted more dangerous than one who had merely distributed pamphlets or painted walls with subversive inscriptions. Beginning in 1978 activists classified as irredeemable were permitted to have visits from their families, while false expectations were created that they would be freed. Subsequently, they were informed of the decision to transfer them to another camp. To assure their cooperation, they were injected with an ostensible tranquilizer that gradually rendered them unconscious. Unable to resist, they were loaded into trucks and transferred to their final destiny: to be hurled into the sea from military airplanes or to be murdered in open fields and special camps built for that purpose.[27]

The repression of virtually all civilian opposition to military rule was something new in Argentina. Torture was revived on a scale hitherto unknown for extracting information from the guilty and instilling terror in the innocent. A clandestine state was erected parallel to the official one, with its own intelligence services, invisible "task forces," and some 340 secret detention centers.[28] Prisoners were hooded or blindfolded during interrogation, their torturers operated under false names, and the authorities denied any knowledge of or participation in these clandestine operations.

The fundamental question is whether any other methods might have proved effective. On this issue military liberals as well as authoritarians coincided. In the war against subversion, they believed, torture was an indispensable condition of victory. The urban guerrillas of the ERP and the Montoneros were under strict orders to reveal nothing until after twenty-four hours had elapsed. This would give their comrades the opportunity to be alerted, to change their identities and locus of operations before being detected. Their typical response when apprehended was to give a declaration that lasted a minute or so, and to repeat it under further questioning. The military had to loosen their tongues before the twenty-four hours expired or their comrades could regroup.[29] Without torture, the ERP and the Montoneros would have continued to launch armed actions. They might have been contained, but not eradicated. That was the military consensus concerning the matter. The justification for torture was a simple one of saving innocent lives. It was a question of trade-offs.

That the military's final solution was really the trump card that made victory possible is confirmed by the guerrillas' accounts of demoralization in the wake of the 1976 coup. If one accepts the claims of the Montonero high command, then only one percent of those taken captive collaborated with the enemy. But this figure is based on earlier estimates, before the imposition of the Military Process. Later, it appeared absurd.[30] From an operational standpoint, the rapid dismantling of guerrilla cells suggested a much higher degree of demoralization. According to one assessment: "This moral deterioration in front of the enemy is a common denominator not only of the Montoneros, but also of the combatants of all the armed organizations in the country, because they too have the same cause"—the defeat brought on by the Military Process.[31]

Besides losing their rear guard, the guerrillas suffered from a sense of impotence and insecurity because they were no longer able to move about "like fish in water." The Military Process gradually undermined their confidence in victory, and when that began to fade, nobody wanted to die for a losing cause. In most cases the betrayal of trust was the result not of moral weakness, but of a realistic appraisal of events—the isolation of the guerrillas and their increasing lack of outside support.[32]

In the conviction that the annihilation of the guerrillas was assured and that no amount of personal sacrifice could stop it, those taken prisoner had no reasonable alternative but to defend their lives in any way they could.[33] Between 1976 and 1978 some six thousand guerrillas were imprisoned in the two largest concentration camps in the capital. But of these "only 5 percent fell because of military intelligence or chance; the other 95 percent because of direct or indirect collaboration."[34]

The military doctrine of the "final solution" was developed by the heads of the three armed services in September 1975. Following the replacement of the Peronist commander of the army, Gen. Alberto Numa Laplane, by Gen. Jorge Rafael Videla in August, military leaders agreed on a secret pact for launching full-scale antisubversive warfare. At the same time they resolved to topple the government of Isabel Perón and to assume total control of the state.

Perhaps the most vocal defender of political genocide was General Camps. Besides identifying the enemy with international subversion, he likened the struggle against subversion to that of Nazi Germany against its own "red menace." Because he took pride in having disappeared some five thousand Argentine citizens in his jurisdiction, he was asked if he was an admirer of Adolf Hitler. Camps replied: "With Hitler I coincide on several points. For example, my humanist concern to save humankind and to struggle against the permanent Communist campaign full of lies."[35]

Duhalde presents a synopsis of Camps's thought. The highlights are the general's characterization of Marxism as the fundamental enemy and the struggle against Marxism as a global one in which the most important field of battle is the conquest of humanity.[36] Although the subversives were defeated militarily, they had yet to be conquered ideologically. "The West lacks the will to victory," because "we are ashamed of our ideals and actions," and because "we end by apologizing for having triumphed."[37] Because the tactics of the dirty war were for the most part repudiated, Camps believed most Argentines lacked the will for national survival.

What, then, was the remedy for this ailment that was leading the West to moral suicide? Camps's answer was to dirty one's hands: "Whoever participates in the war against subversion with the will to win must 'cover himself with mud.' This concept of 'covering oneself with mud' means that the war against subversion is equipped with a new methodology. . . . Everything learned in the manuals and rules of war had to be revised and its application reassessed, since the objective of subversive warfare is not what is considered natural."[38]

Such a strategy began to be applied with Operation Independence against the rural guerrillas in Tucumán in February 1975. Following a secret agreement to take the offensive in September and the extension of the struggle throughout the country in October, the military overcame the last impediment to its strategy by overthrowing the constitutional government. By then the generals realized that the French strategy of counterinsurgency was more viable than the North American, for the "French aimed at a global conception and the North Americans at an exclusively or almost exclusively military response.[39]

This peculiarly Argentine strategy and its origins were described by Peregrino Fernández, a former member of the police corps in the Ministry of the Interior, in a 1 April 1983 declaration in Madrid before the Argentine human rights commission, Comisión Argentina de Derechos Humanos (CADHU). The former policeman attributed the new "Doctrine of War" not only to those the press called military hard-liners, or hawks, but also to army moderates, or doves, such as Gen. Jorge Rafael Videla and Gen. Roberto E. Viola.[40] The final edited version of the "Doctrine of War" was said to be the work of Gen. Cesáreo Cardozo, director of the Superior War College. The doctrine was subsequently approved by the navy and air force, and then made official in the Order of Battle of 24 March 1976.

According to Fernández's testimony, the new doctrine was expounded in detail in a meeting at army headquarters in April 1976, attended by the army's former commanders in chief and retired generals. Basically, it consisted of four points: first, the physical elimination of subversives; second, an ideological orientation rooted in the defense of tradition, family, and property; third, the implantation of generalized terror among the population to prevent the guerrillas from "moving like fish in water"; and finally, the policy of disappearances systematically enforced after the coup.[41]

Concerned about the negative response of the international community to repression under the Franco regime, the military hesitated to resort to mass executions. Since the Argentine people were not prepared for thousands of deaths by firing squads, the generals could not publicly assume responsibility for what might look like political genocide. They preferred a policy of clandestine disappearances, which leaves relatives guessing about the fate of victims, permits unlimited torture with impunity, facilitates the massive application of the death sentence without trial or need of proof, covers up errors, avoids denunciations by victims who turn out to be innocent, frees the government of responsibility for such practices, enables the church to support the military authorities, and dissuades the population from protesting against atrocities because of the generalized climate of fear.[42]

Following his release in 1981 after two years of being disappeared inside the notorious Naval Engineering School, Escuela de Mecánica de la Armada (ESMA), lawyer Martín Gras explained in detail the military's policy of physical extermination.[43] In successive dialogues with his captors he learned that the armed forces aimed to eliminate anybody with a project for social change contrary to their conception of a natural social order. Victory against an enemy that wore no uniforms and occupied no definite space had to violate accepted norms of legality and human rights. To preserve the clandestine apparatus of the armed forces, it was especially necessary to prevent the disappeared from ever reappearing. It was to be a total war not only against the immediate enemy, identified as subversives, but also against those institutions and ideologies that nourished and sustained them.[44]

Targeting the Victims

By "subversion" was understood considerably more than the armed operations of the ERP and the Montoneros. As defined by Gen. Roberto Viola and Brig. Gen. L. A. Jáuregui in a press conference in April 1977, *"subversion is any concealed or open, insidious or violent action that attempts to change or destroy a people's moral criteria and way of life, for the purpose of seizing power or imposing from a position of power a new way of life based on a different ordering of human values."*[45]

This definition acquired general currency within the armed forces. General Videla claimed that "a terrorist is not only someone with a gun or bomb, but also anyone who encourages their use by ideas incompatible with Western Christian civilization."[46] In this perspective the guerrillas constituted only the tip of the iceberg, below which it became imperative to dig out and expose the civilian elements directly and indirectly responsible for social unrest. Although both Videla and Viola had the reputation of being liberals or political moderates, on this issue they found themselves in agreement with Catholic nationalists and military authoritarians the likes of Gens. Luciano Benjamín Menéndez, Ramón Díaz Bessone, and Carlos Suárez Masón, notorious for their "excesses."

There is ample evidence that the generals of the Military Process, liberals as well as authoritarians, had resolved on a final solution to the subversion problem. First, subversion was likened to a highly contagious social disease that had to be eradicated. Second, those infected by the bug of subversion automatically lost their right to citizenship. Third, victims of the infection were considered incorrigible. Last, the accompanying ideas and feelings of resentment and social discontent were intolerable. For all these reasons those slated for extermination included the carriers of the germ and those directly exposed to it as well as those already infected.

Among the curious features of the military's targeting of subversives is that it exempted the Triple A and other right-wing terrorists. They became allies of the armed forces in the struggle against the common enemy. As Rear Adm. César A. Guzzetti expressed the prevailing military view, subversion must not be confused with terrorism.[47] Subversion is pathological, whereas the terrorism that combats it is the healthy reaction of a sick body to the guerrilla germs. Right-wing terrorists were only "antibodies," he observed, in no way comparable to the "microbes" of subversion. Once the pestilence came under control and was exterminated, the actions of these antibodies would presumably cease. There was no reason for the armed forces to turn against right-wing elements. They were healthy; the subversives were the sick ones.

The victims of this social disease were considered aliens. As the commander of the Rosario police announced on the force's 123d anniversary, the life and death struggle with subversion was not exactly comparable to the feud between Cain and Abel: "One cannot and should not recognize the Marxist subversive terrorist as a brother. It is not enough that he be born in our country. Ideologically, he has forfeited the right to call himself an Argentine."[48] President Videla also said as much: "I want to clarify that Argentine citizens are not victims of the repression. The repression is against a minority that we do not consider Argentine."[49]

Subversives were considered unsalvageable. Gen. Cristino Nicolaides declared in no uncertain terms that the "individual who has fought and is committed to subversion *is a delinquent, for me, incorrigible.*"[50] Again, the implication is clear. If unsalvageable, subversives can never become useful citizens. As long as they are alive they will continue to infect others and even their prison guards. Ergo, they must be eliminated. As Col. C. A. Castagno summarized the position of the armed forces, the death of subversives was preferable to their trial and imprisonment: "There is only one form of victory, support for the regular army in the conviction that the delinquents (subversives) cannot live with us."[51]

The meaning of subversion was broadened to include not only overt acts, but also the ideas and feelings inspiring them. To the ordinary classification of crimes was added the bizarre category of ideological criminals. Said Rear Adm. Rubén Jacinto Chamorro: "We cannot allow a miniscule minority to continue perturbing the minds of our youth, inculcating ideas completely alien to our sense of nationality *with an artfully distorted interpretation* of Christian doctrine. All that is subversion."[52] Such sentiments led President Videla to characterize former president Héctor Cámpora as an "ideological criminal."[53] Gen. Adcel Edgardo Vilas also took a dim view of Marxist efforts to influence people's minds, adding that ingenuousness as well as indifference toward the Marxist phenomenon implied "complicity with subversion."[54]

In this perspective, one can understand the final solution proposed by Gen. Ibérico Saint-Jean: "First we will kill all the subversives; then we will kill their collaborators; then their sympathizers; then . . . those who remain indifferent; and finally we will kill the timid!"[55] Since this list covered a majority of the Argentine people, it reinforced the already generalized climate of fear. Nor was Saint-Jean alone in favoring a system of generalized terror. Said Gen. Carlos Suárez Masón: "Faced with the advance of Marxism's *total* operations, it is imperative to have an integral response. . . . It would be absurd to think that we have won the war against subversion just because we have eliminated its armed threat."[56] The next step would be to eliminate its unarmed cadres.

It is remarkable that not even Hitler dared to express such sentiments and that the final solution in Argentina would be directed not against another people with an alien religion—the Jewish nation—but against blood brothers and fellow Catholics. At the same time, there is reason for believing that Hitler's final solution to the Jewish question, as well as the Inquisition's final solution to the heresy problem, strengthened the generals' resolve to launch their own inquisition.

Heritage of the Inquisition

The Montoneros and their allies were among the first to publicize the heritage behind the concentration camp society run by the three branches of the armed services. Rodolfo Walsh, the eminent novelist and essayist who became a captain in the Montonero army, likened the tortures without limit and executions without trial to the persecution of heretics during the Middle Ages. "The absence of habeas corpus has been complemented by the unrestricted use of methods going back to epochs that operated directly on the joints and internal organs of the victims, today with surgical and pharmacological auxiliaries unavailable to the executioners of old. The rack, the wheel, the flayings and suffocations of the medieval Inquisition reappear in contemporary questionings together with the electric prod and the 'submarine.'"[57] The day after he decried these atrocities in his "Open Letter to the Military Junta" (dated 24 March 1977), three army tanks demolished his home in the capital's suburb of San Vicente and disappeared him as well.[58]

The papal Inquisition launched in 1233 and by the Spanish Inquisition in 1478 had set a precedent for the generals' solution to the subversion problem. The fires of the Inquisition had been only momentarily extinguished. As the vice-secretary of the Montoneros'

Cultural Branch of Intellectuals, Professionals, and Artists, Dr. Holver Martínez Borelli, wryly commented: "The Military Trinity that takes hold of Christian symbols and the armature of the Inquisition to officiate the bloody liturgy of a new despotic-salvationist crusade . . . inscribes the cross and the sword on the horizon of the dominant ideology, and in its shadow translates the liberal contradiction 'civilization or barbarism' into 'Western Christian civilization versus unpatriotic and atheistic Marxism.'"[59]

The comparison of the Military Process with a witch-hunt was not farfetched. Torture in the process of interrogation was authorized as early as 1252 by Pope Innocent IV, although death was the exception until the papal inquisitors began appealing to the secular authorities for help in stamping out witchcraft. The identification of witchcraft with heresy or religious subversion was formulated definitively in the writings of the thirteenth-century Scholastics, for whom all magical practices involved an implicit pact with the devil.[60] The inquisitors were unaware that witches were devotees of a pre-Christian religion that should have exempted them from the charge of heresy.[61] Rather than being heretics or internal enemies of the church, they were nonbelievers in the same sense as Jews and Muslims who refused to convert. A similar mistake was made by Argentina's latter-day inquisitors, who insisted that "Marxism is the heresy of the modern world."[62]

The Military Process succeeded the Spanish Inquisition. Unlike the witch trials in North America, witches were not the only or even the principal targets of the Spanish Inquisition and death and torture were not the only punishments. In 1492 the Inquisition was responsible for expelling some two hundred thousand Jews from Spain. The Spanish Inquisition came to the New World on Columbus's second voyage in 1493. Later it extended to Mexico (1532), Lima (1539), and Buenos Aires (1610). In Buenos Aires judicial torture and banishment were used in a campaign to quash all "Jewish" influence. The Inquisition in Latin America also sought to control undisciplined clergy and to keep out Protestantism. In Argentina, as in Spain, the principal victims appear to have been Jews who formally accepted Christianity but who were suspected of apostasy, not those who held fast to their religion.

The immediate prelude to the systematic extermination of heresy was Pope Innocent VIII's bull in 1484. Besides authorizing the bishop of Strasbourg to threaten with excommunication all who hindered the Inquisition, Innocent VIII named two Dominican "hounds of the Lord," Heinrich Kramer and James Sprenger, as inquisitors in special proceedings against witches. They published a text in 1489, *Malleus Maleficarum* (Witches' Hammer), justifying both torture and genocide as a final solution to the heresy problem.

In his introduction to the 1928 edition of the *Malleus*, Montague Somers notes that the subversive ideas of witches and heretics were fundamentally the same as those of Lenin and Trotsky.[63] To the abolition of monarchy and order were added the abolition of private property and inheritance and the total annihilation of religion. Historians may point out dissimilarities in the teachings of the heretical sects, but they were "in reality branches and variants of the same dark fraternity, just as the . . . Anarchists, the Nihilists, and the Bolsheviks are in every sense, save the mere label, identical."[64] Heresy, Somers claims, was "one huge revolutionary body . . . , witches were a vast political movement, an organized society which was antisocial and anarchical, a world-wide plot against civilization."

It was against this complex conspiracy that the Inquisition had to fight. So "who can be surprised if, when faced with so vast a conspiracy, the methods employed by the Holy Office may not seem—if the terrible conditions are conveniently forgotten—a little drastic, a little severe."[65] As if this justification of the torture and annihilation of heretics and subversives throughout Europe and the Americas were not enough, the Reverend Doctor adds: "There can be no doubt that had this excellent tribunal continued to enjoy its full prerogative and the full exercise of its salutary powers, the world at large would be in a far happier and far more orderly position today."

Infused with an acid dose of misogyny, the *Malleus* warns against the sinister role of women in undermining established institutions: "Nearly all the kingdoms of the world have been overthrown by women."[66] Like the subversion and related heresy problem, the problem of women lies in their refusal to be governed.[67] For over three hundred years in Western Europe and America some nine million women were burned at the stake by the Inquisition and its Protestant equivalent on charges of witchcraft.[68] This figure is the one most often cited by scholars in the field, with the extermination ratio of female to male witches somewhere between 20:1 and 100:1. Thus the final solution to the heresy problem included "gynocide" as well as genocide.

The persecution of Jews and witches for heresy did not exhaust the heritage of the Inquisition. Protestants, too, were deemed heretical in a legacy extending from the Council of Trent (1545–1563) to Pope Pius IX's *Syllabus of Errors* (1864). So were modern rationalism, liberalism, democracy, socialism, and communism. Crucial for understanding the final solution to the subversion problem proposed by Catholic nationalists, it was this legacy that inspired General Franco's crusade and won converts among the Argentine military.

In support of Franco's crusade, Pope Pius XI issued his encyclical *Atheistic Communism* (1937). While Pius IX drew the world's attention to the de-Christianizing of modern society as a consequence of modern liberalism, Pius XI concentrated the Vatican's fury on the Communist outcome. The millennia-old struggle between good and evil, he pontificated, had as its contemporary focus the struggle against the "persistent enemies of the Church who from Moscow are directing the struggle against Christian civilization."[69] Wherever communism had asserted its influence, as in Mexico, it had striven to destroy Christian civilization and the Christian religion.[70] Having failed to usher in the promised classless society, subversives had turned to "the only possible substitute . . . terrorism."[71] Thus Pius XI reaffirmed the church's position on heresy, which had been systematized by Pius IX: "Communism is intrinsically wrong, and no one who would save Christian civilization may collaborate with it in any undertaking whatsoever."[72] The Catholic nationalist wing of Argentina's armed forces was indebted to this encyclical.

There is a clear and unbroken line of descent from Pope Innocent VIII's bull in 1484 to Pope Pius IX's *Syllabus of Errors* and Pope Pius XI's encyclical on apostasy in the contemporary world. It is the heritage of the Inquisition behind Donoso's claim that Catholic Christianity constituted the only civilized order, and that there could be no middle ground between it and the church's enemies. Protestantism became the successor to earlier medieval heresies, followed by liberalism, democracy, socialism, and communism. In this perspective, rebellion against church authority ultimately led to the subversive doctrines spread by the Russian Revolution of October 1917. Given the doctrinal continuity between the credo of Argentine nationalists and Donoso's teachings, the ideological roots of the Military Process may be traced to the heritage of the Inquisition.

Ironically, subversives are also indebted to this heritage. Not for nothing did the anarchist Pierre Joseph Proudhon challenge Donoso to rekindle the bonfires of the Inquisition.[73] Subversives were philosophical allies of Donoso in the struggle against the same enemy represented by the combination of liberalism and democracy.[74] Their thinking was dominated by the same finalities, the same sharp antitheses of authority and anarchy, repression and subversion.[75] What was formerly couched in the language of political theology as the showdown between true religion and heresy was now expressed as the final confrontation between the forces of order and social revolution. In terms that apply equally to both sets of contestants, "Donoso's singular importance lies in having grasped—in an ambience of ideological dishonesty and in an epoch of relativizing dissolution of political concepts and antagonisms—the central notion of all great politics . . . the great, historical, and fundamental distinction between friend and enemy."[76] As Mao formulated the fundamental political question: "Who are our friends? Who are our enemies?"[77]

Carl Schmitt, Donoso's principal German interpreter, made a distinction helpful in understanding the military's behavior. What Good and Evil are to morals, Beautiful and Ugly to esthetics, and Profitable and Unprofitable to economics, Friend and Enemy are to politics.[78] The mistake of liberals is to have confused political with other categories, to have "transformed the enemy, from the economic side, into a competitor, and from the ethical side, into a debating adversary."[79] On the contrary, friend and enemy "obtain their real significance from their relation to the real possibility of physical killing."[80] War is thus the consummation of politics. Such is the specifically political legacy of the Inquisition, the legacy of the "final solution" in a fight to the finish, which dominated political thinking during the Military Process and the revolutionary war leading up to it.

The Nazi Example

The specter of heresy and apostasy depicted by Pius XI helps to explain why the Argentine generals revived not only the practices of the Inquisition, but also those of Nazi Germany. According to General Camps, the Argentine military came of age when it added elements of its own to the counterinsurgency doctrines of the French and North Americans.[81] These went beyond the nearly unlimited legal apparatus for handling "emergencies" such as the death penalty, military in place of civilian courts, and the centralization of all security forces under military control. In addition to the legal sanctions for hunting down subversives, the Military Process relied on a secret and illegal apparatus of repression—a "secret state" parallel to the legal one.[82]

Under the supreme authority of the military junta and its de facto president, these two states frequently operated at loggerheads. In the secret state the repression of subversion knew no limits; everything was permitted in dealing with subversives, regardless of the consequences to the innocent.[83] If the legal state ceased to have any jurisdiction over the life and security of the victims, it was because they had been secretly apprehended and subsequently disappeared.

Such was the Argentine military's unique contribution to counter-insurgency warfare. But was it original? The official state's refusal to acknowledge the repressive actions of its parallel organs of security conformed to Nazi techniques in the German zones of occupation.[84] Thus a decree of the Wermacht's chief of staff, the so-called Night and Fog Decree (12 December 1941), sanctioned the disappearance until the end of the war of anyone acting against the reich.[85] Such persons were to be secretly confined and physically isolated in concentration camps without contacts with the outside. The victim having disappeared, there could be no legal recourse for securing his or her release. As Marshal Keitel, chief of the German high command, announced in 1942: "The prisoners shall *disappear* without leaving traces . . . [and] no information shall be released concerning their whereabouts or destiny."[86] But in Argentina, as in Germany, everything became known—"there was no Night and Fog." There was the "great silence," the passive acceptance of the inevitability of violence that transformed the bulk of the nation into an "accomplice."[87]

The Argentine generals also revived Nazi techniques directed against Jews. They considered Jews to be carriers of values subversive to the dominant institutions of the West. In Argentina the persecution of Jews would become a restricted case of the struggle against subversion.

Timerman identifies the extremists or Catholic nationalists in the armed forces as the "heart of Nazi operations in Argentina."[88] There was no question about their anti-Semitism or their acceptance in principle of "the final consequences of Fascist ideology: physical extermination of whoever is considered the enemy . . . the Final Solution."[89] Timerman was saved from disappearing only because the Nazi-minded generals hoped to exploit him as the key witness in their trial against the "international Jewish conspiracy."[90] He believes that a wholly irrational connection existed between the generals' war on subversion and their hatred of Jews: "When the extreme Right combats its natural enemies, its most hated object is the Jew. . . . Its natural enemy is the Left, but its target of hatred is the Jew."[91]

Timerman raises a crucial issue seldom discussed by other commentators on the Military Process. Why did the officers who interrogated him hate Zionism more than communism and consider Israel to be a more dangerous enemy than the Soviet Union?[92] Behind their superficial explanation that communism was more visible than Zionism and therefore easier to detect, he perceived a "reincarnation of Nazi phobias."[93] Their prejudices had been fanned by a reading of the notorious *Protocols of the Learned Elders of Zion*, allegedly by a Jewish infiltrator in the secret inner circle of French Grand Orient Masonry at the turn of the century.[94]

Timerman's interrogators believed that Israel, isolated in a hostile Arab world, needed money and political support from other countries to survive.[95] Toward that end, Zionists had supposedly conspired to create three power centers abroad on which Israel depended for protection.[96] One was the United States, where Jewish money had enabled Jews to acquire political influence. Another was the Soviet Union, where the Kremlin was allegedly still dominated by the Judaized sector of the Communist party, which had played a leading role during the Bolshevik Revolution. The third center of power was Argentina, especially the Patagonian heartland, where Zionist leader Theodor Hertzl had originally planned a Jewish homeland. Considering that New York City and Buenos Aires had more Jews than Tel Aviv, there was a superficial logic to these claims. But again, who would take them seriously who had not been influenced by Nazi ideologues in Argentina?

Most commentators on the Military Process find the generals' anti-Semitism to be too bizarre, fantastic, and irrational to dwell on. Timerman may have exaggerated its importance because he is a Jew and personally suffered from the recrudescence of Nazi ideology since World War II.[97] Yet the issue is central to an accurate understanding of the thinking of Catholic nationalists in the armed forces. To Timerman's credit, he focuses on this concealed dimension of the military iceberg, dismissed by other commentators.

What Timerman overlooks is the specifically rational connection between anti-Semitism and the struggle against subversion. The origin of the hatred of Jews, as persuasively documented by Dennis Prager and Joseph Telushkin in *Why the Jews?* boils down to fear and hatred of Judaism—a religious ideology subverting the core values of Christian civilization.[98] The mere existence of Jews during the past two thousand years, which is to say, their refusal to accept Christ as the Messiah, is perceived as a continuing challenge to the veracity of Christianity.[99] Although hatred of Jews has often reached excessive lengths, the authors believe that it is not irrational or pathological but a reasonable response to an ideological threat.[100]

Since Hitler believed the Jews carried subversive values with them and discharged those values in hostile political ideologies that threatened the fabric of Western civilization, his "Final Solution" to the Jewish question was his final solution to the subversion problem.[101] "It was not the hatred of the Jews as a race that animated the foremost evangelist of radical antisemitism. He hated what the Jews stood for and their success in overturning others' values."[102] In this respect, the Nazis' hostility toward Jews was based on fact. As the authors, both Jews and one an ordained rabbi, conclude: "Only something representing a threat to the core values, allegiances, and beliefs of others could arouse such universal, deep, and lasting hatred."[103]

That Nazi anti-Semitism is tied to hatred of subversives is evident from Hitler's portrait of the Jew in *Mein Kampf*. Because Jews lack the equivalent of the Christian's faith, because they do not believe in survival after death, their cherished Talmud aims to prepare them not for the hereafter but only for success in this world.[104] Therein lies the Jewish content not only of capitalism, but also of Marxist ideology, the professed objective of which is expropriation of the expropriators. With infinite shrewdness the Jew "fans the need for social justice . . . into hatred against those who have been better favored by fortune."[105] Among the Jews' presumed weapons of disintegration are Freemasonry, the liberal press, and the Marxist trade unions and political parties.[106] Thus the Jew works systematically at revolution.

There was a close connection between Hitler's response to the subversion problem and his plans for the solution of the Jewish question. *"In Russian Bolshevism we must see the attempt undertaken by the Jews in the twentieth century to achieve world domination."*[107] Hence the crusade against bolshevism required a corresponding war against international Jewry. That Hitler had plans for the simultaneous and final solution of both questions is evident from what transpired. Indeed, the systematic destruction of European Jewry began during the final week of June 1941, "within hours of the invasion of the Soviet Union."[108]

For evidence that Hitler's anticipated solution to the Jewish question was modeled on his earlier solution to the subversion problem, consider the concluding chapter of *Mein Kampf*. There he laments that Germans went down to bloody defeat in World War I, because "in 1914 and 1915 we did not proceed to trample the head of the Marxist serpent once and for all."[109] In the course of the war German workers became increasingly demoralized by Marxist international propaganda, perceived as playing into the hands of European Jews lacking a homeland of their own. "If at the beginning of the War and during the War twelve or fifteen thousand of these Hebrew corrupters of the people had been held under poison gas . . . , the sacrifice of millions at the front would not have been in vain."[110] Hitler's solution originally applied only to those Jews who were also Marxists, but as potential allies of international bolshevism, all Jews were eventually slated for extinction.

If Jews had not existed they would have had to be invented. Much the same may be said of the devil, the personification of heresy and subversion. As General Camps testified: "What we are witnessing is the present act in the permanent war between Good and Evil."[111] In the general's imagination, God and the devil are still contending for supremacy. Because the Jews were accused of deicide, they had supposedly consorted with the devil, who alone had the power to murder Christ. In twentieth-century Argentina a substitute for the Jews was found in the new Marxist heresy, which satisfied the same human craving for a symbol of radical evil.

Liberal Complicity in the Crusade against Subversion

As a comparatively mild version of Hitler's final solution, the response of the Military Process to subversion had the overwhelming support of Argentine liberals. Although Jews were under suspicion, they were considered "recoverable." But others were not. The role of liberals in the Military Process departed drastically from liberal opposition to Hitler's policies in Germany. German liberals took no part in and refused to defend Nazi atrocities. Argentine liberals, represented by the Radical party and Frondizi's MID, backed their country's dirty war. Thus those who took exception to the hatred of Jews had few if any qualms concerning the emergency measures applied against subversives.

What is remarkable about the composition of the first and second military juntas is that the dirty war was carried out under the direction of military liberals. General Videla and Admiral Emilio Eduardo Massera dominated the first junta until they reached the age of official retirement in July 1978. Although Videla continued as president, his place on the second junta was taken by General Viola and Massera's position was filled by Rear Adm. Armando Lambruschini, both of whom were liberals.

Liberals continued to dominate the military government after Viola was succeeded as army commander in chief by General Galtieri and the second junta gave way to a third. But unlike his army predecessors, Galtieri's liberalism was only skin deep. In September 1981, when Lambruschini retired in favor of the Catholic nationalist Adm. Jorge Isaac Anaya, Galtieri began to show a different face. With President Viola incapacitated by a heart attack, Anaya and Galtieri conspired to replace him.

The liberals managed to hang on after Gen. Horacio Tomás Liendo, a liberal of the same stamp as Videla and Viola, was picked by the junta to serve as provisional president during Viola's illness.

But he lasted barely three weeks. The first coup within the Military Process came on December 11. With the backing of Catholic nationalists Galtieri obliged Viola to resign. Since Liendo refused to continue as provisional president until Galtieri could be sworn in formally, he was replaced by retired admiral Carlos Alberto Lacoste. Thus the first serious fissure in the armed forces saw the emergence of Catholic authoritarians as the hegemonic wing, until a second coup some six months later restored the liberals to power.

Galtieri became president on 22 December, but unlike his liberal precursors his backing by Catholic nationalists allowed him to continue as army commander in chief. In this key role he dominated the third military junta, which turned from internal to external aggression until his bungling of the war over the Malvinas/Falklands led to a second palace coup on 17 June 1982. By a vote of seven to three, the senior generals resolved to end the war and oblige Galtieri to resign. General Cristino Nicolaides was chosen to replace him as the army's top commander. Admiral Anaya was asked to resign, but the navy refused to accept his resignation.

Unable to reach an agreement concerning Galtieri's successor, the senior generals picked Gen. Alfredo Saint-Jean, not to be confused with his Catholic nationalist brother, Ibérico, to serve as provisional president. This precipitated a political crisis responsible for the withdrawal from the junta of the navy and air force. Not until July 1 was a semblance of harmony restored when liberal general Reynaldo Bignone was appointed president by the army alone. Thus the liberals ultimately reasserted themselves in the wake of the disastrous handling of the war, which was blamed on the authoritarians.

From this account it should be evident that military liberals rather than Catholic nationalists dominated the Military Process during the early years, when the war against subversion was at its height. The civilian court that passed sentence on the nine members of the first three juntas in December 1985 concluded that the main responsibility for the repression rested with the liberals. Thus Videla and Massera were given life imprisonment, while General Galtieri and Admiral Anaya were acquitted of charges of repression— although they had to answer to other charges.

Evidently, it had been a mistake to correlate military liberals who called themselves political moderates with doves. From 1975 onward the moderates had posed as doves but were really hawks. The liberal Videla had not minced words when in an address to the Eleventh Conference of Latin American Armies in Montevideo and in anticipation of the military coup he declared: "As many persons must die in Argentina as are necessary to guarantee the country's security."[112]

As matters turned out, political moderates were moderate about everything except the need for repression. General Alejandro Lanusse typified the old school of military liberals, but his type had since been replaced by the likes of General Videla. Lanusse believed in operating within the constitution and the rules of armed warfare. Apprehensive about the turn of events in 1975, he sought to dissuade the armed forces from their project. Hence his warning in November: it is necessary to restore order, but not the order of the cemeteries; it is necessary to achieve peace, but not at the cost of a bloodbath.[113] It is difficult to square this view of an earlier generation of army liberals with the selective genocide advocated by Videla.

Yet one of Videla's principal defenders was also one of his victims. Jacobo Timerman so whitewashes the conduct of the president that the excesses committed during Videla's government appear not to have been his responsibility. Although the central government was dedicated to peace and understanding, Timerman believes that military extremists organized the zones under their control so that they became virtual warlords with their own systems of justice and methods of torture and repression.[114] Despite international pressure, the central government was powerless to free prisoners who had fallen into their hands. As Timerman sums up the predicament of the so-called moderates at the helm, the clandestine state and the parallel system of repression, torture, and disappearances were entirely beyond their control.[115]

The moderates, Timerman believes, represented a minority within the armed forces, whose official leadership they retained solely by virtue of their political intelligence. Kidnapped in April 1977, he was tortured and imprisoned by the extremist sector of the army and tried by a special war council for complicity in an international Jewish conspiracy. But in September the war council ruled there was no evidence of guilt and therefore no existing grounds for detention. President Videla and army commander Roberto Viola tried to secure his freedom. Despite their efforts, he was held under house arrest for another two years.

In September 1979 the Supreme Court of Justice for the second time declared that Timerman should be released. Again the generals conferred and agreed by a broad majority to overrule the Supreme Court's decision. They also tried to compel the justices to resign. It took the president's own threat to resign to induce the army to free Timerman.[116] But it complied on its own terms by illegally stripping him of his Argentine citizenship, confiscating his property, and deporting him. Nor was that the end of the Timerman affair. Furious over President Videla's intervention, General Menéndez staged a military rebellion in Córdoba aimed at expelling the liberals from power—a forty-eight-hour bloodless uprising that failed.

This account of a fundamental split between army liberals and Catholic nationalists is disputed by the French journalist Jean-Pierre Bousquet. He rejects Timerman's characterization of the two currents in the armed forces, the "Pinochetists," disposed to a bloodbath, versus the "legalists," concerned with restoring democracy.[117] As evidence, he cites a speech by Gen. Santiago Omar Riveros to the Inter-American Defense Council on 13 February 1980. Speaking for his fellow nationalist officers, Riveros said they were fed up with Videla's and Viola's hypocritical pretense of being doves.[118] The repression had been based on a carefully elaborated and systematic plan that the generals were ordered in writing to execute down to the last detail. According to Bousquet, there were no warlords or private military jurisdictions. Nor was there a parallel state that operated independently of the official one.[119]

Who is one to believe? Frontalini and Caiati let the generals speak for themselves. Their compilation of statements by the protagonists of the Military Process demonstrates that the dirty war was planned from the top and that Videla and Viola were responsible for its excesses.

8. Resistance to the Military Process

THE MILITARY Process was the Argentine military's systematic response to the Argentine question. It had three principal objectives: restructuring the economy with a view to reversing the slump since 1930 and restoring Argentina's greatness; overcoming political instability by taming organized labor and its political instrument, the Peronist party; and rooting out subversion by intensifying the dirty war. In each of these areas it ran into insurmountable obstacles. Its experiment in economic liberty ruined many of Argentina's large and small businesses by making them compete in an open market dominated by cheap imported goods. Organized labor showed its political teeth, the Peronist party recovered its nerve, and in conjunction with other social forces compelled the military to abdicate. And in response to the dirty war, the guerrillas shifted gears by joining the unarmed resistance.

Although temporarily successful in achieving its immediate objectives, the military had to give up before reaching its ultimate goals. As one astute observer notes, the Argentine military has made political failure a way of life. "In 1930 Uriburu was forced by Justo to give up his corporatist adventure before it had really begun; Aramburu gave way to Frondizi in 1958, a politician whom he did not trust; Illia was never the first choice of the Azules [military liberals], who supervised the election in 1963; and the last thing that Onganía wanted in 1966 was to see his 'revolution' ended by Juan Perón's election seven years later."[1] The Military Process was merely the latest episode in a series of fiascos going back to 1930.

The generals' mismanagement of the economy and blundering over the Malvinas/Falklands seriously disrupted the unity of the military party. But internal divisions were not the only cause of the military's abdication in 1983. The key political factor was resistance. First, there was the armed resistance, important mainly for its indirect effects, such as pushing the military into breaking the laws, deflecting the repression of organized labor onto itself, and catalyzing the resistance of human rights groups. Second, there was the youth resistance supported by the revolutionary vanguards that shifted from military to civil resistance. Third, and most important, there was the trade union resistance supported by the banned and dismantled political parties. Together they were the straw that broke the camel's back.

Was There a Resistance?

The claim of a resistance is still widely disputed. For most Argentines the youth resistance evokes memories of the ERP and the Montoneros, thus qualifying as urban terrorism rather than resistance. Argentina's youth, sectors of the political Left, the Mothers of the Plaza de Mayo, the Relatives of the Disappeared and Detained for Political Reasons, and the combative sector of the trade unions are said to confuse resistance with something else—if not delinquency, then the right of peaceful opposition. Resistance during the Military Process was out of the question, we are told, because of the systematic character, magnitude, and intensity of the repression. The pervasive fear of being tortured and disappeared supposedly paralyzed the will to resist.

Could there have been resistance without the people's recognized leaders at least calling for it? They chose dialogue instead of confrontation. The Peronist and Radical parties supported the war against subversion. The guerrillas were vilified not only by the established parties, but also by leaders of organized labor. Nor was there any feeling of gratitude toward those who risked their lives in the struggle for a democracy that has since persecuted and sentenced their leaders to long years in prison.

At issue is not simply the definition of "resistance." For the most part, both the guerrillas and their antagonists adhere to current usage. Most Argentines believe there was a difference of kind as well as of degree between the 1956–1973 resistance and opposition to the Military Process. That is precisely the rationale for not applying the same name to both.

The first political conversation I had on returning to Buenos Aires in January 1985 reaffirmed the prevailing opinion. On visiting the headquarters of Raimundo Ongaro's Printers' Union (FGB), I asked the new vice-secretary of organization, Osvaldo Villaflor, for his assessment of the resistance. "What resistance?" he retorted. "There wasn't any!" There had been no resistance, he explained, for two reasons: first, because of the systematic character, intensity, and magnitude of state terrorism, the extent of which had never been seen before in Argentina; second, because of the complicity of Peronist political and trade union bureaucrats, who welcomed the dirty war and refused to support a strategy of armed struggle. Resentful of the guerrillas for destabilizing the government of Isabel Perón and for provoking military intervention, most Peronist leaders publicly repudiated them. What they objected to was the military's classification of Peronists as "delinquents."

State terrorism had become so horrendous and pervasive that the masses of workers, according to Villaflor, became cowed by the recognition of their impotence. There was virtually nothing anyone could do against the military's "task forces," which were infinitely more effective than the Triple A. The vicious cycle of detention, torture, confession, and new detentions so crippled the guerrillas that their leaders had to retreat into exile. Unlike the 1956–1973 resistance, the armed struggle petered out and had no popular resonance.

Trade union opposition to the dictatorship stopped short of resistance, Villaflor claimed, because it was limited to narrowly economic objectives. In sum, what the Montoneros and their sympathizers interpreted as a continuation of the resistance of 1956–1973 was disputed by the trade unions, the major political parties, and virtually everybody else.

Why, then, had the military abdicated? I asked. "If it were not for the bungling of the 1982 war over the Malvinas," Villaflor answered, "they would still be in power." It was only after the humiliating defeat by the British that a crisis occurred within the armed forces, aggravated by pressure from the established political parties for a return to constitutional government. But such opposition without economic sabotage, much less armed actions, Villaflor observed, was not enough to constitute resistance.

My final question was whether the Military Process had succeeded in its objective. "It aimed to accomplish two purposes," he replied, "to suppress armed subversion and to break the Peronist monopoly of the popular vote." Evidently, it had succeeded in doing both.

It is curious that Villaflor's assessment from the political Left coincides with that of José Martínez de Hoz, the hated civilian economy minister during the first five years of the Military Process. As Martínez de Hoz commented in a December 1983 interview: "The years of the Military Process were not in vain. . . . Thanks to it, terrorism was defeated and we had the political and social peace necessary for elections."[2] In view of the massive vote for the Radical party in October 1983, people wanted a change from the incompetent Peronist governments of the past. Since without the military regime the Peronists would still be in power, he concluded, the generals performed a legitimate service to their country by overriding the constitutional government.

Villaflor's skepticism concerning a second edition of the Peronist resistance is shared by other political observers. The modernizing dictatorship that called itself the "Argentine Revolution" (1966–1970) was swept aside only after popular uprisings in Córdoba, Rosario, Cipolletti, and elsewhere, while mobilizations of workers and students backed by new guerrilla organizations created a state of emergency for the political system. "In contrast, in 1983 no political or social force could reclaim the laurels for the collapse of the Process of National Reorganization, which reigned for six years without significant resistance and destroyed itself in measuring forces with Great Britain."[3]

However, this assessment is disputed by Ongaro. In a letter from exile to me in January 1977, he outlined the strategy of resistance to the Military Process: "No regime or government can last if one succeeds in annulling the simple reproduction of capital and its profitability for the owners of the means of production—a law we learned less from books than from experience."[4] He had in mind the 1976 work stoppages and sabotage aimed at damaging the capitalist economic structure as a method of bringing down the superstructure. Even then economic paralysis and ruin were serving as levers in a resistance whose long-run objective was to pressure the military to abdicate. When I interviewed Ongaro in January 1985, he claimed success for this strategy.

Carlos Saúl Menem, while governor of La Rioja, also claimed there was a significant resistance and that without it the armed forces might still be in power. "This democracy was not just the gift of a military regime crushed by war in the Malvinas; we Peronists achieved it ourselves, by struggling in the streets."[5] He then added a personal note: "On the thirtieth of March 1982 I was in the street along with the General Confederation of Labor, and again I was imprisoned and a badly beaten victim of repression. There are not many Radical leaders who can say as much."[6] Although many Peronists lacked a clear policy for confronting the regime's violations of human rights and apparently collaborated with the Military Process, "in reality we occupied the front line of the resistance."[7]

Sharing Menem's positive evaluation of the resistance is former Peronist labor lawyer Alvaro Abós. Granted that some labor leaders maintained close relations with the military in a continuing, almost promiscuous, dialogue, these "collaborators" represented only one face of organized labor. In Abós's judgment there was another sector that actively resisted repression. "Every trade union movement has two faces, one that contests and the other that dialogues. . . . That duality was reiterated during the period 1976–1983. Organized labor operated on two fronts, one of confrontation with the regime and the other of conciliation . . . branches of the same trunk. One raised its fist and the other occupied the spaces that the confrontation made available."[8]

Following an army's division of labor, the vanguard concentrated on harassing the enemy while the rear guard covered its back and defended already occupied territory. The subtle interrelation of these two arms of the labor movement, Abós adds, became especially clear toward the end of the Military Process, when both began to cooperate openly and then regrouped in a single reunified CGT in January 1984.

Which was the more consequential wing of organized labor? That question, as Abós interprets it, is tantamount to asking: "Why did a regime, which concentrated such immense powers as did the military dictatorship installed in 1976, return the government to civilian rule?"[9] Part of the answer, he believes, is that during even the worst hours of persecution there were always "embers of resistance that, when the circumstances became propitious, burst into open rebellion."[10] In the end it was the confrontational wing of organized labor that hegemonized the march of events to become the protagonist of a resistance and the principal antagonist of the Military Process.[11]

Abós concedes that the first significant act of mobilization took three years to prepare, because the generalized climate of fear initially paralyzed instead of propelling the resistance. The culmination came with the general strike of April 1979. From then on "the trade union resistance relied on the general strike . . . and massive street mobilizations."[12] But those were not the only symptoms of resistance. During the same three-year period there were 170 other strikes, 300,000 work stoppages demanding wage increases, and more than a billion and a half work-hours eroded by slowdowns.[13] That was no mean feat in the face of a repression the likes of which had not been seen since the terror of Nazi concentration camps during World War II.

That the trade unions came up against a wall of steel, that their struggle acquired momentum only by fits and starts, explains why the Peronist leadership did not undertake the kind of resistance it had against earlier dictatorships. Although General Perón could freely issue instructions for armed struggle in 1956, Isabel Perón was

imprisoned on the eve of the 1976 coup and was not released until
July 1981. During the first resistance Cooke and other members of
the Tactical Command were detained in November 1955, but managed to escape from the Río Gallegos prison in March 1957. Confined to military prisons in 1976, however, the top Peronist political
and trade union leaders remained there throughout most of the Military Process.

Since Isabel Perón was incommunicado, the leadership of the
movement was informally assumed by Deolindo F. Bittel. As governor of the northern province of the Chaco, he had been elected to
replace Angel Robledo as first vice-president of the Justicialist party
less than three weeks before the coup. From prison he assumed strategic leadership of the nascent opposition to the Military Process.
This made him the counterpart of John William Cooke, who had
played a similar role in 1956.

But what a contrast! Cooke, the fiery *porteño*, represented the
Peronist left wing; Bittel circumspectly represented the party's center. Cooke championed the Peronist armed formations; Bittel denounced the Peronist Youth as subversive. Cooke launched both the
armed and popular resistance against the dictatorship from prison;
Bittel did neither.

Bittel outlined his position in a letter from prison to a fellow Peronist on 20 June 1976. The fundamental problem posed by the military coup, he wrote, was the restoration of national unity beginning
with the unity of the armed forces and the working class.[14] The way
to achieve national unity was, first, through a multiparty (*multipartidaria*) alliance and, second, through a multisectoral (*multisec-
torial*) alliance representing the principal organized groups in Argentina. To this he added that it was not the time for thunder but for
dialogue.[15] In effect, Bittel was as far removed from Cooke as the Peronist labor bureaucracy was from Ongaro. Such was the legacy
of Perón's bloodless revolution, but it was not the legacy of the
resistance.

In the same letter Bittel noted there was still no letup from the
guerrillas. With few exceptions the leaders of the Peronist movement had supported and continued to support the armed forces'
countrywide campaign against subversion, which had been signed
into law by the late Peronist government. Bittel was no less committed to repressing the guerrillas than the military. His differences
with the junta hinged on other issues: the unconstitutional character of the coup, the illegal imprisonment of Peronist leaders, and the
proscription of the Peronist party.

Not that Bittel rejected resistance or even armed resistance in principle. On the contrary, in *Qué es el peronismo* he recalled his own clandestine activities after being imprisoned from October 1955 to May 1956.[16] By "resistance" he understood the meaning assigned to it in General Perón's letter to Cooke dated 12 June 1956, an intense struggle in space and time demanding that all, at every place and moment, become combatants against the military regime.[17] He acknowledged the use of bombs and sabotage by Peronists who believed in the tactics of "terrorism," yet he condemned neither. The irony is that he believed armed violence to be illegitimate in 1976, but not twenty years earlier, when it could count on Perón's blessing.

The heads of the Peronist trade unions were no less reluctant than Bittel to have their opposition qualified as "resistance." As victims of the government's campaign of ideological purification, they were intimidated into equating resistance with subversion and both of these with terrorism. Certainly, they could not afford to be charged with all three.

The trade union response from 1976 to 1983 was perceived as neither a revival nor a continuation of the Peronist resistance of 1956–1973. Even those trade union figures who surged into positions of leadership because of their intransigent line—such as Saúl Ubaldini of the Brewers' Union and Roberto García of the taxi drivers—dared not, for reasons of prudence, characterize their struggle as a second edition of the earlier resistance. For Peronists to have characterized their opposition as resistance would have been tantamount to politicizing it, thereby opening themselves to the charge of subversion.

In current usage *resistance* is defined as an organized movement, often underground, of opposition to a government or occupying power perceived as oppressive.[18] Perón added that when resistance becomes collective it is also—economically, politically, and militarily—"intense" and "widespread."[19] But opposition does not have to satisfy all of Perón's conditions to qualify as resistance. Trade union resistance may occur independently of armed resistance and vice versa. As Firmenich observed during my interview in the Villa Devoto Penitentiary on 14 March 1985, the labor upsurge of 1975 was an example of resistance against a formally constitutional government. Consequently, if 1975 was a year of resistance, so was 1982, for the defeat in the Malvinas/Falklands so discredited military rule that labor leaders openly challenged it on political as well as economic grounds.

The year of the "social explosion," 1982, witnessed massive labor mobilizations, marches, and demonstrations in March, September, and December. The third general strike against the military's economic policies differed radically from the two earlier ones in April 1979 and July 1981 in being almost 100 percent effective. Whereas the earlier strikes were separated by more than two years, the general strike of December 1982 was followed by a fourth in March 1983 and a fifth in October. That there were three general strikes in less than a year testifies to mounting opposition to military rule.

But by then little survived of the original Military Process. Following the defeat in the Malvinas/Falklands and the palace coup of June 1982, the third military junta was dissolved. The Military Process came to an inglorious end with the appointment of Gen. Reynaldo Bignone as Galtieri's successor on 1 July 1982. Bignone was designated president by the army after consultation with the major political parties, but without the participation of the navy and air force. The repressive measures of 1976–1982 gave way to a restoration of the electoral process that included the right of virtually all political groups to organize, demonstrate, publish, and distribute their literature. Leading military figures publicly accused of misconduct and of disappearing persons with impunity began to be detained. A general strike and march by the Mothers of the Plaza de Mayo were declared illegal, but they were not repressed. Meanwhile, the number of political disappearances and assassinations dropped to a mere handful.

The mass media attributed the erosion of the Military Process to the armed forces' lack of military as well as economic credibility. But without the resistance leading up to the social explosion of 1982, there is little reason to believe the military would have abdicated. Mass resistance to the regime had already mushroomed before the armed forces launched their battle against Britain. The takeover of the islands appears to have been a last, desperate effort by the discredited junta to garner popular support on the pretext of fighting colonialism.

The Argentine economy was in ruins. Owing to a series of major bankruptcies in 1980, a financial panic ensued. The foreign debt had remained at around $8.5 billion during the early years of the Military Process, but by March 1981 it had jumped to some $25 billion— from a modest 14 percent to over 40 percent of the GDP. Consequently, even before Argentina's defeat in the South Atlantic, the military's economic bungling had contributed to broadening as well as escalating resistance to its continued rule.

By mid-1981 the leading political parties began pressing their demands for a return to democracy. The *multipartidaria* came into being in July. An association of political organizations suspended by the Military Process, it consisted of the Radical, Peronist, Intransigent, and Christian Democratic parties along with former president Frondizi's Movement of Integration and Development. The formation of the *multipartidaria* paved the way for the second general strike, followed in November by the first protest march, led by Saúl Ubaldini with the backing of organized labor. When one considers these three events together, it appears that the deepening of the resistance dates back at least six months before the social explosion (*estallido social*) of 1982.

Unlike the 1956–1973 experience, the 1976–1983 resistance began with armed struggle wedded to a revolutionary war. But with the constitution overridden, the guerrillas became its defenders. They also concentrated on mobilizing a popular counterforce to the illegal dictatorship. By 1977 this strategy prompted the Montoneros to downgrade their revolutionary war to the status of armed resistance. Then, when armed resistance failed to elicit popular support and was effectively annihilated, they switched from armed to unarmed resistance. Meanwhile, the trade union resistance had gotten under way and was continuing under its own steam. Although there was nothing comparable to the combined labor and armed struggles of 1969–1973, trade union resistance continued uninterrupted throughout most of the years of military rule.

The Argentine experience has added a new concept to our political lexicon. First used in connection with the French Resistance to Nazi occupation during World War II and subsequently applied to the Algerian Resistance to French occupation, the word *resistance* came to mean an organized struggle against foreign intervention on behalf of political independence. The less-familiar Argentine resistance, with a small "r," began with the massive opposition to the 1955 coup against Perón and gave the word a different twist. During the ensuing eighteen years the word came to mean a popular struggle against pseudoconstitutional as well as unconstitutional regimes. Later, its meaning was broadened to include resistance to the government of Isabel Perón. Although formally constitutional, her government gave free rein to illegal death squads while instructing the armed forces to eradicate subversion by questionable means.

To end where I began in my conversation with Villaflor, it is evident that he understood by resistance not only massive strikes, slowdowns, and sabotage by organized labor, but also simultaneous armed struggle. On the assumption that trade union and armed struggle must be conjoined, opposition to the military government stopped short of resistance. But common usage does not require their conjunction. It is in this sense that one can speak of resistance not only to the Military Process, but also to the Peronist government that preceded it and the transitional government of 1982–1983, which opened the way to democracy.

From Armed Struggle to Political Resistance

In the still comparatively sparse literature on the armed resistance, too much attention has been given to the guerrillas' military reversals and not enough to their political effectiveness. It is assumed that their resistance ceased once they gave up the armed struggle. But that is not how they assessed their routing on the battlefield.

Paradoxically, those who argue that the guerrillas provoked the March 1976 coup—in the sense that without armed subversion the military would not have intervened—also claim that the guerrillas had virtually no effect in catalyzing the popular resistance. This raises the thorny question of why the guerrillas were consequential in provoking military intervention but inconsequential in resisting it.

Considering that popular support for the guerrillas in 1974–1975 made them a threat to the military, why did it not also contribute to making their resistance effective? The usual reply is that the guerrillas became isolated after the 1976 coup, owing to the scope and intensity of the repression. However, popular backing for armed operations is not the only index of impact. As long as the guerrillas operated militarily, the generals and admirals had to deal cautiously with organized labor. Fear of a repetition of the 1969 *cordobazo* dissuaded the armed forces from accelerating their repression against the trade unions as long as the guerrillas remained a threat.

The military hesitated in formally abolishing the CGT—its greatest blow against organized labor—until November 1979, after the guerrillas had been decisively defeated. It is hardly a coincidence that it waited until the Montoneros were out of commission before launching its final assault on the trade unions. The coup by quotas in 1975–1976 took less than a year to complete. Why then did the taming of organized labor drag out until the end of 1979? The most convincing answer is that armed resistance deflected attention away from the trade unions.

Although the guerrillas suffered serious reverses, including the destruction of a sizable part of their logistic apparatus in 1976, they made headway in other areas. Politically, their campaign of eliciting support for the resistance from the social democratic parties and human rights organisms in Western Europe and the Americas was a success. Even in 1977, when it became evident that armed actions were progressively less frequent and the ERP definitely defeated, the Montoneros "maintained their activity in the form of urban terrorism, domestic and international propaganda, and political intrigues."[20] Thus not until the end of 1977 did the defeat of the armed resistance appear imminent.

The armed resistance came to an abrupt end when in 1979 the Montoneros' long-awaited counteroffensive resulted in the almost total annihilation of their returning troops. Encouraged by the prospect of the first general strike against the military regime in April, the Montoneros concluded that organized labor's retreat since March 1976 was about to turn into an offensive.[21] As the Montoneros perceived the situation, the workers were finally fed up and ready to take to the streets. To bolster the workers' fighting spirit and to maintain their momentum, the Montoneros planned to synchronize months of preliminary agitation and a new wave of armed operations with the anticipated labor explosion.

Up to this point the Montoneros had relied on armed struggle to slow down the enemy advance, thereby enabling the workers to marshal their forces and regroup. By demonstrating the vulnerability of the military to hit-and-run tactics, the armed struggle was expected to encourage workers to organize their own resistance. Although it is impossible to determine the extent to which Montonero armed operations contributed to the trade union resistance, armed struggle led the way.

In the first number of *Vencer* (July-August 1979) Firmenich claimed that as a result of trade union resistance the armed forces had been unable to make their political power legitimate. "Massive, integral resistance has prevented the consolidation of the dictatorial project and is responsible for the political, domestic, and international crisis of the dictatorship. . . . The resulting debility of the regime now permits the launching of a massive counteroffensive initiated necessarily by the working class—the class that began the resistance—but that also includes the national entrepreneurs."[22] The outcome, he predicted, would be to bring down Martínez de Hoz and put an end to the government's policy of dismantling local industries.

The trade union resistance did not emerge *ex nihilo*. Said Firmenich: "On the day following the coup we launched the resistance alone, but after a few months the trade union resistance began developing. Today it is a force of millions . . . [and] our minimum program of pacification and liberation launched on 20 April 1977 is being assumed by Argentina's political and trade union forces as a whole."[23] That was not an exaggeration, but it was misleading, since the trade unions had their own reasons for adopting a policy of intransigence.

The immediate objectives of the Montonero counteroffensive were spelled out in a subsequent interview with the commander of the Montoneros's special infantry troops. Thus Raúl Yäger explained that the purpose of the armed counteroffensive was to assist in promoting a mass insurrection.[24] The conditions were propitious for insurrection, he believed, because the trade union counteroffensive was under way.

The model of a general insurrection was patterned on the insurrectionary strategy that made possible the Sandinista victory in July 1979. Firmenich made a point of traveling to Nicaragua to assimilate the lessons of its revolution. The Montonero counteroffensive was deliberately modeled on the Sandinista final offensive. As Firmenich declared on the eve of the Sandinista victory: *"the solution to the crisis experienced in Argentina is to do what is being done in Nicaragua."*[25]

Montonero support for the popular counteroffensive took three principal forms. First, an armed attack on Martínez de Hoz's economic team coincided with the defense of national sovereignty in opposition to the multinationals. Second, the promotion of trade union solidarity and unification aimed at galvanizing workers and other sectors to confront the dictatorship. Third, the dissemination and implementation of the slogan "To Achieve Trade Union Power Is to Win" became the task of both the special infantry and the special agitational troops.

Was the Montonero intervention a success? Yäger concludes that the decision to undertake it was both correct and opportune. It was correct because to intervene meant to respond to the expectations of the working class and "to question the continuity of the economic plan carried forward by Martínez de Hoz." It was opportune because the workers were mobilizing against the regime and "our absence in those circumstances would have been a costly defection."[26] The presence of the Montoneros may well have added to their credibility, but it seems wishful thinking to believe with Yäger that their diverse forms of struggle provoked General Menéndez's abortive coup in September and undermined civilian support for the dictatorship.

The collaborationist current held the Montoneros' armed struggle responsible for intensifying repression against the labor movement. But armed struggle also focused attention on the guerrillas and took pressure off the trade unions. A panoramic view shows that the resistance became sufficiently generalized by 1979 to bridle and de-

stabilize Martínez de Hoz's project and that the military had to retreat when other sectors of the population joined in the struggle.

The Montoneros' interpretation is not the generally accepted one.
Gillespie claims that "the working class was not yet ready, either
organizationally or politically for a united militant counteroffensive."[27] In view of the divided labor movement and the limited response to the general strike of April 1979, there was little possibility
of workers taking to the streets, recovering the rights of their
unions, bringing down Martínez de Hoz's economic team, splitting
the armed forces, and obliging them to retreat. What was proclaimed
as a popular counteroffensive was not really one and, to add to this
mistake, the results of the Montoneros' labor-oriented initiatives
were "negative."[28]

Unquestionably, the Montoneros' losses were catastrophic. But
were the workers unprepared to launch a counteroffensive? Made
early in 1981, Gillespie's assessment was premature and unsubstan-
tiated by the evidence of trade union activity at the time. It was premature because beginning in November of the same year, the workers took to the streets, they recovered the rights of their unions, and
they contributed to bringing down Martínez de Hoz's economic
team and to splitting the armed forces. "By 1981 the recovery of the
labor movement had become consolidated to such an extent that we
can realistically speak of a labor offensive."[29] Strikes and slowdowns
spread with surprising frequency. The twelve-hour national strike
by automobile workers in July followed by the second general strike
on July 22 placed the new military government of General Viola on
the defensive. The first successful street mobilization against the regime on November 7 precipitated his displacement by a palace coup
in December. "November 7 was no *cordobazo* nor was it enough to
undermine the Military Process, . . . but it is clear from the mobilization on that day that it helped to catalyze the contradictions
within the military dome and to bring down Viola through popular
pressure."[30]

Three crucial events contributed to this turnabout. The first was
the preeminently political document read by Saúl Ubaldini at a dinner of some three hundred Peronist leaders in December 1978. Alvaro Abós interprets this document as the end of the retreat by the
trade unions.[31] The second was the general strike of April 1979,
which, far from being a failure, Abós calls a historical landmark because it defied police and military repression, fostered trade union
solidarity, questioned the foundations of the Military Process, and
had enduring consequences in the struggle by organized labor.[32] The
third crucial event encouraged by the general strike was the emer-

gence in November 1980 of the illegal CGT, reinforcing the determination of the trade unions to take the offensive.[33]

Armed struggle was not the only means the Montoneros used to generalize the resistance. Beginning in 1980 nonviolent methods became the rule. Interviewed in August 1981, Firmenich was asked why the Montoneros no longer operated militarily. Because the objective of Montonero Peronism is the accumulation of power in the most effective way under the circumstances, he replied, and the circumstances in 1981, when labor had taken the offensive, were quite unlike those when its actions were mainly defensive.[34]

That the PRT and the Montoneros were knocked out of the armed struggle did not mean that they stopped being influential in other ways. Their resistance continued to have a crippling effect on Argentina's international relations, because of the combined PRT-Montonero propaganda assault from Paris and other European capitals. Their allegations on radio and television of systematic torture and genocide contributed to discrediting the Military Process.

Unlike the ERP, the Montoneros continued to be a consequential factor back home. With labor's counteroffensive under way, they adopted a new strategy giving priority to semilegal and legal actions. Although *Vencer* had been launched with the expectation of documenting their return and eventual victory, its propaganda became a substitute for military operations. Subsequently, their resistance would take more subtle forms, relying mainly on psychological warfare, support for human rights groups, semilegal strikes, and mass mobilizations aimed at demoralizing and wearing down the dictatorship.

It was not the first time the Montoneros had switched from armed struggle to political activity. They had first done so in 1973, but because of repression during the government of Isabel Perón, they again had to rely on armed struggle as the principal method. After operating underground for more than six years, in 1981 the time had come to politicize the resistance. As Firmenich recalled: "Just as in 1979 we launched the popular counteroffensive and our military actions stood out, so today the fundamental exigency is the participation of the broadest sectors of the working people in an active and decisive way against the dictatorship."[35]

Although an acid critic of the Montoneros, Abós agrees with their general assessment of the events. The year 1979 represented a major turning point, he concludes, because of the shift by organized labor from active self-defense to active offense, tantamount to a counteroffensive.[36] The Montoneros' "triumphalism" was based on an astute assessment of that turning point, confirmed within less than three years by the military's abdication and the return to civilian government.

The PRT-ERP had less to brag about. Against the monstrous apparatus of detentions, torture, confessions, incriminations, dragnets, disappearances, and deaths, it came face to face with an old reality. Guerrillas are able to thrive under conditions of constitutional liberty and semirepressive regimes, but find themselves pinned down, exposed, and vulnerable when confronted with a remorseless and consistent dictatorship. One reverse followed another. Following the military coup in 1976, the PRT's general secretary, Mario Roberto Santucho, issued a call to arms that fell on deaf ears. In July he fell victim to betrayal and assassination. Fearing further lapses in security, the PRT-ERP's leadership then fled into exile.

The annihilation of the principal leaders on 19 July 1976 was an almost fatal blow. It left the PRT confused, disorganized, and in the hands of a substitute leadership incapable of responding to the climate of defeat that was overwhelming and demoralizing the organization. Thus in May 1977, when the ERP's "Interior Direction" was annihilated along with the bulk of its remaining cadres in Argentina, the "Exterior Direction" ordered the survivors to abandon the country.[37]

Following this reversal the PRT ceased to function as a consequential factor in the resistance inside Argentina. Hundreds of cadres were in prison, others had simply disappeared. Those who lost contact with the PRT in 1977 were left to their own resources and did not play an organized role. Unlike the Montoneros', the PRT's military, logistical, and support network was completely dismantled because of information extracted under torture.

Since the armed forces were committed to the physical and political extermination of both organisms, it was enough simply to survive to thwart the military's objectives. Survival signified the persistence of subversion, ergo a continuation of the resistance. Such was the revised objective of the PRT.

Unlike the PRT, the ERP did not survive; therefore, it ceased to resist. But it survived long enough to be consequential. Along with the Montoneros, the ERP's survivors claim credit for bogging down the repressive forces, so that workers were able to catch their breath, regroup under new leaders, and launch their own resistance. "The heroism of militants cost the counterrevolutionary forces a precious loss of time through a kind of unconscious diversionism. Obliged to wipe out the remaining *focos* of armed resistance, military officers saw their own fundamental objective—the annihilation of the workers' vanguard—sidetracked."[38] While they were still combating the armed resistance they were simultaneously harassed by work stoppages, industrial sabotage, impediments to collaboration, errors on assembly lines, resistance to layoffs, and the battle plan of the light and power workers. What would have been a ferociously brutal and immediate blow against organized labor dragged its heels. The delay had repercussions at all levels. Thanks to the armed resistance, the "workers' resistance, which was tenacious and persistent, never allowed the military to fulfill its plans."[39]

Montoneros—To Resist Is to Win

Since the armed forces were committed to the complete eradication of political as well as armed subversion, the Montoneros reasoned that to continue their resistance politically would be to frustrate at least one of the enemy's objectives. Thus in April 1977 they launched the overriding theme of their resistance: "To resist until victory or death!"[40] This meant that, short of annihilation, "To resist is to win!"[41] Although they would continue their armed struggle until the end of 1979, it was only one prong of a two-pronged strategy aimed at bringing down the generals.

Firmenich's objective was to demonstrate to the regime that the Montoneros had not been extirpated by the repression and therefore that the government's final solution had failed. As he noted in a 1979 interview, the generals' final solution was a dismal failure: first, because the Montoneros had managed to survive; second, because the resistance had become generalized.[42]

Safely ensconced in exile, the Montoneros would reflect on their reversals and attempt to learn from the lessons. Frustrated militarily, they embarked on a course of self-criticism designed to pinpoint the theoretical and strategical mistakes of the revolutionary war. In the long run, that would help make their resistance of consequence. It contributed to their survival and it helped transform military defeat into what the generals would later acknowledge to be a political victory.

Unlike the PRT, the Montoneros never acknowledged defeat. But while they made a virtue of necessity, their *mea culpas* testified to intellectual errors to which they traced the mistakes of their armed struggle. Although they chose to call defeat by another name, the conclusions they drew and their resulting shifts in strategy were, objectively speaking, responses to reversals.

The Montoneros' initial response to the 1976 coup was to make a marked swing to the left and to denounce their earlier populist errors. The repression under Isabel Perón's government was traced to

Juan Perón, who had made concessions to the military, had hesitated to expropriate the oligarchy and foreign capital, had opposed the democratization of the Peronist movement, had purged the Peronist Left, and had prepared the way for the Peronist right wing led by López Rega.[43] Justicialist doctrine was supposedly finished because the real needs of the workers could no longer be served by a Peronist pact between labor and capital. Opposed to sharing power with capitalists, the document called for a transition to socialism and the creation of a new revolutionary party, the Montonero party, and proposed that the defunct Peronist movement be rechristened the Montonero movement.

During the period of resistance to the first series of military dictatorships (1966–1973) the Montoneros had characterized Perón as a socialist leader, which fostered illusions concerning the movement he led. As Firmenich acknowledged in July 1976, this characterization was erroneous: "In 1973 we revised the characterization and in 1974 we formulated a self-criticism . . . Perón was not a socialist leader. In the final analysis, his 'Third Position,' by not calling for socialism, can be reduced to bourgeois ideology."[44] Paradoxically, Perón was a bourgeois leader without being a leader of the bourgeoisie.

Further light on the Montonero response to the coup was shed in a 1977 interview with Julio Roqué, the Montonero in charge of military operations in Argentina before being killed in action in May 1977. The military coup revealed the labor bureaucracy for what it really was: an organization unwilling to resist the coming repression. Thus "some fled the country, others fell prisoner in a flock, and in the factories nobody moved, something akin to paralysis."[45] As an ideology, justicialism no longer served to mobilize the masses. Instead, the way to overcome the crisis was "a qualitative leap of Peronism in doctrinal matters, from the doctrine of the Third Position of Perón's 'organized community' to the doctrine of class struggle and the socialist option."[46]

The Montoneros responded to the disintegration of the Peronist movement by organizing its anticipated successor. But the political results of this change of face proved disappointing. Neither their new socialist line, adopted in April 1976, nor their efforts in June to bring together the armed organizations of the non-Peronist Left, nor their attempts to catalyze a trade union resistance in August met with much response.[47] Sensing that they had become dangerously isolated from the Peronist movement, when the supposed corpse showed signs of life, they began to backtrack in an effort to acquire the mass support they desperately needed.

Abandoning their short-lived attempts to build a Montonero movement led by a Montonero party, they turned to the less sectarian task of bringing together the different currents in revolutionary Peronism under the same roof. Signed in Rome on 20 April 1977 by representatives of the Montonero party (PM) and of the former Authentic Peronist party (PPA), the "Treaty of Rome" resulted in a merger called the Movimiento Peronista Montonero (MPM). A mass organization modeled on the official Peronist movement, it incorporated the traditional four branches plus an agrarian and a cultural branch of professionals, intellectuals, and artists. This new organization supposedly struck a balance between the two main revolutionary traditions in Argentina. Thus the Montoneros could boast, like no other comparable organization in the country, of being both a Guevarist political-military vanguard and an integral part of the Peronist movement.

The document of unification defined the popular resistance as the continuation of the Peronist resistance of 1956–1973, which was, in turn, a continuation of the century and a half of Argentine resistance to the native oligarchy and foreign capital.[48] Once again, Perón was dignified as "our leader," although the document added that the Peronist movement since his death had become "an orphan in its strategical leadership and exhausted in its doctrine."[49] Hence the simultaneous back- and forward pedaling promulgated by the new strategy: "Our historical duty consists in rescuing, reaffirming, and continuing with the best of our Peronist past; but simultaneously it is necessary to discover, to propose, and to develop the new in our future as a people."[50]

They further redefined themselves in September 1977, in a document by the Montonero party's National Council. Although they identified their ideology as "dialectical and historical materialism," they reasserted their Peronist "political identity."[51] They also strove for a strategic mix of a Guevarist political-military vanguard and a Peronist mass organization.[52] That the PRT succumbed to the wave of repression during the Military Process was attributed to its failure to reach a synthesis between a class-oriented party of cadres and a movement of masses.[53]

Expressed in terms of Mao's 1937 essay "On Contradiction," the Montoneros survived because "the Peronist Armed Organizations, of which today our Montonero Party is the synthesis, retained in their midst the Guevarism-Peronism contradiction."[54] To retain and yet to overcome this contradiction—that was the seemingly impossible task the Montoneros had set for themselves.[55] To translate this Maoist double-talk into plain English, they opted to preserve the differences while eliminating the incompatibilities between opposing revolutionary currents. Thus they hoped to combine militarism (an armed vanguard) with massism (a popular uprising), ideologism (socialist principles) with reformism (bourgeois-democratic politics), and classism (a Marxist-Leninist party) with movementism (a people's front).

In any synthesis of opposites, Mao contended, one pole must be hegemonic and the other subordinate. But the Montoneros noted that each pole might be hegemonic and each subordinate in different respects.[56] In the contradiction between revolutionary ideology and reformist politics, for example, ideology would be hegemonic in orienting the synthesis but politics would be hegemonic in adapting it to short-term, practical objectives.[57] In this effort at a synthesis of opposites—*contradiction* is the wrong word—they believed they had succeeded.

Where, then, had the Montoneros failed? They had responded to the repression under Isabel Perón by giving too much weight to abstract principles.[58] By insisting on socialism as their goal, they had periodically slipped into the ideologist deviation they associated with Guevarism. The Montoneros' mistake had been to isolate themselves from the Peronist masses by momentarily adopting a non-Peronist political line.

The theoretical problems posed by this self-criticism reflected the Montoneros' disparate ideological origins, a result of their incorporation of the Peronist Youth in 1972 and merger with the Marxist-Leninist FAR in 1973. Although influenced by Guevara, the Peronist Youth were revolutionary Peronists. In contrast, the FAR consisted of Guevarists for whom Peronism was mainly a cover. They were the "infiltrators" in the Peronist movement. Both tendencies concurred on how to handle the militarist-massist polarization, but the Montoneros never completely overcame the margin of difference between the JP's reformist-movementist orientation and the FAR's basically ideological-classist perspective.

Their vaunted synthesis of Peronism and Guevarism looked good on paper, but it did not prevent a major split in the organization in February 1979, followed by a second split in April 1980. In both instances, the dissidents agreed that the overweighting of the Guevarist component was responsible for the Montoneros' final armed counteroffensive and military defeat. In effect, the Peronist-Guevarist synthesis was not a formula capable of overcoming the Montoneros' want of representativeness. To gain a following, they had to play down their Guevarist heritage by mending fences with the Peronist party. In this effort the former Montoneros led the way in a course subsequently traveled by the Montoneros, when they, too, began making overtures to the party and rebuilding their legal fronts in 1982–1983. Such was the new interpretation of "To resist is to win."

As the founder in 1972 of the Peronist Youth–Regional Organizations (JP–R), Rodolfo Galimberti had backed the emerging pro-Montonero tendency, which became the dominant current within the youth movement. More than anyone else, he was responsible for the alliance with the Montoneros in which the JP–R took a backseat. By 1979 he had come to regret that decision. The Montoneros, he argued, had fallen victim to their claim to be the only authentic vanguard in the popular resistance. Calling itself "Peronismo en la Resistencia," Galimberti's tendency sought to insert itself politically into the struggles of Argentine workers from the bottom up rather than from the top down.

The rupture, which took the Montonero leadership by surprise, was sparked by the projected Montonero return to Argentina for the purpose of catalyzing the anticipated "popular counteroffensive." Convinced that the Montoneros had become a liability rather than an asset to the effective prosecution of the resistance, Galimberti made his criticism known to the membership in an open letter dated 22 February 1979 and cosigned by Juan Gelman. Internal discussion of the issue would have been fruitless, they explained, because of the leadership's financial and military control of the rank and file. Thus they and their followers resigned without previous warning, taking with them some seventy thousand dollars. The money was used to finance "Peronism in the Resistance," committed to internal democracy and a strategy compatible with the popular struggles inside Argentina.

Among the reasons given for their resignation was the aggravation of earlier errors never wholly corrected by the leadership. The letter criticized "the resurgence of a militarism, *foquista* in origin," "the reaffirmation of the elitist conception of a party of cadres leading to the organization's progressive isolation from the masses," "the recourse to conspiratorial practices by Montonero party cadres to guarantee their hegemony over the Montonero Peronist movement," "the maniacal sectarianism questioning the representative character of anybody in the people's camp who is not under strict control of the party," "the definitive bureaucratization of all levels of the party's leadership," "the absolute lack of internal democracy," and "an irresponsible triumphalism that convinces nobody."[59]

The letter concluded with a proposal to develop the armed resistance in a popular and democratic way as part of the Peronist mainstream, not outside it. In addition, it called for negotiations aimed at reincorporating the Montoneros into the official Peronist movement based on the understanding that the armed resistance was not the monopoly of any single organization.[60]

Several years later, in a Paris interview Gelman recalled the background leading to the split. His and Galimberti's criticism had been foreshadowed by Rodolfo Walsh, the Argentine novelist and Montonero militant, who had acknowledged earlier errors in a series of papers written in 1976–1977.[61] Like Walsh, Gelman questioned all armed actions that were not directly and unequivocally linked to some immediate interest of the masses. As examples he cited the September 1973 assassination of CGT boss José Rucci, for which the Montoneros were held responsible but which they did not repudiate at the time, and their July 1974 execution of Arturo Mor Roig, the former minister of the interior under Pres. Alejandro Lanusse. He also criticized the leadership for not assisting the masses to organize themselves, for disregarding the people's perception of their interests, and for encouraging a self-defeating elitism that isolated it from those it hoped to serve.[62] According to Gelman, those errors were not merely strategical but followed from a mistaken perception of Argentine political reality.

The open letter of February 1979 was followed in June by what is still the most elaborate criticism of the Montoneros. Known as the "Document of the Rupture," it was signed by Galimberti, Gelman, and seven former Montoneros who had resigned together in February. A document of twenty-three printed pages, legal size, in double columns and small type, it rejected the fundamental premise of Montonero Peronism: the synthesis of the Peronist and the Guevarist revolutionary traditions in Argentina.

The document begins with a summary of the principal intellectual errors resulting from the progressive dissociation of the revolutionary vanguard from the immediate experience of the masses. First, the leadership failed to acknowledge that "the popular resistance, especially that led by the industrial working class by means of strikes, work stoppages, slowdowns, and sabotage, developed in a course parallel to and independent of the armed resistance."[63] Second, it failed to acknowledge that "the only 'immediate result' of all the armed actions in support of trade union conflicts from 1976 forward was the accentuation of the repression of the working class because of the solid alliance between the bosses and the repressive apparatus."[64] These two misperceptions of Argentine reality were allegedly fatal because they alienated labor support and contributed to the Montoneros' isolation from the Peronist movement.

Although the progressive reduction of the Montoneros' political space after 1974 was attributed to the recession of the popular movement, it was in the midst of this recession that the working class developed organizationally superior forms of resistance. Why, then, didn't the Montoneros do likewise? Because their intellectual errors gave rise to strategical ones, to contempt for internal democracy, to political sectarianism, and to reliance on military solutions.[65]

The total absence of collective participation in the formulation of policies, the nonelective character of the leadership, and the deference to authority within the Montoneros' political-military organization, according to the document, invariably clashed with the democratic features of the workers' organizations.[66] While the Montoneros criticized the labor bureaucracy for undemocratic practices, the bureaucratization of the labor leadership paled beside the Montoneros' refusal to recognize elected union officials as representative. As a party of cadres, the Montoneros substituted the principle of authority for that of representation, thereby "guaranteeing that it would never take root organizationally in the working class."[67]

The sectarianism of the Montoneros was presented as another obstacle to an alliance with organized labor. The Montoneros were more concerned with stamping their seal on trade union activity, with imposing their designs on the labor movment by decree than with building a consensus at the grass-roots level.[68] They tried to supplant the organic leaders of the workers with leaders of their own picking and to build parallel trade union organizations that existed mainly on paper. Nor did they hesitate to rely on "avengers" for removing trade union bureaucrats they considered enemies of the working class.[69]

One of the worst expressions of sectarianism arose over the use of funds. In sole control of thirty million dollars remaining from the ransom of the top executives of Bunge and Born, the leadership was unwilling to share it with the rank and file. When repression focused on the famous factory guerrillas, the leadership refused to aid them. It used its monopoly of financial resources to preserve the only source of power it had and for which it never gave an accounting. Financial help was denied "to the strikers fired from their jobs, to the Mothers of the Plaza de Mayo, to the sons of the disappeared, to the widows of the fallen."[70] This was not the way to cement an alliance with other sectors of the resistance, much less lead them.

The Montoneros' interpretation of every political confrontation as a military one was likewise foreign to the workers. The Montoneros repudiated all forms of nonviolent action as reformist. The effect of such thinking was to isolate them even further from the masses: "One begins by negating democracy as 'liberal,' and one ends by denouncing popular sovereignty as 'bourgeois.'"[71] The leaders minimized the political task of preparing the workers for armed resistance. At the same time they mistakenly believed that an armed vanguard was needed to spark a popular insurrection. Thus the Montoneros were faulted for becoming a terrorist alternative, "a Triple A of the Left."[72] At best this would have permitted them to negotiate, in the name of the masses, a settlement favorable to themselves.[73]

Three forces contended for Perón's ear during his third government and for his mantle after he died: *montonerismo* on the Left, *lopezreguismo* on the Right, and *vandorismo* (after the reformist policies of former CGT chief Augusto Vandor) in the Center. In this setting, the only intelligent strategy for the Montoneros was to ally themselves with the Vandorists in an effort to isolate the bloc of Isabel Perón–López Rega.[74] Instead, they interpreted their differences with the labor bureaucracy as antagonistic.[75] By threatening the lives of labor leaders and sabotaging their pact with the national bourgeoisie, they indirectly encouraged the coalition between the trade union and the political bureaucracies. They took on two enemies at once when they should have concentrated on stopping the military from destabilizing the Peronist government.

The Montoneros might have acquired representativeness by formulating answers to the questions of the day, by winning a following through words and deeds acceptable to the masses. But they erred by adopting a massive version of *foquismo:* "You can organize a *foco* with ten or attempt to do so with a hundred thousand: the first was done before 1972; the second was tried after 1972."[76]

As a self-appointed and self-perpetuating revolutionary vanguard, the document claims, the leadership used every means it could to preserve its powers.[77] This resulted in the subordination of the Peronist Youth (JP) to the Montoneros' Organización Político-Militar (OPM) and, after the reorganization of April 1977, of the Montonero Peronist movement (MPM) to the Montonero party (PM). Hierarchically organized along military lines, the party left virtually no initiatives to its mass organizations. The end result was a counterfeit of a Leninist party, "a party of cadres in which the cadres were not cadres and the party was not a party."[78]

The central error behind the leaders' concern to preserve their authority at any cost was the presumption that they were the key to the revolutionary process in Argentina. "This was what justified all the monstrosities committed, beginning with the monarchical structure of the OPM and the farce of the MPM, a monarchical structure hidden by the simple artifice of calling things by another name: 'party' for a paramilitary organization, 'central committee' for a merely advisory board, and 'secretary general' for a military commander."[79] Condemning the original Montonero takeover of the Peronist Youth, Galimberti insisted on its independence.[80] This was tantamount to repudiating the Montoneros' Guevarist heritage. Firmenich, the "monarchical" head of the OPM and its successor, the PM, had finally been challenged by Galimberti as a representative of the Montoneros' mass organizations.

Galimberti's group was not the only thorn in the side of the Montoneros. In April 1980 a second split occurred. Dissidents chafing from the defeat of the vaunted 1979 counteroffensive and calling themselves the Montoneros "17th of October," were led by the Montoneros' former press secretary and the editor in 1973–1974 of their newspaper *Noticias*. Like Galimberti, Miguel Bonasso remained in exile because of criminal charges against him revived by the Radical party (in power from 1983 to 1989).

The substance of Bonasso's criticism was summarized in a telephone interview published in *El Porteño* in April 1985.[81] From Mexico City he recalled that the Montoneros had been divided from the beginning into two main currents: one, Peronist; the other, Guevarist. The Peronist current favored a mass political line, whereas the Guevarist tendency encouraged the formation of a military vanguard. For the most part, the leaders of the Montoneros upheld a vanguardist position. It was their disastrous order to return to Argentina in 1979 for the purpose of sparking the misguided counteroffensive that effectively split the movement in two.

The balance between them had always been precarious, Bonasso indicated, and it was no longer possible to bring them together. The Guevarist tendency was responsible for provoking the Ultra Right and for militarizing a political conflict. While conceding that the Montoneros were obliged in self-defense to operate as a clandestine organization during the government of Isabel Perón, he considered it mistaken to have waged an armed struggle against such a relatively democratic regime. Bonasso called for the integration of former Montoneros and other representatives of revolutionary Peronism who had distinguished themselves in the unarmed struggle against the dictatorship. At the same time he disputed the Montoneros' efforts to preempt their political space.

In criticizing Guevarism, Bonasso focused on its militarist excesses, known as *foquismo*. But from his 1980 criticism of the Montoneros we know that he did not repudiate the vanguardist syndrome interpreted as a political-military tendency with politics in command. Unlike Galimberti, who rejected vanguardism along with its militarist deformation, Bonasso opted for a Leninist conception of the vanguard consistent with the revolutionary Peronism of John William Cooke.[82] The outcome of his self-criticism was thus a new variant of *montonerismo* without *foquismo*, although he has since rejected the term "Montoneros" and vanguardism.

How did Firmenich respond to this barrage of internal criticism? His immediate response was to charge both groups of dissenters with "treason" and to decree death sentences for Galimberti and those who refused to return to Argentina.[83] Although the counteroffensive decimated and paralyzed the Montoneros' armed capability, it was hailed by the leadership as a political victory in stimulating the unarmed resistance.[84] However, it was not long before the Montoneros, too, began making overtures toward other sectors of Peronism. A new retreat and process of de-Guevarization followed the 1979 and 1980 ruptures, ending in the dissolution of the journal *Vencer* in February 1982.

In the last issue of *Vencer* the Montoneros acknowledged by implication their strategical mistakes. First, they had identified the Vandorist labor bureaucracy as the principal enemy within Peronism. Second, when they began identifying the internal enemy with the Lopezreguist conspiracy, they exaggerated its influence over the government. These assessments were used to justify a policy of armed confrontation with Isabel Perón, whereas the correct strategy would have been to focus on their common enemy, "the Lopezreguist conspiracy, which clearly served the oligarchical plan of infiltrating and destroying the Peronist movement."[85]

In this account there was no mention of the labor bureaucracy as an agent of imperialism. López Rega was the main villain, and his conspiracy was directed not just against the Peronist movement but also against Isabel Perón's government. The strategy corresponding to this assessment was not spelled out, but it is not difficult to fathom. The Montoneros would have done better by supporting the Vandorist bureaucracy against the oligarchical counteroffensive and the repressive policies of López Rega.

The Montoneros' change of mind called into question their earlier assessments. In 1974 they had accused the labor bureaucracy of undermining the Peronist movement.[86] "From the heights of the leadership of the 62 Organizations and the Peronist movement, Vandorism undertook the task of isolating Perón from the people, of destroying the organizational forms that permitted him to return to Argentina, of impeding the mobilization of the masses."[87] On June 20, at the Ezeiza International Airport, Vandorist thugs supposedly killed more Peronists than had all the military dictatorships from Perón's fall in 1955 to his return eighteen years later.[88] To implement its repressive policies, the Vandorist elite "infiltrated its agents into the state apparatus."[89] As for López Rega's Ministry of Social Welfare, it did not represent an independent force, but functioned as an ally of the Vandorist bureaucracy.[90]

This version of the enemy within the movement underwent a substantial revision with the publication a year later of a Montonero document in which López Rega appears as the principal villain, independent of the Vandorist elite. "The AAA emerged immediately after the twenty-fifth of May 1973 as the military arm of the policies of the minister of social welfare, José López Rega. The AAA's goal is the destruction of Peronism by the tergiversation of its political values, the emptying of its social content, and the subordination of its economic objectives to those of North American imperialism."[91] From the beginning of President Cámpora's government, López Rega was obsessed with creating a parallel military force comparable to the Nazi SS.[92] It was his overall control of the federal police, who were instructed to allow the Triple A to operate freely, that permitted him to unleash the campaign of kidnappings and assassinations. "If there were no other evidence for making a judgment, the above would be enough to surmise that the Triple A *is the government.*"[93] Although Balbín, the leader of the Radical party, presented Isabel Perón with a partial list of the Triple A's members, she did nothing about it and refused to receive him again.[94]

Unfortunately for the Montoneros' analysis, the Vandorist bureaucracy was staunchly Peronist and the Triple A never took over the government. Thus their justification for armed struggle against Isabel Perón was spurious. They admitted as much in their 1982 reappraisal.

What were the practical consequences of this self-criticism? Briefly, two stages were envisioned in the return to civilian government: first, the restoration of the people's state as it existed during President Cámpora's administration; second, the implementation of a nonsectarian and nonclassist program of political pluralism, social democracy, and a mixed economy.[95] Political pluralism would assure the representation of all social sectors in the government through a multiparty system. Social democracy would assure direct forms of mass participation besides indirect representation through political parties. And a mixed economy would guarantee the initiative for economic development by the people's state without disrupting the private sector. As the document attests: "For this economic model we want a country with a planned and mixed economy, which presupposes . . . centralized and self-managed state enterprises, co-operative enterprises, and private enterprises based on the country's present social structure."[96] Although that is a long way from the Montoneros' socialist project of 1976–1977, resistance to the Military Process had a chance of winning with such a broadly representative program.

The Montoneros had begun to worry over their lack of popular appeal, precisely the issue that led to Galimberti's rupture in February 1979. But the errors pinpointed by Galimberti had yet to be made explicit. Not until he found himself in prison after being extradited from Brazil in October 1984 did Firmenich clearly repudiate the strategy of armed action against Isabel Perón,[97] first, because it did not have the effect intended of protecting the Montoneros and the Peronist Youth from repression, and second, because it reduced the Montoneros' political space by depriving them of a legal front against the government. To this he added the following observations in my prison interview in March 1985: "The return to clandestinity was in practice counterproductive. We became isolated from the Peronist mainstream and our resistance did not acquire the massive response we anticipated. Nor did it help us in mobilizing the people to resist the military coup in March 1976, because by then we had become branded as 'subversives.'"

But by then the Montoneros' *mea culpas* were falling on deaf ears. As Galimberti's sister-in-law Patricia Bullrich remarked during my interview with her: "I am not sure whether I would believe them because of his [Firmenich's] present circumstances. I mean his imprisonment and coming trial. If he has made such a self-criticism, it has come too late, like the sheep that cried 'wolf' too often—until nobody believed it." What Bullrich passed over is that Firmenich's self-criticisms had nothing to do with his imprisonment. They were implicit in the Montoneros' February 1982 document outlining their new strategy. Unwilling to credit the Montoneros with having assimilated Galimberti's criticisms, Bullrich stuck to her original conceptions.

The Montoneros had become deradicalized, but their reputation as left-wing extremists has persisted. In view of their strategical zigzags, this reputation is not unfounded. In my interview with Firmenich, he gave vivid testimony to the tension between principle and strategy. His commitment to socialism had not changed; he had prudently played it down. Nor had he softened his criticism of Isabel Perón, the official head of the Peronist movement, for she had "usurped powers that were clearly unconstitutional" and had "exercised authority through a virtual palace coup." Unlike Galimberti's followers, Firmenich continued to justify the Montoneros' resistance to Isabel Perón's government. It was mainly the resort to armed struggle that he considered premature.

PRT-ERP—To Survive Is to Resist

Since the Military Process was committed to a final solution to the subversion problem, one way of resisting was simply to hold out. Toward this objective the PRT's leadership had ordered the ERP to leave Argentina in 1977. The remaining cadres, cut off from contact with the leadership, fell back on the mass movement, while those in prison attempted to reorganize under new leaders.[98] Such policies helped to preserve the party, so that when the PRT's exiles returned to Argentina in mid-1983, ties were reestablished with those who had remained behind.

In exile the PRT leadership stuck by its decision "to maintain alive the flame of resistance."[99] The survival of the vanguard, if not its armed forces, was considered a sine qua non of prevailing over the military. In accordance with the dictum "To survive is to resist," the PRT not only continued publication of *El Combatiente*, but also established a School of Cadres abroad and made efforts to link up and to restore links with mass organizations inside Argentina. Meanwhile, those comrades who had remained behind, both in and out of prison, engaged in what amounted to a holding operation.[100] Although some believed the PRT had outlived its usefulness and ought to be scrapped, efforts to dissolve the party were branded as "liquidationist."[101]

Frustrated in the effort to continue the resistance, a group of secondary cadres became convinced that the decision to abandon Argentina had been an error.[102] This group was led by Julio Santucho and Roberto Guevara, brothers of Mario and Che, respectively. It gradually displaced members of the former leadership to become the prevailing tendency when a new directorate was elected at the PRT's Sixth Congress in May 1979.

This tendency was not the only source of factionalism. The principal leaders responsible for the May directive, the ERP's commander, Enrique Gorriarán Merlo, and the party's new general secretary, Luis Mattini, had a falling out.[103] Consequently, when the Sixth Congress finally convened, the PRT had already suffered its first and most important split.

In January 1979 Gorriarán, with some fifty to one hundred dissidents, dropped out of the PRT because of differences with the leadership. Two main issues divided them.[104] The first concerned armed support for the Nicaraguan resistance against Somoza. The PRT's leaders, according to Gorriarán, had shown an irresponsible lack of solidarity with the FSLN. As international soldiers of the revolution, he and a handful of other militants left their various countries of exile to assemble in Costa Rica. There they joined the FSLN's forces fighting on the southern front. After the Sandinista victory they also took the initiative of tracking down the former dictator and executing him in a bazooka ambush in Asunción, Paraguay, in September 1980.

The second issue, which prefigured Galimberti's rupture with the Montoneros, concerned the PRT's lack of political representativity. Gorriarán's group supported organizational unity not only with the principal sectors of revolutionary Peronism, but also with other organizations of the resistance in a broad front similar to the FSLN. For the official PRT this signified a defiance of party discipline and the dissolution of the PRT as an independent Marxist-Leninist party.

Gorriarán broke with the PRT because of the party's "sectarianism," its doctrinaire response to the two questions just considered. Following an adaptation of Che Guevara's *foco* strategy to urban guerrilla warfare from 1970 to 1972, the party had adopted a Vietnam-type strategy of prolonged people's war. But it had failed to move to a strategy of generalized or mass insurrection, which had carried the Sandinistas to victory. This was the strategy assimilated by Gorriarán's group through its contacts with the FSLN.

At the PRT's Sixth Congress in La Spezia, Italy, Mattini accepted responsibility for the fateful decision directing all PRT-ERP cadres to abandon Argentina. Although he was retained as the party's general secretary, the party was effectively in the hands of dissidents. Having resolved to return to Latin America, the PRT in January 1980 moved its headquarters to Mexico City. Except for public relations departments set up in France and Sweden, most of the PRT's militants soon followed.

A second major split occurred in Mexico in July–August 1980.[105] The confrontation with Mattini was led by Jorge Oropel over the issue of resuming the resistance inside Argentina. Oropel insisted on the party's immediate return. At the same time he rejected the documents and new line approved at the Sixth Congress as "reformist" for moving too far to the right.

Calling itself the PRT-Argentino, Oropel's group acknowledged only the documents of the Fifth Congress (1970) and the Central Committee and Executive Committee resolutions prior to the abandonment of Argentina in 1977. These had been periodically published in the PRT's weekly, *El Combatiente*. On returning to Argentina, the schismatic PRT began publishing its own edition of *El Combatiente*, beginning with number 142—numbered from the last issue published inside the country. But because of the repression, it had to discontinue publication. Compelled to dissolve, Oropel's group disappeared from sight. It regrouped in May 1986 as the PRT-ERP with a military line committed to reviving the armed struggle.

In August 1980, in the wake of this second split, Mattini asked to be relieved of his responsibilities as general secretary. Pleading ill health and chronic fatigue (*cansancia*) after thirty years of party militancy—although only forty-five—he was allowed to retire. He was succeeded by Amilcar Santucho, supported on the Executive Committee by his brother Julio and by Roberto Guevara. By then all of the original Politburo members responsible for the decision to abandon the country had left the party.[106]

Two years later, in August 1982, a Conference of Cadres convened in place of the scheduled Seventh Congress, but with the powers and attributes of a party congress. Amilcar Santucho was reelected general secretary and plans were made for the PRT's imminent return from exile. By the end of 1982, the crucial year of resistance, the PRT was again in Argentina. But it delayed republishing *El Combatiente* inside the country until March 1984. Between May 1977 and March 1984, when number 298 finally appeared at home, 157 issues had been published abroad.[107]

Roughly paralleling the sequence of Montonero defeats were those experienced by the PRT-ERP. But instead of a series of major reassessments and shifts in political line from 1976 to 1979, the PRT waited until its Sixth Congress to document the kind of self-criticism already evident in Montonero documents from April 1976 to August 1977. This was not the only difference. In February 1982 the Montoneros made a thorough appraisal of the Military Process along with a reappraisal of the Peronist governments since 1973. Not until three years later did the PRT do as much. In each case the Montoneros were quicker to acknowledge their mistakes, quicker to recover from defeat, and also to make political headway after their return to Argentina.

The secret report by the PRT's general secretary, Luis Mattini, at its Sixth Congress reads like a syllabus of errors. Covering the nine years since the Fifth Congress, it traces the party's major setbacks to a faulty assessment of Argentina's ripeness for a socialist revolution. At the same time, the PRT took heed of Gorriarán's principal charges of reneging on its international duty to support the Nicaraguan Revolution and of losing political representativity back home.

Its main strategic error, the PRT acknowledged, was the choice of socialism as an immediate objective.[108] The PRT gave a socialist response to a series of situations that objectively and subjectively required a different orientation aimed at defending democracy and enlarging the scope of democratic participation.[109] "Its errors were not a matter of tactics *but errors of a strategical character with an ideological origin.*"[110] From its main strategic error followed a series of other mistakes: first, in response to the democratic opening and succession of constitutional governments from 1973 to 1976; second, in response to the military dictatorship.

Among the first set of errors, the PRT did not take advantage of the electoral opportunities under the regime of Gen. Alejandro Lanusse (1971–1973).[111] On the mistaken premise that the outcome of elections would be decided by the military, it forfeited the opportunity to elect its own representatives. This meant that its political line for directing the mass movement was subordinated to its military line of confronting the armed forces. Since the decision to abstain during the 1973 elections and to continue the armed struggle did not have the workers' support, it was inevitably counterproductive.

The PRT held a mistaken conception of how to accumulate forces, confusing the latter with the accumulation of combatants and military equipment.[112] As a result, the vanguard was given precedence over the mass organizations, and military operations over political work. The PRT's principal mass organizations, the Frente Antiimperialista por el Socialismo (FAS) and the Movimiento Sindical de Base (MSB), were used for sectarian purposes. Instead of broadening their representation and encouraging initiatives from below, the PRT reduced them to legal appendages of the ERP.

The PRT's military operations were ill-timed and in some instances ill-targeted.[113] The action against the military post of Sanidad in September 1973 prompted the government to outlaw the ERP. The temporary takeover of the army's top base in the town of Azul in January 1974 resulted in repressive legislation. The rural guerrillas being trained in the mountains of Tucumán in 1974 were launched before the sugar workers in the province had been prepared politically. The PRT underestimated not only the obstacles to its armed operations, but also the enemy's capacity to retaliate. The ERP's supporters among the rural population were savagely repressed, and the guerrillas were unable to defend them. The indiscriminate execution of seventeen officers of the armed forces in retaliation for the massacre of ERP militants in Catamarca in August 1974 amounted to a vendetta. And far from dissuading a fascist military coup, the attack on the army's arsenal in Monte Chingolo prompted the armed forces on Christmas Eve 1975 to begin preparations for overthrowing the government. Contrary to the PRT's judgment that the operation was a political victory, it had been disastrous both politically and militarily.

The PRT erroneously believed that the most effective way to forestall a military coup was to upgrade and extend the scope of its military actions.[114] At the same time it misjudged the significance of a prospective coup as a "qualitative leap [forward] in the process of the revolutionary war!"[115]

The PRT mistakenly thought the revolutionary movement of the masses was on the rise throughout 1975.[116] Despite the general strike in July, the tide had already begun to ebb because of the repression at Villa Constitución, the setback in Tucumán, and the mounting terrorism of the Triple A. Thus the PRT continued its offensive when a defensive strategy would have been more appropriate.

The PRT had no response to the power vacuum created by the *rodrigazo*—the June and July 1975 labor demonstrations and general strike that produced the resignation of economy minister Celestino Rodrigo.[117] Nor did it anticipate a democratic transitional phase between capitalism and socialism in its assessment of Argentine reality.[118]

Finally, the PRT was unprepared politically and militarily to confront the coup.[119] Instead of accumulating forces for the coming showdown with the military, it spent most of its strength fighting the government of Isabel Perón.[120] When the coup occurred, the PRT had already suffered a series of defeats and was in no condition to wage an effective armed resistance to the dictatorship.

A second set of strategic errors came in response to the establishment of the first military junta on 24 March 1976. Acknowledgment of these errors was essential if the PRT hoped to survive.

The PRT did not switch to a defensive strategy because the concept of retreat had no place in its calculations.[121] This explains its response without any basis in the objective and subjective conditions of the masses. Failing to perceive that the masses were in retreat, it insisted on taking the offensive. But the call "Argentines to Arms!" and the mobilization of the ERP for a military offensive elicited no popular response.

The PRT believed that as part of a new stage of the revolutionary process, the dictatorship could not survive a victory by the armed resistance.[122] This was expected to issue in a general mass insurrection followed by a struggle for hegemony between the proletariat and the bourgeoisie. None of these scenarios corresponded to what happened.

The PRT leadership succumbed to a process of creeping demoralization and ideological deterioration.[123] As a result of its mistaken anticipations and the crushing repression launched against it in 1976–1977, it lost its bearings through a "right opportunist deviation." This consisted of the decision to seek allies among the bourgeois parties opposed to the military regime and to give up mass agitation and the armed struggle inside Argentina.[124]

The PRT had no coherent plan for responding to the succession of disasters.[125] This led to vacillations in the leadership, to orders and counterorders, to cover-ups, to extreme bureaucratism, to the emergence of factions, to the refusal to engage in self-criticism, and to a policy of expulsions. These errors were compounded by the failure to publish *El Combatiente* on a regular basis and by the general disorganization resulting from the dispersion of exiled militants to different countries. All of this interfered with the party's recovery and efforts to reinsert itself in the workers' struggles.[126] Surely, this was not the way to survive and resist.

The PRT's recommended corrective was to take its cue from Fidel Castro's July 26th movement, which later fused with the pro-Moscow party of Cuba, and from the FSLN, which remained on close terms with Nicaragua's Soviet-type party.[127] Regardless of who would eventually lead the revolutionary process, it concluded, revolutionary unity with the established Communist party in each country was a sine qua non of a successful strategy. From being a merciless critic of the Argentine CP, the PRT had become a fellow traveler.

Most of the strategic errors we have considered were traced by the PRT to an intellectual origin. First, it did not fully assimilate the method and scientific teachings of Marxism-Leninism.[128] Second, this failure was responsible for its misinterpretation of what was happening in Argentina.[129]

The insufficient assimilation of Marxism-Leninism meant a failure to learn from the accumulated experience and creative development of Marxism by the successful Communist and workers' parties. This failure was traced to the PRT's peculiar origins outside the international Communist movement.[130] The only Marxism intimately known to the PRT consisted of the Trotskyist, Cuban, and Vietnamese variants. Trotskyism had waged a continuous polemic against the Marxism of the established Communist parties, while the Cuban and Vietnamese revolutions represented an adaptation of Marxism to specific national conditions that were not those of Argentina. Thus the PRT learned its Marxism secondhand from sources foreign to the experience of its own country.

As the PRT subsequently acknowledged, Marxist theory had to be thoroughly assimilated before it could be intelligently applied to Argentina. Otherwise, strategic mistakes would be made because of a mistaken perception of the country's political reality. To survive and to continue to resist, the PRT would have to reassess what had happened in Argentina since World War II. It did so in a summary of its post-1979 reflections. The sixty-page internal document was presented for discussion in 1984.

Perón's first two governments were described as "bourgeois democratic" and his third government as a "formal democracy."[131] After the momentous role played by the working class on 17 October 1945, the way was cleared for a popular government that, despite its paternalistic elements, was basically democratic. The reforms made during Perón's first government testified to "evident progress in the exercise of democratic know-how until then unfamiliar to the workers."[132] His first two governments represented the "highest point achieved by bourgeois democracy in Argentina."[133] But during Perón's third government the proimperialist financial oligarchy began making inroads into the state apparatus.[134]

The designation "formal democracy" refers to democratic institutions emptied of content, so that they no longer represent the people's interests.[135] "The fascist project in Argentina had its road paved by the repressive measures and legislation of the Peronist constitutional government, which degraded bourgeois democracy in order to control the popular opposition."[136] This was achieved through exceptional laws during the presidencies of Juan Domingo and Isabel Perón and was reinforced by the armed operations of the Triple A. Nonetheless, this deformed or degraded democracy could still be characterized as "constitutional."[137]

The repressive features of Perón's third government and its immediate successor were explained by the transformation of the Argentine economy after 1955 from a semi-independent competitive capitalism into monopoly capitalism dependent on foreign initiatives. Unlike Perón's first two governments which favored small business, his third government and that of Isabel Perón favored the monopolies.[138] Whereas in 1956 only 20 percent of Argentina's industrial production came under the control of monopoly capital, this figure had jumped to 32 percent in 1969, of which more than half represented the share of the multinationals.[139] Technological dependence added to financial dependence on foreign banks and lack of access to foreign markets had combined to reduce the local bourgeoisie to an appendage of the "international financial oligarchy."[140]

Monopoly capitalism, the PRT claimed, had so accentuated the nation's dependence that the fundamental contradiction between wage-earners and capitalists was being expressed as the contradiction between the people's interests and the foreign monopolies supported by the financial and landed oligarchies.[141] By the "people" was understood a bloc of five classes consisting of proletarians, semiproletarians in the city and countryside, nonproletarian salaried employees, poor peasants, and petty bourgeois, including independent craftspeople and self-employed professionals.[142] Based on the PRT's earlier assessment of economic and political forces, socialism had been the strategic objective from 1973 to 1979. However, recognizing its mistake and the advent of a new stage of state-monopoly capitalism epitomized by the political monopoly of the armed forces, in 1979 it redefined its objective as an antioligarchical, anti-imperialist, people's democratic revolution led by the working class.[143]

In conformity with Lenin's thesis that political reaction corresponds to economic monopoly, the PRT associated fascism with a form of state organization characteristic of the monopoly stage.[144] Bonapartist regimes were features of premonopoly capitalism, whereas fascism is the political monopoly corresponding to economic monopoly in its most developed form.[145] Thus fascism first began to germinate during the dictatorship of Gen. Juan Carlos Onganía (1966–1970).[146]

Although the classical Fascist regimes in Italy and Germany had a mass political basis in the petty bourgeoisie, these original fascisms were considered atypical. In contrast to the fascism established from below with mass participation, the PRT distinguished a fascism from above, hegemonized by the military with the backing of big business.[147] Common to both was an alleged dictatorship by the most reactionary and monopolistic sector of the business community animated by a virulent anticommunism and distrust of liberal and democratic institutions.[148] Considering that Perón's third government and that of Isabel Perón made possible the penetration of the state apparatus by the financial oligarchy, it is not surprising that the PRT attributed to them fascistoid features.

The first outright fascist regime, however, had to wait until the coup of March 1976.[149] By then the Argentine economy had reached a new stage, identified as state monopoly capitalism, a consequence of the merger of monopoly capital with the state apparatus.[150] Isabel Perón's government corresponded to an earlier stage undergoing an erosion of democratic forms.[151] But progressive fascisization is not fascism, so a different strategic response was required of each.[152]

Although this account agreed with earlier assessments of the

1973–1976 Peronist governments, it disagreed with the corresponding strategies. In 1974 the prospect of a "transition from parliamentarism to Bonapartism, [and] from Bonapartism to increasing fascisization" was used to justify a strategy of armed confrontation with the governments of Juan Domingo and Isabel Perón.[153] But after the Sixth Congress the revolutionary organizations were faulted for their "unilaterally military response to the difficulties and complexities of the class struggle."[154] The failure to assimilate Marxist strategy presumably lay at the root of this "grave error."[155]

How does the PRT's reassessment of Argentine political reality compare with the Montoneros' reassessment? Although their analytical models differed, they arrived at similar conclusions. Cámpora's regime was likened to a parliamentary democracy by the PRT and to a people's state by the Montoneros. Perón's third government was characterized by the PRT as a formal democracy and by the Montoneros as a government of equilibrium or accommodation between the people and the oligarchy. Isabel Perón's government was an instance of formal democracy with fascistoid tendencies, according to the PRT, and of a government penetrated by oligarchical and imperialist interests, according to the Montoneros. Finally, the Military Process was depicted by the PRT as a fascist regime and by the Montoneros as the government of an armed bureaucracy in the service of the oligarchy and multinational corporations.

In retrospect, the Montoneros and the PRT basically agreed concerning, first, the changing correlation of forces from 1973 to 1976 between the people and the oligarchy, and second, the essential features of the dictatorship that ensued. Where, then, did they differ?

They differed mainly in their assessments of the revolutionary potential of the Peronist movement and of the feasibility of a socialist strategy for Argentina. Peronism was a bourgeois phenomenon from the start that never qualified as revolutionary in the PRT's judgment. This thesis was vigorously contested by the Montoneros. Second, the Montoneros' national revolution is not what the PRT understood by "socialism." Third, these differing assessments were the basis of fundamental differences in strategy. While the PRT's response to its errors was to fall back on the principal mainstays of the Marxist Left, the Montoneros tried to overcome their reputation as extremists by mending fences with the Peronist movement.

Although defeated militarily, the Montoneros and the PRT persisted in their political struggle against the dictatorship. Contrary to the military's expectations, they assimilated at least two lessons of political importance in reflecting on their defeat. Their resistance might still be effective provided they, first, carried on a successful holding operation and, second, recovered political representativity. Consequently, the armed forces' triumph on the battlefield was no guarantee that the military would retain power.

The military had anticipated that by intensifying and extending the scope of repression, the guerrillas would be morally as well as physically destroyed. Pressured into abandoning the armed struggle, however, the Montoneros, the PRT, and former members of the ERP reaffirmed it in principle. Thus Díaz Bessone concludes his book on the following pessimistic note: "By the end of 1978 military victory over the revolutionary war in Argentina was a fact. But the war would continue on the political plane. Perhaps as never before in our country, the aggressor is able to affirm that peace is the continuation of war by other means."[156]

The Youth Resistance

At the head of the youth resistance in Argentina was the Peronist Youth. On 19 August 1983 some forty thousand marchers protested the law of amnesty exonerating the military for its role during the dirty war. The column of the Peronist Youth not only dwarfed that of other youth organizations, including the Radical Youth, but also placed fourth behind the columns of the Communist party, representing some three hundred thousand affiliates, the former Trotskyist Movement toward Socialism, and the Intransigent party in a march in which prudence dictated that both the Peronist and the Radical parties should not participate.[157]

However, by then a sizable section of the Peronist Youth had asserted its independence of the Montoneros. From the moment the Montoneros returned underground in 1974 until the collapse of their ill-fated armed and propaganda offensive in 1979, the Peronist Youth functioned mainly as a guerrilla support group. In 1979 factional differences in the Montoneros led to a corresponding split in its youth section. Thus an independent JP emerged alongside the Montoneros' youth organization at the same time that both began to play an increasingly important role in the resistance.

Patricia Bullrich, Galimberti's sister-in-law and a leader of the Peronist Youth inside Argentina, followed him in 1979 by breaking with Firmenich.[158] She and other disaffected leaders of the Montonero youth branch recovered their autonomy in partnership with Galimberti's self-styled "Peronism in the Resistance." Calling themselves the Peronist Youth in the Resistance, they held their first clandestine congress on an island in the Paraná River in September 1980.

That same month they began publishing *Huelga* (strike) in an effort to mobilize workers of all ages against the military regime. As the first number declared in its editorial, its purpose was to become an alternative press, to voice the aspirations of the workers, and "to contribute to the consolidation of an effective labor and popular resistance."[159] Toward this end, its first task was to rebuild the decimated shop steward organizations and to organize strike committees in each factory.[160]

The Peronist Youth in the Resistance also stole a lead on the Montonero-dominated Peronist Youth–Regional Organizations by reviving in October 1979 the latter's banned journal *JOTAPÉ*. Published intermittently until it began to appear on a regular basis in 1983, the revived *JOTAPÉ* concentrated on propaganda for mobilizing youth against the dictatorship. The first number contained a letter by Galimberti on the crime of being young.[161] It also featured an editorial by Bullrich under the pseudonym of Carolina Serrano, in which she criticized the JP–R for "becoming isolated, clandestinized, and disconnected from the thousands of activists in their workplaces by abandoning universities, factories, neighborhoods, etc."[162] It was the first of six clandestine issues (the last appeared in early 1982). In another six issues she boldly used her real name in defiance of the military.

Galimberti's and Bullrich's contributions dominated the first four issues (October 1979–March 1981).[163] Beginning with the seventh number, in December 1982, through the twelfth in October 1983, Galimberti no longer figured at all—a testimony to Bullrich's increasing political independence. As a former Montonero leader and a fugitive from justice, he had become more of a liability than an asset in Bullrich's efforts to get the Peronist Youth once again recognized as the official fourth branch of the Peronist movement. Thus two years later, reminded of her debt to Galimberti and asked if she still represented his political line, Bullrich replied: "I don't think so. Galimberti is outside the country and today, because of his age, he has very little to do with the Peronist Youth."[164]

What was the role of the Montoneros' youth organization during this period? In 1979 the military's self-styled task forces revised their repressive tactics of detention-torture-information-detention by allowing suspects to remain free for four or five months in order to trap their associates. Thus in an effort to protect their cadres in Argentina, the Montoneros in 1980 launched the slogan "Don't work in groups" (No agruparse).[165] This policy, which prevailed until mid-1982, helped the Montoneros's youth group to make a comeback. Rather than a shift from active to passive resistance, it was a shift from organized to individual resistance based on Perón's overall insurrectional strategy of 1956.

This strategy of survival accounts for the fact that not until two and a half years after the revival of *JOTAPÉ* did the JP–R begin publishing *JP ¡Presente!* The first number appeared in February–March 1982 on the heels of the extinct *Vencer,* first on a bimonthly and then on a monthly basis. By then the Montoneros had decided in favor of anonymity by ceasing to publish a journal of their own.

In its new journal the JP–R hammered away at the imperative of mobilizing workers and pressuring the military to call elections. Under the slogan "Mobilization is the only road" the first five numbers, through October 1982, disseminated the Montoneros' new strategy, which since November 1979 had displaced their original reliance on military operations.[166] The special supplement to the fifth number reiterated this message in an interview with veteran Peronist leader Andrés Framini. Asked what strategy should be adopted to guarantee the military's withdrawal, he replied. "I believe that with one eye we should be looking at recruiting affiliates and with the other—which is the most important and must not be abandoned—at mobilization. The people's best weapon for demonstrating its strength to the enemy is mobilization. . . . Even if there is a coup and the present generals are replaced by others, they will be unable to stop the elections."[167]

A major document published in the fifth number of *JP ¡Presente!* claims that the youth resistance helped in toppling both the second and third military juntas. "The heroic resistance of the first years following the 24 March 1976 coup led by the most combatant and consequential sectors of the labor movement, by the popular organizations and relatives of the victims of repression, laid the groundwork for the recovery of the popular forces and sealed the Peronist Youth's revolutionary commitment with the blood of the best sons of the people. This commitment showed itself in the mobilizations that put an end to the 'continuist' plans of Viola and Galtieri."[168] Viola's government was destabilized by the general strike of July 1981 and by the March of Protest to the Church of San Cayetano in November. Galtieri's government was destabilized in a similar way by popular demonstrations during the first half of 1982, in which the JP–R again played a significant role. The reorganization of the Peronist Youth, its reappearance as an organized force, "made its numerical and mobilizing weight felt in the march to San Cayetano, in the street fights during the criminal repression on March 30 of this year in almost all the country's cities, and in the mobilization of June 15 that finished off Galtieri."[169]

The JP–R mobilized again on September 22 and then in the March for Life by the Mothers of the Plaza de Mayo in October. While the collaborationist current within the trade unions and the political parties cautioned, "Don't rock the boat," the JP–R boldly went ahead with its strategy of preventing the military from achieving an orderly retreat.[170] In open repudiation of a policy of accommodation, it called for continued struggle toward a "national and popular revolution, not a pact with tyrants and traitors."[171] Mimicking the military's policy of disappearances, the JP–R proposed its own final solution to the subversion problem: "There can be no solution for the country without 'disappearing' the oligarchy."[172]

In February 1983 the JP sector loyal to the Montoneros staged its first national congress since the military takeover. Assembling in the capital of San Juan Province, the JP–R made its bid to become the fourth branch of the Peronist movement.[173] Reviewing the popular mobilizations of 1982, it claimed a share of the fruits based on its participation in the events that beginning on March 30 effectively destabilized the regime. "Thus March 30, June 14, September 22, the March for Life on October 5, the multisectoral mobilizations in San Juan and Mendoza, the neighborhood marches that reached a climax in the *lanusazo*, the general strike of December 6, and the march of resistance were stepping-stones in the growing struggle and popular mobilization."[174] But it was to be a new and transformed Peronist movement with which the JP–R hoped to become reunified.[175]

For Bullrich's sector of the JP loyal to the official party, this smacked of "Montonero Peronism." Indeed, Galimberti's *La revolución peronista*, a sixty-three-page booklet published in May 1983, called into question the "rupturist trans-Peronism" of the "fake 'revolutionaries' who had betrayed the movement."[176] As Bullrich later commented: "The JP–R conceals the stigma of the Montoneros, and this invalidates many political alliances."[177] Galimberti's political ambitions had also suffered from this stigma.

That both sectors of the Peronist Youth played a consequential role in destabilizing the military regime is evident from the Montoneros' documentary film *The 16th of December*.[178] Used in training Montonero youth, the documentary focuses on the youth resistance during the decisive year, 1982. Beginning with the second March of Protest, organized by the CGT on March 30, the viewer is led through a series of spectacular events in which the Argentine people and the youth in particular mobilized against the dictatorship. One witnesses the occupation of the Plaza de Mayo on April 10 in support of the liberation of the Malvinas/Falklands and the restoration of democracy, followed by the violent ejection of the youth from the Plaza on June 15, when they interrupted President Galtieri's speech announcing Argentina's defeat. The work stoppage on September 22 in open defiance of the dictatorship, in which the trade union youth also distinguished themselves, further discredited the regime. So did the March for Life, in which some 10,000 persons converged on the Plaza de Mayo on October 5, and the convocation of the Peronist masses at the Peronist party rally in Atlanta Stadium on October 18. But December was the crucial month. The general strike mobilized some 6 million workers on December 6, the March of Resistance mobilized more than 100,000 people on December 10, and the March for Democracy brought together more than 150,000 on December 16. Only during this final episode, organized by the *multipartidaria*, did the crowd get out of hand, when some 300 youth struggled to break through the military cordon protecting the Government House. Understandably, the government blamed the Montoneros for the violence.

Altogether, the youth resistance added to the military's headaches. This was partly a function of its size. According to the "Final Document" of the military regime released in May 1983, the guerrillas reached a peak capacity of 15,000 militarily trained and fully armed combatants.[179] But there were another 100,000 or more supporters among the youth. Díaz Bessone claims that "the guerrillas with their sympathizers and ideological supporters did not exceed 150,000."[180] A majority belonged to the pre-1979 Peronist Youth.[181]

The military's estimates appear to err on the low side. The circulation figures of the Peronist Left and PRT-ERP publications provide a rough guide to the level of active support for the guerrillas. The Peronist Youth weekly *El Descamisado* had a circulation of more than 100,000 before it was banned in April 1974, while the Montonero daily *Noticias* sold 150,000 copies on a regular basis before it was shut down in August.[182]

But these periodicals represented only one sector of the Peronist Left, that which came to terms momentarily with the Peronist government. The weekly *Militancia*, with a circulation of forty thousand, appealed to a different political constituency, which favored an alliance with the PRT-ERP against the government.[183] And it is a fair guess that before being suppressed in March 1974 the ERP-oriented daily *El Mundo*, if not its fortnightly *Nuevo Hombre*, at least matched the circulation of *Militancia*.

Since the circulation figures of *El Descamisado* and *Noticias* overlap, the Montonero-JP sector of the resistance was probably no larger than 150,000. Even so, the guerrillas together with their logistical and ideological supporters would also have included the 40,000 readers of the PRT-oriented journals.

As former Córdoba governor Ricardo Obregón Cano summarized the relative importance of the principal forms of resistance to the Military Process, next to the resistance by organized labor the most important resistance was the youth resistance.[184]

The Trade Union Resistance

The same institutional factors that destabilized the government of Isabel Perón upset the military regime that replaced it. In each case the principal catalyst was organized labor's demand for a share of political influence and the national income corresponding to its numbers and role in Peronist doctrine. Although not the only organized opposition, it was the most influential.

Economically, labor had the greatest stake in the resistance. Perón had anticipated a 50 percent share of the national pie for labor by 1977 and a 52 percent share by 1980.[185] But what promised to be a modest step for organized labor proved to be too much for the military. In the conviction that the trade unions had exceeded their bounds by demanding and getting excessive wages and benefits, the armed forces imposed an austerity plan designed to restore the status quo prior to the entire Peronist era, dating back even before World War II.[186]

The Military Process set Argentina back more than three decades. The proportion of wages and salaries in the national income fell from 47.3 percent in 1974 to 30.8 percent in 1977—a level roughly maintained through 1978.[187] Although 1979 showed a slight improvement, former minister of economy Aldo Ferrer claimed that labor's share had fallen from 48 percent to 35 percent from 1976 to 1979.[188] These were the golden years of the Military Process. Thus labor's share was substantially below levels prior to the coup.

This reduction was matched by an absolute fall in real wages. Real wages were reported as having fallen some 40 percent between March 1976 and the end of 1978.[189] The real minimum wage of an unskilled worker was reduced by 40 percent during 1976 alone.[190] Worse still, by the end of 1978 the average wage had fallen to 36 percent of wages paid to skilled workers in 1974 and to 29 percent of wages paid to unskilled workers.[191]

The sharply escalating inflation under Isabel Perón's government had been halted, but it was achieved at the cost of slowing down the economy. The fall in real wages was accompanied by a drastic curtailment of investment, a corresponding reduction in the GNP, and an absolute reduction in the number of wage and salary earners from approximately 76 percent of the total work force in 1970 to 61 percent in 1980.[192] Possibly, this was a world record. No other country to my knowledge had so restructured its economy that it had ended not just poorer instead of richer by the turn of the decade, but also with a smaller percentage of wage and salary earners than it began.

Although the level of employment remained stable during the period 1976–1979, it was achieved with the help of low wages and the reemergence of a class of self-employed workers. The regressive restructuring of the work force was evident in the growth of this archaic class from some 6 percent of the work force in 1970 to 20 percent in 1980.[193] Other factors contributing to the maintenance of high employment levels were the compulsory displacement of foreign workers, mostly Paraguayans, Chileans, and Bolivians, and the flight of several hundred thousand "political undesirables" who sought sanctuary abroad.[194] But a severe recession was around the corner. By 1980–1981 unemployment had become a major problem reminiscent of the Great Depression. By October 1980 total unemployment had soared above 10 percent of the economically active population and had climbed to approximately 12 percent by April 1981.[195]

Trade union resistance to the Military Process was predicated on these and similar developments. New leaders, surging up from the ranks in replacement of old leaders who had been jailed, complained of the suicidal course taken by the "Process of National Disorganization." However, there were at least two features of the Military Process that did not figure in their denunciations: first, the improvement in salary levels of professional, scientific, and administrative employees; second, the expansion of the public sector, despite the regime's vaunted economic liberalism and denationalization of selective enterprises.[196]

The forcible reduction in real wages was mainly a blow at organized labor and did not adversely affect the compensation of highly qualified professionals and administrators. In 1980 there was an increase in wage and salary differentials "in favor of the categories of 'qualified worker,' 'supervisors and foremen' in factory personnel, and for the highest category of administrative personnel."[197] That same month the average compensation of workers received a boost of 39 percent, in part to catch up with inflation. But it was distributed unequally and contributed to a further rupture in employee solidarity. Thus the increase for factory workers was only 26.6 percent, compared to 44.5 percent for administrators.[198]

The new minister of economy, José Martínez de Hoz, was directly responsible for the reform of the wage and salary structure. As he explained the motives of the reform, it was indispensable for overcoming the downward leveling typical of labor policies during the 1973–1976 period.[199]

This leveling process had allegedly destroyed incentives for improving skills, acquiring professional competence, and assuming greater responsibilities. Owing to collective bargaining, the beginning wage of unskilled workers in some instances exceeded the salaries of the most capable and qualified officials.[200] The Military Process aimed at reestablishing order, thereby "reimplanting the hierarchical structure in the field of labor."[201] The "Wizard of Hoz," as he was affectionately dubbed by the international business community, repudiated the wage and labor policies of the Peronist labor bureaucracy as partial to nonprofessional workers and an obstacle to higher technification. "If we compare the wage and salary structure to a pyramid in which the base is broad and represented by the larger number of low-level wages for less specialized work, but gets progressively narrower as salaries become greater, then this pyramidal structure changed during 1976–80: the base became smaller and it fattened out in the middle because of the increasing number of better paid, technically qualified and specialized jobs available."[202]

The restructuring of this pyramid was not confined to the private sector. Martínez de Hoz made a special point of applying it to state enterprises and to the rest of the public sector. Consequently, professional military officers transformed into government administrators doubly benefited. The top military brass had not clamped down on the trade unions merely to increase capital's share of the national income; their own salaries were at stake.

The assault on collective bargaining was a victory of capital over labor, but it was also a victory for the emerging professional and managerial class and its vanguard—the armed forces. Professional soldiers questioned what they perceived as the privileges of a spoiled and undisciplined working class, privileges made possible through collective bargaining—a right denied to military officers. They lamented the tendency of labor contracts to narrow income differentials between professional and nonprofessional workers. They especially resented the high salaries of trade union officials, bureaucrats like themselves but without their social background and education.

The first restructuring of the wage and salary pyramid occurred in November 1976 with the objective of correcting distortions in the collective contracts of 1975, which had been imposed through political pressures.[203] This reform was followed by a second in March 1977, introducing a greater spread and differentiation in wage and salary scales. The third reform, in April 1978, widened further the gap between the minimum wage and top salaries for managers and professionals.[204]

Figures on the redistribution of income at the expense of labor and to the benefit of capital effectively conceal the extent to which professional and managerial strata and other members of the so-called new class benefited from the wage and labor policies of the Military Process. This is because the statistical category of professional salaries is misleadingly included in labor's share. Since there are few data covering the increased share of the technobureaucratic class in national income during the 1976–1983 period or before, it has been uncritically assumed that big business was the only beneficiary of the government's new high-tech policies.

During the months leading up to the military coup, Argentine labor had acquired a share of political power never before matched in the country's history. The trade unions controlled the governments of the three most important industrialized provinces (Buenos Aires, Córdoba, Santa Fe), they held key cabinet posts in the Ministry of Labor (Carlos Ruckauf) and the Ministry of Economy (Antonio Cafiero), and they were directly represented on the Supreme Council of the Peronist movement by Lorenzo Miguel and Casildo Herreras. This situation became intolerable to the top military brass, who looked on labor bureaucrats as social upstarts. Thus the powers of the state were used to intervene the unions and to replace their leaders with military appointees.

When the generals took over in 1976, the political offices shared by the Peronist political and trade union bureaucracies were monopolized and divided among the three branches of the armed forces. In effect, one set of bureaucrats replaced another. As Argentine sociologist Francisco Delich concludes: "The trade union bureaucracy was shoved aside and replaced by the state bureaucracy."[205] At issue was an interbureaucratic struggle for power rather than a contest between labor and capital. Even so, big capital became the principal economic beneficiary of the Military Process, while labor became the principal victim.[206] It was against this background that the trade unions took the initiative in organizing and mobilizing what became the chief force of the resistance.

The resistance had to contend with obstacles never before encountered. The Military Process differed from previous military experiments in the extent of its economic, institutional, and physical attacks on organized labor. In the past, trade union resistance had been coordinated with armed struggle under the overall leadership of General Perón. This time there was no supreme conductor to guide

it, and the only surviving Peronist armed formation, the Montoneros, had been discredited as subversive by most Peronists. Thus
repression reached levels hitherto unheard of, but for organized labor the means of combating it excluded the use of violence.

In a speech to the International Labor Organization in Geneva in
May 1980, the general secretary of the Plastic Workers' Union, the
"moderate" Jorge Triaca, claimed that from 1976 to 1980 Argentine
workers had had some fifty billion dollars in wages and salaries expropriated by the military regime's nullification of collective contracts.[207] As early as April 1976 the Ley de Contrato de Trabajo (LCT)
had been revised, suspending the right of collective bargaining,
which had been the source of most of labor's gains from 1973 to
1976. The new Contract Law abolished automatic wage increases
designed to keep up with inflation.[208] It imposed penalties for poor
performance and harsh measures for absenteeism without a signed
medical excuse. It gave the employer the right to alter working conditions, including the length and intensity of the working day, without consulting the workers. It abolished the special privileges
awarded by collective contracts, such as the six-hour day, discounts
for company products, low-interest loans, free clinics, maternity
benefits, nursery lunch rooms, scholarships and leave for technical
education. With the abrogation of collective contracts also went
workers' control and participation in the management of their
enterprises.

To this unprecedented assault on the workers' standard of living
was added the institutional violence toward their organizations. In
November 1979 the government revised the legal basis of trade
union power, the Ley de Asociaciones Profesionales (LAP).[209] The
CGT was formally dissolved and the trade unions forbidden to ad-
minister their pension and welfare funds. The closed shop and dues
checkoff systems were declared illegal.

The revised law of professional associations prohibited unions
from engaging in political activity, from receiving subsidies from political organizations, and from supporting candidates for political
office. It decreed that unions could not have jurisdiction beyond a
single province and the federal capital, thereby contributing to their
geographical division. In forbidding persons with police records
from occupying union posts, it removed by a single stroke virtually
all leaders of the Argentine labor movement, who at one time or another had been imprisoned for labor activism. The new law also prohibited supervisory, scientific, and managerial employees from belonging to the same unions as manual workers—a decree aimed at
further fragmenting the work force and at increasing income differ-

entials to the advantage of professional workers and officers in the armed forces.

These setbacks were attended by physical violence against union leaders and labor activists accused of aiding subversion. The government's campaign of psychological warfare against the unions, the persecution, imprisonment, kidnapping, assassination, and disappearance of labor activists, had never before been carried out systematically. Trade union leaders with suspected Marxist or Guevarist sympathies were mercilessly exterminated, unless, like Ongaro, they found refuge in exile. René Salamanca, the revolutionary head of the Córdoba auto workers Sindicato de Mecánicos y Afines del Transporte Automotriz (SMATA), was arrested on the day of the coup and never heard of again.[210] A similar fate overtook Jorge Di Pasquale, the militant leader of the Pharmacy Workers' Union, in December 1976.

Orthodox Peronists also disappeared, notwithstanding their anticommunism. Oscar Smith, the militant head of the Light and Power Workers' Union, was kidnapped and disappeared in February 1977.[211] According to a statement by the Relatives of the Disappeared and Detained for Political Reasons, "40 percent of the detained-disappeared are workers from almost all the trade unions, some union leaders, others factory delegates, the majority simply workers who struggled to redeem their rights."[212] This figure was based on a document issued by the Permanent Assembly of Human Rights, covering some five and a half thousand disappearances between 1975 and 1982.

A major concern of the Military Process was to eradicate so-called factory guerrillas and subversives within the labor movement.[213] As the new minister of labor Gen. Horacio Tomás Liendo indicated in his May Day message of 1976, any effort to resist the Process of National Reorganization was tantamount to allying oneself with subversion. Among the symptoms of subversion he included individual and group indoctrination among the rank and file and the support of false grievances and artificial conflicts aimed at confronting managers and discrediting the workers' responsible leaders.[214] In the conviction that labor protest was the work of infiltrators in the labor movement, Liendo warned Argentine workers not to become their accomplices.

The penalties for playing into the hands of subversion initially terrorized almost all organized labor into passivity. Delich recalls how labor activists—thousands of them—were fired, imprisoned, killed, disappeared, and forced into exile. "There were executions in the factories, and physical and psychological violence was used to frighten the workers. Assemblies and meetings were forbidden. . . . Labor recruitment became provisional and did not acquire stability until the intelligence services responded to the information provided by employers."[215] Consequently, a record as an activist blocked the way to continued employment.

In response to the first wave of labor conflicts in Ford, General Motors, FIAT, Peugeot, and Chrysler in September 1976, culminating in strikes at both the Ford and the General Motors plants, the government announced that it would imprison for six years those who participated in a strike; whoever instigated one would serve ten years. The Ford plant, with some four thousand workers, was occupied by the army. At gunpoint workers were forced to return to their jobs.[216] A hundred union delegates were jailed, along with subdelegates and labor activists, some of whom permanently disappeared.[217]

The generals had portrayed themselves as defenders of civilization against a government and a popular movement they considered lawless, corrupt, and ultimately responsible for subversion. They had also been touting their commitment to Christian values. The trade unions followed suit by supporting the military's war against subversion and appealing to the social doctrines of the church as a buffer against repression.

Support for trade union resistance was forthcoming from the Latin American Bishops' Conference in January 1979 in Puebla, Mexico. The bishops examined and rejected three ideologies: capitalist liberalism, Marxist collectivism, and the doctrine of national security.[218] There could be no question of identifying Peronism with any one of them. But the military junta was committed to the doctrine of national security, which the bishops condemned for violating church teachings concerning natural rights. Sensing that the bishops were on their side, the trade unions appealed to church doctrine in their confrontations with the military regime.[219]

Subsequently, the trade unions invoked in their defense Pope John Paul II's 1981 encyclical *Laborem Exercens,* which made an even stronger impression on the labor rank and file.[220] Celebrating the ninetieth anniversary of Pope Leo XIII's *Rerum Novarum,* John Paul II's encyclical followed the guidelines of Vatican II in recognizing the presence of objectively unjust situations that cry out for radical and urgent change.[221] At the core of the encyclical was the pope's insistence on the priority of labor over capital on the ground that capital is ultimately derived from labor. Notwithstanding his opposition to Marxism, his sketch of a basic Christian and humanist understanding of work had considerably more in common with Marx's labor theory of value than with traditional economic theory.[222]

It also shared a commitment to Marx's model of socialism managed by freely associated producers, the model advocated by the Polish Solidarity movement. Like Solidarity, the Polish pope wanted democracy and socialism in the workplace as well as in government: "For it must be noted that merely taking these means of production (capital) out of the hands of their private owners is not enough to ensure their satisfactory socialization. . . . Converting the means of production into state property in the collectivist system is by no means equivalent to 'socializing' that property. We can speak of socializing only when . . . on the basis of his work each person is fully entitled to consider himself a part-owner of the great workbench at which he is working with everyone else."[223]

Here was the rationale for resistance and for a Christian national syndicalism that the Peronist trade unions had been looking for. It is hardly a coincidence that the first general strike against the Military Process occurred in the immediate wake of the Puebla Conference, while the first massive protest march took place some two months after John Paul II's encyclical. Both the Polish labor movement and the pope's backing of it provided fuel for the trade union resistance in Argentina.

As Alvaro Abós acknowledged: "During those years many of the partial strikes were 'Polish in character.' Strikes characterized in these terms were accompanied by peaceful mobilizations in the train of an image of the Virgin of Luján, and in many cases counted on the protective presence of the local priest. It was an adaptation to our circumstances of the epic struggle of the Polish trade union Solidarity, whose similarities with the Argentine situation were immediately recognized by our workers."[224] The emphasis *Laborem Exercens* placed on the right to strike and on the indispensable role of trade unions in contemporary societies was interpreted by Argentine trade unionists as a "vote of condemnation against the antilabor policies of the junta and as a moral passport legitimizing the actions of the unions."[225]

Although the main body of the Catholic clergy opted for dialogue with the military regime, at least three bishops publicly denounced its policies as incompatible with the social teachings of the church. Archbishop Zaspe of the province of Santa Fe criticized the junta's intervention of the trade unions as incompatible with church doctrine; Bishop Hesayne of Viedma in the province of Río Negro denounced the suppression of collective contracts as sinful; and Bishop Angelelli in the province of La Rioja paid with his life for his strictures against the un-Christian character of the military regime.[226] Parish priests also voiced their dissent. On 4 June 1976 two priests and three Irish seminarians were gunned down in St. Patrick's Church in Belgrano "R," a suburb of the nation's capital, allegedly for subversion under the cover of Christian values.

The trade union resistance may be interpreted in part as an ideological struggle to determine who were the authentic defenders of the church in Argentina. The ideological underpinnings of Peronist social and political doctrine coincided with church teachings concerning the social question as reinterpreted by Pope John XXIII and Vatican II (1962–1965). Although the military's vaunted defense of Western Christian values agreed with traditional church doctrine, it had not kept pace with the times. Thus the support received from recent church teachings inspired trade unionists to defy the Military Process by means of illegal strikes and marches that risked not only their jobs, but also their freedom and in some instances their lives.

The 1956–1973 resistance had seen three main currents of trade union opposition to the repressive policies of military and pseudo-constitutional regimes. There was a collaborationist current committed to business unionism and to dialogue with the government aimed at negotiating the workers' hours, wages, health, and other social services within the existing institutional framework. Opposed to it was a current committed to political action, to presenting a solid front against the government, and to restoring the Peronist homeland, with the trade unions in key government positions. Opposed to both of these was a revolutionary current represented by the combative trade unions with socialist aspirations. Although the political action current relied on a variety of tactics, including dialogue, semilegal slowdowns, and illegal strikes and sabotage, only the revolutionary current responded to Perón's earlier call for absolute intransigence, full-scale civil resistance, and support for the clandestine organizations preparing for armed struggle.

All three currents reappeared within a year of the 1976 coup. But because the revolutionary current had sparked the 1969 *cordobazo* and had been linked to armed subversion, it suffered the same fate as the Montoneros and the ERP.

Originally led by Amado Olmos, head of the Sanitation Workers' Union, the revolutionary current was responsible for the transitional socialist program adopted by the CGT at its 1962 national conference in Huerta Grande, Córdoba. When a CGT split occurred in 1968, this program was reaffirmed by the newly constituted CGT of the Argentines (CGTA) under Raimundo Ongaro's leadership. After the *cordobazo* the CGTA was outlawed and Ongaro went to prison for his role in the resistance. Later, he fell afoul of Isabel

Perón's government and went into exile. Because the intensified persecution of his followers effectively crippled the revolutionary current, it could not play the leading role against the Military Process that it had during the earlier resistance.

With the revolutionary current out of sight, the political action current became the principal focus of opposition to the Military Process. Representing the views of seventy-eight unions, the first major document of the trade union resistance declared on 5 January 1977: "Extremism, represented as much by the unpatriotic and suicidal guerrillas of the Left as by right-wing groups intent on imposing their own conception of justice with a violence no less inhumane, is the expression of an elitism that disdains the people."[227] It then added that both kinds of extremism served foreign interests intent on the division and destruction of the nation. Even so, this affirmation of patriotism did not sit well with the military government, which denounced the document as subversive and obliged the commission responsible for it to dissolve.

The political action current was repudiated by the military regime for claiming the right to represent the workers' interests at the state level, thereby demanding a key role in shaping government policy. At the same time, its economic demands were abhorrent to the generals, for it also claimed an exclusive right to negotiate wages and working conditions by concentrating trade union power in the General Confederation of Labor. It was the current representing Perón's views concerning organized labor. The three pillars of his trade union doctrine were unity in a single union of workers in each branch of industry and a single federation of trade unions to coordinate their economic struggles; solidarity, to overcome the political differences among workers; and organization of, by, and for the workers to guarantee their independence.[228]

During the first Peronist resistance Rogelio Coria, head of the Unión Obrera de la Construcción de la República Argentina (UOCRA), personified the collaborationist current. His place was taken during the 1976–1983 resistance by Jorge Triaca, head of the plastic workers. As the moving spirit behind the Negotiation and Labor Commission launched in April 1978 by some of the largest unions intervened by the government, he became general secretary of the Comisión Nacional de Trabajo (CNT), founded with the government's blessing in August 1978. Triaca was the single most influential leader of organized labor until the trade union resistance began building up momentum with the illegal revival of the CGT in November 1980.[229] During the war in the Malvinas/Falklands the CNT decided to transform itself into a rival CGT, the CGT–Azopardo, named after the street that housed it. It, too, was under Triaca's leadership.

The political action current during the 1956–1973 resistance was personified by Augusto Vandor, nicknamed "el Lobo" (the Wolf). He was secretary of the powerful Metalworkers' Union (UOM). By artfully combining negotiation and intransigence, Vandor distinguished himself as the key figure in the "62 Organizations"—the political arm of the Peronist trade unions—after Amado Olmos's brief sway over it during the early 1960s. Following Vandor's assassination by pre-Montonero guerrillas in June 1969, his shoes were filled by the UOM's new secretary, José Ignacio Rucci. After the Montoneros assassinated Rucci in September 1973, Lorenzo Miguel occupied both posts.

On the eve of the military coup the Peronist trade union bureaucracy was divided between those who sought an accommodation with the military and those loyal to Isabel Perón. As the head of the 62 Organizations, Lorenzo Miguel cast his lot with the latter. Rodolfo Audi was the only journalist present when Miguel reported the news of the president's arrest by the army. As he recalled the event: "Miguel stood up and . . . decreed the revolutionary general strike in defense of the institutional order."[230] The decree was broadcast within minutes, but it was quickly silenced by the military-imposed censorship.

Because of his political role as head of the 62 Organizations, Miguel was imprisoned by the military for almost four and a half years. Only after his release in April 1980 was he in a position to take charge of the developing trade union resistance. But by then the leadership of the political action current had crystallized under two new figures, Roberto García of the Taxi Drivers' Union and Saúl Ubaldini of the tiny Brewers' Federation.

García was the principal organizer of the Commission of the 25, the first enduring trade union federation of the resistance. Launched in March 1977, it antedated Triaca's organization by more than a year. In July 1978 he also founded the ill-fated Movimiento Sindical Peronista (MSP), proscribed by the government barely two months later as reedition of the illegal 62 Organizations.[231] But it continued functioning underground until 1983, when it became the trade union nucleus of Antonio Cafiero's Movimiento de Unidad, Solidaridad y Organización (MUSO), which backed Cafiero's bid as the Peronist party's candidate for president.[232] In 1983 García became the principal trade union leader in the camp of the renovators, which included Cafiero and other Peronists who hoped to democratize the Peronist movement. Until then a leading exponent of "verticalism"—the Peronist principle of authority according to which Peronists are expected to obey the directives of their leader—he subsequently adopted a pronounced antiverticalist position.

Ubaldini, a fellow verticalist who later replaced García as the principal spokesman of the Commission of the 25, emerged from obscurity to become the key figure in the trade union resistance.[233] Press secretary of the Brewers' Federation, he was elected general secretary of the illegally revived CGT, subsequently the CGT–Brasil, named after the street in which it was headquartered to distinguish it from the rival CGT–Azopardo. Ubaldini became famous for recovering the passionate rhetoric and mystique of union solidarity that had been Ongaro's claim to fame. He also was the only union leader during the resistance to approach the Mothers of the Plaza de Mayo and to embrace their leader, Hebe de Bonafini, in a gesture identifying labor's cause with the movement for human rights.

Interpreting the history of the trade union resistance is no easy task. Its ups and downs hinge on what factors are taken as decisive. How the resistance is divided into stages depends on the weights assigned to the intensity and scope of the resistance at any given moment and the role of the trade unions' legal and illegal organizations, mobilizations, and public declarations.

Alvaro Abós argues that the turning point of the resistance came in November 1978 with the publication of a document by the Commission of the 25 calling for an end to the Military Process.[234] The decisive factors, as he perceives them, were not the scope and intensity of labor mobilizations that came later, but the organization of political activists in the Commission of the 25 and their subsequent agreement on a strategy of defiance articulated in the national press. Thus "the consolidation of the CNT as a dialoguing entity pushed the 25 to adopt a posture of open confrontation with the regime."[235] At issue was who would become the recognized leaders of the working class: the temporizers, or the intransigents. Both made their bids in November 1978 in major statements to the press.[236] But the document of the 25 read by Ubaldini at a dinner of three hundred leading Peronists tipped the scales.

Granted that November 1978 was a turning point of the resistance, the accumulated evidence of trade union activity from March 1976 to December 1983 testifies against its being the only turning point. Instead of one big retreat until November 1978 followed by a single great advance, the trade unions responded piecemeal to the military's piecemeal assault. As they perceived the struggle, it consisted of a series of small advances followed by partial retreats and then by new starts. It was aptly summarized in the slogan "Barajar y dar de nuevo" (shuffle and deal again).[237]

It appears that this reshuffling by organized labor occurred several times. The first wave of resistance from September 1976 to November 1977 came in response to the worst setback the trade unions had experienced in their history. Trade union leaders hesitated to risk their liberty by supporting strikes, slowdowns, and other illegal mobilizations. Following a second retreat, the second wave of resistance from November 1978 to November 1979 went beyond mere economic demands in calling for the restoration of democracy and an end to government repression. By then the intransigents were prepared to serve jail terms for illegal activities. For the first time the continued existence of the Military Process was questioned. After another year of retreat, the third wave of resistance, from November 1980 to December 1983, directly mobilized workers in political confrontations with the regime.[238] During this last stage the political activists moved from sporadic illegal activities to permanent confrontation symbolized by their revival of the illegal CGT.

The story of this resistance by quotas is that of a prolonged struggle between labor's David and the army's Goliath. After five months of dejection and inertia, Argentine workers suddenly showed signs of life in a rash of conflicts over wages leading to a series of strikes in the auto industry in September 1976. This singular response was followed in October by a still more acute struggle by light and power workers, who protested enforcement of the new Labor Contract Law. In retaliation for their strike in October, the army detained the leaders and occupied the electric plants. The workers then resorted to slowdowns to protest the fate of those who had been arrested, fired, kidnapped, or tortured.

This state of affairs continued through the beginning of January 1977. On January 26, five thousand intervened light and power workers gathered in front of their union hall in the first massive demonstration against the regime. Frequent acts of industrial sabotage were reported in the press. From January 29 to February 4 the press reported damage to electrical transformers, fires and floods in power plants, and repeated cuts in electricity. On February 8 the workers again struck in open defiance of the government. More detentions and kidnappings of union delegates followed. Finally, on February 11 the union's general secretary was disappeared.

In response to this mounting wave of labor militancy, trade union leaders organized a commission representing the smaller unions that were not intervened. In an open letter to the minister of labor, the commission demanded wage increases, worker participation in the determination of wages, the return of collective bargaining, the end of government intervention in the trade unions, the immediate restoration of the CGT, the release of trade unionists imprisoned without cause, the publication of a list of those detained stating their whereabouts, the end of massive hiring and firing on ideological grounds, and a substantial change in the government's economic policies.[239]

In March it was replaced by the Commission of the 25, consisting initially of twenty medium-sized unions that were soon joined by five others.[240] It provided the leadership for the second rash of strikes in October and November 1977, when several hundred thousand workers struck the railways, subways, ports, airlines, buses, gas and petroleum installations, bottling plants, textile factories, banks, and credit institutions. Most of these strikers limited their demands to wage increases and, in most cases, despite the illegal nature of the strikes, the government complied with the strikers' demands. The result was a temporary respite in a class struggle that had yet to acquire a political character.

The world football match hosted by Argentina and the impending war with Chile over unsettled boundaries in the Beagle Channel tended to overshadow other issues in 1978. It was a year of recession for the resistance, a year of relative stagnation in labor activism marked by the normalization of the collaborationist current. Thus Triaca's Negotiation and Labor Commission founded the CNT, recognized by the government as the principal representative of organized labor because of its commitment to dialogue. Although the Commission of the 25 responded by organizing the Peronist Trade Union movement, the latter's political character was sufficiently transparent that the government outlawed it. Some thirty-five representatives were temporarily jailed in the first mass arrest of top union leaders since March 1976.

A reshuffling occurred in November, which interrupted the lull in labor activism and led directly to the first general strike in April 1979. The statement of the 25, read by Ubaldini at a dinner of top Peronists and then widely circulated by the press, supplemented earlier economic demands with a call for elections, democracy based on social justice, and an end to military government.[241] Although the document was denounced by the authorities, this time the authors refused to back down.

Before the general strike could materialize, its instigators were arrested. Jailed on April 23, some were not released until several months later. Their place was taken by a clandestine Commission of the 25, which went ahead with plans for the strike. But the strike did not have the support of the CNT. Its scope was limited to the industrial belt around the federal capital, where the influence of labor activists was strongest.

The failure of the strike elsewhere prompted the intransigents to negotiate with the moderates in an effort to overcome the division within the labor movement. In September the CNT and the Commission of the 25 momentarily buried their differences by founding a new umbrella organization, the Conducción Unica de los Trabajadores Argentinos (CUTA), but six months later the political activists deserted it because of its conciliatory tactics. Then came the biggest blow organized labor had suffered since the revision of the Law of Contract in April 1976. On 16 November 1979 the new Law of Professional Associations outlawed the CGT.

In 1980 there was a noticeable decline in trade union mobilizations, but it was to be the last major reversal under the Military Process. The internal division of the labor movement persisted with the effective dissolution of the CUTA in March. Then came the activist boom—three consecutive years of steady and mounting advances linked to the illegal restoration of the CGT.

The revival of the CGT was the prelude to the second general strike, on 22 July 1981.[242] Although the *multipartidaria* refrained from backing the strike, the Peronist party and several lesser parties supported it. But again the negative of the CNT kept the strike from becoming anything more than partial. It was confined to the industrial cordon around the capital. On this occasion the detention of the instigators lasted only three days.

This action was followed on November 7 by the first protest march against the government. Under the slogan "Bread, peace, and work," Ubaldini led a procession toward the Church of San Cayetano, where a mass in the open air was celebrated by the local curate.[243] Some ten thousand workers participated, but without support from either the *multipartidaria* or the CNT. This demonstration was a notorious success and, for the first time, its authors were not sanctioned, despite their open defiance of the authorities.

The *estallido social*, the social explosion that contributed to toppling the military regime, occurred in 1982. It began with a second protest march and trade union mobilization on March 30. This was followed, in the wake of the disastrous war over the Malvinas/Falklands, by another mobilization and march on September 22. Then came the third general strike, on December 6, at the initiative of the CGT–Azopardo, which had joined the bandwagon. Supported by the *multipartidaria* and by political activists in the CGT–Brasil, this strike was an overwhelming success, as was the March for Democracy on December 16, organized by the *multipartidaria* with the backing of both CGTs.

By then the armed forces had become concerned mainly with retiring gracefully and protecting themselves from judicial prosecution. But there was to be no letup by the resistance. Two more general strikes were declared, on March 28 and October 4, 1983, again almost 100 percent effective.

One need not agree with the Montoneros' assessment of their role in the resistance to appreciate their view of the principal stages leading to the denouement of the Military Process. As they depicted these stages in a seventeen-page document dated June 1983: "Taking a panoramic view of the almost eight years of this oligarchical tyranny, one sees that in 1976 we took charge of the resistance, that the resistance became sufficiently generalized to put a brake on and destabilize Martínez de Hoz's project, and that in unison with the social and political vanguard of the organized labor movement we launched in 1979 the popular counteroffensive . . . and obliged the dictatorship to retreat when all the other social sectors of the national and popular camp joined the struggle."[244] In this account a key role was played by the trade union resistance.

Although it would be rash to conclude that trade union resistance toppled the military regime, it contributed, along with the government's bungling of the economy and of the war in the Malvinas / Falklands, to inducing the military to step down. Thus labor's strategy of "shuffle and deal again" paid off. Said Saúl Ubaldini in a CGT declaration on 2 November 1983, published on the heels of the Peronist electoral upset in October: "There has been only one winner, the Argentine people!"[245] Besides welcoming the return of democracy, he defended the resistance of organized labor in an emotional homage to those who died in the struggle against the Military Process "in the streets, the factories, and the churches."[246]

As Raimundo Ongaro has reiterated, the accumulated force and momentum of trade union resistance is not spontaneous, but the result of months, sometimes years, of painstaking preparation. That was his experience in 1969 in connection with the first *cordobazo*— a lesson repeated on the occasion of the first general strike against the Military Process a decade later.[247] Said Ongaro in a message from exile in celebration of this first general strike: "This day of national protest is not the work of an inspired group. It is the expression of the people's dignity in a national strike against a group of military elitists, who scorned the collective and national conscience of the Argentines. It is not a general strike surging forth from a spectacular paroxysm. It is the first coordinated response throughout the entire country. After taking three years to prepare, day by day, with the anonymous actions of millions of workers flowing together in a massive torrent of liberty, it will inundate the commandos of repression."[248]

His words were a token of things to come.

9. The Final Humiliation

THE OUTCOME of the Military Process did not conform to the generals' expectations. The trial and punishment of the guilty began with the abdication of the military in December 1983. Argentina's equivalent of the famous Nuremburg Trials after World War II, the trials of the generals, admirals, and air force brigadiers responsible for the Military Process, set a precedent not only in Argentina, but also for the rest of Latin America. Never before had the three branches of the armed services had to account to civilians for allegedly criminal behavior and a surfeit of patriotic zeal in the exercise of military duties.

The members of the three military juntas were first tried by their peers in the Armed Forces Supreme Council, a military court whose judges had been appointed during the Military Process. Understandably, the judges stood behind their former colleagues in the dock and acquitted them by refusing to reach a negative verdict. In line with President Alfonsín's amendments to the Military Code of Justice, their cases then came before a civilian court, the Federal Court of Criminal Appeals. Throughout these new trials military leaders continued to protest their innocence while disputing the jurisdiction of a civilian court in military matters. Former president Videla boycotted his trial by refusing to designate defense counsel, and the defense attorneys of other members of the three military juntas likewise insisted that the trial was unconstitutional. The trials were further denounced for encouraging a new wave of subversion.

The armed services had been disgraced and the military party had to bear the consequences. But it was not the military's only humiliation. Its final humiliation was to see its work undone, to witness the revival of subversion through a continuation of the resistance against the new Radical government, as if nothing had happened between 1976 and 1983. To add to this affront, the Montoneros survived the holocaust and the ERP's former members began to regroup. They also became active in a variety of legal fronts, which they created or penetrated. Thus the military's worst fears were becoming a reality. The victors in the war against subversion were being displaced by the vanquished.

The Resistance Continues

For two hours on 22 April 1985 I watched some fifty thousand marchers led by the Mothers of the Plaza de Mayo followed by the principal youth organizations and the parties of the revolutionary Left. Tantamount to the fifth march of resistance, this Mobilization for the Trial and Punishment of the Guilty clamored for the release of political prisoners. Denounced for their backing of political subversives during the Military Process, the Mothers had become the principal thorn in the side of the new Radical regime.

Who were these "Mothers" who had become an independent political force in Argentina? From their first demonstration in the Plaza de Mayo opposite Government House in April 1977, the Mothers mounted an uncompromising campaign for their sons' and daughters' live reappearance. Their show of solidarity with the families victimized by state terrorism pointed an accusing finger at the military government. Identified by their white kerchiefs, they continued to convene there every Thursday afternoon for a decade to demand information concerning the thousands of disappearances, punishment of those responsible for genocide, and freedom for political prisoners. Linked to the guerrillas by sympathy and blood, the Mothers also covered for them politically. Their professedly humanitarian concerns transcended political labels, but the underlying reality of their resistance presupposed a major restructuring of society. Their resistance, like that of the youth, did not end with the military regime but continues to the present day.

The Mothers' campaign had the backing of other human rights groups. The list is an impressive one: the Relatives of the Disappeared and Detained for Political Reasons; the Asamblea Permanente por los Derechos Humanos (APDH); the Movimiento Ecuménico por los Derechos Humanos (MEDH); the Centro de Estudios Legales y Sociales (CELS); and the Servicio de Paz y Justicia (SERPAJ).[1] Through their combined efforts the courts were flooded with suits and petitions against the illegal privation of human freedom. The Mothers' original list of eight hundred disappearances, compiled in December 1977, rose to twenty-five hundred in May 1978 and some four thousand by September 1979; it has since doubled.

As they became bolder, the Mothers organized so-called marches of resistance. On the heels of the first massive human rights demonstration in October 1982, they launched the one hundred thousand–strong first March of the Resistance in December. It would not be the last. Two more marches of resistance occurred in 1983 and a fourth in December 1984. Thus the psychological warfare launched against the military regime did not suddenly stop with the inauguration of a democratic government.

As an argument for continuing their struggle, the Mothers pointed to Alfonsín's December 1983 presidential edict against the heroes of the resistance who, instead of being rewarded for their efforts, were being brought to trial with the generals. In an effort to placate the armed forces, Alfonsín chose to deal harshly with acts of subversive terrorism. Thus the Mothers found themselves at loggerheads with a constitutional government that had authorized new antisubversive legislation.

The president of Argentina declared all forms of terrorism to be equally reprehensible. This explains the government's repeated affirmations that there were no political prisoners. But the Mothers of the Plaza de Mayo, the Grandmothers of the Plaza de Mayo, and the Relatives of the Disappeared and Detained for Political Reasons did not share this opinion. They believed that in likening the political-military vanguards to the forces of chaos and in persecuting the leaders of the armed resistance as "criminal," Alfonsín's government was continuing in the footsteps of the military.

President Alfonsín was unswervingly committed to the rule of law. His commitment helped fuel the opposition to the Military Process, but it also made him question any opposition besides his own. "For Alfonsín the trade unions were not antagonists of the regime but, on the contrary, its prolongations or, worse, its even more totalitarian excrescence."[2] This explains why the president did not repeal the repressive decrees against organized labor enacted by his military predecessors: "Between the real legality of the labor movement . . . trampled by the dictatorship in 1976 and the formal legality assigned to it by the dictatorial regime in 1979, Alfonsín gave priority and preeminence to the latter."[3] In this perspective, the new democratic Leviathan had become a cover for the monstrous and repressive labor policies of the military Behemoth it replaced.

Before abdicating, the military government decreed amnesty for those responsible for the dirty war. Although the law was rescinded by the Radical government, Alfonsín bowed to the generals' request that the officers be tried by a military court. The results were predictable. Even before the verdict was announced the Mothers and their human rights supporters were protesting the procedure as an example of continuity with the military past.

Adolfo Pérez Esquivel, a leading human rights activist and winner of the Nobel Peace Prize, explained why he refused to participate in the government's National Commission on the Disappearance of Persons, headed by novelist Ernesto Sábato. "Under no conditions could we accept that the military should be judge in its own case."[4] What would it mean for the military's top brass to be tried for war crimes, when the tribunal itself was a military one? Esquivel interpreted it as a sign that the Radical government was proceeding with great caution so as not to offend the armed forces. In effect, the latter continued to exercise a veto in political matters.

In response to the president's decision to permit the trial of generals and admirals by a military court, the leader of the Intransigent party denounced the procedure as unconstitutional. Dr. Oscar Alende, the party's head, also questioned the president's record on human rights. "In December 1977, despite occasional appearances at meetings of the Permanent Assembly for Human Rights (APDH), Dr. Alfonsín publicly gave his support to General Videla and requested that the repression be unified!"[5]

The military trials turned into a fiasco. The council of twenty retired officers charged with courts-martial deliberated for almost five months before reaching a verdict in September 1984. They found no one guilty. Here was additional evidence of continuity with the military regime, which reinforced the Mothers' decision to continue their resistance.

A year after Alfonsín came to power, the Mothers' grievances had still to be resolved: "No to amnesty. Trial and punishment of the guilty. Reappearance alive. Freedom for political prisoners. Return of children to their families"![6] The government finally had recourse to civil prosecutions, but they did not begin until April 1985, and when the verdicts were announced in December, the top military brass literally got away with murder.

In August 1985 one of the leaders of the dissolved Montonero Peronist movement, former governor Ricardo Obregón, was sentenced to ten years for membership in an "illicit organization." And in November the public prosecutor demanded life imprisonment for Firmenich, whose reputation as Public Enemy Number One did not count in his favor. Thus the constitutional government continued the work of its unconstitutional predecessor by refusing to release political prisoners and by indicting and sentencing new ones. As the Mothers of the Plaza de Mayo responded to this "continuism" in a December editorial in their *Madres de Plaza de Mayo:* "The Resistance Continues!"[7]

The treatment accorded to Firmenich is instructive. In exile in Mexico with other members of the Montoneros' national leadership, Firmenich had eluded efforts by Argentine intelligence and security forces to capture or eliminate him. It was Alfonsín's supposedly tolerant and benign government that succeeded in trapping him.

Firmenich arrived in Brazil with his wife and child in November 1983 to attend an international conference of popular and democratic parties. After his wife gave birth to a second son, he visited the Argentine consul in Rio de Janeiro in February 1984 to legalize the infant's nationality. The consul demanded his arrest, the Brazilian authorities complied, and President Alfonsín asked for his extradition.[8] Despite a massive campaign in Brazil for his release, he was extradited in October on condition that his penalty would not exceed that under Brazilian law—a total of twenty-five years. This condition was ignored by his prosecutors.

The fact that from March 1976 onward he had led an armed resistance against the military dictatorship did not exonerate him. Firmenich was indicted for the September 1974 kidnapping of corporate executives Juan and Jorge Born, for the October 1979 attempt on the life of treasury secretary Juan Alemann, and for the November 1979 slaying of Argentine executive Francisco Soldati.[9] For the Radical party in power, that was enough to make him a terrorist.

The "continuism" between the military and the democratic governments was denounced not only by the Mothers, but also by political analysts. As one commentator complained about the repressive legislation carried over from the Military Process: "The evils of yesterday may bear fruit with today's complaisance."[10] Among the most glaring examples of this "dirty postwar" was the government's deference to the military establishment in August 1984. Instead of demoting and punishing, the government promoted to the rank of general those who had tortured journalists, burned books, and provisioned the army's and navy's concentration camps.[11]

Although the Radicals made a fetish of human rights, they showed more concern for ending censorship and the laws against pornography than for restoring the rights of workers. Apparently, trade union demands for untrammeled collective bargaining, for freedom of action without constant interference from the Ministry of Labor, for workers' self-management, and for a share in the profits did not figure in the radicals' conception of rights. Three years after assuming power, the Radical government had still not repealed the Labor Contract Law, which arbitrarily suspended the right of collective bargaining, or the sinister attack on the rights of organized labor made by the Law of Professional Associations. Although these survivals of military repression were seldom enforced, they remained on the books ready to be applied in case of emergency.

A similar assessment of the Radical government's continuity with the Military Process was being diffused by the Montoneros' youth branch. The new government was lambasted for absolving the oligarchy of responsibility for the tragic events of the past decade. Thus in an internal document the JP–R defined the conjunctural option as "REAL DEMOCRACY OR OLIGARCHICAL CONTINUISM."[12]

Commenting on the proposed March of Resistance on 20 December 1984, to be followed by the March in Defense of Democracy on the twenty-first, Firmenich urged the JP–R to participate massively in both. In an article submitted in December but published after the two events, he wrote: "Without resistance . . . democracy would not have been restored, and without resistance it cannot be defended on the likely day that the oligarchical minority attempts another gorilla strike."[13]

Operating with greater caution since its leaders had yet to be indicted by the new government, the PRT did not announce its intentions of continuing the resistance until a year and a half later. Then, responding to the resurgence of right-wing terrorism, the PRT urged: "Advance the Popular Resistance. . . . The increasing attacks demonstrate that a democracy that does not strengthen itself economically must inevitably fall back on social and political repression."[14]

Despite the democratic fanfare, there was an underlying continuity between the new Radical government and the military governments that preceded it. Because of military blackmail, the fate of the new government depended not only on punishing the guerrillas, but also on preventing the rebirth of subversion. This scenario prompted Argentina's returning exiles to continue their resistance against repressive laws surviving from the Military Process. Like the Montoneros and Galimberti's tendency, both the PRT and Gorriarán's followers began preparing for a protracted struggle against these unconstitutional hangovers.

The Quest for Political Allies

Toward this objective during the three years following the restoration of democracy, the quest for new political allies and the restructuring of old alliances became one of the former guerrillas' main concerns. By then they had assimilated the principal lesson of the Nicaraguan Revolution, that revolutionaries cannot succeed by themselves: "The experience of the Nicaraguan Revolution, and the

Cuban Revolution for that matter, demonstrates that the only kind of alliance that can succeed is one in which the revolutionary forces have *the backing and fronting of political moderates."*[15] Widespread support for the Mothers of the Plaza de Mayo and of other human rights groups vividly confirmed the advantages of the new strategy.

This strategy had worked miracles in Nicaragua.[16] Convinced that it could not win without support from other social classes, the FSLN in 1977 surreptitiously organized a support group of professionals and businesspeople calling itself the Group of Twelve. As an integral part of the broad opposition organized in the Frente Amplio de Oposición (FAO), the Group of Twelve represented FSLN interests among the social forces seeking a negotiated settlement with Somoza. A year later the Sandinistas further broadened their support by organizing the Movimiento Pueblo Unido (MPU), which eventually included twenty-two trade unions and civic and political associations. Finally, in 1979 they created the Frente Patriótico Nacional (FPN), embracing a number of small but influential political parties.

How did Argentina's returning exiles respond to the Nicaraguan example? The PRT's "classist" response was to rebuild its organization in 1983–1984 and to support the Frente del Pueblo (FREPU), organized in September 1985. At the initiative of Osvaldo Villaflor, survivors of the former Peronist Armed Forces and rank-and-file Peronism also joined the People's Front (FP) coalition.[17] This infusion of Peronist blood, according to Pablo Giussani, contributed to the front's predominantly populist ideology. Although Communists represented the strongest single force in the alliance, its political language was "70 percent Peronist, 25 percent Trotskyist, and only 5 percent Communist."[18] But it polled only 2 percent of the vote, and the PRT was demonstrably upset by the concessions made to Peronist doctrine.

The other former guerrillas opted for a "movementist" response. Following Gorriarán's guidelines, former members of the ERP laid the groundwork for a new populist alternative that invoked the intransigent legacy of the Radical and Peronist movements. Meanwhile, those responsive to Galimberti made common cause with the reformists in the Peronist establishment who were clamoring for internal democracy and a renovation in doctrine and leadership. Alone among the returning exiles, the Montoneros experimented with a multiplicity of options.

In October 1984 Gorriarán gave an extensive interview in Cali, Colombia, in which he steered a middle course between the Radical party's option of "Democracy or Dictatorship" and the alternative of "Liberation or Dependence" posed by revolutionary Peronism. By calling for the convergence of revolutionary currents in support of both democracy and liberation, he evoked fears that his followers were engaged in a new kind of subversion aimed at destabilizing the constitutional government.

The fundamental error of the guerrillas, Gorriarán recalled, was their lack of the kind of revolutionary unity that won the day in Nicaragua.[19] Asked about the feasibility of reconstituting the revolutionary organizations of the previous decade, he replied: "We believe that the political tendency in Argentina is oriented toward something new . . . a unitary synthesis of the progressive wings of the traditional parties and the surviving remnants of the revolutionary current, plus the new generation and the sectoral organizations that emerged during the last few years—all united in a great social and political movement committed to leading the struggle for authentic national liberation."[20]

Gorriarán envisioned a movement patterned on the example of the Sandinistas and hegemonized by new social forces outside the dominant two-party system. Although the fundamental obstacle faced by these social forces was their lack of political unity, he was confident of overcoming it. "What divided and divides us is an identification with a political party. . . . We think the solution requires an end to all sectarianism and a concentrated effort to build a national revolutionary political organization, which will allow its members to maintain their previous political identification even when they unite. . . . I mean to say that a Peronist, a Socialist, or a Christian will not have to cease being one in order to come together."[21]

The monthly *Entre Todos* became a striking example of the efforts by Gorriarán's followers to chart a new course from outside the two major parties. Committed to the unity of the progressive forces, it has contributed to spearheading a third political alternative in Argentina. *Entre Todos* began publishing in December 1984. Its subtitle, "Those Who Want Liberation," is followed by a list of supporting groups suggesting an Argentine counterpart of the Sandinista Front of National Liberation. It attempts to bring together Peronists, Radicals, Intransigents, Christians, Socialists, Communists, and independents such as the Mothers of the Plaza de Mayo and the various human rights groups, into a kind of people's front. Whereas *El Combatiente* aimed at building the vanguard, *Entre Todos* championed a mass line.

Gorriarán was the only former leader of the PRT on the government's most-wanted list, but he was also the least sectarian. Unlike their former comrades, his followers were not constrained by classist preconceptions. When they returned from exile they adopted a policy of "entrism" into the Juventud Intransigente (JI), the youth sector of Oscar Alende's Intransigent party. The press cited this strategy of infiltration as evidence of a "subversive rebirth."

The strategy of entrism into the Intransigent Youth was shared with other dissident elements likewise dissociated from the PRT. These included former followers of Mattini who left the party in August 1980, former political prisoners, most of whom lost contact with the party during confinement, and the free elements (*sueltos*) who had to shift for themselves after May 1977.[22] This was a sizable group and accounts for what the mass media called the effective "takeover" of the Intransigent Youth by former members of the PRT-ERP. In any case, the JI became the principal mass organization at the disposal of these former guerrillas.

Nelson Marinelli, a militant in the Partido Obrero (PO), the Trotskyist Labor party affiliated with the Fourth International (International Committee), credits the former cadres of the PRT-ERP with having built the Intransigent Youth movement.[23] Virtually nonexistent prior to reorganizing in 1983, this thriving youth sector represented a challenge to the party's old guard. Thus when the JI won the elections in a party local in Greater Buenos Aires, the local was closed down by PI authorities.

At its Fourth National Congress in 1984 in Alta Gracia, Córdoba, the JI presented a Marxist-Leninist analysis of the Argentine situation strongly suggestive of this new influence.[24] Besides unity of the popular forces in a "third historical movement," it insisted on the hegemony of the working class as a prerequisite of victory. "The revolutionary transformation of the system . . . depends on the vanguard role of the workers, because they possess the most advanced degree of national consciousness in having suffered most from the contradictions of imperialism."[25]

In its scenario of a third historical movement, the document of the Fourth Congress faulted radicalism for failing to incorporate the working class in a populist coalition, and Peronism for losing the support of intermediate strata. "Despite their achievements, these movements failed to overcome both the ties of dependence on imperialism and the economic basis of oligarchical power."[26] They also failed in a misguided effort to unify the popular forces under a single party. "The third historical movement is not the exclusive patrimony of any political party [and] . . . the Intransigent party does not pretend to dominate it."[27]

The scenario of a third historical movement was brought to national attention during Raúl Alfonsín's presidential campaign in

1983, but it had ceased to be a monopoly of the Radical party. Alfonsín envisioned a successor to the first popular movement led by Hipólito Yrigoyen and the second under Juan Domingo Perón.[28] The first came to represent a decisive majority because of its defense and implementation of political democracy; the second, because it responded to the workers' demands for economic and social justice. But the first historical movement failed because it did not respond to a mushrooming labor force demanding economic reforms and protective social legislation.[29] The second failed because its authoritarian and corporativist tendencies were incompatible with democracy.[30]

Alfonsín hoped to overcome the limitations of radicalism and Peronism through a new movement committed to social justice and democracy. A coalescence of the Radical and Peronist parties in an electoral front would be futile, he argued, because an electoral compromise would effectively perpetuate instead of eradicating their respective errors.[31] Consequently, he proposed to reform the Radical party in the expectation of transforming it into the desired political synthesis. But despite the initial appeal, the Radical project never got off the ground.

A different kind of movementist option was that of the former Montoneros and their youth sector, transformed from the Peronist Youth in the Resistance into the Unified Peronist Youth. Founded on the heels of the military's abdication in December 1983, the JPU in November 1984 launched a new *JOTAPÉ* (Second epoch), which continued to be published on a bimonthly basis.

Despite Bullrich's disclaimers concerning Galimberti, the JPU leadership included several of Galimberti's former "lieutenants." In my interview with Daniel Llano and the JPU's secretary of organization, Jorge Reyna, they acknowledged Galimberti's continuing influence.[32] Llano was in weekly touch with Galimberti in Paris by telephone. Moreover, in my subsequent interview with Bullrich, she admitted to sharing Galimberti's general orientation.

In May 1985 the top offices in the JPU were still nonelective. It could not be otherwise for a clandestinely created organization that had only recently emerged from underground. Although its first congress had been held in January, its top leaders were carry-overs from the former "Peronist Youth in the Resistance." Within the new organization Bullrich shared with Pablo Unamuno a position tantamount to general secretary.

Hostility toward the Montoneros and the JP–R was a feature of this new organization as well as its predecessor. Interviewed in January 1985, Bullrich was asked for her opinion of the Montoneros: "It is an organization with more international links than with a real idea of how to transform Argentina. It has changed into something clownish, into a clownish minority without any clear definition but with a persistent sense of the messianic. . . . It was a bad joke for those who fell because of their beliefs; and for the survivors of that experience it is a betrayal."[33] Concluding that the Montoneros had become a fossil like the PRT and that Firmenich was the image of defeat, she had decided to keep her distance from both.

At the same time, Bullrich rejected the temptation of joining other youth groups to build a third historical movement.[34] Her group had other plans. In September 1982, after the military's defeat in the Malvinas/Falklands and in response to the electoral opening that followed, Bittel and other veteran Peronists encouraged the formation of a new current called the Movement of Unity, Solidarity, and Organization (MUSO). Among its founders were former minister of economy Antonio Cafiero and labor minister Miguel Unamuno. Unamuno was the father of Pablo Unamuno, who shared with Bullrich the leadership of Galimberti's youth sector.

MUSO brought together the different verticalist tendencies in traditional Peronism, which had been loyal to Isabel Perón and had distinguished themselves by their resistance to the Military Process. Unlike the party's other electoral currents, MUSO based its program on Perón's political testament in *El proyecto nacional*. Supported initially by Lorenzo Miguel and the 62 Organizations, the *musistas* expected to dominate the party's primaries and prevail in the national elections. Such was the star to which the Peronist Youth in the Resistance attached itself to become, with the backing and fronting of Cafiero and Miguel Unamuno, the MUSO's youth sector.

In an interview with Mona Moncalvillo and Alberto Fernández, Cafiero identified MUSO with the first attempt at renovating the party's project and methods. He recalled MUSO's official review *Movimiento*, in which a new kind of Peronism was first discussed. "There was the nucleus of the central idea that, if Peronism did not renew its project and methodology, if it did not assimilate the changes that had occurred in Argentine society, if it did not explicitly renounce violence, if it did not clearly repudiate the military regime, then it would have no future in the country's political scenario."[35] It was to Cafiero's credit that with Bittel's encouragement he launched what would later become the renovating current in Peronism. Thus to have become MUSO's youth sector was a tour de force for Galimberti's tendency.

Calling themselves the "renovators," the dissidents convoked a congress of their own in Río Hondo, Santiago del Estero, in February 1985. In repudiation of the marshals of defeat responsible for the electoral fiasco of October 1983, this congress elected a new national leadership. Backed to the hilt by Galimberti's youth group, reorganized as the Unified Peronist Youth, the renovators rewarded the latter by promising to restore the youth branch of the Peronist movement.

From the backing and fronting of MUSO to that of the renovators—that has been the political trajectory of Galimberti's tendency since 1982. But with the exception of Cafiero, the other two leading renovators in the congressional renewal elections of November 1985, Carlos Grosso and Saúl Menem, retained their distrust of the former Montoneros. Unlike Cafiero's homecoming, to the prodigal sons and daughters of Peronism Grosso and Menem turned a cold shoulder. In a series of interviews they were asked how they proposed to assimilate the youth led by Bullrich and Unamuno. Grosso responded that it was not enough that they had won representativity in the news media, since they still had to compete in internal elections.[36] Menem's response was downright hostile: "Patricia and Unamuno are part of revolutionary Peronism and have been disqualified by the youth and by the majority of the party's leaders. . . . They want to return to old methodologies, but Montonerism has no place in our political community!"[37]

In the end the JPU's leaders saw that they might have to renounce their resistance if they hoped to cement their fragile alliance with the renovators. Tantamount to a rupture with Galimberti, this prospect was already the subject of heated discussions within the JPU's inner circle when I became privy to it in April 1985. I did not anticipate the outcome. By the end of the year both Pablo Unamuno and Jorge Reyna had made their peace with the Montoneros by joining the National Executive Board of Revolutionary Peronism alongside Mario Firmenich and Roberto Perdía.[38]

How well did the JPU leadership apply the lessons of the Nicaraguan Revolution? While the FSLN exercised effective control over the organizations of political moderates that backed and fronted for it, this was not the kind of tie that bound the Peronist Youth in the Resistance to MUSO nor the JPU to the renovators. The JPU hoped to continue its resistance in alliance with the renovators, but in doing so it had to take a back seat to Perón's posthumous social democratic orthodoxy. In part that explains the desertions of Pablo Unamuno and Galimberti's "lieutenant" in favor of the Montoneros' independent strategy vis-à-vis the Peronist establishment.

The Special Case of the Montoneros

In a statement to the press in December 1983, the Montoneros announced their decision to dissolve the Montonero Peronist movement. For most Argentines this meant the dissolution of the Montoneros as a revolutionary vanguard. Imagine their surprise when, on 2 April 1984, a Montonero column appeared alongside the former combatants in the Malvinas/Falklands in a march commemorating the second anniversary of Argentina's repossession of the islands.[39] According to one account, the Montoneros' resurrection was not an improvised event but the "patiently prepared implementation of a strategy adopted at a summit meeting in Mexico in mid-1983, a strategy for recovering from their smashing political and military defeat beginning in 1976."[40]

Only a few days before, according to an insistent rumor, the Montonero leadership had met secretly in Córdoba with the leaders of the ERP to assess the political situation and to agree on a common strategy for confronting the new democratic government. Although the accusation proved unfounded, other charges of a subversive rebirth (*rebrote subversivo*) continued to surface during the following year. In January 1985 the press reported that the Peruvian guerrillas known as Sendero Luminoso (Shining Path), in collaboration with the Montoneros and the ERP, were infiltrating political organizations on the Left, including the Peronist Youth and the Intransigent party. It was further reported that the Montoneros under Firmenich's leadership had decided to postpone the armed struggle until a more opportune moment. Firmenich denied any substance to this rumor.[41]

In April the monthly *El Porteño* ran a lead article exposing the "feverish visions of a subversive rebirth."[42] According to testimony by former *erpistas*, the ERP had dissolved and there were no plans to revive it.[43] Among other rumors laid to rest was one that the Montoneros were preparing reprisals for the imprisonment of Firmenich. The editors also reproduced his article on the alleged terrorist conspiracy.[44] But in the course of defending the Montoneros against accusations of renewed violence, they failed to note that the Montonero leader was committed to continuing the resistance.

While acknowledging that the ERP no longer existed, Firmenich explained that the Montoneros did exist and would continue to play a role in Argentine political life.[45] After ten years of state terrorism at the service of the oligarchy and dependence, the questioning of the status quo was being revived by the popular sectors, including the Montoneros. That was the deeper significance behind accusations of a "subversive rebirth."[46]

As Firmenich noted in a printed handout in November 1983, "even the elementary manuals of strategy point out two possible responses to defeat: unconditional surrender and dispersion of one's forces or, on the contrary, regrouping under a new strategy."[47] The Montoneros opted for the latter. Consequently, after giving up the armed struggle, they began currying favor with revolutionary Peronists loyal to the official party. This sector was better able to survive repression and, beginning in March 1981, began to replace the Montoneros as the principal influence on the Peronist Left. Represented by Peronist Intransigence (IP), founded by Vicente L. Saadi in July 1981, it later adopted the name Peronist Intransigence and Mobilization (IMP).

Here was the initial backing and fronting the Montoneros needed to regain political credibility and influence. But as Ongaro quipped: "It was neither intransigent nor mobilizing."[48] For the sake of party unity Saadi had welcomed back the Montoneros, but he also made significant concessions to the party's right wing. In keeping with Perón's strategy of embrace and absorb, Saadi worked for a solid front of all Peronists first against the Military Process and then against the government of Raúl Alfonsín.

A coalition with Peronist Intransigence became the Montoneros' strategic objective once they formally abandoned the armed struggle and began rebuilding their legal fronts. Hoping for its cooperation, they sought to revive their former legal cover, the Authentic Peronist party (PPA). Only after this effort failed did they make overtures to other groups in exploratory efforts to galvanize a third historical movement. Then they attempted a rapprochement with the renovators opposed to the official Peronist leadership. Later, they sought an agreement with the party's official leaders. Finally, they turned to the CGT for help.

It was in response to the Peronist electoral defeat in October 1983, when the crisis of the Peronist party had become visible, that Firmenich proposed the first strategy. In an article published under the pseudonym of "Darío Quiroga," he attributed the loss of votes among the labor and popular sectors to the failure by the party's leaders to uphold the movement's revolutionary tradition and to incorporate new revolutionary proposals suited to the present stage: "return of the disappeared, settlement of accounts, and reparation of damage."[49] The adoption of these proposals also aimed to broaden the movement's support base.

Firmenich concluded that the electoral fiasco indicated a loss of confidence in the Peronist party and its leadership. As Italo Luder had commented on the principal difference between himself and Alfonsín in the presidential campaign, a vote for Peronism meant support for the social doctrines of the Catholic church.[50] Peronism's loss of revolutionary élan had reduced itself to this. Hence the imperative of establishing a revolutionary alternative to the official party.

Hoping to build a viable alternative, the Montoneros invited other revolutionary Peronists to join in refloating the PPA. Declared illegal by Isabel Perón's government in December 1975 because of ties to the Montoneros, it was temporarily resurrected in December 1983.

Their proposal to relaunch the PPA was outlined in a document presented to the press by those who had backed and fronted for the Montoneros in 1975. Released by the former governor of Buenos Aires Oscar Bidegain after arriving at the Ezeiza airport on 20 December 1983, the document explained the Montoneros' decision to build an alternative Peronist party instead of working to transform the official one from within. "Forced into exile, we founded the Montonero Peronist movement as a political organism of opposition to the tyranny installed in Argentina, . . . but in these new circumstances in which the oligarchical-military regime has been defeated and the rule of law restored, there is no reason to maintain that structure. Therefore, together with the dissolution of the Montonero Peronist movement, we have come to recuperate the political and juridical personality of the Authentic party."[51]

Thus ended the Montonero Peronist movement, an "illicit" organization that stood in the way of the Montoneros' unification with the rest of revolutionary Peronism. The Montonero Army had already dissolved, so all that was left of the Montoneros was a revolutionary vanguard with a political heritage—since the self-styled Montonero party was not a party in the electoral sense.

The Montonero project received the immediate backing of its youth organization. According to the JP–R, the successive defeats of September 1955, March 1976, and October 1983 were rooted in the failure of Peronism to articulate and promote a global plan for eradicating the oligarchy and the country's dependence on imperialism.[52] This failure was compounded by the disorganization of the Peronist movement, its inability to find a substitute for the unipersonal and charismatic leadership of its founder. Until those problems were solved and the movement became reorganized along democratic lines, the JP–R maintained, there was no hope for revolutionary Peronism.[53]

According to the document, the answer was to participate actively in the transformation of Peronism by rebuilding its revolutionary nucleus; that meant to escape from the bonds of the two-party system, from the populist fossils that played into the hands of the oligarchy.[54] This system of tweedledum and tweedledee offered no revolutionary alternative for voters, most of whom had backed one or the other of the established parties in the October elections.[55]

In response to the JP–R document, the Agrupación Peronismo Auténtico (APA) and the Agrupación "Sabino Navarro" were formally constituted in April 1984 as bases for reviving the Authentic Peronist party.[56] However, other sectors of revolutionary Peronism were wary of the Montoneros' intentions. The Montoneros were said to be a divisive factor within Peronism. As former congresswoman Nilda Garré, a leader of Peronist Intransigence and Mobilization, said in May: "It is our understanding that the Montonero project is definitely and absolutely exhausted. Thus we agree with the document that Oscar Bidegain made public on his arrival in the country, announcing that the Montonero Peronist movement had dissolved and that it was necessary to re-create new effective forms of organization."[57] However, the agreement ended there. "Concerning the relaunching of the Authentic party announced by Bidegain, which presupposes that Peronism is no longer viable, or at least that the Justicialist party has exhausted itself as an electoral instrument, we profoundly disagree. That is because we believe the struggle must be made within the Peronist movement, since it continues to be the reference point of the popular bases."[58]

Although Peronist Intransigence assumed the task of regrouping the Peronist Left in 1981, by inviting the Montoneros to participate it ran into a predicament. As Nilda Garré recalled: "It was our understanding that the space we hoped to create within the Peronist movement would be shared with all the cadres of combative Peronism. . . . It was our understanding that there would be no exclusions and that everyone could join us who satisfied those requisites [intransigence and mobilization]. But we understand that in recent documents—apparently issued in the name of 'revolutionary Peronism'—there is again talk of the viability of the 'Montonero project,' which is incongruous and a political delirium."[59] Worse still, the Montoneros were competing with Peronist Intransigence and Mobilization for the same political space.

It was not an easy matter to revive a political party whose leaders were detained on arrival at the Ezeiza airport. Charged with belonging to a Montonero underground organization, Bidegain managed to elude his captors and flee into exile. However, the former governor of Córdoba, Ricardo Obregón Cano, was not that lucky. Thus confronted with mounting obstacles, the Montonero leadership decided to abandon the seemingly hopeless project.

In June 1984 a new experimental strategy would take its place. The Montoneros who visited Brazil and conferred with Firmenich in prison, prior to his extradition hammered out a new policy. In an internal document launched from Rio de Janeiro based on their reassessment of the situation in Argentina, they posed the crucial question of how to carry on the revolutionary project of the past fifteen years.[60] Concerned with restructuring their web of alliances and overcoming their dependence on a Peronist movement that had failed them, they called for a political alternative tantamount to a third historical movement.[61]

The idea of a third historical movement was not original to Alfonsín and is now generally recognized as having been an electoral gimmick. As Firmenich commented in my interview: "It goes back almost 20 years to an effort by the then Revolutionary Armed Forces (FAR) to develop an alternative to both Radicalism and Peronism. The concept was originally formulated by Jorge Omar Lewinger, who subsequently became a Montonero and the editor of our journal *Vencer.* When the FAR merged with the Montoneros in October 1973 the original concept was discarded in view of the regeneration of the Peronist movement."

The collapse of efforts to refloat the PPA would revive interest in this alternative proposal. The Montoneros acknowledged a revolutionary heritage that was not exclusively Peronist but included contributions made by the Radical party under President Yrigoyen.[62] The labor and welfare legislation of the Peronist era was only the most recent expression of this intransigent legacy.

How was this heritage to be preserved? The Montoneros had tried to give their revolutionary current a mass basis by inserting themselves within the Peronist movement. At the same time, they had struggled to make Peronism the vehicle of a socialism suitable to Argentine national traditions.[63] In the course of their armed struggle against unconstitutional and repressive regimes they helped to develop the revolutionary current, but for a variety of reasons failed to transform the Peronist movement into a revolutionary force.

Was there any chance that they would eventually do so? As the document pointed out, there was less chance than when Perón was alive because the movement was leaderless, its doctrines went unheeded, and the political and labor bureaucracies refused to fill old bottles with the wine of new generations.[64] Even though important popular elements remained faithful to its project, "Peronism today

is in decadence."[65] The weaknesses that kept Perón from confronting the oligarchy when he was alive had become so aggravated that
Peronism no longer represented a clear majority of the Argentine
people, but had degenerated into another run-of-the-mill political
party. Thus the Montoneros wanted to establish a political space
for themselves that would embrace the intransigent current within
Peronism, but that would go beyond the limits of the Peronist
movement.

The document proposed a political realignment of revolutionary
Peronism with the youth who voted for Alfonsín's plans of renewal
and change, a youth destined to become disillusioned to the extent
that the Radical party did not live up to its campaign promises.[66] It
suggested further that the Montoneros should seek allies among
those closest to themselves politically, notably the Intransigent
party, the humanism and liberation current within Christian democracy, and the Marxist-Leninist Left.[67] "Today, our project no
longer consists in following the guideposts of a leader and strategist
like General Perón, who has ceased to exist, but rather in retaining
his historical guidelines, in rooting ourselves in the movement's
most dynamic social and political bases of support, and in addressing ourselves to those other sectors that are becoming the protagonists of the social change our country needs."[68]

As an alternative to becoming politically irrelevant in a movement that was no longer revolutionary, the document proposed to
develop a "third political space."[69] Because of Alfonsín's inability to
build a third historical movement for which he lacked support in his
own party, the Montoneros decided to make this Radical scenario
their own. Thus their new goal was to become the political alternative to a decadent Peronism and a frustrating radicalism.

The Montoneros' immediate task was to acquire representativity.[70] That would come not from infiltrating the leadership of
trade union and youth organizations, but from winning over their
organic leaders. To gain representativity would be to meet the aspirations of mass organizations by struggling to recover rights lost
under the military dictatorship.[71]

Originally, the Montoneros relied on the Peronist movement to
bring about a form of national socialism in response to the revolutionary surge of the masses who had followed Perón's leadership. But
the popular euphoria was gone and the political and labor bureaucracies could not agree on concrete steps for implementing a socialist
transformation. Since the Peronist movement had lost interest in
such a transformation, the Montoneros looked to a third historical
movement to chart the way.

But without assurance of controlling the proposed alliance, the new strategy made the Montoneros look like reformers rather than revolutionaries. In the first published interview with Firmenich following his extradition from Brazil, Jorge Asís was surprised to find a person whose words indicated he was anything but the ultraradical, bomb-throwing terrorist the press had pictured him to be. *"I would say more: if Firmenich of the decade of the seventies, of its beginnings, would have conversed with the present Firmenich, he would have dismissed him as a lukewarm reformist."*[72] Firmenich had so distanced himself from Marxism that his current political ideology and program seemed to have little in common with that other Firmenich, characterized by the authorities as Public Enemy Number One.

Because Firmenich was awaiting trial for a series of crimes that included murder as well as kidnapping, he had to be circumspect in what he said. Thus he claimed that most of the informal charges against him were fables, that the Montoneros were responsible for José Rucci's assassination, that the financier David Graiver had laundered the sixty million dollars in ransom from the kidnapping of the Born brothers, that Admiral Massera had met with him in Paris as the prelude to a series of crimes perpetrated against top government functionaries.[73] But why take Firmenich's word? asked Asís. He also wondered whether Firmenich's diffuse ideology of liberation, which distinguished the Montoneros from the Marxist-Leninist Left but obliterated their differences with the Intransigent party, represented his real views.[74] And why believe the spate of documents signed by Firmenich in view of his pending trial?

Asís suspected that the change in Firmenich's ideology was a case of special pleading coincident with the latter's imprisonment. But we have seen that Montonero efforts to recover representativity began several years prior to his October 1984 extradition. A new program had been launched with the publication in January–February 1982 of the final issue of *Vencer*, which identified the Montoneros' course with that of the Radical party under Yrigoyen and the Justicialist party under Perón. Its call for political pluralism and a mixed economy was part of the reformist program that took Asís by surprise. Thus Firmenich's imprisonment postdated rather than predated his new political line.

The foregoing strategy looked good on paper, but it was soon superseded by another strategy in response to an unprecedented split in the Peronist party. At the party's congress in the Odeón Theater in December 1984, Lorenzo Miguel tried to ram through his slate of hand-picked candidates. This move boomeranged when former members of the now-defunct MUSO, joined by Triaca's collaborationist sector and by Saadi's tendency, deserted the theater and made plans for a new congress. Although Triaca and Saadi were at best fair-weather allies of the fomer *musistas*, from December 1984 to July 1985 the renovators had a definite edge over the official party. Such was the context in which the Montoneros decided to make another about-turn.

In response to the Odeón split, the Montoneros called for an effective alliance with the renovators based on a new six-point program of "DOCTRINAL ACTUALIZATION, NATIONAL PROJECT, GENERATIONAL REJUVENATION, INTERNAL DEMOCRACY, STRATEGY OF POWER, AND REMOVAL OF THE COUP-MONGERING CABAL."[75] At issue was the creation of a new Peronist alternative akin to the defunct Authentic Peronist party but with a broader political base. Since it had proved impossible to remove the old leadership democratically, the Montoneros recommended the organization of a rival Peronist party in the capital and in the province of Buenos Aires, where the marshals of defeat were entrenched. Simultaneously, efforts would be made to rout the forces of Lorenzo Miguel and his allies in future party congresses. "If the transformation is achieved by defeating . . . Miguel in party congresses, so much the better. If not, and if another Peronist party competes in the coming elections, that is only to express 'externally' what was plugged 'internally.'"[76]

The political crisis of Peronism was compounded by the predicament confronting Alfonsín's party, which received only the government, not power. According to the Montonero analysis, the radicals were tied down, unable to fulfill their promises to the electorate and at the same time unwilling to resort to repression. The country was drifting toward social and political chaos: "Thus, after two, three, or at most four years of constitutional government, the conditions will have been created for a new military coup."[77]

Under these circumstances the Radical government could only be a government of transition, a "confusing and contradictory presence in which the continuist policies of the dictatorial past, imposed by those sectors that still retain power, coexist with the transformative policies imposed by the people on the dictatorship in retreat."[78] Hence, the question: Where will and should the transition end? To this the Montoneros responded that without a transforming and revolutionary alternative, the inverse course would be followed.[79]

With the prospect of another coup before Alfonsín completed his term in office, the Montoneros urged the reformist wing in the Justicialist party to put an end to verticalism, thuggery, sectarianism, and the attempts of each sector of the movement to monopolize power for itself.[80] That was the prospect the Justicialist Congress should have considered, but it did not heed the message. The result was two parties instead of one, with the Montoneros publicly supporting the renovators.

As Firmenich noted during my interview in the Villa Devoto Penitentiary, "The contradictions within the Movement stemming from its multiclass composition are currently being resolved owing to its newly acquired pluralist or democratic character." He was referring to the congress of the renovators in February, which agreed on a program first championed by the Montoneros in 1973. Is it not ironic, I remarked, that their program should have borne fruit more than a decade later? Firmenich retorted: "It was a matter *not* of historical irony, but of a correct strategy! . . . The electoral defeat of October 1983 contributed, more than anything else, to the emergence of the 'renovators.' They had to adopt our original proposals or otherwise face defeat in the congressional elections scheduled for November." Here supposedly was the transformative and renovative Peronism the Montoneros had been calling for, a party that no longer turned its back on the revolutionary current but promised to restore the Peronist Youth as the fourth official branch of the movement.

Firmenich's assessment of the renovators bordered on triumphalism. In fact, the Montoneros were not welcomed back. The renovators represented a new orthodoxy, which was only slightly less hostile to them than the old. An amnesty for political prisoners did not figure in the calculations of either the renovators or the corporativists in the labor movement. The expectation that the renovators would make their peace with the Montoneros turned out to be illusory.

This realization eventually led to another shift in strategy. Within four months of my interview with Firmenich, he had jumped from an alliance with the renovators to an equally makeshift coalition with the followers of Miguel and Herminio Iglesias—the latter in control of the party machine in the key province of Buenos Aires. At the July "Unity Congress" in Santa Rosa, La Pampa, a new official party emerged that was actually a rehash of the old, with Saadi, the senator from Catamarca, fronting for Miguel-Iglesias and also for the Montoneros![81]

In a discussion of the mysteries of revolutionary Peronism, Giussani denounced Saadi's political somersault at Santa Rosa, which catapulted him into the top position of the nominally reunified party—the reward for his deserting the renovators.[82] At first it was thought that he had broken his ties to the Montoneros in an effort to promote his political ambitions. Nothing of the kind. The Montoneros gave their unqualified support to his unholy alliance with the fascistoid Iglesias and the former collaborationist Jorge Triaca, who also figured in the party's new leadership.[83] In a move characterized by Giussani as a pearl of political surrealism, the senator from Catamarca "jumped through the political hoop with the Montoneros on his back."[84]

At Santa Rosa, Isabel Perón was reaffirmed as the party's titular president, Saadi became its first vice-president, Triaca its second vice-president, and Iglesias was reelected as the party's general secretary. The question asked by many Argentines was what motivated the Montoneros, after their vendetta against the last Peronist government and their resistance to a dirty war that had been publicly defended by both Triaca and Iglesias, to make common cause with their mortal enemies. Ideologically, they had more in common with the renovators and with the Commission of the 25 than with former president Frondizi's Movement of Integration and Development and other groups to the right instead of the left of the Peronist party, with which they were now allied. There is only one explanation of this anomaly: political opportunism. Having established a beachhead in the party's leadership, the Montoneros were not going to sacrifice it for the sake of principle.

Cultivating the backing and fronting of political moderates was hardly a new strategy for the Montoneros, who had begun their political debut by inserting themselves in the Peronist movement. But there was a startling difference between their early practice of entrism, when they could count on strong support from Perón, and the most recent example, in which Saadi became a pawn of a party over which he had virtually no control and the Montoneros even less. This time their hoped-for backing and fronting by the official movement was a phantom.

The Montoneros had sacrificed their alliance with the renovators in the hope of becoming reinstated by the Peronist movement. But in the November 1985 elections the renovators in both the capital and the province of Buenos Aires ran their own candidates and outperformed the official party. In response to the party's electoral defeat, followed by the dissolution of its newly formed "national front" with Frondizi's MID, Saadi had the good sense to resign as first vice-president. Thus the Montoneros were left with little to show for their efforts.

When Saadi resigned in November 1985, the Montoneros again

found themselves in the role of outsiders. But in testimony to their resilience, they did not take long to recover. From having failed to establish a foothold among both the renovators and the officialists, they turned to an alliance with the CGT, which under Saúl Ubaldini's direction had kept a prudent distance from both wings of the divided party.

In January 1984 the CGT had become reunified under four general secretaries—Triaca was one of them—but Ubaldini captured the stage. During the mobilizations in May 1985, Ubaldini declared on repeated occasions that "either the government must change its economic policy or it must go!"[85] For the first time since Ongaro's leadership of the rebel CGTA in 1968–1969, the CGT came to terms with sectors of the continuing resistance to oligarchical hegemony.[86] Once again the CGT appealed to the youth, human rights groups, and the marginal political parties of the Left to defend democracy and resist the oppressive policies of a nonlabor government. Finally, in December it launched an emergency program of twenty-six points with the intention of mobilizing public opinion and repealing the repressive legislation surviving from the Military Process.[87]

With the exception of the Radical Youth, the country's other youth organizations, headed by the JPU, responded in January 1986 by endorsing the CGT's emergency program. And in February the newly created National Executive Board of Revolutionary Peronism announced its public support of the twenty-six points.

Here was a new twist. If any organization had an opportunity of becoming the nucleus of a third historical movement, it was the CGT. Although the Intransigent party had doubled its representation by sending three more delegates to Congress in 1985, that was hardly an impressive figure. To hope that it might become the nucleus of a third political alternative was grasping at straws. The renovators had done considerably better, but had yet to welcome back the Montoneros. With Ubaldini, who had personally supported the Mothers of the Plaza de Mayo during the resistance, the Montoneros seemed to stand a better chance.

Thus the resistance continued but not in the form of armed or illegal struggles. The Montoneros did not propose to destabilize the government of Raúl Alfonsín. First, they aimed to recover rights extinguished by the military dictatorship, to ensure that those guilty of genocide would be punished, and to obtain the release of political prisoners. Second, they remained in a state of alert ready to engage in drastic forms of civil disobedience in the event of another showdown. Finally, they hoped to carry the resistance to its ultimate, or socialist, conclusion.

An End to the Military Era?

Gen. Ramón Camps, the Catholic nationalist police chief in charge of repression in the province of Buenos Aires from April 1976 to December 1978, believed that subversion was far from over. "We defeated subversion militarily. Politically, we lost the war because of the timidity of certain members in our camp. Subversion is clearly starting to spread again. Our experience has been globally positive and we shall know how to use it on another occasion."[88] This is the same general who, in a prison interview with former *Buenos Aires Herald* editor Robert Cox, declared: "On returning to power, my hand will not tremble when I sign the order of execution of Raúl Alfonsín!"[89]

Originally published in *Harper's* (May 1985), Cox's prison interview gives his reassessment of Argentine democracy. When he returned to Buenos Aires in mid-1984, he reached the sad conclusion that democracy was not the miracle he had expected and that it could not, any more than military solutions, offer a way out of the country's economic impasse. It seemed to him that democracy had not liberated Argentina from the past, because Argentines do not associate democracy with civil rights. The majority of military officers may not think like General Camps, that it was necessary to execute President Alfonsín for aiding and abetting Marxism and that the country was moving toward a civil war. However, Cox became convinced that they expected to return to power and that the people would again acclaim them for saving the country. Although the generals had been defeated, there was no victorious army to subdue or discipline them. According to Cox, that explains why eight and a half months passed before the coup's leader, Gen. Jorge Rafael Videla, was even arrested, and why Gen. Reynaldo Bignone, the last military president, completely eluded the government's justice.

The chief of the *New York Times* bureau in Buenos Aires, Edward Schumacher, had a similarly dour prognosis of the Argentine situation. He attributed the nation's frustrating tale of failure to the primacy of politics over economics.[90] Although as late as World War II Argentina was the economic equal of Australia and not far behind Canada in development, political factors interfered with the country's continued growth. Not the least of those factors was the Argentine military, whose only oath of allegiance was to the flag.[91] Its supreme duty was to defend the nation, not the Constitution. However, the armed forces were not the only ones responsible for the country's predicament. One of the sad features of Argentina is that the people had taken to the streets "to cheer the rise and fall of every government, military or civilian!"[92]

In Argentina an end to the military era is still not in sight. With armed subversion eradicated, the military has shifted its sights to cultural subversion. There is no end to the struggle against international communism, it believes, because armed subversion is at the end of a line that begins by infiltrating popular organizations, undermines respect for church, family, and political authority, and then waits for conditions to become ripe for launching mass violence backed by acts of terrorism. Although the nation's watchdog, the armed forces refuse to be harnessed to civilian authority.

This explains the phenomenon referred to by the Argentine Left as *continuismo* (continuism). Nobel Peace Prize winner Adolfo Pérez Esquivel declared to the press in March 1984: "The arrival of democracy in Argentina provoked no break with the past. . . . The Mothers of the Plaza de Mayo are persecuted and have been assaulted. Two of my collaborators have received death threats, now, under democracy."[93]

Many hoped 1984 would bring the end of the military era; however, nationalist civilian organizations continued to goad the military to intervene. On May 13, in the heart of the nation's capital, a group of Catholic militants invaded the General San Martín Theater on Corrientes Avenue to disrupt a performance considered insulting to the pope and to Catholic doctrine. Shouts of "Bolshies, get out!" were intermixed with the chant, "May the disappeared never reappear!"[94] The demonstrators were identified with two ultranationalist organizations, Opus Dei and Falange of the Faith.

This was a prelude to the reactivation of nationalist commandos. On June 9 a bomb was discovered on the jumbo jet that was to take former president Isabel Perón back to Madrid.[95] A barometer-type device, it would have detonated with a change in atmospheric pressure and was clearly the work of professionals. In August some fifty bombs targeted at the CGT, the Justicialist party, the Peronist Youth, and human rights organizations were set off in the provincial capital of Córdoba.[96] The provincial government indicated that the bombings were linked to military units, because the explosives were available only to the armed forces. But the matter ended there and there were no detentions.

August also witnessed the reappearance of military task forces associated with torture and the disappearance of persons during the Military Process. The Jorge Cáceres Monié Task Force, representing the Comando Nacionalista Argentino (CNA), distributed leaflets in downtown Buenos Aires on August 23. The leaflets informed the public of the CNA's intention to defend the two most-respected institutions in Argentina, the church and the armed forces, against their detractors.[97] The government of Raúl Alfonsín was charged with freeing terrorist delinquents who had bloodied the land and with indicting military patriots who had defended the country against atheistic subversion. Compelled to take matters into its own hands, the task force announced its decision to condemn to death Mario Eduardo Firmenich and the principal supporters of the Montonero-Marxist project. The death warrants included Oscar Alende, head of the Intransigent party, Vicente Leonidas Saadi, leader of the Peronist bloc in the Senate, and Ernesto Sábato and Emilio Mignone—the last two because of their work on behalf of human rights. The leaflet concluded with a reaffirmation of the nationalist commitment to "defend our Western and Christian way of life."

A few days later the CNA's Occident for Victory Task Force added to the list of condemned the names of four national congressmen, Augusto Conte (Christian Democrat), Federico Storani (Radical), Miguel Unamuno and Julio César Araóz (Peronists), along with the Peronist governor of Catamarca and four Argentine journalists. The names of others already sentenced by the CNA's Superior Court of Honor and Justice would be announced at a later date. All had been sentenced for being "agents of the antinational Marxist and Montonero project."[98]

The leaflets were distributed in Ford Falcons, the automobiles used by the armed forces' security and intelligence services in thousands of kidnappings during the Military Process, which strongly suggested that the nationalist commandos had military connections. The government declared as much in a statement to the press and proceeded immediately to provide twenty-four-hour police protection for those condemned to death. But the government's response was mainly token. Thus Oscar Alende characterized the operations as the work of clandestine forces biding their time and as a "resprouting of the Triple A encouraged by the government's negligence."[99]

These events, combined with isolated kidnappings, assaults, disappearances, bombings, and a rash of other threats against members of the Peronist Youth, set the stage for the spectacular takeover and bombing of the Belgrano radio station in the nation's capital on 29 April 1985. This was the single most audacious and organized operation of its kind since the abdication of the armed forces in December 1983. A group of ten armed men, five in police uniforms and the remainder with stockings over their heads, subdued the two regular policemen and radio station guard at the transmission plant, after which they detonated explosives and hurled incendiary bombs at the transmitters. The station was kept off the air for some eight hours until another radio station furnished the equipment for renewed broadcasts.

For months Radio Belgrano had been denounced by nationalist elements as a "subversive *foco.*" Its early morning program "Without Anaesthesia," directed by a journalist having close contacts with Radio Sandino in Nicaragua and radio announcers in Cuba, was the principal target of the verbal attacks and threats that preceded the bombings. Like the attempted bombing of Isabel Perón's plane, these efforts were the work of professionals. But on this occasion leaflets were also scattered throughout the plant with the misleading inscription: "Now more than ever: Democracy or MARXISM."[100]

Systematic threats of this kind and a smaller-scale series of bombings of public administration offices and universities followed the assault on Radio Belgrano. Public protest finally led to drastic government action. In October 1985 the president imposed a sixty-day state of siege—a response that some perceived as the beginning of a new reign of terror.

When he assumed office in December 1983, Alfonsín was aware that his projected war crimes tribunal would be resisted by the armed forces, so he settled for a trade-off. On December 13 he issued two decrees. The first, number 157, called for the detention and trial of seven subversive terrorists for criminal acts dating back to 25 May 1973. Decree number 158 indicted the nine heads of the first three military juntas for illegal homicide, detention, and torture for which they were ultimately responsible; however, they would be tried by a military court.

But the military court reached a verdict of not guilty. Since the armed forces had fought a war to save the country from subversion, the judges concluded, their excesses were not crimes but the price of victory. Under popular pressure, the president then arranged for civil prosecutions. In March 1985 a federal prosecutor announced that the members of the first three military juntas would be tried on 711 counts ranging from torture to homicide. Their attorneys countered by showing that ultimate responsibility rested on the shoulders of civilians; whatever atrocities had been committed were traced to the government of Isabel Perón, which in February 1975 had authorized the dirty war.

As might have been expected, the sentences handed down in December 1985 were extremely lenient. Except for General Videla and Admiral Emilio E. Massera, the leaders of the three military juntas were in effect exonerated. Brigadier General Orlando R. Agosti, the air force member of the first junta, got off with four and a half years. From the second military junta, General Roberto Eduardo Viola and Rear Admiral Armando Lambruschini were sentenced to seventeen and eight years, respectively, but air force Brigadier Omar D. Graffigna was acquitted. Also acquitted were all three members of the third military junta, although they would later be convicted by a military court for their bungling of the war in the Malvinas/Falklands.

The effective exoneration of others responsible for "war crimes," the reappearance of nationalist commandos, the temporary reimposition of a state of siege, and the scattered military rebellions beginning in Holy Week of 1987 and continuing through 1988 suggest that the military establishment was still operating as an autonomous entity. Although subversion was not the obsession that it was during the 1960s and 1970s, remnants of the army's and navy's task forces continued to harass persons not even remotely associated with the Marxist and Montonero projects.

The scale of repression and subversion has been reduced, but it promises to escalate and to bring on military intervention as social unrest increases. This is the great fear in Argentina—a social explosion in response to deteriorating living conditions that show no signs of recovering because of the protracted economic crisis. Unless that crisis can be resolved, workers may shift their allegiance from the labor bureaucrats in the General Confederation of Labor to new leaders impregnated with Marxist ideas. There are few signs that the distribution crisis will be resolved on the workers' terms, so the prospects for democracy in Argentina are unquestionably bleak.

Is the military era over? Since the resistance continues, such a conclusion would be premature. In view of the guerrilla assault by former members of the ERP on the military base at La Tablada in January 1989, armed struggle still seems to be a temptation—although this particular attack was surely ill-advised. The important consideration is that remnants of the ERP and the Montoneros are geared to return underground should the military again threaten a constitutional government. There is a general consensus among former militants of both organizations that the road of armed struggle is still viable, that the presence of guerrillas immensely strengthens a popular resistance, and that their eclipse during the 1970s was due to "mistakes in application of a line that was basically correct."[101] The military is understandably worried.

Without any resolution of the Argentine question in sight, we are back where we started with Alfonsín's "iron dilemma": a military obsessed with fighting subversion, a Peronist movement that has only partly broken with its authoritarian past, a financial oligarchy even more dependent on foreign interests, a Radical party still deaf to the claims of social justice, and a subversive undercurrent awaiting new opportunities to bring down the superstructure.[102] Since the military expects to return to power, its "final humiliation" may not be the final one.

Conclusion

THIS BOOK has investigated the origins and outcomes of Argentina's dirty war, the intellectual foundations of that war and their impact on the ensuing opening of and return to democracy. The principal ideologies and actions of the three main protagonists—the armed forces, the guerrillas, and organized labor—have been traced to their roots in the Catholic church and its leading apologists, to the doctrines of modern liberalism, to the legacy of the Bolshevik Revolution, and to the Fascist and National Socialist precursors of justicialism. Notwithstanding the military's repeated appeals to Argentina's national being, the ideologies that immediately inspired the dirty war have stamped on them the imprimatur of the Vatican and "made in the U.S.A."

The precursor to this book predicted not only further military rebellions of the kind that occurred at Monte Caseros in January 1988 and Villa Martelli in December, but also the guerrillas' return prepared by the subversive rebound of 1982–1983.[1] Most commentators expressed skepticism concerning the possibility and were completely taken by surprise when the guerrillas reappeared at La Tablada in January 1989. Their indifference to the guerrillas' mindset and the lessons of the revolutionary war only partly accounts for their complacence. Their fundamental mistake was to have discounted the social question at the root of Argentina's ills.

In Argentina the presence of economic decline and political instability since 1930 has made the social question increasingly acute. Initially, Peronist ideology served to woo workers away from revolution, but in the long run it contributed to the intensification of their discontent. Organized labor's resistance during the 1950s and 1960s and the revolutionary war that emerged from the Peronist resistance confirmed the military's fears.

Then came the dirty war and its offspring, the Military Process.

While crushing the guerrillas militarily, they added fuel to the fire. But neither the Military Process's collapse nor the return to democracy provided a respite from social unrest. Disillusioned with military intervention, the comfortable classes temporarily concluded that to live with subversion was a more reasonable option than to eradicate it. Meanwhile, unrest intensified and today threatens to break out in a social explosion.

It took the Military Process to defeat the guerrillas. Convinced that a total war with no holds barred was necessary, the military overrode the Constitution and imposed a system of state terrorism that effectively "disappeared" potential troublemakers. Prior to the new system of generalized terror, the guerrillas continued relentlessly with their armed operations. Military hard-liners were noticeably impatient with the progress of repression. The March 1976 coup and the Military Process aimed at bringing the dirty war to a successful conclusion.

That the dirty war alone did not suffice was a conviction shared by the established leaders of the Radical party, traditional liberals, the political Right, and the guerrillas. Today this claim is disputed by leaders of the reconstituted Radical and Peronist parties, prominent intellectuals, and an influential sector of the Argentine press. Who has the stronger case? The record shows that the Military Process was in fact necessary for victory. Whether the guerrillas could have been crushed without it is a matter of speculation. *If* there had been no imposition of state terrorism, *if* thirty thousand Argentines had not disappeared, *if* two hundred thousand had not been tortured, who knows what might have happened?

The strategy of the dirty war boomeranged. Initially, it enjoyed the support of most Argentines. But when the war officially ended in 1978 and the truth emerged concerning the magnitude of kidnappings, torture, and disappearances, the military was hard-pressed to defend itself. Its predicament was insurmountable. The generalized terror provoked a popular resistance that directly challenged the Military Process.

The outcome might have been predicted. The dictatorship collapsed and the guerrillas won a political victory. Thus the Military Process cut two ways. It was both the Achilles' sword that defeated the guerrillas militarily and the Achilles' heel that ultimately caused the generals to abdicate.

The subsequent transition and return to democracy beginning in June 1982 confirms the paradoxical outcome to this complex and contradictory process. Thus to the trials and imprisonment of its top leaders was added the military's humiliation and the continuation of the resistance in a new key under the deceptively benevolent government of President Alfonsín.

Were the military's responses to subversion excessive or unreasonable, as critics insist? Since the kidnappings, tortures, and disappearances were needed to assure the guerrillas' military defeat, the means were adequate to the end in view. But they proved to be the military's political undoing.

The generals misperceived the impact of armed subversion on the values of Western civilization. The Catholic faith and the Roman Church were not at issue. The Montonero leaders were practicing Catholics, in some instances, fanatical in their faith. Nor was the ERP intent on abolishing institutional religion. Like the Marxists in the PRT, the ERP's militants professed a form of socialist humanism compatible with Christian humanism during the Renaissance. Socialist values are no more threatening to Western civilization than are liberal values and by now are an integral part of the Western cultural heritage.

The generals confused Soviet-style Marxism-Leninism with communism. The communist legacy antedates Marxism and in many instances is incompatible with it. Anarchists and communists are committed to leveling from the top down; the established Communist parties are not.[2] The generals had no reason to quarrel with a graded society based on knowledge. Leveling communism, not a socialist meritocracy, was their fundamental enemy.

The generals failed to distinguish socialist from communist subversion. Guillén became the mentor of Raimundo Ongaro, virtually the only influential labor leader with a communist orientation. But the Montoneros had no use for Ongaro's egalitarianism and made fun of his communist mystique. Among the guerrillas only the ERP shared some of Guillén's and Ongaro's premises.

Are the guerrillas finished militarily? Did the generals put an end to guerrilla warfare in Argentina—once and for all?

On 23 January 1989, at 6:15 A.M., armed insurgents attacked the military garrison at La Tablada, twenty miles southwest of Buenos Aires. The fighting lasted nearly thirty hours.

The titular head of the guerrillas was Jorge Baños, a respected Buenos Aires lawyer dedicated to human rights cases and a leader of the Movimiento Todos por la Patria (MTP). Organized in March 1986 by the founders of the monthly *Entre Todos*, the MTP embraced clergy, journalists, university professors, students, and former cadres of the ERP, including Enrique Gorriarán. But only a small sector of the movement knew that an assault would take place.

Those who organized the attack were experienced guerrillas from the demobilized ERP led by Francisco Provenzano.

The attack failed. Baños and several others who surrendered were taken aside and summarily shot. There are pictures taken by journalists of his detention, before the army announced he was killed in action. Once again the army was shooting prisoners, this time under cover of a widely celebrated "rule of law."

After the attack, there was a huge mobilization and witch-hunt launched by the combined forces of the Right. They screamed that Gorriarán and the ERP had arisen, that Fidel and Ortega had planned the operation. The police went wild with huge dragnets, knocking down over fifty houses and arresting scores on the Left. On the basis of army reports, the Argentine media claimed that the attackers were equipped with the latest rocket launchers from Russia and China, with grenade launchers and automatic rifles. This later turned out to be false: the guerrillas had some old machine guns and other obsolete equipment.

Almost a week later came an announcement from neighboring Uruguay by an organization nobody had heard of, the Frente de Resistencia Popular (FRP). It claimed credit for the attack, explaining that the army at La Tablada was preparing a coup, which the action aimed to forestall. Meanwhile, the witch-hunt went on and President Alfonsín prepared a new law to let the army back into national security affairs.

Additional details were given in a statement released by the FRP on 12 March 1989, again from Uruguay. For the first time people learned of the international composition of the guerrilla band, that two Paraguayans and a Brazilian were killed in the assault, and that a Bolivian died after being taken prisoner. Finally, there was the ominous message for the Argentine military—the FRP swore "to continue the struggle until victory."[3]

What the FRP's statements did not reveal was that the MTP had become disillusioned with the policies pursued by other sectors of the resistance. On 4 December 1988, while the coup at Villa Martelli was still in progress, the principal human rights groups had launched a new organization with the intention of creating civil defense groups throughout the country. Calling itself Democratic Initiative for Civil Resistance, it was modeled on Mahatma Gandhi's nonviolent opposition to British rule in India. This explains the energetic repudiation of the attack on La Tablada in a communiqué issued on the same day by human rights groups. Although ridiculing the "theory of two devils" for making no distinction between guerrilla terrorism and state terrorism, the communiqué testified to the first open split of the resistance between the partisans of armed and unarmed struggle.

With few exceptions the Argentine Left joined the national chorus, denouncing the return of armed subversion as madness. But facile accounts of the guerrillas' mistakes based on a cost-benefit analysis have little relevance to the complex web of events in which the FRP and the MTP became entangled and obliged to respond. The owl of Minerva, Hegel reflected, flies at dusk.[4] Wisdom is acquired and mistakes are discovered only after the rush of events is over. In armed struggle as in national wars there is no way of avoiding risks.

As recently as 1985, the former guerrillas I interviewed were re-affirming their faith in armed struggle—not that they had ever lost it. Engineering such a venture is not like building a bridge; the odds are that the venture will collapse. To succeed, guerrillas know that more than violence and deception of the enemy are necessary; the timing of their operations is crucial, and in revolutionary warfare chance or fortune plays a role in shaping political outcomes. Hence their current strategy of wait and see.

Will there be a repetition of the events at La Tablada? At issue is not the role of international communism or the export of the Cuban and Nicaraguan revolutions, which fired up the ERP and the Montoneros in the 1970s and 1980s. There may be no more dirty wars, but as long as there is an Argentine question there will be a military era, protracted resistance, and the potential for armed struggle in Argentina.

Appendix. Prison Interview with Mario Firmenich

Federal Penitentiary of Villa Devoto, Buenos Aires, 14 March 1985

BECAUSE NO paper, pens, pencils, or other recording devices were permitted by the prison authorities, the interview had to be reconstructed after the event. It has been checked for accuracy by my wife and coworker, Deborah Hepburn, and by the executive adviser to the monthly *Latino América,* Alicia Giraudo, who were present at the interview.

D.H.: How do you conceptualize the recent resistance? Do you date it from your return underground in September 1974 or from the military coup that toppled the last Peronist government in March 1976?

M.F.: I have never maintained that the resistance resumed in March 1976. The government of Isabel Perón–López Rega not only violated the Constitution through its illegal measures against the government's critics, but also exercised authority through a virtual palace coup. It was the government that secretly organized the Triple A. In doing so, it usurped powers that were clearly unconstitutional. The silencing of opposition and the assassination of political opponents amounted to a *golpe de estado* [coup]. López Rega was responsible for the Ezeiza massacre in June 1973 and the coup against the government of President Cámpora in July. By his own admission he was an admirer of Hitler and was a proponent of a fascist version of "national socialism." Perón was 78 years old and helpless. Chronically ill, his physicians advised him against running for the presidency. He was like a "package" wrapped up and carried about by López Rega with Isabel in attendance. When Perón was present, Isabel addressed the minister of social welfare as "López" who in turn addressed her as "Señora." But in his absence it was "Daniel" and "Isabel." He must have sensed the intimacy. At the same time they shielded him from political contacts. They misadvised and misinformed him. Together they exercised a form of political blackmail over the old man.

D.H.: You seem to have acknowledged two palace coups, one against President Cámpora in July 1973 and another after Perón's death in July 1974.

M.F.: There were two coups against which we had to defend ourselves. But as long as Perón lived we could count on some support from him and from the government, which remained within the bounds of the Constitution. That is why we defended him against attacks from the Left. The coup against Cámpora was not instigated by Perón but by López Rega and the Peronist Right.

D.H.:   But would you say that resistance to the coup of July 1974 had the popular backing of the resistance to the coup of March 1976?

M.F.:   The character of the resistance changed as a result of the military coup. Thus one may speak of two periods of the resistance, that before and after March 24. Support for each varied, depending on the circumstances.

D.H.:   In your article in *La Voz* that appeared on February 2nd, 1985, you acknowledge that it was a mistake to have engaged in armed actions against the government of Isabel Perón. First, because they did not have the effect intended of protecting the Montoneros and Peronist Youth from repression; and second, because they reduced your political space by depriving you of a legal front against the government. How much popular backing did you have?

M.F.:   The return to clandestinity was in practice counterproductive. We became isolated from the Peronist mainstream and our resistance did not acquire the massive response we anticipated. Nor did it help us in mobilizing the people to resist the military coup in March 1976, because by then we had become branded as "subversives."

D.H.:   In a book recently published by the Center of Legal and Social Studies (CELS), *El Mito de la Guerra Sucia,* the escalation of state terrorism under the first military junta is presented not as a war but as a witch-hunt. What is your opinion?

M.F.:   The resistance to the military dictatorship was part not just of a 7-year war from 1976 to 1983 but of an intermittent 150-year war that is still inconclusive. However you interpret the so-called "dirty war," it was part of a larger struggle between the Argentine people on one side and the oligarchy supported by foreign interests on the other, a virtual civil war that began as early as 1828 with the struggle between Unitarians and Federalists over the control of our country's destiny. We consider ourselves to be the continuators of the Federalists and the gaucho montoneros who resisted the "liberalism" of the port city of Buenos Aires, which continues to play into the hands of foreign interests.

D.H.:   That is to say, the war was an interrupted one.

M.F.:   It was an interrupted war that periodically cooled off but then heated up in the clash between rival armies, as during the military insurrection by the Radicals in 1905, the bombing of Plaza de Mayo by the naval air force in June 1955, etc. The struggle against the native oligarchy has yet to be resolved in this country as it was in Mexico. After roughly 10 years of military struggles the oligarchical regime gave way to the institutionalization of the Mexican Revolution in 1920. In the context of Mexican politics, the Argentine situation has been described as what might have happened in Mexico if the Institutional Party of the Revolution (PRI) continued winning the elections while the conservative National Action party (PAN) controlled the armed forces. Under such conditions Mexico would not have exhibited the political stablity of the past 65 years. As in Argentina, instability and political stalemate would have become the norm. After 1916 the Conservative party was not able to win a single presidential election. However, it seduced the armed forces into "substituting" for it. The "military party," as Perón called it, has been the party of the oligarchy ever since. It prevented the Radicals under Yrigoyen and the Justicialists under Perón from carrying through popular reforms. Thanks to a succession of reactionary military coups, the oligarchy is still a power in Argentina.

D.H.: Isn't there some evidence that Perón consciously sought to emulate the Mexican example, that he tried to make a Mexican-type revolution in Argentina but without the bloodshed?

M.F.: Unfortunately, he did not go far enough. If Perón had succeeded, Argentina would not be faced with its current predicament. The Mexican Revolution awakened an entire continent.

D.H.: From 5th place in 1929 in per capita real income ahead of Italy and Japan as well as the Soviet Union, Argentina has sunk to 43rd or 44th place within the international community.

M.F.: Behind Brazil as well as Mexico. Argentina no longer holds first place even in Latin America.

D.H.: Would you say that Perón's failure to consummate the national revolution may be attributed in part to the limitations of his political thought? Granted that his liberal critics were mistaken in calling him a "fascist," wasn't there a fascist component in his doctrine? Didn't it contribute to his formulation of a Third Position equidistant from both capitalism and socialism, which may have discouraged him from taking stronger measures against the oligarchy?

M.F.: Perón claimed to be an admirer of Mussolini. But besides his sympathy for Italian fascism, he also assimilated elements of Stalinism. I recall him saying of Mao that the little Chinaman had stolen some of his ideas!

D.H.: There may even have been a "laborite" element in his thought. Wasn't Perón an admirer of the British Labor Party and didn't he rely initially on a working class party built on the British model?

M.F.: You could say that Perón was a social democrat. Even more than the British influence, he made a point of following the Swedish model.

D.H.: Would you agree, then, that the complexities and even inconsistencies of Perón's thought help to explain the "contradictions" within the Peronist Movement? In other words, wasn't Perón himself responsible for the continuing struggle between the Movement's left and right wings?

M.F.: There were obvious weaknesses in Perón's thought as there are today in Peronist orthodoxy, which the Montoneros have made an effort to transcend. But at least Perón's thought was suited to his times and to the low level of political consciousness of Argentina's native-born workers, especially from the interior. The same cannot be said of Peronist orthodoxy today. What was useful and credible in the 40s and 50s came in response to conditions that no longer exist. The original Peronist ideology has degenerated into a set of dogmas, into a cosmovision or philosophy concerning the way things are. Many people confuse ideology with philosophy.

D.H.: What do you mean by ideology?

M.F.: Unlike philosophies that explore the nature of physical and social reality, ideologies arise in response to the question "What do we want?" The answer to that question changes from generation to generation. What the Third Position meant for Perón served for the 40s and 50s, but can no longer fulfill our present needs. The same may be said for Perón's understanding of "national socialism." The original multiclass objectives of the Peronist Movement should likewise not be confused with the pluralism we presently advocate. The contradictions within the Movement stemming from its multiclass composition are currently being resolved owing to its newly acquired pluralist or democratic character based on the hegemony of the working class.

D.H.: In a recent issue of *Latino América* (December 1984) there is an article on the doctrinal transformation of Peronism that makes some of the points you just mentioned. Among other things, it proposes the construction of a national form of socialism based on a revised conception of the Third Position. Does that mean that the Montoneros' position of nonalignment with respect to the East-West conflict has also undergone a shift? Do you still believe, for example, that the socialist camp represented by the Warsaw Pact offers no more hope than the so-called Free World represented by NATO? As socialists, I would expect you to have more in common with the socialist countries.

M.F.: The confrontation between NATO and the Warsaw Pact is not an Argentine question. It is out of our hands. Any action that might involve us in a nuclear war would prove disastrous for Argentina. That is why we favor nonalignment. Although we have more in common with the socialist camp, we don't call ourselves "socialists." Perón realized the controversial and divisive connotations of this word and substituted another for it. Although we occasionally talk of building socialism, we prefer the term Justicialism. Is it accurate, for example, to call a llama a camel without a hump on its back? Although that is what llamas initially appeared to Europeans, llamas are not a special breed of camels. Nor is Justicialism an adaptation of European social democracy to Argentina. We do not follow foreign models but rely on our own resources.

D.H.: But isn't there a strong dose of Marxism-Leninism in your thinking?

M.F.: Marxism-Leninism is defined by a particular philosophy. Since we do not share that philosophy, we are not Marxist-Leninists. The so-called "laws of dialectics" working through nature as well as history have been falsified by events. According to those laws the human brain should not be operating at under-capacity. Nonetheless, only a small part of the brain is ever put to use. Nor are we committed to a Marxist-Leninist ideology in the sense I have already indicated. For Marxist-Leninists that ideology was given its definitive form by Lenin and has remained static ever since. It has not responded to the changing times. As for the method of economic and political analysis derived from Marx, it has become part of the scientific and intellectual legacy of mankind. Its acceptance is now almost universal and has little to do with Marxism.

D.H.:   But is it only the method you accept? What of Marx's fundamental premises and conclusions concerning history and its development?

M.F.:   That history has taken the form of class struggles, that workers are exploited, and that "surplus value" exists not only under capitalism but also under socialism—in the sense of an economic surplus or fund for accumulation—are universal truths that nobody, who understands what is being asserted, would contest. But is that enough to make one a Marxist? In Latin America revolutionaries are still confronted with a dilemma. On the one hand, practically the only revolutionary theory known to them is European, whether the philosophy of Rousseau and the Jacobins during the Great French Revolution or the philosophy of Marx, Lenin, and the Russian Revolution of October 1917. Unfortunately, these European imports have never fitted or have only partly fitted our own social and political reality. On the other hand, Latin America has yet to produce a Lenin of its own. And that means that we are still fumbling around for guidance.

D.H.:   Speaking of European models and influences, the British author of *The Soldiers of Perón* claims on the basis of interviews with the Montoneros that the two most important works shaping your strategy during the resistance were Clausewitz's *On War* and Abraham Guillén's *Strategy of the Urban Guerrilla*. Were those works really that influential?

M.F.:   We were familiar with the relevant sections of Clausewitz's major work, but we never studied it thoroughly. As for Guillén, I remember reading that urban guerrillas should operate by night and never by day. So that is how we began. But that was almost 20 years ago until we learned that guerrillas can be just as effective, even more effective, by operating in broad daylight and among large crowds where they are not readily detectable. I also recall a passage in which the *gallego* claimed that guerrilla warfare in the cities is ultimately ineffective unless backed up by rural guerrillas. But there are few rural areas in Argentina where guerrilla warfare is appropriate. The attempt by the People's Revolutionary Army (ERP) to build a rural base in Tucumán proved disastrous and we criticized the effort from the start. That was the extent of Guillén's influence, as far as I am aware. Why must everything significant come from Europe? Actually, the main intellectual influence on the Montoneros had a native origin. It was our reading of Argentine history that shaped our strategy as well as our ideology. Our principal guides were Juan José Hernández Arregui, José María Rosa, Arturo Jauretchi, and Rodolfo Puiggrós. We also owe a singular debt to John William Cooke, our original mentor.

D.H.: Among the figures just mentioned, who was the most influential?

M.F.: You could say that we learned most from Puiggrós.

D.H.: But both he and Cooke were Marxist-Leninists!

M.F.: You omitted to add that they were also Peronists. Both successfully adapted their Marxism to Argentine national conditions. Their method was derived from Marxism, not their ideology.

D.H.: What of the influence of the Cuban Revolution and, for that matter, the victorious Nicaraguan Revolution? You noted that Latin America has yet to produce a Lenin of its own. But wouldn't Fidel Castro fit that role?

M.F.: If there was a direct Marxist influence on us, it came from reading the works of Mao Tse-tung. The Chinese Cultural Revolution made a profound impression on us, as it also did on Perón. One can hardly compare Fidel Castro's thought with that of Mao. Fidel has yet to write anything systematic. Regis Debray tried to capture Fidel's thought but completely misinterpreted the strategy that led to victory against Batista. His influence on Latin American revolutionaries bordered on the suicidal and set us back several years. If the Cubans have adopted a dogmatic version of Marxism-Leninism, it is because Cuba is a miserable country without rivers, petroleum, iron ores, etc. They are dependent for survival on the U.S.S.R. Argentina is in a different category altogether. We follow our own path. Cuba is an anomaly and there is little chance of its revolution ever being imitated elsewhere. The Nicaraguan Revolution is something else.

D.H.: Nonetheless, revolutionary movements have a way of influencing one another especially when they are successful. The fact that the strategy of mass insurrection or "movementist" tendency within the Sandinista Front of National Liberation (FSLN) became the prevailing one by 1977 makes me wonder if the Montoneros may have been partly responsible for the change. Surely, the example of the *cordobazos* and the successful Peronist resistance of the late 60s and early 70s must have weighed in the balance. The Montoneros' recent emphasis on political pluralism and a mixed economy following the Sandinista victory in 1979 suggests that the FSLN has had a reciprocal effect. Was there in fact a mutual influence?

M.F.: Rather than a cause and effect relationship, both the FSLN and the Montoneros developed their strategies in response to fundamentally similar social and political conditions. Although we had contacts with the FSLN going back to the late 60s, to my knowledge there was little mutual influence. The FSLN's insurrectional strategy was adopted, as in our own case, only after a Debrayist or *foco* strategy had failed. It was their own day-to-day revolutionary experience that finally decided in its favor. As for the Montoneros, we had already developed a program in favor of political pluralism and a mixed economy as early as 1973. Although expressed in somewhat different terms, it came to the same thing. Moreover, our insurrectional strategy had a Peronist origin that likewise antedated the insurrectional strategy of the FSLN.

D.H.: Isn't it ironical that the program you fought for in 1973, especially your championing of political pluralism and internal democracy within the Peronist Movement, should finally have borne fruit at the Congress of Río Hondo in February 1985? That is, that your program is now accepted by both the political center and left of center of the Peronist leadership?

M.F.: It was a matter *not* of historical irony but of a correct strategy!

D.H.: Are you saying that the "correctness" of your strategy was a determining factor? In other words, that the corporative and verticalist structuring of the Peronist Movement so discouraged democratic participation by the Peronist bases that they finally repudiated the Party's political as well as labor bureaucracies?

M.F.: The electoral defeat of October 1983 contributed, more than anything else, to the emergence of the "renovators." They had to adopt our original proposals or otherwise face defeat in the congressional elections scheduled for November.

D.H.: Evidently, the democratization of the Peronist Movement is a powerful factor in your favor. Does, then, the recent acceptance of the Peronist Youth as a fourth official branch of the Movement—with a right to 25% representation at all levels—indicate that the Montoneros are in a position to recover the ground lost during the Military Process?

M.F.: I wouldn't say that. The past 7 years of repression have taken their toll. There is no comparison between the popular support we enjoyed in 1974–75 and what we represent today. We were almost completely decimated and it will take years to recover what we lost.

D.H.: I noted that very few youth between the ages of 18 and 30 attended the public demonstration organized by the Peronist Youth in Plaza Once on March 11. The 12 thousand or so present represented mainly an older generation.

M.F.: The Peronist Youth was completely wiped out by the Military Process. As late as 1982, the decisive year of the resistance, there was no JP. We have had to rebuild it under almost impossible conditions, because our youth educated under the Military Process was subjected to a systematic and insidious propaganda that made us appear to be malefactors and delinquents. Today the Radical Party continues to present us in the same light as "subversive terrorists." We have had to contend with the "theory of the two devils," which lumps together and makes no distinction between our use of violence in defense of the Constitution and the practice of genocide by the military dictatorship. But the youth are beginning to realize that there is a difference and that this is a country of lies. Our money is a lie. That the military process had for one of its objectives the elimination of corruption in public office, when it turned out to be the most corrupt government in our nation's history, was a lie. That its purpose was to uphold the Constitution, which it brazenly violated under the guise of rooting out subversion, was a lie. That it represented the national interest, that it was not partial to the oligarchy, and that it was not directed against the Argentine working class were lies, etc. We have made our self-criticism by recognizing our errors. The military has yet to do so. The Argentine nation must now make its self-criticism by rejecting the lies of the past decade. The democratization of the Peronist Movement has been a step in that direction.

D.H.: It appears that the Radical Party's Movement of Renewal and Change has also made an effort at self-criticism. Alfonsín's electoral campaign in support of a "Third Historical Movement" succeeded in assimilating, at least rhetorically, the Peronist program in most of its essentials. Is there any difference between this movement and Peronist efforts to organize a "National Front"?

M.F.: The "Front" refers to efforts to revive the political coalition responsible for the Peronists' overwhelming victory at the polls in September 1973—the Justicialist Liberation Front (FREJULI). In sharp contrast, the "Third Historical Movement" refers to the Radicals' campaign to supersede not only the mass movement built by Yrigoyen, but also the Peronist movement that replaced it. Surely, the Peronists are not going to agree to become obsolete. That explains why they counterpose a revived "National Front" to the Radicals' "Third Historical Movement."

D.H.: Even so, it would appear that the "renovators" at Río Hondo have gone beyond the original Peronist Movement in assimilating the Radicals' emphasis on democracy. Am I right in believing that they, rather than the Radicals, represent a third historical option?

M.F.: You are right about the convergence of the two party platforms. Disillusioned with the mafia of political and labor bureaucrats in control of their party's apparatus, many rank and file Peronists voted for Alfonsín rather than Luder. In part, they were deceived by the propaganda for a "Third Historical Movement." Today they have grounds for being disillusioned with the Radical party, because Alfonsín ended by betraying his campaign promises. Radical talk about a "Third Historical Movement" is now generally recognized to have been an electoral gimmick. Nobody in the Radical Party now takes it seriously. Besides, Alfonsín failed to acknowledge that this concept was not his own, that it did not originate with his Movement for Renewal and Change. It goes back almost 20 years to an effort by the then Revolutionary Armed Forces (FAR) to develop an alternative to both Radicalism and Peronism. The concept was originally formulated by Jorge Omar Lewinger, who subsequently became a Montonero and the editor of our journal *Vencer*. When the FAR merged with the Montoneros in October 1973 the original concept was discarded in view of the regeneration of the Peronist Movement.

D.H.: I notice from your articles in *La Voz* that you are critical of the Radical Party not only for erecting what you call a merely formal democracy, but also for failing to dismantle the repressive apparatus carried over from the Military Process. I understand what you mean by formal democracy, but in what respects is the old repressive apparatus still functioning?

M.F.: The intelligence services have been left intact along with their files on so-called "subversives." We are being indicted by a Radical government under conditions dictated by the military juntas. In this respect the Radical government is continuous with that of the dictatorship.

D.H.: It seems that the Radical Party was successful where the Military Party failed. I have in mind your imprisonment and that of Ricardo Obregón Cano.

M.F.: We did not anticipate that a democratic government would treat us on the same level with those responsible for the "disappearance" of thousands of our fellow Argentines, with professional torturers, etc.

D.H.: Does that mean that your efforts to return to Argentina were premature? Ricardo Obregón returned in December 1983 only a few weeks after Alfonsín assumed the presidency, and was detained at the Ezeiza Airport. He has been in prison ever since. And you were detained in Brazil in February 1984 and extradited to Argentina at the request of the Argentine government in October. You must have known that the Brazilian intelligence services were working hand in glove with their Argentine counterparts. Why, then, did you risk returning before the repressive apparatus had been dismantled?

M.F.: The choice was between political death in exile or the struggle to recover political credibility and influence by returning to Argentina. Who would listen to me from Mexico, operating from Chihuahua or perhaps Querétaro? Since political death for me is worse than physical death or imprisonment, my only option was to return. At least here I am able to make myself heard through *La Voz* and *Latino América*. Even in prison I am politically useful.

D.H.: During the presidential campaign of 1983 it was widely believed that the Montoneros had disappeared as a political force in Argentina. Are you thinking of disbanding or reorganizing under another name?

M.F.: Not at all. Although in 1983 we seriously considered disbanding, our movement has been reorganized under our own name, we have established a network of political alliances, and we are in the process of becoming reaccepted as a revolutionary tendency within the Peronist Movement. Whatever happens to me, the Montoneros still have an important role to play in Argentine politics. . . .

Prison guards (interrupting): "The interview is at an end!"

Notes

1. The Argentine Question

1. Raúl Alfonsín, *La cuestión argentina*, 9. All translations are mine unless otherwise indicated.

2. See Alfonsín's characterization of the Military Process based on the armed forces' declaration on 24 March 1976 and Gen. Jorge R. Videla's speech of March 30, ibid., 40–41. For Alfonsín's solution to the Argentine question, see ibid., 148–149.

3. Ibid., 9.

4. Rogelio Frigerio, *Diez años de la crisis argentina: diagnóstico y programa del desarrollismo*, 47–48.

5. Ibid., 45–47.

6. Ibid.

7. Carlos Waisman, *Reversal of Development in Argentina: Postwar Counterrevolutionary Policies and Their Structural Consequences*, 5–6, 9.

8. Ibid., 5, 9.

9. Ibid., 9.

10. David Rock, *Argentina 1516–1982: From Spanish Colonization to the Falklands War*, xxiv–xxv.

11. Ibid., 378.

12. Gustavo Polit, "The Industrialists of Argentina," 400.

13. Fernando H. Cardoso and Enzo Faletto, *Dependencia y desarrollo en América Latina*, 59–64.

14. Rodolfo Terragno, foreword to Eduardo Crawley, *A House Divided: Argentina 1880–1980*, xii.

15. Carlos Escudé, *Gran Bretaña, Estados Unidos y la declinación argentina, 1942–1949*, 14–15, 28–29, 73–76, 245–248, 329–330, 375–383.

16. Waisman, *Reversal of Development*, 106–109.

17. Ibid., 119–122.

18. Ibid., 126–127.

19. Ibid., 164–165.

20. Ibid., 171.

21. José A. Martínez de Hoz, *Bases para una Argentina moderna 1976–1980*, 21–22.

22. Cited by Alfonsín, *La cuestión argentina*, 40.

23. Martínez de Hoz, *Bases*, 30–31, 109–111.

24. Aldo Ferrer, "La economía argentina bajo una estrategia 'preindustrial,'" in Rouquié, *Argentina, hoy,* 105–106, 124–128.

25. Martínez de Hoz, *Bases,* 219–220.

26. Waisman, *Reversal of Development,* 9.

27. Frigerio, *Diez años,* 107.

28. Torcuato S. Di Tella, "Stalemate or Coexistence in Argentina," 250.

29. Richard Gillespie, *Soldiers of Perón: Argentina's Montoneros,* 1–2.

30. Leopoldo Lugones, "Propósitos," 188.

31. Alain Rouquié, *Poder militar y sociedad política en la Argentina,* I, 12–21; II, 379–386.

32. For the Magna Carta of "Intransigent Nationalism," see Federico Ibarguren, *Orígenes del nacionalismo argentino,* 187–192.

33. Juan Domingo Perón, *Perón-Cooke correspondencia,* II, 381, 385.

34. Enrique Pavón Pereyra, *Perón tal como es,* 25.

35. Samuel Blixen, *Treinta años de lucha popular: conversaciones con Gorriarán Merlo,* 23.

36. Leopoldo Lugones (hijo), *Mi padre,* 334–335; Ernesto Che Guevara, "Mensaje a los pueblos del mundo a través de la Tricontinental," *Obras 1957–1967,* II, 584.

37. James Neilson, "Los Camps y los Firmenich," 33.

38. Piero Gleigeses, "¿Qué pasa en Argentina? Decadencia y amenaza latente de militarismo," 13.

39. Thomas Hobbes, BEHEMOTH, 356–358.

40. Alexis de Tocqueville, *Democracy in America,* I, 238.

41. Ibid.

42. Perón, *Perón-Cooke correspondencia,* I, 22.

43. *La Razón,* 6 October 1981.

44. Alfonsín, *La cuestión argentina,* 169.

45. Ibid., 171.

46. Ibid., 173.

47. Frigerio, *Diez años,* 107.

48. Ibid., 108.

49. Errico Malatesta, *His Life & Ideas,* 224.

50. Ronaldo Munck et al., *Argentina: From Anarchism to Peronism,* 36, 50.

51. Malatesta, *Life & Ideas,* 183.

52. Ibid., 196.

53. Ibid.

54. José Peter, *Crónicas proletarias,* 58.

55. Ibid., 28.

56. Ibid., 29.

57. Ibid., 58.

58. Karl Marx, "Critical Marginal Notes on the Article by a Prussian," in Marx and Engels, *Collected Works,* III, 193, 203–204.

59. Ibid., 194, 197.

60. Ibid., 196, 206.

61. Karl Marx and Frederick Engels, "Manifesto of the Communist Party," *Selected Works,* I, 65.

62. Karl Marx, "The Civil War in France," *Selected Works,* I, 541.

63. V. I. Lenin, "Imperialism, the Highest Stage of Capitalism," in *The Lenin Anthology,* 236.

64. Hobbes, BEHEMOTH, 282.

65. Juan Domingo Perón, *Doctrina revolucionaria*, 103.
66. Juan Domingo Perón, *Doctrina peronista*, 224.
67. Ibid., 223.
68. Pavón Pereyra, *Perón*, 234.
69. Ibid.
70. Waisman, *Reversal of Development*, 21–23, 88–93, 122, 126, 285–286.
71. Ibid., 190–206.
72. Hannah Arendt, *On Revolution*, 108.
73. "Otra vez los archivos de los campos de concentración."
74. Raimundo Ongaro, letter to the author (8 January 1977), in Donald C. Hodges, *Argentina, 1943–1987: The National Revolution and Resistance*, ix.

2. The Military Era

1. Munck et al., *Argentina*, 87, 91–93, 95–97; Peter, *Crónicas proletarias*, 96, 113, 127–128, 140–155; and Rouquié, *Poder militar*, I, 207–208.
2. Alfredo Rocco, "The Political Doctrine of Fascism," 317–320.
3. Peter, *Crónicas proletarias*, 153.
4. Joseph Page, *Perón: A Biography*, 20–21.
5. Alexis de Tocqueville, *Recollections*, 85–87.
6. Ibid.
7. Tocqueville has left a vivid description of the central figures of the Second French Republic and their political confrontations (ibid., 145–154, 163–165, 180–188).
8. Rock, *Argentina 1516–1982*, 184.
9. Alphonse de Lamartine, "Manifesto to Europe," 195.
10. Rock, *Argentina 1516–1982*, 184–185.
11. Ibid., 185.
12. Ibid.
13. John Stuart Mill, *On Liberty*, xx–xxi, 4.
14. Cited by Enrique Zuleta Alvarez, *El nacionalismo argentino* I, 140–141.
15. Mill, *On Liberty*, 11–12.
16. Ibid., xx.
17. Steven Seidman, *Liberalism and the Origin of European Social Theory*, 16.
18. Rouquié, *Poder militar*, I, 223–224; see also table, 232.
19. Ibid., 221–222.
20. Ibid., 208.
21. Leopoldo Lugones, *La grande Argentina*, 129, 189–191.
22. Rouquié, *Poder militar*, I, 244.
23. Ibid., 333.
24. Ibid., 330.
25. Ibid., 336 n.
26. Ibid., 335.
27. Ibid., II, 20.
28. Ibid., 72.
29. Ibid.
30. Frank Owen, *Perón: His Rise and Fall*, 92, 103.
31. Ibid., 92.
32. Ibid., 116.
33. Ibid., 117.

34. David D. Cruz, *El recambio de los dioses*, 65.
35. Owen, *Perón*, 149–150, 152, 157.
36. Rock, *Argentina 1516–1982*, 305.
37. Owen, *Perón*, 123.
38. Ibid.
39. See Rouquié, *Poder militar*, II, 195, 199.
40. Ibid., 248.
41. Brian Crozier, *Franco: A Biographical History*, 89.
42. Rouquié, *Poder militar*, II, 264.
43. Daniel Poneman, *Argentina: Democracy on Trial*, 28.
44. Ibid., 28; and Cruz, *El recambio*, 164.
45. Rouquié, *Poder militar*, II, 246.
46. Gary W. Wynia, *Argentina: Illusions and Realities*, 96.
47. Rouquié, *Poder militar*, II, 241.
48. Ibid., 273.
49. James Kohl and John Litt, eds., "The Argentine Guerrillas Speak," *Urban Guerrilla Warfare in Latin America*, 395.
50. Ibid., 398.
51. Ibid., 399.
52. "El partido militar," 3.
53. Ibid.
54. Wynia, *Argentina*, 93.
55. Ibid., 98.
56. Darío Canton, *La política de los militares argentinos: 1900–1971*, 107.
57. Ibid., 115.
58. Ibid.
59. Ibid.
60. Rouquié, *Poder militar*, II, 287.
61. Canton, *La política de los militares*, 116.
62. Wynia, *Argentina*, 113.
63. Ibid.; and Poneman, *Argentina*, 101.
64. Poneman, *Argentina*, 101.

3. The Peronist Phenomenon

1. Perón, *Doctrina revolucionaria*, 68–70.
2. Ibid., 70, 72.
3. Ibid., 72.
4. Ibid.
5. Ibid., 72–74.
6. Ibid., 69.
7. Ibid., 70.
8. Ibid., 69–70. See also Juan Domingo Perón, *Filosofía peronista*, 270.
9. Ibid., 75.
10. Ibid., 73.
11. Ibid.
12. For the following account, see the summary at the end of ibid., 149–150.
13. Juan Domingo Perón, *La tercera posición argentina*, 49.
14. Pavón Pereyra, *Perón*, 62.
15. Juan Domingo Perón, *La hora de los pueblos*, 121–122.
16. Pavón Pereyra, *Perón*, 180–181.

17. Perón, *La hora,* 144–145.

18. Ibid., 144.

19. Ibid., 122.

20. Pavón Pereyra, *Perón,* 62.

21. Ibid., 64.

22. Eugenio P. Rom, *Asi hablaba Juan Perón,* 148.

23. Ibid., 149–150.

24. Benito Mussolini, "The Doctrine of Fascism," 174.

25. Ibid., 175.

26. Ibid.

27. James Gregor, *The Ideology of Fascism,* 345. See Benito Mussolini, "Segnalazione," *Opera omnia,* XXVI, 84; idem, "Atto quinto finora," ibid., XXIX, 63.

28. Pavón Pereyra, *Perón,* 171.

29. Ibid., 210.

30. Ibid.

31. Oswald Spengler, *The Hour of Decision,* 204.

32. Arnold J. Toynbee, *A Study of History,* V, 152–194, 319–337.

33. Perón, *La hora,* 5.

34. Ibid., 5, 12, 31–32.

35. Waisman, *Reversal of Development,* 164–206.

36. Perón, *Doctrina revolucionaria,* 70.

37. Perón, *Filosofía,* 121.

38. Ibid., 265, 267.

39. Ibid., 270, 272.

40. Juan Domingo Perón, *Apuntes de historia militar,* 139.

41. Ibid., 139–143.

42. Fermín Chávez, introduction to Juan Domingo Perón, *El proyecto nacional: mi testamento político,* 8–9. See also Deolindo F. Bittel, *Qué es el peronismo,* 27–28.

43. Bittel, *Qué es el peronismo,* 27–28.

44. Perón, *Proyecto,* 24.

45. Ibid., 25.

46. Juan Domingo Perón, *La comunidad organizada,* 20.

47. Ibid., 87–89; and idem, *Filosofía,* 42, 180.

48. Perón, *La comunidad,* 108.

49. Ibid.

50. Ibid., 109–110.

51. Ibid., 95.

52. Ibid., 96.

53. Ibid., 70–74, 81.

54. Ibid., 113.

55. Ibid., 90–91.

56. Ibid., 91.

57. "Las veinte verdades del justicialismo," in Perón, *La tercera posición,* 99.

58. Perón, *Filosofía,* 20.

59. Ibid., 26.

60. Ibid., 42.

61. Ibid., 43.

62. Pavón Pereyra, *Perón,* 281–282.

63. Ibid., 326.

64. Ibid., 111–112.

65. Perón, *Filosofía*, 272.
66. Ibid., 265.
67. Ibid., 272.
68. Ibid., 277.
69. Rom, *Perón*, 147.
70. Ibid., 148.
71. Perón, *Doctrina revolucionaria*, 48, 73.
72. In *Five Great Encyclicals*, 8–9, 12, 16–24.
73. Perón, *Doctrina revolucionaria*, 204.
74. *Five Great Encyclicals*, 144.
75. Ibid., 137.
76. Ibid., 156.
77. Perón, *La hora*, 167.
78. Perón, *Filosofía*, 161.
79. Perón, *Doctrina peronista*, 359–360.
80. José Antonio Primo de Rivera, *Revolución nacional (puntos de falange)*, 311–376.
81. Ibid., 371.
82. Ibid., 369, original emphasis.
83. Ibid., 243.
84. Ibid., 293, original emphasis.
85. Ibid., 36.
86. Ibid., 37.
87. Ibid., 159–160, 175–176, 191, 193.
88. Mussolini, "Relativismo e fascismo," *Opera*, XVII, 266–267.
89. Juan Domingo Perón, *Conducción peronista*, 89.
90. Ibid., 90.
91. Perón, *Filosofía*, 265.
92. Mussolini, "The Doctrine of Fascism," 175–178.
93. Perón, *Doctrina revolucionaria*, 79, 82.
94. From Enrique Pavón Pereyra's *Vida de Perón* as cited by Crawley, *A House Divided*, 65–66.
95. See Adolf Hitler, *Mein Kampf*, 209–210, 213; and Torcuato Luca de Tena et al., eds., *Yo, Juan Domingo Perón: relato autobiográfico*, 28.
96. Gottfried Feder, *Manifiesto contra la usura y la servidumbre del interés del dinero*, 11–13, 25–26, 74.
97. Ibid., 51.
98. Ibid., 26.
99. Perón, *Doctrina peronista*, 55.
100. Ibid.
101. Ibid., 237.
102. Ibid., 243.
103. Hitler, *Mein Kampf*, 213.
104. Feder, *Manifiesto*, 21.
105. Ibid.
106. Perón, "Las veinte verdades," in *La tercera posición*, 97.
107. Perón, *Doctrina revolucionaria*, 76.
108. Ibid., 137–138.
109. Perón, *La tercera posición*, 22.
110. Perón, *Proyecto*, 27, 33, 92.
111. Ibid., 24–25.

112. Ibid., 101–103.
113. Ibid., 107.
114. Ibid., 84–86.
115. Ibid., 84.
116. Ibid., 129.
117. Perón, *Conducción*, 88–89.
118. Ibid., 89.
119. Perón, *Doctrina peronista*, 106.
120. Ibid., 223, 237.
121. Ibid., 260.
122. Ibid., 359–360.
123. Ibid., 131, 359–361.
124. Ibid., 171.
125. Ibid., 172.
126. Ibid., 109–110.
127. Ibid., 69.
128. Perón, "Las veinte verdades," in *La tercera posición*, 99.
129. Perón, *Doctrina peronista*, 110–114.
130. Ibid., 115.
131. Ibid., 116, 123, 259.
132. Perón, *Doctrina revolucionaria*, 95–96.
133. Perón, *Doctrina peronista*, 142.
134. Ibid., 164–165.
135. Ibid., 166.
136. Perón, *Conducción*, 91–93.
137. Perón, *Doctrina peronista*, 156.
138. Ibid., 156–157.
139. Ibid., 188.
140. Ibid., 189.
141. Ibid., 175.
142. Ibid., 141.
143. Ibid., 140.
144. Ibid., 171.
145. Ibid., 248.
146. Ibid., 237.
147. Ibid.
148. Cited by Alberto Belloni, *Del anarquismo al peronismo*, 50.
149. Pavón Pereyra, *Perón*, 108–109.
150. Ibid., 109.
151. Pablo Giussani, *Montoneros: la soberbia armada*, 170.
152. Ibid., 172.
153. Ibid.
154. Perón, *Conducción*, 138.
155. Pavón Pereyra, *Perón*, 268–269. See also Perón, *Conducción*, 138–139.
156. Munck et al., *Argentina*, 133.
157. Ibid.
158. Ibid., 182–183.
159. Ibid., 133–134.
160. Juan Domingo Perón, *Juan Perón en la Argentina 1973: sus discursos, sus diálogos, sus conferencias*, 366.
161. Ibid., 160.

162. Owen, *Perón*, 213.
163. Ibid.
164. Juan Domingo Perón, *Correspondencia*, II, 51.
165. Ibid., 51–53.
166. Cited by Corvalán Nanclares, *Justicialismo: la hora de la verdad*, 60.
167. Juan Domingo Perón, *Juan D. Perón 1973–1974: todos sus discursos, mensajes y conferencias*, II, 231.
168. Perón, *Correspondencia*, II, 83–84.
169. Perón, *En la Argentina*, 157.
170. Ibid.
171. Pavón Pereyra, *Perón*, 218.
172. Perón, *Perón-Cooke correspondencia*, I, 34.
173. Ibid., 35.
174. Ibid.
175. Ibid., 37.
176. Ibid., 35.
177. Ibid., 43.
178. Ibid., 51.
179. Ibid., 119.
180. Ibid., 319.
181. Ibid., 137.
182. Ibid., 190.
183. Ibid., II, 390.
184. Luca de Tena, *Yo, Juan Domingo Perón*, 45.
185. Salvador Ferla, *El drama político de la Argentina contemporánea*, 254.
186. Ibid.
187. Perón, *Perón-Cooke correspondencia*, I, 33.
188. Ibid., 30.
189. Ibid.
190. Ibid., II, 136.
191. Ibid., I, 49.
192. Ibid.
193. "The Cooke-Guillén Guerrilla Plan of 1955," appended to Hodges, *Argentina, 1943–1987*, 315–320.
194. Perón, *Perón-Cooke correspondencia*, I, 50.
195. "Instrucciones generales para los dirigentes," ibid., II, 389–398.
196. Hodges, *Argentina, 1943–1987*, 318–319.
197. Perón, *Perón-Cooke correspondencia*, I, 306–312.
198. Ibid., 307.
199. Hodges, *Argentina, 1943–1987*, 319.
200. Perón, *Perón-Cooke correspondencia*, I, 319.
201. Ibid.
202. Ibid., 320.
203. Hodges, *Argentina, 1943–1987*, 319.
204. "Directivas generales para todos los peronistas," Perón, *Perón-Cooke correspondencia*, II, 378–383.
205. Ibid., I, 11.
206. Ibid., II, 379.
207. Ibid., 378.
208. Ibid., 379.
209. Ibid.

210. Ibid., 379–380.
211. Ibid., 380.
212. Ibid., 381.
213. Juan Domingo Perón, *Actualización política y doctrinaria para la toma del poder*, 7–8.
214. Ibid., 13.
215. Ibid., 21.
216. Ibid., 26.
217. Ibid., 43.
218. Perón, *Perón-Cooke correspondencia*, II, 191.
219. Ibid., 201.
220. Ibid., 213.
221. Ibid., 221.
222. Ibid., 222.
223. Ibid., 276.
224. Perón, *En la Argentina*, 50.
225. Ibid., 83.
226. Munck et al., *Argentina*, 134.
227. Ibid., 142.
228. Ibid., 202.
229. Leonardo Lezcano, "La resistencia estaba en todas partes," *La lucha por la democracia sindical en la UOM de Villa Constitución*, 57–58.
230. Guido Di Tella, *Argentina under Perón, 1973–76*, 5–6.
231. Ibid., 6.
232. Ibid.
233. Waisman, *Reversal of Development*, 122.
234. Di Tella, *Argentina*, 206.
235. Ibid., 207.
236. Ibid.
237. Ibid., 16–17.

4. The Revolutionary War

1. Perón, *Perón-Cooke correspondencia*, II, 9–10.
2. V. I. Lenin, "The Symptoms of a Revolutionary Situation," from "The Downfall of the Second International," *The Lenin Anthology*, 275–276.
3. Georges Sorel, *Reflections on Violence*, 142–145.
4. Perón, *Perón-Cooke correspondencia*, I, 306–312; II, 10.
5. Ibid., II, 10.
6. Ibid.
7. Ibid.
8. Ibid., 11.
9. Ibid.
10. Guevara, *Obras 1957–1967*, I, 31.
11. John William Cooke, *La lucha por la liberación nacional*, 104.
12. Ibid., 104–105.
13. Ibid., 106–107.
14. Ibid., 92.
15. Ibid., 93.
16. Ibid., 13.

17. Ibid., 14–16.
18. Ibid., 16–17.
19. Ibid., 25.
20. Ibid., 103.
21. Ibid., 91.
22. Perón, *Perón-Cooke correspondencia*, II, 193.
23. Ibid.
24. Ibid., 193–194.
25. Cooke, *Liberación nacional*, 104.
26. Ibid., 105.
27. Perón, *Perón-Cooke correspondencia*, II, 156.
28. Ibid., 156–157.
29. Ibid., 184.
30. Ibid., 199.
31. Ibid., 186–187, 203.
32. Ibid., 192.
33. Ibid.
34. Ibid., 191–192.
35. Ibid., 192–193.
36. Ibid., 195.
37. Ibid., 195–196.
38. Ibid., 195.
39. Ibid., 194.
40. Ibid., 195, 203.
41. Ibid., 194.
42. Ernesto Che Guevara, "The Duty of a Revolutionary Doctor," *Selected Works*, 257.
43. Ibid.
44. Ibid., 258.
45. Guevara, "Cuba: Exceptional Case or Vanguard in the Struggle against Colonialism," *Selected Works*, 60–62.
46. Ibid., 62.
47. Guevara, "Socialism and Man in Cuba," *Selected Works*, 159.
48. Ibid., 159, 163.
49. Ramón Genaro Díaz Bessone, *Guerra revolucionaria en la Argentina (1959–1978)*, 11–12.
50. Ibid., 29, 31.
51. Ibid., 39.
52. Ibid., 19–20.
53. Ibid., 25.
54. Ibid., 25, n 17.
55. Ibid., 82–83.
56. Ibid., 83.
57. Ibid., 60–73, 87, 91–92, 103–105.
58. Ibid., 73.
59. Ibid., 74.
60. Ibid., 75.
61. Ibid., 76.
62. Ibid., 104–105.
63. Ibid., 258.
64. Ibid., 261.

65. Ibid., 259–262.

66. Ibid., 257–258.

67. Ibid., 281–302.

68. "La violenta historia de los Montoneros—primera parte," 53.

69. Ibid., 55.

70. Ibid., 53.

71. Díaz Bessone, *Guerra revolucionaria*, 136, original emphasis.

72. Jorge Asís, "Conversación con Firmenich en la cárcel," 3.

73. "Cámpora: su gobierno, sus hombres, su historia," *Gente*, 14. See also Munck et al., *Argentina*, 193.

74. Guevara, "Guerrilla Warfare: A Method," *Selected Works*, 93.

75. Ibid., 95.

76. Ibid.

77. Díaz Bessone, *Guerra revolucionaria*, 193–195.

78. Ibid., 169, 175.

79. Ibid., 169.

80. Cited in Gerardo López Alonso, *1930–1980: cincuenta años de historia argentina*, 368.

81. Jacobo Timerman, *Prisoner without a Name, Cell without a Number*, 20, 80.

82. Alfonsín, *La cuestión argentina*, 173.

83. *Webster's New Universal Unabridged Dictionary* (1979), 1884; and *The Concise Columbia Encyclopedia*, 839–840.

84. *A Dictionary of the Social Sciences*, ed. Julius Gould and William L. Kolb, 719.

85. Giussani, *Montoneros*, 74–75 n.

86. Ibid., 75 n.

87. Carlos A. Brocato, *La Argentina que quisieron*, 170.

88. Ibid., 170–171.

89. Ibid., 96–97, 99–100.

90. Ibid., 102–103, 170–171.

91. Ibid., 97, 108–109.

92. Ibid., 186–187, n 65.

93. Ibid., 96–97.

94. Giussani, *Montoneros*, 99.

95. Machiavelli, *The Prince and Other Works*, 148–149.

96. Ibid., 150.

97. Gillespie, *Soldiers of Perón*, 217.

98. Ibid., 218–222.

99. Ibid., 221.

100. Ibid., 227, 270–271.

101. Giussani, *Montoneros*, 97–101.

102. Ibid., 100.

103. Guevara, "Socialism and Man in Cuba," *Selected Works*, 169.

104. V. I. Lenin, "'Left-Wing' Communism—An Infantile Disorder," *The Lenin Anthology*, 602.

105. V. I. Lenin, "From an Obituary: Ivan Vasilyevich Babushkin," *Communist Morality*, 43–44.

106. V. I. Lenin, "Enemies of the People," *The Lenin Anthology*, 306.

107. Leon Trotsky, *Their Morals and Ours*, 41.

108. Ibid., 42.

109. Guevara, "La guerra de guerrillas," *Obras,* 43.
110. Ibid.
111. Mario Eduardo Firmenich, "Otra vez 'la conspiración terrorista internacional.'"
112. Edward S. Herman, *The "Real" Terror Network,* 219.
113. Juan Carlos Marín, *Los hechos armados: un ejercicio posible,* 123.
114. Ibid., 120.
115. Ibid., 165.
116. Ibid., 175.
117. Ibid., 174–175.
118. "La violenta historia de los Montoneros," 46.
119. Ibid.
120. Ibid.
121. Timerman, *Prisoner,* 18–21, 56, 124.
122. Giussani, *Montoneros,* 93–95, 217–218.
123. Robert Cox, "Souring on the Democratic Dream," *Harper's* (May 1985).
124. Horacio Daniel Rodríguez, *"Che" Guevara. ¿Aventura o revolución?* 8–9.
125. Timerman, *Prisoner,* 20; Giussani, *Montoneros,* 87–88.
126. Alan M. Wald, *The New York Intellectuals: The Rise and Decline of the Anti-Stalinist Left from the 1930s to the 1980s,* 268. See also Bruno Rizzi, *La lezione dello stalinismo,* 46.
127. Page, *Perón,* 250.
128. Eva Perón, *La razón de mi vida,* 211.
129. Fidel Castro, "Discurso del 18 de octubre de 1967."
130. Guevara, *Selected Works,* 169.
131. Ibid., 177–180.
132. A. James Gregor, *The Fascist "Persuasion" in Radical Politics,* 15–16, 301–304, 320–321 n, 397–398. For the characterization of Mussolini as a Marxist "heretic," see A. James Gregor, *Young Mussolini and the Intellectual Origins of Fascism,* xi, 58.
133. Gregor, *The Fascist "Persuasion,"* 5.
134. Ibid., 320.
135. Ibid., 300–301.
136. Ibid., 15–16, 18–21.
137. For the alleged common denominator of Perón's "fascism," Castro's "fascism," and Guevarism, see ibid., 310, 410.
138. Guevara, "Guerrilla Warfare: A Method," *Selected Works,* 93–95.
139. Julio Santucho, *Los ultimos guevaristas: surgimiento y eclipse del ejército revolucionario del pueblo,* 224.
140. Ibid., 222.
141. Juan Gasparini, *Montoneros: final de cuentas,* 198–199.
142. Di Tella, *Argentina,* 201.
143. Ibid.
144. Brocato, *Argentina,* 84.
145. Di Tella, *Argentina,* 47–48.
146. Firmenich, "Otra vez 'la conspiración terrorista'"; PRT, *VI° Congreso Mayo 1979,* 18–19; and Enrique Gorriarán, *Democracia y liberación,* 21–24.
147. Alvaro Abós, *El posperonismo,* 37.
148. Ibid.
149. Ibid.

150. Alvaro Abós, *Las organizaciones sindicales y el poder militar (1976–1983)*, 95–96; Francisco Delich, "Después del diluvio, la clase obrera," 136; Eduardo Luis Duhalde, *El estado terrorista argentino*, 53–54, 59–60; Daniel Frontalini and María C. Caiati, *El mito de la guerra sucia*, 81–82, 103–104.

151. Abós, *Las organizaciones sindicales*, 95; Duhalde, *El estado terrorista*, 60; Rouquié, "Hegemonía militar, estado y dominación social," *Argentina, hoy*, 47.

152. Rock, *Argentina 1516–1982*, 366.

153. Martínez de Hoz, *Bases*, 21–28.

154. Ibid., 15.

155. Brocato, *Argentina*, 200–202.

156. Duhalde, *El estado terrorista*, 76–78. See also chapter 5, this book.

157. Mona Moncalvillo and Alberto Fernández, eds., *La renovación fundacional*, 111.

158. Ibid., 112.

159. Ibid., 112–113.

160. Corvalán Nanclares, *Justicialismo*, 31.

161. Ibid., 32, original emphasis.

162. Antonio Cafiero et al., *Hablan los renovadores*, 35–36.

163. Ibid., 36.

164. Ibid., 29–30.

165. Ibid.

166. Ibid., 36.

167. Ibid., 37–38.

168. Díaz Bessone, *Guerra revolucionaria*, 10–12.

169. Ibid., 13–14.

170. Gillespie, *Soldiers*, 270.

171. Ibid., 238.

172. Díaz Bessone, *Guerra revolucionaria*, 9.

173. Marín, *Los hechos armados*, 30, 95. See Gillespie, *Soldiers*, 238, 270.

174. Ibid., 63–65.

175. Munck et al., *Argentina*, 174–176, 180–182.

176. Alejandro Lanusse, *Mi testimonio*, 3–4, 15–16, 192–193, 198–208, 264.

177. Ibid., 230–231, 294–295; Marín, *Los hechos armados*, 70–71.

178. Ibid., 73.

179. Ibid., 73–74 n, 151.

180. Ibid., 98.

181. Cited in ibid., 95–96.

182. Ibid., 96.

183. Ibid., 99–100.

184. Ibid., 100.

185. Ibid., 101.

186. Ibid., 94–95, 114–116.

187. Ibid., 70–71, 101–104.

188. Ibid., 104.

189. Frederick Engels, preface to the first English edition of Karl Marx, *Capital*, I, 17.

190. Marín, *Los hechos armados*, 65.

191. Ibid., 66–68.

192. María Matilde Ollier, *El fenómeno insurreccional y la cultura política (1969–1973)*, 117–119.

193. Ibid., 119.
194. Ibid., 117–118.
195. Marín, *Los hechos armados*, 165.
196. Ibid., 30.
197. Frontalini and Caiati, *Guerra sucia*, 65–67; Abós, *Las organizaciones sindicales*, 95.
198. Díaz Bessone, *Guerra revolucionaria*, 342–350. See also Gillespie, *Soldiers*, 232–237.

5. Battleground of World War III

1. Richard M. Nixon, *The Real War*, 19–50; Duhalde, *El estado terrorista*, 32–35; Michael Klare and Nancy Stein, *Armas y poder en América Latina*, 16; Frontalini and Caiati, *Guerra sucia*, 9–10.
2. *La Nación* (14 April 1976).
3. Duhalde, *El estado terrorista*, 35–36.
4. Cited by Frontalini and Caiati, *Guerra sucia*, 35, original emphasis.
5. Cited by Duhalde, *El estado terrorista*, 79.
6. Cited by Frontalini and Caiati, *Guerra sucia*, 14.
7. Ibid., 31.
8. Ibid., 31–32.
9. Ibid., 32.
10. Timerman, *Prisoner*, 100–103.
11. Ibid., 102.
12. Cited by Duhalde, *El estado terrorista*, 81.
13. Ibid., 115.
14. Ibid., 118–119.
15. Ibid., 115, 128 n 58. See also Frontalini and Caiati, *Guerra sucia*, 17.
16. Duhalde, *El estado terrorista*, 122.
17. Ibid., 120, 124.
18. Ibid., 76.
19. Cited by Frontalini and Caiati, *Guerra sucia*, 15.
20. Ibid.
21. Ibid., 45.
22. Ibid., 57–67.
23. Ibid., 44.
24. Ibid., 44, 57.
25. Ibid., 43.
26. Ibid., 44.
27. Ibid., 58.
28. Ibid., 63.
29. *Webster's Unabridged Dictionary*, 2059.
30. Karl von Clausewitz, *De la guerra*, 27.
31. Ibid., 13.
32. Ibid., 18.
33. Cited by Frontalini and Caiati, *Guerra sucia*, 41.
34. George H. Nash, *The Conservative Intellectual Movement in America since 1945*, 91.
35. Cited by Samuel T. Francis, *Power and History: The Political Thought of James Burnham*, 127.

36. Nash, *The Conservative Intellectual Movement*, 92.
37. Cited by Francis, *Power and History*, 83 n 4; and Townsend Hoopes, *The Devil and John Foster Dulles*, 181.
38. Francis, *Power and History*, 67.
39. Ibid.
40. Ibid., 127.
41. Nash, *The Conservative Intellectual Movement*, 97.
42. James Burnham, *The Struggle for the World*, 1.
43. Ibid., 2.
44. Ibid., 3.
45. James Burnham, *The Coming Defeat of Communism*, 67.
46. Ibid., 69.
47. Ibid., 70.
48. Ibid.
49. Clausewitz, *De la guerra*, 189.
50. André Malraux and James Burnham, *The Case for De Gaulle: A Dialogue between André Malraux and James Burnham*, 7–8, 21, 23.
51. Ibid., 21.
52. Ibid., 61.
53. Ibid., 31–32, 67–68.
54. Ibid., 75–76.
55. Frontalini and Caiati, *Guerra sucia*, 31.
56. Ibid.
57. Gasparini, *Montoneros*, 94.
58. Ibid.
59. Ibid.
60. Ibid.
61. Ibid.
62. Brian Crozier, *The Struggle for the Third World*, 137–140, 146.
63. Crozier, *Franco*, 268, 506–512.
64. Brian Crozier, *A Theory of Conflict*, 201.
65. Ibid., 202.
66. Ibid., 203.
67. Ibid., 205.
68. Ibid., 210.
69. Ibid.
70. Ibid., 84–86.
71. Brian Crozier, *Strategy of Survival*, 199–200.
72. Ibid., 200–201.
73. Ibid., 201.
74. Ibid., 205.
75. Ibid.
76. Ibid., 206.
77. Ibid., 208.
78. Ibid., 209.
79. Cited by Duhalde, *El estado terrorista*, 81; from *La Semana* (April 1982).
80. Ibid., 82.
81. Crozier, *Theory of Conflict*, 82.
82. Ibid., 84.
83. Crozier, *Strategy of Survival*, 23.
84. Ibid., 123, 156.

85. Ibid., 23.

86. Ibid.; and Díaz Bessone, *Guerra revolucionaria*, 53. The citation is from Rosa Luxemburg.

87. Díaz Bessone, *Guerra revolucionaria*, 50. See Marx and Engels, "Manifesto," *Selected Works*, I, 45.

88. Díaz Bessone, *Guerra revolucionaria*, 50.

89. Ibid., 60.

90. Ibid., 63.

91. Crozier, *Strategy of Survival*, 146.

92. Cited by Duhalde, *El estado terrorista*, 116.

93. Frontalini and Caiati, *Guerra sucia*, Appendix, 106–107.

94. Nixon, *Real War*, 19.

95. Ibid., 335.

96. Ibid., 251, 263, 265.

97. Ibid., 354.

98. Ibid., 20.

99. John A. Garraty and Peter Gay, eds., *The Columbia History of the World*, 1085.

100. Nixon, *Real War*, 21–22, 41.

101. Ibid., 21.

102. Ibid.

103. Garraty and Gay, *The Columbia History*, 1084–1085.

104. Ibid., 1082, 1085–1086.

105. William J. Pomeroy, *Guerrilla and Counter-Guerrilla Warfare: Liberation and Suppression in the Present Period*, 41.

106. Ibid., 100–102.

107. Clausewitz, *De la guerra*, 189.

108. D. F. Fleming, *The Cold War and Its Origins 1917–1960*, I, 439.

109. Ibid., 455.

110. Ibid., 446.

111. Ibid.

112. Ibid., 249.

113. Burnham, *Struggle for the World*, 1.

114. Ibid.

115. Richard M. Nixon, *Real Peace*, 96–97.

6. The Defense of Western Civilization

1. Cited by López Alonso, *1930–1980*, 368.

2. Cited by Frontalini and Caiati, *Guerra sucia*, 98. See the similar statement by Gen. Alejandro Lanusse (28 July 1972) appended to Rubén A. Sosa, *La magia toma el poder en Argentina*, 256.

3. Pedro Eugenio Aramburu and Isaac F. Rojas, *La revolución libertadora*, 8.

4. Ibid., 22–24.

5. Ibid., 48–49.

6. Ibid., 67.

7. Ibid., 48.

8. Lanusse, *Mi testimonio*, 4.

9. Ibid.

10. Ibid.

11. Ibid., 91.

12. Ibid., 17.
13. Ibid., 129.
14. Cited by López Alonso, *1930–1980*, 368.
15. Lanusse, *Mi testimonio*, 284.
16. Ibid., xvi.
17. Ibid., xvii.
18. Ibid., 230.
19. Ibid., 230–231.
20. Ibid., 294.
21. Ibid., 295.
22. Rouquié, *Poder militar*, II, 188, 206 n 19, 286, 351.
23. Lanusse, *Mi testimonio*, 227, 240.
24. Ibid., 234.
25. Ibid., 240.
26. Ibid., 251.
27. Ibid., 218.
28. Ibid., 220.
29. Ibid., 253.
30. Cited by Frontalini and Caiati, *Guerra sucia*, 18.
31. Burnham, *Struggle for the World*, 21.
32. Ibid., 22–23.
33. James Burnham, *Suicide of the West*, 15.
34. Ibid.
35. Ibid., 16.
36. Ibid., 17.
37. Ibid., 20–22.
38. Ibid., 17–18.
39. Ibid., 26; see also 297, 315.
40. Ibid., 22–24.
41. Ibid., 24.
42. Ibid., 291.
43. James Burnham, "Joys and Sorrows of Empire," *National Review* (13 July 1971).
44. James Burnham, *The Machiavellians*, viii.
45. Ibid.
46. Burnham, *Suicide*, 159–160.
47. Ibid., 160–161.
48. Ibid., 160.
49. Ibid., 161.
50. Ibid., 175.
51. Ibid., 161.
52. Ibid., 174, 288.
53. Ibid., 174–175.
54. Burnham, *Machiavellians*, 120–122, 125–126.
55. Burnham, *Suicide*, 178–180, 184.
56. Ibid., 288.
57. Ibid., 48, 51.
58. Ibid., 201.
59. Ibid., 189.
60. Ibid., 189–190.
61. Ibid., 190.

62. James Burnham, *Congress and the American Tradition*, 296–298.
63. Ibid., 12, 285–289.
64. Ibid., 337.
65. Ibid., 338.
66. Ibid., 282.
67. Ibid., 283.
68. Ibid.
69. Ibid., 337.
70. Cited by F. Ibarguren, *Orígenes*, 121.
71. Ibid., 121–122.
72. Ibid., 12–13; and Arturo Jauretche, *Política nacional y revisionismo histórico*, 121–122.
73. Shlomo Ben-Ami, *Fascism from Above: The Dictatorship of Primo de Rivera 1923–1930*, 69 n 82.
74. Ibid., 282–286.
75. Ibarguren, *Orígenes*, 21.
76. Ibid., 27.
77. Ibid., 24.
78. Ibid.
79. *Five Great Encyclicals*, 150–151.
80. Ibid., 151.
81. Primo de Rivera, *Revolución nacional*, 134–135.
82. Ibid., 159–160, 163.
83. Ibid., 163.
84. Ibid., 220.
85. Ibid., 205.
86. Ibid., 219–222.
87. Ibid., 159–160.
88. Ibid., 162, 166.
89. Ibid., 240, 242.
90. Ibid., 241.
91. Jordán B. Genta, *Testamento político*, 30–33.
92. Perón, *Filosofía*, 46–49.
93. Ibid., 44, 92.
94. Ibarguren, *Orígenes*, 14.
95. Ibid.
96. Carlos Ibarguren, *La historia que he vivido*, 369.
97. Ibid.
98. Ernst Nolte, *Three Faces of Fascism*, 115, 119.
99. Ibid., 120–121.
100. Ibid., 131.
101. Ibid.
102. Zuleta Alvarez, *El nacionalismo argentino*, I, 213–214.
103. Ibid., 214.
104. Ibid.
105. Ibid., 215.
106. Ibid.
107. Carl Schmitt, *Interpretación europea de Donoso Cortés*, 31.
108. Ibid.
109. Ibid., 30, 93–94.
110. Ibid., 125–126.

111. Ibid., 138—140, 142.

112. Ibid., 139—140.

113. Juan Donoso Cortés, "Discurso sobre la dictadura," *Obras completas*, II, 203—204.

114. Ibid., 203.

115. Ibid., 197.

116. Ibid., 204.

117. Ibid., 197—200.

118. Ibid., 199.

119. Ibid., 197—198.

120. Donoso Cortés, "Correspondencia con el Conde de Montalembert," *Obras completas*, II, 207.

121. Ibid., 208. See also Donoso Cortés, "Ensayo sobre el catolicismo, el liberalismo y el socialismo," *Obras completas*, II, 412—414.

122. Donoso Cortés, "Correspondencia," *Obras completas*, II, 209; idem, "Polémica con la prensa española," *Obras completas*, II, 215.

123. Ibarguren, *Orígenes*, 24.

124. Ibid.

125. Donoso Cortés, "Discurso sobre Europa," *Obras completas*, II, 306.

126. Ibid., 304, 312.

127. Ibid., 306.

128. Ibid., 307.

129. Ibid., 308.

130. Ibid.

131. Ibid., 308—309.

132. Ibid., 309.

133. Ibid., 306.

134. Ibid., 310—311.

135. Ibid., 313—314.

136. Ibarguren, *Orígenes*, 26.

137. Timerman, *Prisoner*, 94—98.

138. Cited by Frontalini and Caiati, *Guerra sucia*, 78.

139. *Protocols of the Learned Elders of Zion*, 9—11, 18, 20, 23, 33, 35, 42—43, 51.

140. Ibid., 22, 48.

141. See Julio Meinvielle, *Los tres pueblos bíblicos en su lucha por la dominación del mundo*; idem, *Entre la iglesia y el reich*; idem, *El judío en el misterio de la historia*; and idem, *El comunismo en la revolución anticristiana*.

142. See Jordán Bruno Genta, *Guerra contrarrevolucionaria: doctrina política*; idem, *Principios de la política: la guerra subversiva en nuestra patria*.

143. Meinvielle, *El judío*, 37.

144. Marysa Navarro Gerassi, *Los nacionalistas*, 113.

145. Ibid.

146. Ibid., 113—114.

147. Ibid., 114—115.

148. Ibid., 230.

149. Genta, *Testamento*, 33.

150. Ibid., 28.

151. Ibid., 12.

152. Ibid., 11.

153. Ibid., 12—13.

154. Lothrop Stoddard, *The Revolt against Civilization*, 142.
155. Ibid., 143–145.

7. The Military's "Final Solution"

1. Duhalde, *El estado terrorista*, 46–47.
2. Ibid., 47.
3. Ibid.
4. Giussani, *Montoneros*, 235 n 56.
5. Ibid.
6. Duhalde, *El estado terrorista*, 47.
7. Ibid., 48.
8. Sosa, *La magia*, Appendix VI, 275–278.
9. Ibid.
10. Ibid., 278.
11. Ibid., 157.
12. Alejandro Horowicz, *Los cuatro peronismos*, 234.
13. Ibid.
14. Brocato, *Argentina*, 51–52 n 14.
15. Ibid.
16. López Alonso, *1930–1980*, 315.
17. Duhalde, *El estado terrorista*, 48–49.
18. Ibid., 49.
19. Cited by Frontalini and Caiati, *Guerra sucia*, 107–108.
20. Ibid., 49.
21. Ibid., 74.
22. Duhalde, *El estado terrorista*, 75. Based on testimony by a former aide to Gen. Albano Harguindeguy.
23. Frontalini and Caiati, *Guerra sucia*, 25. Based on a statement by General Videla.
24. Comisión Nacional Sobre la Desaparición de Personas (CONADEP), *Nunca más*, 479.
25. "Las trampas del Nunca Más." Cited in CONADEP, *Nunca más*, 238–239.
26. Duhalde, *El estado terrorista*, 240–247.
27. "Otra vez los archivos de los campos de concentración," 65.
28. "Genocidio," 17; Poneman, *Argentina*, 36.
29. Santiago Aroca, "Los 5000 desaparecidos de Camps," 12.
30. "Reflexiones críticas y autocríticas acerca de la lucha armada en la Argentina y de la estrategia en Montoneros para la etapa actual," cited by Gasparini, *Montoneros*, 145–146.
31. Ibid., 146.
32. Ibid., 151, 153.
33. Ibid., 147.
34. Ibid.
35. Aroca, "Los 5000 desaparecidos de Camps," 12.
36. Duhalde, *El estado terrorista*, 81.
37. Ibid., 82.
38. Ibid., 83–84.
39. Frontalini and Caiati, *Guerra sucia*, 146–147.
40. Ibid.

41. Ibid., 33.
42. Duhalde, *El estado terrorista,* 146–147.
43. Ibid., 76–78.
44. Ibid., 78.
45. Frontalini and Caiati, *Guerra sucia,* 75, original emphasis.
46. Ibid., 24.
47. Ibid., 21.
48. Ibid., 22.
49. Ibid.
50. Ibid.
51. Ibid., 23.
52. Ibid., original emphasis.
53. *Clarín* (5 May 1979).
54. Frontalini and Caiati, *Guerra sucia,* 25.
55. Gillespie, *Soldiers,* 250.
56. Frontalini and Caiati, *Guerra sucia,* 19.
57. Rodolfo Walsh, "Carta abierta de un escritor argentino a la junta militar," 19.
58. "La cultura de la liberación: Rodolfo Walsh," 17.
59. Holver Martínez Borelli, *La trinidad militar: política e ideología,"* 5–6.
60. H. C. Eric Midelfort, *Witch Hunting in Southwestern Germany 1562–1684: The Social and Intellectual Foundations,* 17–18.
61. Margaret A. Murray, *The God of the Witches,* 17–22.
62. Interview with Ramón Camps in *La Semana* (April 1982), cited by Duhalde, *El estado terrorista,* 81.
63. Heinrich Kramer and James Sprenger, *Malleus Maleficarum,* xvii.
64. Ibid., xviii.
65. Ibid.
66. Ibid., 41, 46.
67. Ibid., 47.
68. Andrea Dworkin, *Our Blood: Prophecies and Discourses on Sexual Politics,* 16–17.
69. *Five Great Encyclicals,* 179.
70. Ibid., 184.
71. Ibid., 185.
72. Ibid., 199.
73. Schmitt, *Interpretación europea,* 67.
74. Ibid., 138.
75. Ibid., 94.
76. Ibid., 141–142.
77. Mao Tse-tung, "Analysis of the Classes in Chinese Society," *Selected Works,* I, 13.
78. Carl Schmitt, "The Concept of 'the Political,'" 326.
79. Ibid., 327.
80. Ibid., 328.
81. Frontalini and Caiati, *Guerra sucia,* 31.
82. Duhalde, *El estado terrorista,* 28–30.
83. Frontalini and Caiati, *Guerra sucia,* 92.
84. Ibid., 84.
85. Ibid., 92–93.
86. Ibid., 93.

87. Timerman, *Prisoner*, 51.
88. Ibid., 29–30.
89. Ibid., 99.
90. Ibid., 30.
91. Ibid., 64.
92. Ibid., 100.
93. Ibid., 102.
94. Ibid., 74.
95. Ibid., 73–74.
96. Ibid., 74.
97. Ibid., 64–65, 77, 100–101, 133.
98. Dennis Prager and Joseph Telushkin, *Why the Jews?* 22–23.
99. Ibid., 23.
100. Ibid., 24.
101. Ibid., 153–154.
102. Ibid., 159.
103. Ibid., 24.
104. Hitler, *Mein Kampf*, I, 306.
105. Ibid., 319.
106. Ibid., 315, 320–323.
107. Ibid., II, 661, original emphasis.
108. Martin Gilbert, *The Holocaust: A History of the Jews of Europe during the Second World War*, 18. See also Karl Dietrich Bracher, *The German Dictatorship: The Origins, Structure, and Effects of National Socialism*, 424.
109. Hitler, *Mein Kampf*, II, 678.
110. Ibid., 679.
111. Cited by Duhalde, *El estado terrorista*, 81.
112. Cited by Frontalini and Caiati, *Guerra sucia*, 25.
113. Cited by Duhalde, *El estado terrorista*, 126 n 43. A similar statement occurs in Lanusse, *Mi testimonio*, 129.
114. Timerman, *Prisoner*, 26.
115. Ibid., 27.
116. Ibid., 128.
117. Jean-Pierre Bousquet, *Las locas de la Plaza de Mayo*, 37–38.
118. Ibid., 172.
119. Ibid., 170.

8. Resistance to the Military Process

1. Wynia, *Argentina*, 109.
2. "Reportaje a Martínez de Hoz," 69.
3. Horacio Verbitsky, *La posguerra sucia*, 10.
4. Hodges, *Argentina*, ix.
5. Cited by Gustavo Beliz, *Menem: Argentina hacia el año 2000*, 190–192.
6. Ibid., 192.
7. Ibid., 208.
8. Abós, *El posperonismo*, 152.
9. Ibid., 155.
10. Ibid.
11. Ibid.
12. Ibid., 156.

13. Ibid., 255 n 51.
14. Bittel, *Qué es el peronismo,* Appendix, 219.
15. Ibid., 220.
16. Ibid., 109–110.
17. Ibid., 112. See Cooke, *Correspondencia Perón-Cooke,* I, 14.
18. *Webster's Unabridged Dictionary* (1983), 1541.
19. Cooke, *Correspondencia Perón-Cooke,* I, 14–15.
20. Díaz Bessone, *Guerra revolucionaria,* 352, 360.
21. Fernando Vaca Narvaja, "Take the Street."
22. "Entrevista al Comandante Firmenich," 6–7.
23. Ibid., 7.
24. "Entrevista con el Comandante Raúl Yäger: los obreros movilizados acabarán con la tiranía," 4.
25. Cited by Gasparini, *Montoneros,* 184, original emphasis.
26. "Entrevista con el Comandante Raúl Yäger," 4.
27. Gillespie, *Soldiers,* 262–263.
28. Ibid., 265.
29. Munck et al., *Argentina,* 219.
30. Fernando Vaca Narvaja, "*Balance 81:* el camino es la movilización," 8.
31. Abós, *Las organizaciones sindicales,* 46–47.
32. Ibid., 55–56.
33. Ibid., 75–76.
34. "Firmenich responde: la victoria es esencialmente política," 35.
35. Ibid., 34.
36. Abós, *Las organizaciones sindicales,* 56, 103.
37. "Balance y perspectivas," 1.
38. PRT, *Aporte para la discusión política,* 24.
39. Ibid., 25.
40. The theme of the First Rome Conference (April 1977) was elaborated in the so-called Treaty of Rome. See Movimiento Peronista Montonero, *Resistir y vencer para ganar la paz en la Argentina,* 4.
41. The slogan of the Second Rome Conference (November 1977) of the Montonero Peronist movement was "Resistir es vencer." See the English edition of *Vencer,* nos. 2–3 (1979): 7; and "Montoneros hoy," 37.
42. "Entrevista al Comandante Firmenich," 4.
43. Partido Montonero, *Hacia una nueva política para la conquista del poder por los trabajadores y el pueblo peronista,* based on an original draft in *El Montonero,* no. 11 (24 April 1976).
44. Mario Eduardo Firmenich, "Firmenich: A Political Analysis," 18.
45. Julio Roqué, "'Argentina país en guerra': hablan los Montoneros," 94.
46. Ibid., 89.
47. Gillespie, *Soldiers,* 241.
48. Movimiento Peronista Montonero, *Resistir y vencer,* 3–4.
49. Ibid., 4.
50. Ibid.
51. Montonero Party, *Statement of the Montonero Party's September 1977 National Council,* xxviii, n 1.
52. Ibid., iii.
53. Ibid., iii–iv.
54. Ibid., iii. See Mao Tse-tung, "On Contradiction," *Selected Works,* I, 331–337.

55. Montonero Party, *Statement,* iv.
56. Ibid.
57. Ibid., xxx, n 8.
58. Ibid., x.
59. "Carta abierta de Galimberti y Gelman (París, 22 de febrero de 1979)," 43.
60. Ibid., 44.
61. "Juan Gelman: entrevista exclusiva realizada en París por Roberto Mero," 27. See also Rodolfo Walsh, *Los papeles de Walsh,* 17.
62. "Juan Gelman," 27–28.
63. Rodolfo Galimberti et al., *La ruptura,* 7.
64. Ibid.
65. Ibid., 10.
66. Ibid.
67. Ibid.
68. Ibid., 11.
69. Ibid., 12.
70. Ibid.
71. Ibid., 13.
72. Ibid. On the Montoneros' option for "terrorism," see also 15.
73. Ibid., 14.
74. Ibid., 19.
75. Ibid., 20.
76. Ibid., 19.
77. Ibid., 20.
78. Ibid., 21.
79. Ibid., 22.
80. Ibid.
81. Miguel Bonasso, "No hay que confundir el enemigo," 15.
82. Gillespie, *Soldiers,* 268.
83. Ibid., 268–269.
84. Fernando Vaca Narvaja, "Take the Street," 3. See also the interview with Roberto Perdía, "Conquering Workers' Hegemony," 5, 9.
85. Mario E. Firmenich et al., "Bases para la alianza constituyente de la nueva Argentina," 34.
86. Montoneros, *Reencauzar el movimiento peronista como eje de la liberación. Reconstruir el frente bajo la hegemonía de los trabajadores. Recuperar el gobierno para el pueblo y para Perón,* 5–9.
87. Ibid., 6.
88. Ibid., 5.
89. Ibid., 6.
90. Ibid., 5, 9.
91. Montoneros, "Radiografía de la Triple A," 245–246.
92. Ibid., 247.
93. Ibid., 251.
94. Ibid.
95. Firmenich et al., "Bases para la alianza," 56–58.
96. Ibid., 65.
97. Firmenich, "Otra vez 'la conspiración,'" in *El Porteño* (April 1985), 13.
98. "*Combate* entrevista a la dirección del PRT," 13.
99. "Informe del Comité Central saliente al VI Congreso del PRT reunido en mayo de 1979," 38.

100. "*Combate* entrevista," 13.
101. "Informe del Comité Central," 39–40.
102. "Balance y perspectivas," 2.
103. Interview with María Seoane, former ERP militant aligned with the tendency led by Julio Santucho and Roberto Guevara, Buenos Aires, 25 April 1985.
104. The following account is based on Seoane's testimony. For Gorriarán's own account, see Blixen, *Gorriarán Merlo*, 247–274.
105. Interview with Norberto Rey of the PRT National Directorate, Buenos Aires, 29 April 1985.
106. "Balance y perspectivas," 2.
107. Interview with Norberto Rey.
108. "Informe del Comité Central," 35.
109. Ibid., 26.
110. Ibid., 32.
111. Ibid., 18.
112. Ibid., 19.
113. Ibid., 19–20.
114. Ibid., 27.
115. Ibid., 28.
116. Ibid., 27–28.
117. Ibid., 25.
118. Ibid., 35.
119. Ibid., 29.
120. Ibid., 35.
121. Ibid., 29, 31.
122. Ibid., 30.
123. Ibid., 38–39, 42.
124. Ibid., 38, 40.
125. Ibid., 39.
126. Ibid.
127. PRT, "Nuestra línea internacional," 94.
128. "Informe del Comité Central," 31. See also "*Combate* entrevista," 12.
129. "Informe del Comité Central," 34.
130. Interview with Norberto Rey.
131. PRT, *Aporte para la discusión*, 17–18.
132. Ibid., 17.
133. Ibid., 18.
134. Ibid., 22–23.
135. Ibid., 6.
136. Ibid., 11.
137. Ibid., 24.
138. Ibid., 22–23, 32–33.
139. Ibid., 33. Based on figures provided by Gerardo Duejo, *El capital monopolista y las contradicciones secundarias de la sociedad argentina*.
140. PRT, *Aporte para la discusión*, 33–34.
141. Ibid., 36, 42.
142. Ibid., 46, 51.
143. Ibid., 44–46.
144. Ibid., 9.
145. Ibid., 9–10.
146. Ibid., 56.

147. Ibid., 11.
148. Ibid., 10.
149. Ibid., 35.
150. Ibid., 56.
151. Ibid., 9–10.
152. Ibid., 23.
153. PRT, "Parliamentarismo y fascismo," 5–6.
154. PRT, *Aporte para la discusión*, 23.
155. Ibid.
156. Díaz Bessone, *Guerra revolucionaria*, 359.
157. Verbitsky, *La posguerra sucia*, 37–38.
158. Interview with Patricia Bullrich.
159. "A formar comisiones de lucha en cada fábrica," 1.
160. Ibid., 3.
161. Rodolfo Galimberti, "El delito de ser joven," 7–8.
162. Carolina Serrano, "Editorial," 2–4.
163. See their respective articles: Carolina Serrano, "El modelo de la juventud" and Rodolfo Galimberti, "Queridos compañeros de la Juventud Peronista," *JOTAPÉ*, no. 2 (February 1980), 1–2 (5), 3–4 (6); Carolina Serrano, "Resistencia peronista a la dictadura videlista" and Rodolfo Galimberti, "Queridos compañeros de la Juventud Peronista," *JOTAPÉ*, no. 3 (August–September 1980): 1–3, 4–7; and Carolina Serrano, "Editorial" and Rodolfo Galimberti, "Y ahora Viola," *JOTAPÉ*, no. 4 (March 1981): 2–5, 6–9.
164. "Es Bullrich, pero lidera a los peronistas," 7.
165. Interview with Montonera militant Alicia Giraudo, Buenos Aires, 8 March 1985.
166. Altogether five numbers of *JP ¡Presente!* appeared in 1982—in February–March, April–May, June–July, August–September, and October.
167. "Andrés Framini," 12.
168. "Bases políticas para la acción y organización de la Juventud Peronista," 2.
169. Ibid., 13.
170. Ibid., 2.
171. Ibid., 3.
172. Ibid., 6.
173. JP, *Boletín Informativo* (April 1983): 21.
174. Ibid., 9.
175. Ibid., 17.
176. Rodolfo Galimberti, *La revolución peronista*, 30.
177. "Patricia Bullrich," 74.
178. The following depiction of the film is based on a private showing in a Montonero house in a working-class suburb of Buenos Aires, 13 March 1985.
179. See Frontalini and Caiati, *Guerra sucia*, 6–7.
180. Díaz Bessone, *Guerra revolucionaria*, 25 n 17.
181. As early as February 1973 attendance at Montonero-oriented JP rallies reached almost 100,000 (Gillespie, *Soldiers*, 120). The numbers continued to grow.
182. Ignacio González Janzen, *Argentina: 20 años de luchas peronistas*, 219–220.
183. Gillespie, *Soldiers*, 127 n 9.
184. Interview with Ricardo Obregón Cano, Buenos Aires, 18 March 1985.

185. Perón, "Síntesis del Plan Trienal 1974–1977," *En la Argentina*, 279, 308.
186. Ferrer, "La economía argentina," 105.
187. *Coyuntura y Desarrollo*, no. 9 (May 1979): 53. Cited by Carlos M. Vilas, "On the Crisis of Bourgeois Democracy in Argentina," 20.
188. Ferrer, "La economía argentina," 122.
189. *La Nación* (19 December 1978). Cited by Santiago Senén González, *Diez años de sindicalismo argentino (de Perón al Proceso)*, 107.
190. Vilas, "On the Crisis of Bourgeois Democracy," 20.
191. Ibid.
192. *Coyuntura y Desarrollo*, no. 38 (October 1981): 39. Cited by Vilas, "On the Crisis of Bourgeois Democracy," 20 n 9.
193. Ibid.
194. Francisco Delich, "Después del diluvio," 137.
195. *Coyuntura y Desarrollo* (October 1981): 39. Cited by Vilas, "On the Crisis of Bourgeois Democracy," 20 n 9.
196. Ferrer, "La economía argentina," 119, 121, 123–124.
197. Cited by Delich, "Después del diluvio," 139. From *El Economista* (28 March 1980).
198. Ibid., 139 n 11. From *Mercado* (5 November 1980).
199. Martínez de Hoz, *Bases*, 110–111, 114–116.
200. Ibid., 111.
201. Ibid.
202. Ibid., 114.
203. Ibid., 116.
204. Ibid., 117.
205. Delich, "Después del diluvio," 142–143.
206. Ibid., 135.
207. Senén González, *Diez años*, 134.
208. The following account of the LCT is based on Abós, *Las organizaciones sindicales*, 42–43.
209. See Abós's account of the LAP, ibid., 64–66.
210. Ibid., 13–14.
211. Ibid., 22.
212. Cited by Duhalde, *El estado terrorista*, 89.
213. Abós, *Las organizaciones sindicales*, Appendix, 112, 115.
214. Ibid., 115.
215. Delich, "Después del diluvio," 140.
216. Abós, *Las organizaciones sindicales*, 12.
217. Ibid.
218. Phillip Berryman, *The Religious Roots of Rebellion*, 353.
219. Abós, *Las organizaciones sindicales*, 82–83.
220. Ibid., 83.
221. Cited by Berryman, *The Religious Roots*, 288–289.
222. Ibid., 290.
223. Ibid., 291–292.
224. Abós, *Las organizaciones sindicales*, 83.
225. Ibid.
226. Ibid., 84.
227. Ibid., Appendix, 123.
228. Juan Domingo Perón, "Unidad, solidaridad y organización," *El pensa-*

miento político de Perón, 93–94; and idem, *Doctrina peronista,* 274, 276–277.

229. On the formal dissolution of the CGT in November 1979 and its illegal revival in November 1980 alongside the 62 Organizations, see Senén González, *Diez años,* 125–127, 142–143.

230. Alfredo Carazo and Rodolfo Audi, *Siete años de lucha contra la dictadura,* 19.

231. Abós, *Las organizaciones sindicales,* 39.

232. Ibid.

233. Ibid., 76–78.

234. Ibid., 46–47. Munck et al. concur with this assessment of the turning point, *Argentina,* 215.

235. Abós, *Las organizaciones sindicales,* 46.

236. See Senén González, *Diez años,* Appendix, 102–112.

237. Ibid., 70.

238. Munck et al. describe it as a "labor offensive," *Argentina,* 219.

239. Abós, *Las organizaciones sindicales,* Appendix, 124–125.

240. Ibid., 34.

241. Senén González, *Diez años,* 110–111.

242. Abós, *Las organizaciones sindicales,* 75–76, 78–80.

243. Ibid., 80.

244. Movimiento Peronista Montonero, *La política que hemos venido desarrollando y los golpes del enemigo,* 4.

245. Cited by Mora Cordeu et al., *Peronismo, la mayoría perdida,* 220.

246. Ibid.

247. Interview with Raimundo Ongaro in Lima, 2–3 March 1976, and Madrid, 19 September 1978. Agustín Tosco gives a similar account of the *cordobazo.* See Blixen, *Gorriarán Merlo,* 84.

248. Cited by Abós, *Las organizaciones sindicales,* 54, 108 n 19. From Madrid's *El País* (28 April 1979).

9. The Final Humiliation

1. "*Combate* entrevista a los organismos de defensa de los derechos humanos en Argentina," 38. In the past the Mothers also worked on close terms with the Communist-controlled Argentine League for Human Rights (Liga Argentina por los Derechos Humanos—LADH). See Bousquet, *Las locas,* 53.

2. Abós, *El posperonismo,* 154.

3. Ibid.

4. "Esquivel formuló severas críticas."

5. "Alfonsín apoyó a Jorge Videla," 5.

6. "A la 4ª marcha de la resistencia," 1.

7. Cited by Pablo Giussani, *Los días de Alfonsín,* 411.

8. "Una historia que empezó en febrero."

9. Ibid.

10. Verbitsky, *La posguerra sucia,* 10–11.

11. Ibid., 10.

12. JP–R, *Aportes para una síntesis política,* 12.

13. Mario E. Firmenich, "Unidad nacional y pluralismo ante los reclamos de justicia."

14. "Impulsar la resistencia popular," 2, 4.

15. Interview with Daniel Llano, propaganda and press secretary of the Unified Peronist Youth (Juventud Peronista Unificada—JPU), Buenos Aires, 12 April 1985.

16. John A. Booth, *The End and the Beginning: The Nicaraguan Revolution*, 102–103, 152–154.

17. Giussani, *Los días de Alfonsín*, 367.

18. Ibid., 366.

19. Gorriarán, *Democracia y liberación*, 43–44, 67–69.

20. Ibid., 45–46.

21. Ibid., 46.

22. Interview with Maria Seoane.

23. Interview with Nelson Marinelli, Buenos Aires, 9 April 1985.

24. JI, *Apuntes para la liberación*, 10–14.

25. Ibid., 11.

26. Ibid., 13.

27. Ibid., 14.

28. Alfonsín, *La cuestión argentina*, 148–149.

29. Ibid., 130–134.

30. Ibid., 134–145.

31. Ibid., 192–194.

32. Joint interview with Daniel Llano and Galimberti's "lieutenant" Jorge Reyna, Buenos Aires, 11 April 1985.

33. *La Semana* (26 January 1985).

34. Ibid.

35. Moncalvillo and Fernández, *La renovación fundacional*, 116.

36. Cafiero et al., *Hablan los renovadores*, 77.

37. Ibid., 112.

38. Roberto C. Perdía and Fernando Vaca Narvaja, *Existe otra Argentina posible*, 270.

39. "Vuelven los Montoneros," 36.

40. "Montoncros hoy," 36.

41. Firmenich, "Otra vez la 'conspiración.'"

42. "ERP y Montoneros: adiós a las armas," 11.

43. Ibid., 17.

44. "Mario Eduardo Firmenich: 'Los Montoneros sí existen,'" 12–13. Reproduced from Firmenich, "Otra vez la 'conspiración.'"

45. Ibid., 12.

46. Ibid., 12–13.

47. Mario E. Firmenich, *Aportes del peronismo revolucionario para la transformación del movimiento*, 3.

48. Interview with Raimundo Ongaro, Buenos Aires, 26 January 1985.

49. Mario E. Firmenich [Darío Quiroga, pseud.], "Rescatar las banderas revolucionarias y marchar hacia la transcendencia histórica," 6.

50. Cited by Prensa Obrera, *El Partido Obrero y el peronismo*, 155.

51. Mario E. Firmenich et al., "Al pueblo argentino," 1.

52. JP–R, *Aportes para una síntesis*, 4–5.

53. Ibid., 6–7.

54. Ibid., 7–10.

55. Ibid., 8.

56. "Lanzamiento de la APA," and "No arriar las banderas: la Agrupación 'Sabino Navarro' resaltó el peronismo auténtico."

57. Nilda Garré, "El montonerismo, hoy, es un delirio político," 14.

58. Ibid., 15.

59. Ibid.

60. Montoneros, *A los compañeros del peronismo montonero y del peronismo revolucionario*, 1.

61. Ibid., 3, 6.

62. Ibid., 1.

63. Ibid., 2–3.

64. Ibid., 2.

65. Ibid.

66. Ibid., 3.

67. Ibid.

68. Ibid.

69. Ibid., 6.

70. Ibid., 7.

71. Ibid., 6.

72. Asís, "Conversación con Firmenich en la cárcel," 3, original emphasis.

73. Ibid.

74. Ibid., 4.

75. Mario E. Firmenich et al., *Análisis y propuestas para los militantes y activistas del peronismo transformador y revolucionario*, 7.

76. Ibid.

77. Ibid., 10.

78. Ibid., 11.

79. Ibid.

80. Ibid., 14–15.

81. Giussani, *Los días de Alfonsín*, 274–276.

82. Ibid., 294–295.

83. Ibid., 295.

84. Ibid.

85. Ibid., 108; see also 112–113.

86. Ibid., 119–121.

87. Perdía and Vaca Narvaja, *Existe otra Argentina*, 261–265.

88. Aroca, "Los 5000 desaparecidos de Camps," 12.

89. *Gaceta de Hoy* (25 April 1985).

90. Edward Schumacher, "Argentina and Democracy," 1072.

91. Ibid., 1075.

92. Ibid.

93. "No hay un corte con el pasado," 11.

94. "Infierno en el teatro."

95. "Silencio en Ezeiza."

96. "La violencia política," 15.

97. "Por la calle y con los Falcón," 7.

98. "Ya actuan los 'grupos de tareas,'" 7.

99. Ibid.

100. *La Voz* (30 April 1985).

101. Blixen, *Gorriarán Merlo*, 263–265; Gasparini, *Montoneros*, 210–212; and Santucho, *Los últimos guevaristas*, 226.

102. Alfonsín, *La cuestión argentina*, 171, 173.

Conclusion

1. See "Farewell to Arms" in Hodges, *Argentina*, 210–240.
2. See Donald C. Hodges, *The Bureaucratization of Socialism*, 174–189.
3. "Acusa el FRP de complicidad en torturas a jueces y políticos," *La Jornada* (Mexico) (13 March 1989).
4. G. W. F. Hegel, *The Philosophy of Right*, 13.

Bibliography

Interviews

Hugo Bressano (pseud. Nahuel Moreno), secretary general of the PRT (Verdad), Buenos Aires, 15 May 1971.

Nubelio Valentín Brizuela, secretary of state of the province of La Rioja and secretary general of the Justicialist party of La Rioja, La Rioja, 21 February 1985.

Patricia Bullrich, visible head of the Unified Peronist Youth, Buenos Aires, 16 April 1985. Published as "The Peronist Youth Stage a Comeback—Without the Montoneros," *South Eastern Latin Americanist*, March 1986, vol. 29, no. 4: 13–20.

Jorge Cepernic, former governor of Santa Cruz and newly appointed editor of *La Voz*, Buenos Aires, 25 March 1985.

Ana Comas, Montonera militant and defense lawyer, Tallahassee, Florida, 18–19 October 1976, Cuernavaca, Mexico, 7 February 1978.

Ricardo Curten, editor of the Montonero monthly *Latino América*, Buenos Aires, 7 March 1985.

Mario Eduardo Firmenich in the Federal Penitentiary of Villa Devoto, Buenos Aires, 14 March 1985. Condensed version published as "The Montoneros' Past, Present, and Future," *South Eastern Latin Americanist*, March 1986, vol. 29, no. 4: 1–13.

Silvio Frondizi, Buenos Aires, 24 May 1971.

Nilo Gambini, organizational secretary of the Peronist Youth-Regional Organizations, Buenos Aires, 11 April 1985.

Alicia Giraudo, executive counsel of *Latino América* and director of the Montonero archives, Buenos Aires, 8 March 1985.

Carlos González, cosecretary-general of the Peronist Youth-Regional Organizations, Buenos Aires, 21 April 1985.

Juan Martín Guevara, former member of the PRT-ERP and Che Guevara's younger brother, Buenos Aires, 28 March 1985.

Abraham Guillén, Montevideo, 3–4 June 1971, Lima, 1–3 March, 1976, Madrid, 16–18 September 1978.

Ricardo Lazcano, coeditor of *Latino América*, Buenos Aires, 26 March 1985.

Daniel Llano, secretary of press and propaganda of the Unified Peronist Youth, Buenos Aires, 11–12 April 1985.

Nelson Marinelli, journalist for *El Tiempo* and militant in the Trotskyist Labor party (PO), Buenos Aires, 9 April 1985.

Isauro Molina, 2d vice-president of the Justicialist party of Catamarca and former national congressman, Catamarca, 20 February 1985.

Ricardo Obregón Cano, former governor of Córdoba and member of the Supreme Council of the Montonero Movement, in the Federal Penitentiary opposite the Colón Theater, Buenos Aires, 18 March 1985.

Raimundo Ongaro, Lima, 2–3 March 1976, Madrid, 19 September 1978, Buenos Aires, 26 January 1985.

Francisco Provenzano and Norberto Rey, PRT militants, Buenos Aires, 26 April 1985.

Adriana Puiggrós, functionary of the Peronist Youth and daughter of Rodolfo Puiggrós, Cuernavaca, Mexico, 16 December 1974, Mexico City, 12 June 1975, Cuernavaca, Mexico, 13 January 1978.

Norberto Rey, Buenos Aires, 29 April 1985.

Jorge Reyna, secretary of organization of the Unified Peronist Youth, Buenos Aires, 11 April 1985.

Irene Rodríguez, member of the national secretariat and the politburo of the Communist party of Argentina, Buenos Aires, 21 April 1985.

María Seoane (pseud. Laura Avellaneda), former member of the PRT-ERP, Buenos Aires, 25 April 1985.

Ernesto Tiffenberg and Daniel Molina, editors of the monthly *El Porteño*, Buenos Aires, 9 April 1985.

Osvaldo Villaflor, former labor secretary of the FAP, Lima, 2 March 1976.

Osvaldo Villaflor and other militants of the FAP and PB, Lima, 3 March 1976.

Osvaldo Villaflor, currently organizational vice-secretary of the Printers' Union of Buenos Aires, 17 January 1985.

Newspapers and Periodicals

Ahora. Buenos Aires, 28 March 1985, no. 76.

El Auténtico. Buenos Aires, 10 December 1975, 24 December 1975.

Avanzada Socialista. Buenos Aires, June 1973–July 1974, nos. 64–111.

Caras y Caretas. Buenos Aires, October 1983–September 1984.

El Caudillo. Buenos Aires, March 1974–December 1975, nos. 16–73.

Chicago Tribune. Chicago, 12 March 1947.

Clarín. Buenos Aires, January 1976–April 1985.

Combate. Stockholm, January–February 1985, nos. 116–117.

El Combatiente. Buenos Aires, August 1973–July 1974, nos. 85–124; March 1984–February 1989, nos. 298–370.

Commentary. New York, November 1979.

Con Todo. Buenos Aires, May 1974, nos. 1–2; Mexico City, April 1978, no. 1.

Convergencia Justicialista. December 1984–March 1985, nos. 1–4.

Coyuntura y Desarrollo. Mexico City, May 1979, October 1981.
Cristianismo y Revolución. Buenos Aires, September 1971.
Cuadernos Políticos. Mexico City, January–March 1977, no. 11.
De Frente. Buenos Aires, May–July 1974, nos. 1–10.
El Descamisado. Buenos Aires, June 1973–April 1974, nos. 6–46.
El Diecisiete. Buenos Aires, November 1983–April 1984, nos. 1–4.
El Economista. Buenos Aires, 28 March 1980.
Entre Todos. Buenos Aires, December 1984–April 1985, nos. 1–5.
Estrella Roja. Buenos Aires, August 1973–July 1974, nos. 23–35.
Evita Montonera. Buenos Aires, October–November 1974.
Fichas. Buenos Aires, April 1964, no. 1.
Foreign Affairs. Washington, D.C., Summer 1984.
La Gaceta de Hoy. Buenos Aires, 25 April 1985.
Gente. Buenos Aires, 5 July 1976, no. 572; 29 July 1976, no. 575.
Il Giornale d'Italia. Milan, 25 September 1973.
Intercontinental Press. New York, January 1970–January 1985.
Intransigencia y Movilización Peronista. Buenos Aires, June 1983, no. 1.
La Jornada. Mexico City, 21 September 1988.
JOTAPÉ. Buenos Aires, February–April 1974, nos. 1–3; 1st epoch, October 1979–October 1983, nos. 1–12; 2nd epoch, November 1984–April 1985, nos. 1–3.
JP ¡Presente! Buenos Aires, January–October 1982, August 1984.
Latin American Perspectives. Riverside, Calif., fall 1974, no. 3; fall 1982, no. 35.
Latin America Political Report. London, October 1975–May 1979.
Latin America Weekly Report. London, March 1980–March 1986.
Latino América. Buenos Aires, March 1984–April 1985, nos. 1–14.
Libre. Buenos Aires, 3 July 1984, no. 25; 13 November 1984, no. 44; 9 March 1985, no. 62.
Lucha Peronista. Mexico City, April 1975, no. 1.
Madres de Plaza de Mayo. Buenos Aires, December 1984–April 1985, nos. 1–5.
Mayoría. Buenos Aires, December 1975–February 1976.
Mercado. Buenos Aires, 5 November 1980.
Midstream. New York, May 1987.
Militancia. Buenos Aires, June 1973–March 1974, nos. 1–38.
El Montonero. Buenos Aires, 24 April 1976.
El Mundo. Buenos Aires, February–March 1974, nos. 134–165.
La Nación. Buenos Aires, 24 May 1931, January 1976–December 1982.
NACLA's Latin America and Empire Report. San Francisco, January 1977.
National Review. New York, 13 July 1971.
New York Times. New York, February 1944–October 1945.
Noticias. Buenos Aires, May–June 1974, nos. 184–198.
Nuevo Hombre. Buenos Aires, 1st series, September 1973–June 1974, nos. 47–65; 2nd series, November 1975–February 1976, nos. 1–8.
El Obrero. Buenos Aires, April 1974, no. 1.

La Opinión. Buenos Aires, 25 March 1976.

El País. Madrid, 28 April 1979.

Panorama. Buenos Aires, 14 April 1970.

Patria Socialista. Buenos Aires, July 1973–February 1974, nos. 1–5.

El Periodista. Buenos Aires, February–April 1985, nos. 23–30.

El Peronista. Buenos Aires, April–May 1974, nos. 2–4.

¡Por Esto! Mexico City, 3 September 1981, no. 10; 10 September 1981, no. 11; 17 September 1981, no. 12; 15 July 1982, no. 55.

El Porteño. Buenos Aires, May 1984–May 1985, nos. 29–41.

Posición. Córdoba, November 1973–April 1974, nos. 10–13.

La Prensa. Buenos Aires, August–December 1977, December 1980–January 1981.

Prensa Confidencial. Buenos Aires, August 1973–January 1976, nos. 284–402.

Primera Plana. Buenos Aires, 2d epoch, 15 June 1984, no. 59.

Primícia Argentina. Buenos Aires, July 1974, no. 23.

Proceso Internacional. Mexico City, 2 April 1979, no. 126.

La Razón. Buenos Aires, May 1979–October 1981, August–September 1985.

Redacción. Buenos Aires, January–February 1985, nos. 143–144.

La Semana. Buenos Aires, December 1983–January 1985.

Semana Política. Buenos Aires, December 1975–February 1976, nos. 62–67.

Sin Censura. Buenos Aires, 2d epoch, 8–19 December 1983, no. 15.

Tiempo Argentino. Buenos Aires, 6 February 1985, no. 803.

The Times. London, 4 January 1978.

El Trabajador. Buenos Aires, April–July 1974, nos. 4–6.

Unidos. Buenos Aires, December 1984, no. 4.

Unomásuno. Mexico City, 17 March 1979.

Vencer. Mexico City, September 1979–February 1982, nos. 1–12.

Vocero Popular. Buenos Aires, January–April 1974, nos. 37–38.

La Voz. Buenos Aires, September 1982–May 1985.

Books and Documents

Abós, Alvaro. *El Posperonismo.* Buenos Aires: Legasa, 1985.

———. *Las organizaciones sindicales y el poder militar (1976–1983).* Buenos Aires: Centro Editor de América Latina, 1984.

Acossano, Benigno. *Eva Perón, su verdadera vida.* Buenos Aires: Lamas, 1955.

"Acusa el FRP de complicidad en torturas a jueces y políticos." *La Jornada* (13 March 1989).

"A formar comisiones de lucha en cada fábrica." *Huelga,* no. 1 (September 1980): 1–4.

"A la 4ª marcha de la resistencia." *Prensa Obrera* (18 December 1984): 1.

Alende, Oscar, et al. *El ocaso del "Proceso."* Buenos Aires: El Cid, 1981.

Alexander, Robert. *The Perón Era.* New York: Columbia University Press, 1951.

Alfonsín, Raúl. *La cuestión argentina*. Buenos Aires: Torres Agüero, 1980.
"Alfonsín apoyó a Jorge Videla." *La Voz* (15 August 1984): 5.
A los compañeros del peronismo montonero y del peronismo revolucionario. Rio de Janeiro, 1984.
Altamira, Jorge. *La Estrategia de la Izquierda en la Argentina*. Buenos Aires: Prensa Obrera, 1989.
Altmann, Werner. *El proyecto nacional peronista*. Mexico City: Extemporáneos, 1981.
América Latina en Armas (Documentos). Buenos Aires: Ediciones M.A., 1971.
Amnesty International. *Torture in the Eighties*. London: Amnesty International Publications, 1984.
"Andrés Framini." *JP ¡Presente!* no. 5 (October 1982): 8–13.
Aramburu, Pedro Eugenio, and Isaac F. Rojas. *La revolución libertadora (discursos en 12 meses de gobierno)*. Buenos Aires, 1956.
Arbelos, Carlos A., and Alfredo M. Roca. *Los muchachos peronistas*. Madrid: Emiliano Escolar, 1981.
Arendt, Hannah. *On Revolution*. New York: Viking, 1965.
———. *The Origins of Totalitarianism*, 2d ed. New York: Meridian, 1958.
Aristotle. *The Politics of Aristotle*. Translated by Ernest Barker. Oxford: Clarendon Press, 1948.
Arnaud, Pascal. *Estado y capitalismo en América Latina: casos de México y Argentina*. Mexico City: Siglo Veintiuno, 1981.
Aroca, Santiago. "Los 5000 desaparecidos de Camps." *La Semana* (29 December 1983): 12.
Artesano, Eduardo. *Ensayo sobre el justicialismo a la luz del materialismo histórico*. Rosario, 1953.
Asís, Jorge. "Conversación con Firmenich en la cárcel." *Revista Libre*, no. 44 (13 March 1984): 1–4.
Baily, Samuel L. *Nationalism and Politics in Argentina*. New Brunswick: Rutgers University Press, 1967.
Bakunin on Anarchy: Selected Works. Edited by Sam Dolgoff. New York: Knopf, 1972.
"Balance y perspectivas." *El Combatiente*, no. 298 (March 1984): 1–7.
"Bases políticas para la acción y organización de la Juventud Peronista." *JP ¡Presente!* no. 5 (October 1982): 1–17.
Bashansky, Enrique. *1982, el año en que se derrumbó el "Proceso."* Buenos Aires: Anteo, 1984.
Bayer, Osvaldo, *Los vengadores de la Patagonia trágica*. 3 vols. Buenos Aires: Galerna, 1974.
Beliz, Gustavo. *Menem: Argentina hacia el año 2000*. Buenos Aires: Galerna, 1986.
Belloni, Alberto. *Del anarquismo al peronismo*. Buenos Aires: Peña Lillo, 1960.
Ben-Ami, Shlomo. *Fascism from Above: The Dictatorship of Primo de Rivera, 1923–1930*. Oxford: Oxford University Press, 1983.
Bernetti, Jorge Luis *El peronismo de la Victoria*. Buenos Aires: Legasa, 1983.

Berryman, Phillip. *The Religious Roots of Rebellion.* Maryknoll, N.Y.: Orbis, 1984.

Binder, Leonard, et al. *Crises and Sequences in Political Development.* Princeton: Princeton University Press, 1971.

Bittel, Deolindo F. *Qué es el peronismo.* Buenos Aires: Sudamericana, 1983.

Blanksten, George I. *Perón's Argentina.* Chicago: University of Chicago Press, 1953.

Blixen, Samuel. *Treinta años de lucha popular: conversaciones con Gorriarán Merlo.* Buenos Aires: Contrapunto, 1988.

Bonasso, Miguel. "No hay que confundir el enemigo." *El Porteño* (April 1985): 15.

―――. *Recuerdo de la muerte.* Buenos Aires: Bruguera, 1984.

Booth, John A. *The End and the Beginning: The Nicaraguan Revolution.* Boulder: Westview, 1983.

Bousquet, Jean-Pierre. *Las locas de la Plaza de Mayo,* 5th ed. Buenos Aires: El Cid, 1984.

Bracher, Karl Dietrich. *The German Dictatorship: The Origins, Structure, and Effects of National Socialism.* New York: Praeger, 1970.

Braun, Oscar, ed. *El capitalismo argentino en crisis.* Mexico City: Siglo Veintiuno, 1973.

Brocato, Carlos A. *La Argentina que quisieron.* Buenos Aires: Planeta, 1985.

Burke, Edmund. *Reflections on the Revolution in France.* New York: Liberal Arts, 1955.

Burnham, James. *The Coming Defeat of Communism.* New York: John Day, 1949.

―――. *Congress and the American Tradition.* Chicago: Henry Regnery, 1959.

―――. "Joys and Sorrows of Empire." *National Review* (13 July 1971): 749.

―――. *The Machiavellians,* 2d ed. New York: Gateway, 1970.

―――. *The Managerial Revolution.* New York: John Day, 1947.

―――. *The Struggle for the World.* New York: John Day, 1947.

―――. *Suicide of the West,* 2d ed. New Rochelle, N.Y.: Arlington, 1975.

―――. *The War We Are In: The Last Decade and the Next.* New Rochelle, N.Y.: Arlington, 1967.

―――. *The Web of Subversion: Underground Networks in the U.S. Government.* New York: John Day, 1954.

Burns, Jimmy. *The Land That Lost Its Heroes: The Falklands, the Post-War and Alfonsín.* London: Bloomsbury, 1987.

Bychkova, N., et al., eds. *Communist Morality.* Moscow: Progress Publishers, n.d.

Cafiero, Antonio, and Carlos Grosso, with Carlos Saúl Menem. *Hablan los renovadores.* Buenos Aires: Galera, 1986.

Cafiero, Antonio, and José Manuel De La Sota, with Juan Pablo Feinmann and Sancho Alvarez. *La renovación fundamental.* Buenos Aires: El Cid, 1986.

Cámpora, Héctor. *El mandato de Perón.* Buenos Aires: Quehacer Nacional, 1975.

———. *La revolución peronista*. Buenos Aires: Editorial Universitaria de Buenos Aires, 1973.

"Cámpora: su gobierno, sus hombres, su historia." *Gente* (3 July 1976): 14–18.

Camus, Albert. *The Rebel*. New York: Vintage, 1956.

Canton, Darío. *La política de los militares argentinos: 1900–1971*. Buenos Aires: Siglo Veintiuno, 1971.

Carazo, Alfredo, and Rodolfo Audi. *Siete años de lucha contra la dictadura*. Caracas: Nuevo Horizonte, 1984.

Cárdenas, Gonzalo, et al. *El peronismo*. Buenos Aires: Cepe, 1969.

Cardoso, Fernando Henrique, and Enzo Faletto. *Dependencia y desarrollo en América Latina*. Mexico City: Siglo Veintiuno, 1969.

Carranzo, Mario. *Fuerzas armadas y estado de excepción en América Latina*. Mexico City: Siglo Veintiuno, 1978.

"Carta abierta de Galimberti y Gelman (París, 22 de febrero de 1979)." In "Renuncian los líderes: desviaciones del movimiento montonero," *Proceso Internacional* (2 April 1979): 43–44.

Castoriadis, Cornelius. *La sociedad burocrática*. 2 vols. Barcelona: Tusquets 1976.

Castro, Fidel. "Discurso del 18 de octubre de 1967." In Guevara, *Obras*, I, 11–24.

Cerrutti, Costa, Luis E. *El sindicalismo*. Buenos Aires: Trafac, 1969.

Ciria, Alberto. *Partidos y poder en la Argentina moderna (1930–1946)*. Buenos Aires: La Flor, 1975.

———. *Perón y el justicialismo*. Buenos Aires: Siglo Veintiuno, 1971.

Clausewitz, Karl von. *De la guerra*. Havana: Ciencias Sociales, 1975.

Codovilla, Victorio. *Vigencia y proyección: breve selección de trabajos*. Buenos Aires: Fundamentos, 1970.

Cohen, Carl. *Communism, Fascism and Democracy*. 2d ed. New York: Random House, 1972.

"*Combate* entrevista a la dirección del PRT." *Combate*, nos. 116–117 (January–February 1985): 6–7.

"*Combate* entrevista a los organismos de defensa de los derechos humanos en Argentina." *Combate*, nos. 116–117 (January–February 1985): 38–51.

Comisión Nacional sobre la Desaparición de Personas (CONADEP), *Nunca más*. Buenos Aires: Editorial Universitaria de Buenos Aires, 1984.

Conducción Nacional de la Juventud Peronista-Regionales. *Aportes para una síntesis política*. Buenos Aires: 1984.

Conducción Nacional del Movimiento Peronista Montonero. *La política que hemos venido desarrollando y los golpes del enemigo*. Buenos Aires: 1983.

Consejo Superior del Movimiento Peronista Montonero. "Bases para la Alianza Constituyente de la Nueva Argentina." *Vencer*, no. 12 (January–February 1982): 1–95.

———. *Grupos económicos oligárquicos en la Argentina*. Mexico City, 1982.

———. *1943–1973. Tres décadas de luchas del pueblo contra la oligarquía*. *Vencer*, no. 11 (November–December 1981): 1–32.

El control político en el cono sur, 2d ed. Edited by the Instituto Latino-
americano de Investigaciones Sociales. Mexico City: Siglo Veintiuno,
1976.
Cooke, John William. *Apuntes para la militancia.* Buenos Aires: Schapire,
1972.
———. *Correspondencia Perón-Cooke.* 2 vols. Buenos Aires, 1971.
———. *La lucha por la liberación nacional.* Buenos Aires: Granica, 1971.
———. *Peronismo e integración.* 3d ed. Buenos Aires: Aquarius, 1974.
———. *Peronismo y revolución.* Buenos Aires: Granica, 1971.
Corbière, Emilio J. *El mito alfonsinista.* Buenos Aires: Icaria, 1985.
Cordeu, Mora, with Silvia Mercado and Nancy Sosa. *Peronismo, la mayoría
perdida.* Buenos Aires: Planeta, 1985.
Corradi, Juan E. *The Fitful Republic: Economy, Society, and Politics in Ar-
gentina.* Boulder: Westview, 1985.
Corvalán Nanclares, Ernesto. *Justicialismo: la hora de la verdad.* Buenos
Aires: Temática, 1984.
Cox, Robert. "The Souring of the Argentine Dream." *Harper's* (May 1985):
49–57.
Crawley, Eduardo. *A House Divided: Argentina 1880–1980.* London:
Hurst, 1984.
Crozier, Brian. *Franco, A Biographical History.* London: Eyre & Spottis-
woode, 1967.
———. *Franco, historia y biografía.* Madrid: Magisterio Español, 1969.
———. *Occidente se suicida.* Buenos Aires: Atlantida, 1979.
———. *Los solo rivales: la lucha por el tercer mundo.* Buenos Aires: Mary-
mar, 1967.
———. *Strategy of Survival.* London: Temple Smith, 1978.
———. *The Struggle for the Third World.* London: Bodley Head, 1966.
———. *Teoría del conflicto.* Buenos Aires: Emece, 1977.
———. *A Theory of Conflict.* London: Hamilton, 1974.
Cruz, David D. *El recambio de los dioses.* Buenos Aires: Sur, 1984.
Cueva, Agustín. *El desarrollo del capitalismo en América Latina,* 3d ed.
Mexico City: Siglo Veintiuno, 1979.
"La cultura de la liberación: Rodolfo Walsh." *Con Todo* (April 1978): 17.
Davidowicz, Lucy S. *The War against the Jews 1933–1945.* New York: Holt,
Rinehart and Winston, 1979.
Debray, Régis. *La crítica de las armas.* 2 vols. Mexico City: Siglo Veinti-
uno, 1975.
———. *Revolution in the Revolution?* Translated by Bobbye Ortiz. New
York: Monthly Review Press, 1967.
Delich, Francisco. "Después del diluvio, la clase obrera." In Rouquié, *Ar-
gentina, hoy,* pp. 129–150.
Díaz Alejandro, Carlos F. *Essays on the Economic History of the Argentine
Republic.* New Haven: Yale University Press, 1970.
Díaz Bessone, Ramón Genaro. *Guerra revolucionaria en la Argentina
(1959–1978).* Buenos Aires: Fraterna, 1986.

Di Tella, Guido. *Argentina under Perón, 1973–76.* London: Macmillan, 1983.

Di Tella, Torcuato S. *Reflections on the Argentine Crisis.* Washington, D.C., 1982.

———. "Stalemate or Coexistence in Argentina." In Petras and Zeitlin, *Latin America: Reform or Revolution?* pp. 249–263.

Donoso Cortés, Juan. *Obras Completas de Don Juan Donoso Cortés, Marqués de Valdegamas.* Edited by Juan Juretschke. 2 vols. Madrid: Editorial Católica, 1946.

Duejo, Gerardo. *El capital monopolista y las contradicciones secundarias en la sociedad argentina.* Buenos Aires: Siglo Veintiuno, 1973.

Duhalde, Eduardo Luis. *El estado terrorista argentino.* Buenos Aires: Argos Vergara, 1983.

Dworkin, Andrea. *Our Blood: Prophecies and Discourses on Sexual Politics.* New York: Putnam's, 1976.

Ebenstein, William. *Great Political Thinkers: Plato to the Present*, 3d ed. New York: Holt, Rinehart and Winston, 1969.

———. *Modern Political Thought: The Great Issues.* New York: Rinehart, 1957.

El Kadri, Envar, and Jorge Rulli. *Diálogos en el exilio.* Buenos Aires: Foro Sur, 1984.

Encuentro Nacional de Juventud Peronista "Atilio López." Córdoba, 26–27 January 1985.

Engels, Frederick. *The Origin of the Family, Private Property and the State.* New York: International Publishers, 1972.

"Entrevista al Comandante Firmenich." *Vencer*, no. 1 (1979): 4–13.

"Entrevista con el Comandante Raúl Yäger: los obreros movilizados acabarán con la tiranía." *Vencer*, no. 4 (1980): 4–7.

"Es Bullrich, pero lidera a los peronistas." AHORA (28 March 1985): 6–7.

"ERP y Montoneros: adiós a las armas." *El Porteño* (April 1985): 10–17.

Escudé, Carlos. *Gran Bretaña, Estados Unidos y la declinación argentina, 1942–1949.* Buenos Aires: Belgrano, 1983.

"Esquivel formuló severas críticas." *La Voz* (20 June 1984).

Familiares Peronistas de Presos Detenidos-Desaparecidos Mártires de la Repressión. *Argentina: Ni Olvido, Ni Amnestía, Aparición con Vida.* Buenos Aires, November 1983.

Farrés, María Teresa, et al. *Elecciones y participación: análisis de las elecciones del 30 de octubre de 1983 en la capital federal.* Buenos Aires: COPEDE, 1984.

Fava, Athos. *Qué es el partido comunista.* Buenos Aires: Sudamericana, 1983.

Fayt, Carlos S. *El político armado: dinámica del proceso político argentino, 1960–1971.* Buenos Aires: Viracocha, 1971.

———, ed. *La naturaleza del peronismo.* Buenos Aires: Viracocha, 1968.

Feder, Gottfried. *Manifiesto contra la usura y la servidumbre del interés del dinero.* Buenos Aires: Maxim, 1984.

Feinmann, José Pablo. *El peronismo y la primacia de la política.* Buenos Aires: Cimarrón, 1974.

Ferla, Salvador. *El drama político de la Argentina contemporánea.* Buenos Aires: Lugar, 1985.

Fernández, Arturo. *Ideologías de los grupos dirigentes sindicales (1966–1973).* 2 vols. Buenos Aires: Centro Editor de América Latina, 1986.

Ferrer, Aldo. "La economía argentina bajo una estrategia 'preindustrial.'" In Rouquié, *Argentina, hoy,* pp. 105–128.

Firmenich, Mario Eduardo. "Aportes del peronismo revolucionario para la transformación del movimiento." *La Voz.* (November 1983).

———. "Firmenich: A Political Analysis." *NACLA Report* (January 1977): 17–22.

———. "Firmenich responde: la victoria es esencialmente política." *¡Por Esto!* (17 September 1981): 34–38.

———. "Otra vez 'la conspiración' terrorista internacional." *La Voz* (2 February, 1985). In *El Porteño,* "Los Montoneros sí existén" (April 1985): 12–13.

———. "Propuesta del peronismo montonero durante el conflicto: ante el agravamiento de la crisis anglo-argentina por la reivindicación de nuestra soberanía nacional sobre las Islas Malvinas." Buenos Aires, 28 April 1982.

———. [Darío Quiroga, pseud.] "Rescatar las banderas revolucionarias y marchar hacia la transcendencia histórica." *La Voz* (8 November 1983): 6.

———. "Unidad nacional y pluralismo ante los reclamos de justicia." *La Voz* (23 December 1984).

Firmenich, Mario Eduardo, et al. "Al pueblo argentino." Buenos Aires, 20 December 1983.

———. "Análisis y propuestas para los militantes y activistas del peronismo transformador y revolucionario." Buenos Aires, 6 December 1984.

———. "Bases para la alianza constituyente de la nueva Argentina." *Vencer,* no. 12 (January–February 1982): 1–97.

Five Great Encyclicals. New York: Paulist Press, 1939.

Fleming, D. F. *The Cold War and Its Origins, 1917–1960.* 2 vols. Garden City, N.Y.: Doubleday, 1961.

Francis, Samuel T. *Power and History: The Political Thought of James Burnham.* Lanham, Md.: University Press of America, 1984.

Franco, Juan Pablo, and Fernando Alvarez. *Peronismo: antecedentes y gobierno.* Buenos Aires: Antropología 3er Mundo, 1972.

Frigerio, Rogelio. *Diez años de la crisis argentina: diagnóstico y programa del desarrollismo.* Buenos Aires: Planeta, 1983.

Frondizi, Silvio. *La realidad argentina.* 2 vols. Buenos Aires: Praxis, 1955–56.

Frontalini, Daniel, and María Cristina Caiati. *El mito de la guerra sucia.* Buenos Aires: CELS, 1984.

Galimberti, Rodolfo. "El delito de ser joven." *JOTAPÉ,* no. 1 (17 October 1979): 7–8.

———. *Frente a la crisis nacional.* Buenos Aires, 1982, pp. 1–13.

————. *Movimiento peronista y programa de liberación: una crítica a las propuestas de alvearización.* Buenos Aires, 1982, pp. 1–51.

————. *El peronismo y la crisis de la dictadura.* Paris, 1981, pp. 1–16.

————. "Queridos compañeros de la Juventud Peronista." *JOTAPÉ*, no. 2 (February 1980): 3–4, 6; no. 3 (August–September 1980): 4–7.

————. *La revolución peronista.* Buenos Aires: Fondo Editorial de la Revolución Peronista, 1983.

————. "Y ahora Viola." *JOTAPÉ*, no. 4 (March 1981): 6–9.

Galimberti, Rodolfo, et al. *La ruptura.* Paris, 1979, pp. 1–23.

Gálvez, Manuel. *Vida de Hipólito Yrigoyen.* Buenos Aires: Editorial Universitaria de Buenos Aires, 1973.

García Lupo, Rogelio. *La rebelión de los generales.* Buenos Aires: Jamcana, 1963.

Garraty, John A., and Peter Gay, eds. *The Columbia History of the World.* New York: Harper and Row, 1972.

Garré, Nilda. "El montonerismo, hoy, es un delirio político." *El Porteño* (May 1984): 14–15.

Garré, Nilda, et al. *El peronismo unido y organizado: la alternativa nacional y popular.* Buenos Aires, 1981.

Gasparini, Juan. *Montoneros: final de cuentas.* Buenos Aires: Puntosur, 1988.

"Genocidio." *JP ¡Presente!* (August 1984): 17.

Genta, Jordán Bruno. *Guerra contrarrevolucionaria: doctrina política.* Buenos Aires: Nuevo Orden, 1965.

————. *Principios de la política: la guerra subversiva en nuestra patria.* Buenos Aires: Editorial Cultura Argentina, 1970.

————. *Testamento político.* Buenos Aires: Buen Combate, 1984.

Ghioldi, Rodolfo. *La plataforma de Martínez de Hoz.* Buenos Aires, 1976.

Gilbert, Martin. *The Holocaust: A History of the Jews of Europe during the Second World War.* New York: Holt, Rinehart and Winston, 1985.

Gillespie, Richard. *Soldiers of Perón: Argentina's Montoneros.* Oxford: Oxford University Press, 1982.

Giussani, Pablo. *Los días de Alfonsín.* Buenos Aires: Legasa, 1986.

————. *Montoneros: la soberbia armada.* Buenos Aires: Planeta, 1984.

Gleigeses, Piero. "¿Qué pasa en Argentina? Decadencia y amenaza latente de militarismo." *La Jornada* (21 September 1988): 13–14.

Godio, Julio. *La caída de Perón de junio a setiembre de 1955,* 2d ed. Buenos Aires: Granica, 1973.

————. "Perón y los Montoneros." Maracaibo, 1977, unpublished.

Goldwert, Marvin. *Democracy, Militarism, and Nationalism in Argentina, 1930–1966.* Austin: University of Texas Press, 1972.

González, Ernesto. *Qué fue y qué es el peronismo.* Buenos Aires: Pluma, 1974.

González Janzen, Ignacio. *Argentina: 20 años de luchas peronistas.* Mexico City: Patria Grande, 1975.

Gorriarán Merlo, Enrique. *Democracia y liberación.* Buenos Aires: Reencuentro, 1985.

Gould, Julius, and William L. Kolb. *A Dictionary of the Social Sciences.* New York: Free Press, 1964.

Graham, John T. *Donoso Cortés: Utopian Romanticist and Political Realist.* Columbia: University of Missouri Press, 1974.

Gregor, A. James. *Contemporary Radical Ideologies: Totalitarian Thought in the Twentieth Century.* New York: Random House, 1968.

———. *The Fascist "Persuasion" in Radical Politics.* Princeton: Princeton University Press, 1974.

———. *The Ideology of Fascism.* New York: Free Press, 1969.

———. *Italian Fascism and Developmental Dictatorship.* Princeton: Princeton University Press, 1979.

———. *Young Mussolini and the Intellectual Origins of Fascism.* Berkeley and Los Angeles: University of California Press, 1979.

Guevara, Ernesto Che. *Obras 1957–1967.* 2 vols. Havana: Casa de las Américas, 1970.

———. *Selected Works.* Edited by Rolando E. Bonachea and N. P. Valdés. Cambridge: MIT Press, 1969.

Guillén, Abraham. *Estrategia de la guerrilla urbana,* 1st ed. Montevideo: Manuales del Pueblo, 1966. 2d revised ed. Montevideo: Liberación, 1969.

———. "El pueblo en armas: estrategia revolucionaria." Montevideo, 1972, unpublished.

———. *Teoría de la violencia.* Buenos Aires: Jamcana, 1965.

Gutiérrez, Guillermo. *Explotación y respuestos populares.* Buenos Aires: El Cid, 1974.

Hegel, G. W. F. *The Philosophy of Right.* Translated by T. M. Knox. Oxford: Clarendon Press, 1967.

Heiden, Konrad. *Der Fuehrer: Hitler's Rise to Power.* Boston: Houghton Mifflin, 1944.

Herman, Edward S. *The "Real" Terror Network.* Boston: South End Press, 1982.

Hernández, Pablo. *Conversaciones con el Teniente Coronel Aldo Rico.* Buenos Aires: Fortaleza, 1989.

———. *La tablada: El regreso de los que no se fueron.* Buenos Aires: Fortaleza, 1989.

Hernández Arregui, Juan José. *Peronismo y socialismo.* Buenos Aires: Plus Ultra, 1972.

"Una historia que empezó en febrero." *La Voz* (22 October 1984): 2.

Hitler, Adolf. *Mein Kampf.* Translated by Ralph Manheim. Boston: Houghton Mifflin, 1943.

Hobbes, Thomas. *BEHEMOTH: The History of the Causes of the Civil Wars in England,* in *The English Works of Thomas Hobbes of Malmesbury,* vol. 6. Edited by Sir W. Molesworth, London, 1839–1845.

———. *LEVIATHAN,* Parts I and II. Edited by H. Schneider. New York: E. P. Dutton, 1958.

Hodges, Donald C. *Argentina, 1943–1987: The National Revolution and Resistance.* Revised and enlarged ed. Albuquerque: University of New Mexico Press, 1988.

————. *The Bureaucratization of Socialism.* Amherst: University of Massachusetts Press, 1981.

————. *Intellectual Foundations of the Nicaraguan Revolution.* Austin: University of Texas Press, 1986.

————. "Interviews with Patricia Bullrich and Mario Eduardo Firmenich." *South Eastern Latin Americanist* (March 1986): 1–20.

————. *The Latin American Revolution.* New York: William Morrow, 1974.

————. *The Legacy of Che Guevara.* London: Thames and Hudson, 1977.

————. *Marxismo y revolución en el siglo veinte.* Mexico City: El Caballito, 1978.

————. *Socialist Humanism: The Outcome of Classical European Morality.* St. Louis: Warren H. Green, 1974.

————, ed. *Philosophy of the Urban Guerrilla.* New York: William Morrow, 1973.

Hodges, Donald C., and Abraham Guillén. *Revaloración de la guerrilla urbana.* Mexico City: El Caballito, 1977.

Hoopes, Townsend. *The Devil and John Foster Dulles.* Boston: Little, Brown, 1973.

Horowicz, Alejandro. *Los cuatro peronismos.* Buenos Aires: Legasa, 1985.

Ibarguren, Carlos. *La historia que he vivido.* Buenos Aires: Editorial Universitaria de Buenos Aires, 1969.

Ibarguren, Federico. *Orígenes del nacionalismo argentino.* Buenos Aires: Celcius, 1969.

Imaz, José Luis de. *Los que mandan,* 1st ed. Buenos Aires: Editorial Universitaria de Buenos Aires, 1964.

"Impulsar la resistencia popular." *El Combatiente,* no. 329 (September 1986): 1–4.

"Infierno en el teatro." *La Voz* (14 May 1984): 16.

"Informe del Comité Central Saliente al VI Congreso del PRT reunido en mayo de 1979." *VI° Congreso mayo 1979. Comité Central "20 aniversario" enero 1985,* 9–44.

Intransigencia Peronista. *Propuesta para la Intransigencia Peronista.* Buenos Aires, 1981.

James, Daniel. *Resistance and Integration: Peronism and the Argentine Working Class, 1946–1976.* Cambridge: Cambridge University Press, 1988.

Jauretche, Arturo. *F.O.R.J.A. y la década infame.* Buenos Aires: Coyoacán, 1962.

————. *Política nacional y revisionismo histórico.* Buenos Aires: Peña Lillo, 1982.

Jones, Joseph F. *The Fifteen Weeks.* New York: Viking, 1955.

Jouvenel, Bertrand de. *On Power: Its Nature and the History of Its Growth.* Translated by J. F. Huntington. Boston: Beacon, 1962.

"Juan Gelman: entrevista realizada en París por Roberto Mero." *Caras y Caretas* (October 1983): 23–28, 62–63.

Juventud Intransigente: apuntes para la liberación. Buenos Aires: Editorial Apuntes para la Liberación, 1985.

Juventud Peronista—17 de Octubre. *Por un peronismo del futuro para construir la Argentina liberada.* Buenos Aires, December 1983.
Juventud Peronista—Regionales. *Aportes para una síntesis política.* Buenos Aires, 1984.
———. *Bases políticas para la acción y la organización.* Buenos Aires, 1982.
———. *Boletín Informativo.* Buenos Aires, April 1983.
———. *Democracia real o continuismo oligárquico.* Buenos Aires, 1984.
Juventud Peronista Unificada. *Conclusiones del Congreso de la J.P. (Córdoba, 26–27 de enero).* Buenos Aires, 1985.
Kirkpatrick, Jeane J. *Dictatorships and Double Standards.* New York: Simon and Schuster, 1982.
Klare, Michael, and Nancy Stein. *Armas y poder en América Latina.* Mexico City: Era, 1978.
Kohl, James, and John Litt. *Urban Guerrilla Warfare in Latin America.* Cambridge: MIT Press, 1974.
Kramer, Heinrich, and James Sprenger. *Malleus Maleficarum.* New York: Dover, 1971.
Lamartine, Alphonse de. "Manifesto to Europe." In Postgate, *Revolution from 1789 to 1906,* pp. 193–197.
Lanusse, Alejandro A. *Mi testimonio.* Buenos Aires: Laserre, 1977.
"Lanzamiento de la APA." *La Voz* (27 April 1984): 8.
Laqueur, Walter, *Terrorism.* Boston: Little, Brown, 1977.
———, ed. *The Guerrilla Reader: A Historical Anthology.* New York: Meridian, 1977.
———, ed. *The Terrorism Reader.* Philadelphia: Temple University Press, 1978.
Laqueur, Walter and George L. Mosse, eds. *International Fascism 1920–1945.* New York: Harper, 1966.
Lechner, Norbert, ed. *Estado y política en América Latina.* Buenos Aires: Siglo Veintiuno, 1981.
Lehning, Arthur. *From Buonarroti to Bakunin.* Leiden: Brill, 1970.
Lenin, V. I. "Imperialism, the Highest Stage of Capitalism." In *The Lenin Anthology,* pp. 204–274.
———. *The Lenin Anthology.* Edited by Robert C. Tucker. New York: Norton, 1975.
———. *Selected Works.* 3 vols. New York: International Publishers, 1967.
Lesseps, Mariano, and Lucia Traveler. *Argentina: un país entregado.* Madrid: Castellote, 1978.
Lezcano, Leonardo. "La resistencia estaba en todas partes." In *La lucha por la democracia sindical en la UOM de Villa Constitución,* pp. 57–58.
Lichtheim, George. *The Origins of Socialism.* New York: Praeger, 1969.
López, Alonso, Gerardo. *1930–1980. Cincuenta años de historia argentina. Una cronología básica.* Buenos Aires: Belgrano, 1982.
Luca de Tena, Torcuato, with Luis Calvo and Esteban Peicovich, eds. *Yo, Juan Domingo Perón: relato autobiográfico.* Barcelona: Planeta, 1976.
La Lucha por la democracia sindical en la UOM de Villa Constitución.

Supplement to *Hechos y protagonistas de las luchas obreras argentinas.* Buenos Aires, 1985.

Ludwig, Emil. *Colloqui con Mussolini,* 3d ed. Verona: Mondadori, 1950.

Lugones, Leopoldo. *El estado equitativo.* Buenos Aires: Editora Argentina, 1932.

———. *La grande argentina.* Buenos Aires: Babel, 1930.

———. "Propósitos." In Ibarguren, *Orígenes del nacionalismo argentino 1927–1937,* pp. 187–192.

Lugones, Leopoldo (hijo). *Mi padre.* Buenos Aires: Centurión, 1949.

Luna, Félix. *Argentina de Perón a Lanusse 1943–1973.* Buenos Aires: Planeta, 1974.

———. *Golpes militares y salidas electorales.* Buenos Aires: Sudamericana, 1983.

Machiavelli. *The Prince and Other Works.* Edited and translated by Allan H. Gilbert. New York: Farrar, Straus, 1946.

Mackinder, Halford J. *Democratic Ideals and Reality.* New York: Henry Holt, 1942.

Malatesta, Errico. *His Life & Ideas.* Edited by Vernon Richards. London: Freedom Press, 1965.

Malraux, André, and James Burnham. *The Case for De Gaulle: A Dialogue between André Malraux and James Burnham.* New York: Random House, 1948.

Mao Tse-tung. *Selected Works of Mao Tse-tung.* 5 vols. Peking: Foreign Languages Press, 1965–1977.

Mariátegui, José Carlos. *Defensa del marxismo.* Lima: "Amauta," 1967.

Marín, Juan Carlos. *Los hechos armados: un ejercicio posible.* Buenos Aires: CICSO, 1984.

Martín, Alexis (pseud.). *Las técnicas de la guerra oculta.* Buenos Aires: Flamarión, 1963.

Martínez Borelli, Holver. "La Trinidad Militar: política e ideología." *Con Todo* (April 1978): 5–8.

Martínez de Hoz, José A. *Bases para una Argentina moderna 1976–1980.* Buenos Aires: Martínez de Hoz, 1981.

Marx, Karl. *Capital.* 3 vols. Edited by Frederick Engels. New York: International Publishers, 1967.

Marx, Karl, and Frederick Engels. *Collected Works,* vol. 3. New York: International Publishers, 1975.

———. *Selected Works.* 2 vols. Moscow: Foreign Languages Publishing House, 1958.

Meinvielle, Julio. *El comunismo en la revolución anticristiana.* Buenos Aires, Theoría, 1961.

———. *Concepción católica de la política.* Buenos Aires: Theoría, 1961.

———. *Entre la Iglesia y el Reich.* Buenos Aires: Adsum, 1937.

———. *El judío.* Buenos Aires: Antidoto, 1936.

———. *El judío en el misterio de la historia.* Buenos Aires, Theoría, 1959.

———. *Política argentina, 1948–1956.* Buenos Aires: Trafac, 1956.

————. *Qué saldrá de la España que sangra*. Buenos Aires: Talleres Gráficos San Pablo, 1937.

————. *Los tres pueblos bíblicos en su lucha por la dominación del mundo*. Buenos Aires: Adsum, 1937.

Menem, Carlos Saúl, and César Arias. *Renovación a fondo*. Buenos Aires: El Cid, 1986.

Menem, Carlos Saúl, and Eduardo Duhalde. *La revolución productiva*. Buenos Aires: Peña Lillo, 1989.

Methvin, Eugene J. *The Rise of Radicalism: The Social Psychology of Messianic Extremism*. New Rochelle, N.Y.: Arlington, 1973.

Midelfort, H. C. Eric. *Witch Hunting in Southwestern Germany 1562–1684: The Social and Intellectual Foundations*. Stanford: Stanford University Press, 1972.

Mill, John Stuart, *On Liberty*. Edited by Elizabeth Rapaport. Indianapolis: Hackett, 1978.

Moncavillo, Mona, and Alberto Fernández, eds. *La renovación fundacional*. Buenos Aires: El Cid, n.d.

Montonero party. *Statement of the Montonero Party's September 1977 National Council*. English edition of *Vencer*, nos. 2–3 (1979): 1–32.

Montoneros. *A los compañeros del peronismo montonero y del peronismo revolucionario*. Rio de Janeiro, 1984.

————. "Radiografía de la Triple A." In González Janzen, *Argentina: 20 años de luchas peronistas*, pp. 245–254.

————. *Reencauzar el movimiento peronista como eje de la liberación. Reconstruir el frente bajo la hegemonía de los trabajadores. Recuperar el gobierno para el pueblo y para Perón*. Buenos Aires, 1974.

"Montoneros hoy (primera parte)." *La Semana* (26 April 1984): 36–40.

Moreno, Nahuel. *1982: empieza la revolución*. Buenos Aires: Solidaridad, 1988.

Movimiento Peronista Montonero. *La Política que hemos venido desarrollando y los golpes del enemigo*. Buenos Aires, 1983.

————. *Resistir y vencer para ganar la paz en la Argentina (tratado de Roma)*. Rome, 1977: 1–15.

Movimiento Unidad, Solidaridad y Organización (MUSO). *Transformamos la derrota de octubre en una victoria política*. Buenos Aires, 1984.

Munck, Ronaldo, with Ricardo Falcón and Bernardo Galitelli. *Argentina: From Anarchism to Peronism*. London: Zed, 1987.

Murmis, Miguel, and Juan Carlos Portantiero. *Estudios sobre los orígenes del peronismo*. Buenos Aires: Siglo Veintiuno, 1971.

Murray, Margaret A. *The God of the Witches*. London: Oxford University Press, 1970.

Mussolini, Benito. *My Autobiography*. New York: Scribner's, 1928.

————. "The Doctrine of Fascism." In Oakeshott, *The Social and Political Doctrines of Contemporary Europe*, pp. 164–179.

————. *Fascism: Doctrine and Institutions*. Rome: "Ardita," 1935.

————. *Opera Omnia*. 36 vols. Florence: La Fenice, 1951–1961.

Nadra, Fernando. *Un año de gobierno peronista*. Buenos Aires: Sílaba, 1974.

Nash, George H. *The Conservative Intellectual Movement in America since 1945.* New York: Harper, 1976.

National Leadership of the Montonero Peronist Movement. *To the People of Argentina: Social Justice and Popular Self-Government Lead the Way towards Democracy and Peace.* (20 April 1980). English edition of *Vencer*, no. 4. (1980).

Navarro Gerassi, Marysa. *Los nacionalistas.* Buenos Aires: Jorge Alvarez, 1969.

Neilson, James. "Los Camps y los Firmenich." *La Semana* (29 December 1983): 32–33.

Neumann, Franz. *Behemoth: The Structure and Practice of National Socialism 1933–1944,* 2d ed. New York: Harper, 1944.

Nietzsche, Friedrich. *The Complete Works of Friedrich Nietzsche.* 18 vols. Edited by Oscar Levy. Edinburgh: Foulis, 1910–1927.

Nixon, Richard. *Real Peace.* Boston: Little, Brown, 1983.

———. *The Real War.* New York: Warner, 1981.

"No arriar las banderas: la agrupación 'Sabino Navarro' resaltó el peronismo auténtico." *La Voz* (27 April 1984): 8.

"No hay un corte con el pasado." *Clarín* (22 March 1984): 1.

Nolte, Ernst. *Three Faces of Fascism.* Translated by Leila Vennewitz. New York: Holt, Rinehart and Winston, 1965.

North American Congress on Latin America (NACLA). *Argentina in the Hour of the Furnaces.* New York: NACLA, 1975.

Oakeshott, Michael, ed. *The Social and Political Doctrines of Contemporary Europe.* New York: Macmillan, 1942.

Obregón, Cano, Ricardo. *Análisis y propuestas para el movimiento peronista.* Buenos Aires, 1984.

O'Donnell, Guillermo, *1966–1973: el estado burocrático autoritario.* Buenos Aires: Belgrano, 1982.

———. *Modernization and Bureaucratic Authoritarianism: Studies in South American Politics.* Berkeley: Institute of International Studies, 1973.

———. *Reflexiones sobre las tendencias generales de cambio en el estado burocrático-autoritario.* Buenos Aires: CEDES, 1975.

O'Donnell, Guillermo, and Delfina Linck. *Dependencia y autonomía: formas de dependencia y estrategias de liberación.* Buenos Aires: Amorrortu, 1973.

Ollier, María Matilde. *El fenómeno insurreccional y la cultura política (1969–1973).* Buenos Aires: Centro Editor de América Latina, 1986.

Ongaro, Raimundo Alfredo. *Argentina: algunos apuntes para un amplio debate popular.* Madrid, 1978.

———. *Como decíamos ayer. . . . Solo el pueblo salvará al pueblo.* Buenos Aires: Agrupación Lista Verde de los Gráficos, 1982.

"Otra vez los archivos de los campos de concentración." *La Semana* (29 December 1983): 57–66.

Owen, Frank. *Perón: His Rise and Fall.* London: Cresset, 1957.

Page, Joseph. *Perón: A Biography.* New York: Random House, 1983.

Pan, Luis. *La agonía del régimen de junio a setiembre.* Buenos Aires, 1956.

Parry, Albert. *Terrorism: From Robespierre to Arafat.* New York: Vanguard, 1978.

Partido Intransigente. *Aportes para el proyecto nacional.* Córdoba, 1975.

Partido Montonero. *Hacia una nueva política para la conquista del poder por los trabajadores y el pueblo peronista.* Buenos Aires, 1976.

Partido Revolucionario de los Trabajadores (PRT). *Aporte para la discusión política.* Buenos Aires, 1984.

———. "Nuestra línea internacional." *VI° Congreso Mayo 1979. Comité Central "20 aniversario" enero 1985,* pp. 91–94.

———. "Parliamentarismo y fascismo." *El Combatiente,* no. 106 (6 February 1974): 5–7.

———. "El partido militar." *El Combatiente* (August 1987): 1–8.

———. *El peronismo ayer y hoy.* Mexico City: Diógenes, 1974.

———. *VI° Congreso Mayo 1979. Comité Central "20 aniversario" enero 1985.* Buenos Aires, 1985.

"Patricia Bullrich." *Revista Libre* (19 March 1985): 67–74.

Pavón Pereyra, Enrique. *Perón tal como es.* Buenos Aires: Macacha Güemes, 1972.

Payne, Robert. *The Terrorists: The Story of the Forerunners of Stalin.* New York: Funk and Wagnalls, 1957.

Pehme, Kalev. *Argentina's Days of Rage: The Genesis of Argentine Terrorism.* New York: Argentina Independent Review, 1980.

Peralta Ramos, Mónica. *Acumulación del capital y crisis política en Argentina 1930–1974.* Mexico City: Siglo Veintiuno, 1978.

Peralta Ramos, Mónica, and C. H. Waisman, eds. *From Military Rule to Liberal Democracy in Argentina.* Boulder: Westview, 1987.

Perdía, Roberto. "Conquering Workers' Hegemony." *Vencer,* nos. 2–3 (1979): 4–9.

Perdía, Roberto C., and Fernando Vaca Narvaja. *Existe otra Argentina posible.* Buenos Aires: Enrique González Olguín, 1986.

Perelman, Angel. *Como hicimos el 17 de octubre.* Buenos Aires: Coyoacán, 1961.

Perlmutter, Amos, and Valerie Plava Bennett, eds. *The Political Influence of the Military.* New Haven: Yale University Press, 1980.

Perón, Eva. *La razón de mi vida.* Buenos Aires: Peuser, 1951.

Perón, Juan Domingo. *Actualización política y doctrinaria para la toma del poder.* Buenos Aires: 25 de Mayo, 1983.

———. *Apuntes de historia militar.* Buenos Aires: República Argentina, 1951.

———. *La comunidad organizada.* Buenos Aires: Cepe, 1974.

———. *Conducción política.* Buenos Aires: Reconstrucción, 1973.

———. *Correspondencia.* 2 vols. Buenos Aires: Corregidor, 1983.

———. *Correspondencia Perón-Frigerio 1958–1973: análisis crítico de Ramón Prieto.* Buenos Aires: Macacha Güemes, 1975.

———. *Del poder al exilio: como y quienes me derrocaron.* Buenos Aires: Ediciones Argentinas, 1974.

————. *Directivas generales para todos los peronistas.* Buenos Aires, 1956.

————. *Doctrina peronista.* Buenos Aires: Macacha Güemes, 1973.

————. *Doctrina revolucionaria.* Buenos Aires: Freeland, 1974.

————. *Filosofía peronista.* Buenos Aires: Freeland, 1974.

————. *El frente oriental de la Guerra Mundial en 1914.* Buenos Aires: Instituto Geográfico Militar, 1931.

————. *La fuerza es el derecho de las bestias.* Buenos Aires: Síntesis, 1958.

————. *La hora de los pueblos.* Buenos Aires: Baires, 1974.

————. *Instrucciones generales para los dirigentes.* Buenos Aires, 1956.

————. *Juan Perón en la Argentina 1973–1974: sus discursos, sus díalogos, sus conferencias.* Buenos Aires: Síntesis, 1974.

————. *Juan D. Perón 1973: todos sus discursos, mensajes y conferencias.* 2 vols. Buenos Aires: Reconstrucción, 1974.

————. *Latinoamérica: ahora o nunca.* Montevideo: "Diálogo," 1967.

————. *El pensamiento político de Perón.* Buenos Aires: Kikiyón, 1972.

————. *Perón-Cooke Correspondencia.* 2 vols. Buenos Aires: Granica, 1973.

————. *El proyecto nacional: Mi testamento político,* 5th ed. Buenos Aires: El Cid, 1984.

————. *El pueblo quiere saber de qué se trata.* Buenos Aires: Freeland, 1973.

————. *El pueblo ya sabe de qué se trata.* Buenos Aires: Freeland, 1973.

————. *La tercera posición argentina.* Buenos Aires: Baires, 1974.

————. *Tres revoluciones militares.* Buenos Aires: Síntesis, 1972.

————. *Los vendepatria.* Buenos Aires: Freeland, 1972.

Peronismo de Base (PB). *Sindicalismo y clasismo. Militancia,* no. 33 (31 January 1974).

Peter, José. *Crónicas proletarias.* Buenos Aires: Esfera, 1968.

Petras, James, and Maurice Zeitlin, eds. *Latin America: Reform or Revolution?* New York: Fawcett, 1968.

Pion-Berlin, David. *The Ideology of State Terror: Economic Doctrine and Political Repression in Argentina and Peru.* Boulder: L. Rienner, 1989.

Polit, Gustavo. "The Industrialists of Argentina." In Petras and Zeitlin, *Latin America: Reform or Revolution?* pp. 399–430.

Pomeroy, William J. *Guerrilla and Counter-Guerrilla Warfare: Liberation and Suppression in the Present Period.* New York: International Publishers, 1964.

Poneman, Daniel. *Argentina: Democracy on Trial.* New York: Paragon, 1987.

"Por la calle y con los Falcón." *La Voz* (25 August 1984): 7.

Postgate, Raymond. *Revolution from 1789 to 1906.* Boston: Houghton, 1921.

Potash, Robert A. *The Army and Politics in Argentina.* 2 vols. Stanford: Stanford University Press, 1980.

Prager, Dennis, and Joseph Telushkin. *Why the Jews?* New York: Simon and Schuster, 1985.

Prawdin, Michael (pseud.) *The Unmentionable Nechayev: A Key to Bolshevism.* New York: Roy, 1961.

Prensa Obrera. *El Partido Obrero y el peronismo.* Buenos Aires: Prensa Obrera, 1983.

Prieto, Ramón. *De Perón a Perón (1946–1973).* Buenos Aires: Macacha Güemes, 1974.

Primo de Rivera, José Antonio. *Revolución nacional (puntos de falange).* Madrid: Prensa del Movimiento, 1949.

Protocols of the Learned Elders of Zion. Translated by Victor E. Marsden. Union, N.J.: Christian Educational Association, 1922.

Puiggrós, Rodolfo. *El peronismo: sus causas.* Buenos Aires: Cepe, 1969.

———. *Pueblo y oligarquía.* Buenos Aires: Corregidor, 1974.

Quinterno, Carlos Alberto. *Militares y populismo (la crisis argentina desde 1966 hasta 1976).* Buenos Aires: Temas Contemporáneos, 1978.

Ramos, Jorge Abelardo. *De octubre a setiembre.* Buenos Aires: Peña Lillo, 1959.

———. *Revolución y contrarrevolución en la Argentina.* 5 vols. Buenos Aires: La Reja, 1961–1974.

Rauschning, Hermann. *The Revolution of Nihilism.* New York: Alliance, 1939.

"Reportaje a Martínez de Hoz." *La Semana* (29 December 1983): 68–69.

Rizzi, Bruno. *La lezione dello stalinismo.* Rome: Opere Nuova, 1962.

Roberts, J. M. *The Mythology of the Secret Societies.* London: Secker and Warburg, 1972.

Rocco, Alfredo. "The Political Doctrine of Fascism." In Cohen, *Communism, Fascism, and Democracy,* pp. 315–328.

Rock, David. *Argentina 1516–1982: From Spanish Colonization to the Falklands War.* Berkeley and Los Angeles: University of California Press, 1985.

———. *Politics in Argentina, 1890–1930: The Rise and Fall of Radicalism.* London: Cambridge University Press, 1975.

Rodríguez, Carlos J. *La idea peronista: contenido ideológico del justicialismo.* Córdoba: Libra, 1981.

Rodríguez, Horacio Daniel. *"Che" Guevara: ¿aventura o revolución?* Barcelona: Plaza and Janes, 1968.

Rodríguez Sánchez, Margarita. *Gravitación política de Perón.* Mexico City: Extemporáneos, 1981.

Rom, Eugenio P. *Asi hablaba Juan Perón.* Buenos Aires: Peña Lillo, 1984.

Roqué, Julio. "'Argentina país en guerra': hablan los Montoneros." *Cuadernos políticos* (January–March 1977): 87–102.

Rouquié, Alain, ed. *Argentina, hoy.* Mexico City: Siglo Veintiuno, 1982.

———. *Poder militar y sociedad política en la Argentina.* 2 vols. Buenos Aires: Emecé, 1983.

Rousseau, Jean-Jacques. *On the Social Contract. Discourse on the Origin of Inequality. Discourse on Political Economy.* Translated and edited by Donald A. Cress. Indianapolis: Hackett, 1983.

Santucho, Julio. *Los últimos guevaristas: surgimiento y eclipse del ejército revolucionario del pueblo.* Buenos Aires: Puntosur, 1988.

Schmitt, Carl. "The Concept of 'the Political.'" In Ebenstein, *Modern Political Thought*, pp. 326–328.

———. *The Concept of the Political*. New Brunswick, N.J.: Rutgers University Press, 1976.

———. *Interpretación europea de Donoso Cortés*. Madrid: Rialp, 1952.

———. *Political Theology*. Cambridge, Mass.: MIT Press, 1985.

Schramm, Edmund. *Donoso Cortés. Su vida y su pensamiento*. Madrid: Espasa-Calpe, 1936.

Schumacher, Edward. "Argentina and Democracy." *Foreign Affairs* (Summer 1984): 1070–1095.

Seidman, Steven. *Liberalism and the Origins of European Social Theory*. Berkeley and Los Angeles: University of California Press, 1983.

Senén González, Santiago. *Breve historia del sindicalismo argentino 1857–1974*. Buenos Aires: Alzamor, 1974.

———. *Diez años de sindicalismo argentino (de Perón al Proceso)*. Buenos Aires: Corregidor, 1985.

———. *El sindicalismo despues de Perón*. Buenos Aires: Galerna, 1971.

Serrano, Carolina [Patricia Bullrich]. "Editorial." *JOTAPÉ*, no. 1 (17 October 1979): 2–4; no. 4 (March 1981).

———. "El modelo de la juventud." *JOTAPÉ*, no. 2 (February 1980): 1–2, 5.

———. "Resistencia peronista a la dictadura videlista." *JOTAPÉ*, no. 3 (August–September 1980): 1–3.

"Silencio en Ezeiza." *La Voz* (10 June 1984).

Smith, Peter H. *Argentina and the Failure of Democracy: Conflict among Political Elites 1904–1955*. Madison: University of Wisconsin Press, 1974.

———. *Politics and Beef in Argentina*. New York: Columbia University Press, 1969.

Snow, Peter G. *Political Forces in Argentina*. New York: Praeger, 1979.

Somos la vida. Buenos Aires: Respuesta, 1985.

Sorel, Georges. *Reflections on Violence*. Translated by T. E. Hulme. New York: Peter Smith, 1941.

Sosa, Rubén A. *La magia toma el poder en Argentina*. Mexico City: Posada, 1975.

Spengler, Oswald. *The Hour of Decision*. New York: Knopf, 1934.

Stalin, Joseph. *Selected Writings*. New York: International Publishers, 1942.

Statistical Yearbook for Latin America (1983). New York: United Nations, Economic Commission for Latin America, New York, 1983.

Stoddard, Lothrop. *The Revolt against Civilization*. New York: Scribner's, 1922.

Stoetzer, Carlos. *Two Studies on Contemporary Argentine History*. New York: Argentina Independent Review, 1980.

Strasser, Carlos, ed. *Las izquierdas en el proceso político argentino*. Buenos Aires: Palestra, 1959.

Strubbia, Mario. *¿Por qué fracasó Alfonsín?* Rosario: Fundación Ross, 1989.

Terragno, Rodolfo H. *Los 400 días de Perón*. Buenos Aires: La Flor, 1974.

———. *De Cámpora a Videla*. Buenos Aires: Peña Lillo, 1981.

Thomas, Clive Y. *The Rise of the Authoritarian State in Peripheral Societies.* New York: Monthly Review, 1984.

Timerman, Jacobo. *Prisoner without a Name, Cell without a Number.* Translated by Toby Talbot. New York: Vintage 1982.

Tocqueville, Alexis de. *Democracy in America.* Translated by Henry Reeve, 2 vols. New Rochelle, N.Y.: Arlington, n.d.

———. *Recollections.* Translated by Alexander Teixera de Mattos. New York, 1896.

Tosco, Agustín. *Presente en las luchas de la clase obrera.* Buenos Aires: Jorge O. Lannot y Adriana Amantea, 1984.

Toynbee, Arnold J. *A Study of History.* 6 vols. London: Oxford University Press, 1939.

Trinquier, Rougier. *Guerra, subversión, revolución.* Buenos Aires, 1975.

Trotsky, Leon. *Their Morals and Ours.* New York: Pathfinder, 1966.

Turner, Frederick C., and José Enrique Miguens, eds. *Juan Perón and the Reshaping of Argentina.* Pittsburgh: University of Pittsburgh Press, 1983.

Vaca Narvaja, Fernando. "Balance 81: el camino es la movilización." *Vencer,* no. 11 (November–December 1981): 6–16.

———. "Take the Street." *Vencer,* nos. 2–3 (September–October 1979): 2–3.

Vasconi, Tomás Amadeo. *Gran capital y militarización en América Latina.* Mexico City: Era, 1978.

Vazeilles, José Gabriel. *La ideología oligárquica y el terrorismo de estado.* Buenos Aires: Centro Editor de América Latina, 1985.

Verbitsky, Horacio. *La posguerra sucia.* Buenos Aires: Legasa, 1985.

Vicens, Luis. *Loperreguismo y justicialismo.* Buenos Aires: El Cid, 1983.

Vilas, Carlos M. "On the Crisis of Bourgeois Democracy in Argentina." *Latin American Perspectives* (Fall 1982): 5–30.

"La violencia política." *Clarín* (26 September 1984).

"La violenta historia de los Montoneros—primera parte." *La Semana* (29 December 1983): 44–56; "Segunda y última parte." *La Semana* (5 January 1984): 63–74.

"Vuelven los Montoneros." *El Porteño* (May 1984): 12–16.

Vyshinsky, Andrei Y., ed. *The Law of the Soviet State.* Translated by H. W. Babb. New York: Macmillan, 1948.

Waisman, Carlos H. *Reversal of Development in Argentina: Postwar Counterrevolutionary Policies and Their Structural Consequences.* Princeton: Princeton University Press, 1987.

Wald, Alan M. *The New York Intellectuals: The Rise and Decline of the Anti-Stalinist Left from the 1930s to the 1980s.* Chapel Hill: University of North Carolina Press, 1987.

Walsh, Rodolfo. "Carta abierta de un escritor argentino a la junta militar." *Con Todo* (April 1978): 19–23.

———. *Los papeles de Walsh.* Edited by Rodolfo Galimberti. Paris, 1979.

Webster, Nesta H. *The French Revolution.* 1919. Reprint, Hollywood, Calif.: Angriff, n.d.

―――. *Secret Societies and Subversive Movements.* 1924. Reprint, Hawthorne, Calif.: Christian Book Club of America, 1967.

―――. *World Revolution.* Boston: Small, Maynard, 1921.

Whitaker, Arthur P. *The United States and the Southern Cone: Argentina, Chile, and Uruguay.* Cambridge: Harvard University Press, 1976.

Wynia, Gary W. *Argentina: Illusions and Realities.* New York: Holmes and Meier, 1986.

―――. *Argentina in the Postwar Era.* Albuquerque: University of New Mexico Press, 1978.

"Ya actuan los 'grupos de tareas.'" *La Voz* (1 September 1984): 7.

Zuleta Alvarez, Enrique. *El nacionalismo argentino.* 2 vols. Buenos Aires: La Bastilla, 1975.

Index

DATE DUE

MAY 0 6 1997	
DEC 0 6 2001	
DEC 1 2 2003	